What Causes Men's Violence Against Women?

Michèle Harway • James M. O'Neil Editors

What Causes Men's Violence Against Women?

Foreword by U.S. Senator Joseph R. Biden, Jr.

Sage Publications, Inc.
International Educational and Professional Publisher
Thousand Oaks ■ London ■ New Delhi

For information:

Sage Publications, Inc.
2455 Teller Road
Thousand Oaks, California 91320
E-mail: order@sagepub.com

Sage Publications Ltd.
6 Bonhill Street
London EC2A 4PU
United Kingdom

Sage Publications India Pvt. Ltd.
M-32 Market
Greater Kailash I
New Delhi 110 048 India

Printed in the United States of America

Library of Congress Cataloging-in-Publication Data

Main entry under title:

What causes men's violence against women? / edited by Michèle
   Harway, James M. O'Neill; forword by Joseph R. Biden.
      p.   cm.
   Includes bibliographical references (p.) and index.
   ISBN 0-7619-0618-5 (cloth: acid-free paper)
   ISBN 0-7619-0619-3 (pbk.: acid-free paper)
   1. Abusive men.   2. Men—Socialization.   3. Sex-role.
4. Women—Abuse of.   5. Wife—Abuse.   I. Harway, Michèle.
II. O'Neill, James M.   III. Biden, Joseph R.
HV1441.4.W48   1999
362.83'92-dc21   99-6400

This book is printed on acid-free paper.

99   00   01   02   03   04   10   9   8   7   6   5   4   3   2   1

Contents

Senator Joseph R. Biden, Jr.

Foreword

I introduced the Violence Against Women Act in 1990 for one fundamental reason—because, at the time, violence against women, unlike any other form of violence, was virtually ignored by government agencies, social institutions, and society at large. As I stated then, the key aim of the Violence Against Women Act was to confront—and condemn—the attitudes of denial and neglect that have allowed this problem to exist and grow. The centerpiece of the bill was a new legal remedy for victims of violence that was rooted in discrimination against women. This new remedy offered victims a legal tool—including the right to file civil suits for monetary or other damages—to fight back against such violence. This new remedy sent a powerful message that violence based on gender—in the same way as violence based on race or religion—assaults an ideal of equality shared by our entire nation.

Enacting this legislation was not easy: It took 4 years of contentious negotiation, persistence, and, finally, compromise. Why was it such a struggle? I believe it is because the Violence Against Women Act addressed such a fundamental aspect of our society: long-held attitudes about relationships between men and women. There is no more profound relationship in our culture than that between men and women. Exploring the many facets of this relationship is what this book is all about. It is not a straight path. This mission lends itself to the exploration of provocative and controversial hypotheses. Indeed, I find myself in wholehearted disagreement with some of the conclusions contained in this book. At the same time, I am convinced that the important mission of *What Causes Men's Violence Against Women?* must be undertaken if we are to continue to make strides against violence against women.

Let us face a fundamental fact: This type of violence has been allowed to continue because the problem has been protected by a wall of silence, denial, and neglect. Therefore, whether it be a beating in the home, a rape by a neighbor, or an assault on the street, we cannot hope to respond effectively to violence against women unless we openly confront and condemn the attitudes that nurture the violence. We must end the silence. The Violence Against Women Act did just that, with a bold, national declaration that violence against women is unacceptable. This book continues the journey by exploring various aspects of relationships between men and women that may contribute to it. It is not an easy search; we may not like or agree with the theories that have been put forward to explain why people engage in this violence. However, I believe we have no choice but to ask the questions and examine the theories.

In addition to helping to redefine attitudes about violence against women, the Violence Against Women Act has provided the practical components necessary to protect women from violence. On this score, the experts were unanimous: We had to do everything. In the fight to end domestic violence and sexual assault, we had to enlist the time and talents of more police, prosecutors, judges, and victim's advocates; we had to strengthen laws against rape and domestic violence; and we had to provide rape crisis centers and battered women's shelters, which can literally make the difference between a woman living or being killed.

On this more practical front, the tangible successes of the Violence Against Women Act are many. Since being signed into law in 1994, the Act has provided shelter to more than 90,000 battered women and their children. The National Domestic Violence Hotline received over 120,000 calls in its first year and a half of operation. Police are now trained to arrest abusers and to guide victims to help. Prosecutors are trained to pursue evidence and convictions. The results have been astounding—according to the FBI, the murder rate for wives, ex-wives, and girlfriends at the hands of their intimates fell to a 19-year low in 1995.

The Violence Against Women Act changed our laws and committed $1.6 billion over 6 years to transform the culture that permitted this epidemic to grow. Although we have made significant progress, we still have much more work to do. Congress should strengthen and build on its successes. We should improve interstate enforcement of "stay away" orders; tackle the particular problems of violence encountered by women on college campuses; get tough on users of "date rape" drugs; and help employers understand the burdens of violence and how they can help women overcome them.

As a society, we are finally starting to recognize that violence against women is not a private matter and that it requires continued action by the criminal justice, health care, social services, and educational institutions throughout our nation. As such, the struggle to end this violence must be waged on several different fronts, and members of the academic community have much to contribute.

The struggle to end violence against women is far from over. We must gain a better understanding of the fundamental causes and the best ways to address them. *What Causes Men's Violence Against Women?* makes important strides in this direction. It offers a comprehensive discussion of the many interrelated factors that contribute to this violence. It provides an important knowledge base that all who seek to reduce violence against women should master. Just as important, this book charts an important course for future research on this national problem. Only if we are armed with understanding can we ever look forward to the day when this violence is eradicated from our midst, and, surely, if we shrink from this quest for understanding, we can have no effect but to sentence millions of women to lives shattered by violence.

Joseph R. Biden, Jr.
United States Senator

Preface

The first steps of this book were, metaphorically speaking, a trust walk. We were long-time acquaintances, but never workmates. However, we were invited to present *together* at an American Psychological Association (APA) Miniconvention on men's violence in the family (O'Neil & Harway, 1994a). Fortunately, we were given plenty of lead time, and we needed it, because not only did we have to prepare a presentation, but first we had to develop a working style, a relationship, and a common area of focus. Early in the process, we discovered that we both loved the world of ideas and were particularly excited about using a dialogue to resolve any differences in our perspective on violence against women. We decided that, in addition to writing a paper, we would present our ideas as a public dialogue during the miniconvention presentation. We recognized that in psychology, men and women were having a difficult time dialoguing on the issues of violence against women. Consequently, we felt that our public dialogue could demonstrate that men and women can be partners in discussing this issue and in finding solutions.

Furthermore, Michele's two books (Harway & Hansen, 1994; Hansen & Harway, 1993) on family violence and spouse abuse, and Jim's research program on men's gender-role conflict (O'Neil, Good, & Holmes, 1995) convinced each of us that scholars had *not* always been asking some of the critical questions about violence against women. The largest body of literature on relationship violence explored why women stay in violent relationships. Because that research contributed little to stopping violence, researchers and theorists shifted to asking, "What are batterers like?" We thought a better question might be, "*Why do men batter?*" This question was more relevant, because asking what batterers are like yields descriptions of batterers, but it does not explain how battering behaviors develop. Identifying the characteristics of batterers and understanding how battering occurs are, of course, related, but the former has no explanatory power and, therefore, it does not allow us to set up prevention programs. If instead, the focus shifted to *why men batter*, prevention strategies are more easily created. So we decided to move in that direction with our dialogues. The specific focus of our dialogues became the factors that explain men's violence against women.

Early on, we realized that the topic of men's violence against women is one of the most difficult topics in America today and that it is one that has the possibility of polarizing the sexes, as well as ethnic communities. We also understood that violence touches each of us in a very personal way by prompting examinations of our own potential to be victims and/or victimizers. Furthermore, we recognized that having a dialogue on a sensitive topic with a colleague with whom you have never worked before has its complexities. It is even more difficult when you live at opposite ends of the country and the dialoguing must occur over the phone. As we dialogued, we found many areas of agreement and disagreement. There were times when our defenses interfered with our communication process. Many times there was silence on the line as we pondered how to resolve a seemingly unresolvable difference on the causes of violence against women. Points of silence occurred most often when the discussion shifted to a consideration of how interactional and relational factors between men and women might contribute to the violence. During the silences, we internally questioned whether we could trust each other. We explored our feelings of defensiveness and insecurity when we failed to communicate our critical points clearly. We wondered how to reconcile our differing points of view. At various times, one or the other of us struggled to follow the other's logic in explaining relationship violence. Over a period of many months, we stuck with this difficult task. We explored and stretched each other's thinking and generated possible causal connections between antecedent factors in men's lives and violence against women.

The outcome was positive because we generated a multivariate model of factors related to men's violence against women that we presented at an APA Presidential Miniconvention (O'Neil & Harway, 1994a). We further refined the model and it was published in the journal *Violence Against Women* (O'Neil & Harway, 1997). Then it occurred to us that we needed to expand the dialogue further. We invited two of our colleagues (Gary Brooks and Marsali Hansen) to dialogue with each other and to present with us at another APA conference (O'Neil, Harway, Brooks, & Hansen, 1995). We believed that these types of dialogues, especially across gender lines, were important to continue.

How did we keep the dialogue on this most difficult topic going over a 5-year period? We identified the following key factors:

 – having respect for each other;

 – sharing common political beliefs (a humanistic and feminist orientation);

- sharing common professional interests in men's and women's issues;
- having common training as psychologists;
- being from the same age cohort;
- having the same mentors at the University of Maryland who had instilled in us a belief that violence and societal oppression are important issues;
- having mutual commitments to eradicating violence between men and women;
- having similar intellectual styles in terms of scientist–practitioner ways of thinking about clinical issues, research, and personal–political issues.

As we completed the first few phases of our dialogue, we also decided that a book was warranted where experts on violence against women could critique the factors and hypotheses we had developed. In this way, the dialogue was further expanded to other experts on violence against women. The book you are reading is not only an outcome of our dialogues, but also an outcome of our extended dialogues with the chapter authors.

A book such as this rarely gets written without the involvement of many people. In our case, these people span two coasts.

Some people we want to acknowledge together. They include our original editor, C. Terry Hendrix, and the staff at Sage Publications, who provided much guidance and support during the entire process. We also want to thank the chapter authors, who put many long hours into their chapters and responded well to our ongoing critiques. We also are grateful to Lenore Walker, whose early reactions to our convention paper and journal article (O'Neil & Harway, 1997) were a catalyst for thinking about a book on men's violence against women. Going back a little further chronologically, we want to thank Ron Fox, Ph.D., President of the APA in 1994, and the Miniconvention Planning Committee who invited us to participate in Ron's Presidential Miniconvention on the Family. As we described earlier, this invitation was instrumental in our working together and developing the original ideas in the book.

We also want to acknowledge our graduate school professors and mentors at the University of Maryland in the Department of Psychology, the Department of Counseling and Personnel Services, and especially those on the staff in the University Counseling Center. Our mentors have shaped our thinking about critical social issues and have molded us into the professionals we have become. In particular, William Sedlacek, Ph.D., is fondly remembered and thanked. Thomas M. Magoon, Jim's mentor, is fondly acknowledged for crystallizing Jim's interest in research and professional involvement in psychology.

At the Phillips Graduate Institute, Michele wants to thank Sandy Cushman for transmitting drafts on an emergency basis and for other forms of assistance during the manuscript preparation. Sally Peace was helpful in facilitating Michele's transition from one word-processing software to another, right in the middle of the project. Ed Cox is also acknowledged for his support of Michele's writing.

Michele's husband, Bruce E. Antman, was a steadfast supporter and cheer-leader who provided helpful suggestions. His gentle nature and his professional training as a mediator provided the perfect counterpoint for the content of this book.

At the University of Connecticut, Jim would like to thank his undergraduate students in Men and Masculinity: Psychosocial Perspectives (HDRF 259) and those graduate students who have participated in his summer gender-role journey workshops (EPSY 325) over the last 15 years. These students have offered many insights and personal experiences that explain how relationship violence occurs. Jim also would like to thank the many men and women in the Society for the Psychological Study of Men and Masculinity (Division 51 of the American Psychological Association) who have supported his work on explaining men's gender-role conflict. Dr. Glenn Good of the University of Missouri—Columbia and Dr. James Mahalik of Boston College have been particularly influential and supportive.

Finally, Jim would like to thank Marina Chebotayev O'Neil for her careful editing of the entire manuscript and for enduring the many long hours devoted to writing this book. Without her partnership, encouragement, and support, the book would not have been possible.

As with our related publications on this topic, we decided on the ordering of the editorship by a toss of the coin. Our work together was truly a collaborative endeavor.

Michele Harway, Ph.D.
James M. O'Neil, Ph.D.

PART I

Book Context and Critiques of O'Neil and Harway's Multivariate Model Explaining Men's Violence Against Women

Introduction

P art I provides an overall orientation to the book's goals and includes four chapters. Chapter 1 gives a brief history of the controversial issues related to men's violence against women. We present a theoretical rationale for the book and describe our collegial process of dialogue in preparing the book. The overall organization of the book is described, as well as the different sections and chapters.

In Chapter 2, we present the preliminary multivariate model that describes the factors that explain men's violence against women (O'Neil & Harway, 1997). Four content areas or factors are defined, including macrosocietal, biological, gender-role socialization, and relational. Thirteen hypotheses are also specified about the causes of men's violence against women. This multivariate model provides a common set of ideas for critique by the chapter authors and a structure for them to make their own hypotheses about the causes of men's violence against women.

Amy Marin and Nancy Felipe Russo consider the important contributions of feminist writers and theorists in explaining men's violence against women in Chapter 3. As Marin and Russo point out, feminists emphasize gender, power, and structural dimensions of violence. Marin and Russo are most interested in the role of the contributions of societal institutions to male violence. They consider men's violence against women to be a form of social control and they emphasize the social construction of male violence. Like many other feminists, they view various forms of male violence against women (battering, rape, sexual harassment) as related phenomena, all resulting, at least in part, from male power and privilege. These notions are explored in detail in Chapter 3, and a feminist lens is used to critique the four content areas of the O'Neil and Harway model.

In Chapter 4, Richard Gelles critiques two prevailing theories about men's violence: the feminist and the sociological models. He notes that neither of these models focuses on the perpetrators of the violence against women. Gelles describes limitations of the existing research to explain battering. This research includes clinical data, official report data, and surveys conducted by social scientists. He then critically reviews data on known risk and protective factors related to men's violence against women. He concludes his chapter with an analysis of the hypotheses found in the O'Neil and Harway multivariate model.

What Causes Men to Be Violent Against Women?

The Unanswered and Controversial Question

MICHELE HARWAY
JAMES M. O'NEIL

"If the leading newspapers were to announce tomorrow a new disease that, over the past year, had afflicted from 3 to 4 million citizens, few would fail to appreciate the seriousness of the illness. Yet, when it comes to the 3 to 4 million women who are victimized by violence each year, the alarms ring softly. . . . We live in a nation where crimes against women are still perceived as anything but crime—as a family problem, as a private matter, as 'sexual miscommunication'." So said Senator Joseph R. Biden, Jr. (Biden, 1993, p. 1059), the chief architect of the Violence Against Women Act (VAWA), in describing societal reactions to relationship violence. The legislation he has championed will affect the millions of women who are victims of violence in their own home and in other settings. The Violence Against Women Act treats violence motivated by gender as a violation of civil rights, changes existing family violence laws, increases funding for services to victims, and encourages states to respond to domestic violence as a crime, not as a private matter (see U.S. Senate Judiciary Committee, 1990, 1991).

Senator Joseph Biden's legislation has made violence against women a national priority and one where social scientists can make a significant difference. Social scientists with their research knowledge and theories are best suited to create prevention programs, provide services for victims and their families, and conduct research on critical questions related to violence against women.

The primary goal of this book is to address one critical question: "Why do men commit acts of violence against women?" The previous literature has focused primarily on why women stay in battering relationships and the development of typologies of batterers. Both of these topics are important, but they do not address the causes of men's violence or explain the risk factors for men who use violence as a relational tool. Full multivariate models that explain the cause of men's violence against women have been slow to develop over the last three decades. Our primary rationale for focusing on the single question, "Why do men batter?" is that answers to this question could decrease the amount of violence against women significantly. Furthermore, we need to answer this question to create comprehensive prevention programs for boys and girls, and men and women of all ages.

In this first chapter, we review recent history related to understanding men's violence against women. Second, we provide a theoretical rationale for the book and discuss the professional process of writing the book. Finally, the book's organization is discussed to orient readers to the different sections and chapters.

PAST CONTROVERSIES RELATED TO EXPLAINING MEN'S VIOLENCE AGAINST WOMEN

In the United States, historically, relationship violence or battering was not considered a serious problem and was judged to be a private matter. However, since the late 1970s, research clearly documents that battering exists across all age, class, race, and socioeconomic levels and that it usually has dangerous outcomes (Okun, 1986). Even with hard data on the existence of battering and the damage that results from it, the larger society in the 1970s and 1980s was mainly in denial about battering. For the most part, the public hoped that violence toward women was an aberration that affected only seriously pathological families. Several notorious domestic violence cases have helped the American public accept battering as a significant societal problem.

Battering remains a difficult topic for men and women to discuss. On a personal level, dialogues between the sexes on the causes of violence against women have been limited and fraught with conflict and controversy. Many men have avoided discussing the epidemic of battering in America because it has activated shame, guilt, fear, and defensiveness in them. Similarly, women may have wanted to discuss this serious problem with men, but may have feared men's reactions. These interpersonal dynamics explain the dearth of productive inter-gender dialogue on men's violence against women. This topic has been an easy one for men and women to avoid.

Threat and defensiveness when discussing inter-gender violence is an important dilemma to acknowledge and remediate. For us, discussing and writing about it brought up our own periodic discomfort. We hope that addressing this issue directly does not add to the problem. Likewise, the reader also may be uncomfortable with our views about why men and women have had difficulty dialoguing on the causes of men's violence against women.

Within the academic community, the issue of relationship violence also has been controversial. Academics have had difficulty dialoguing on this topic (Avis, 1994; Barnett, Miller-Perrin, & Perrin, 1997; Bograd, 1992; Dutton, 1994; Gelles, 1993c; Gelles & Loseke, 1993; Hamberger & Renzetti, 1996; Hansen, 1993; Johnson, 1995; Moltz, 1992). Part of the problem has been that the academic controversies in several disciplines never have been resolved. Typical of this were the initial debates about the appropriateness of working with batterers in couples' therapy (Bograd, 1988b; Goldner, 1985b; Hare-Mustin, 1978; Pressman, 1989). This debate resulted in a great deal of emotionality, but little agreement. There was limited theory and research to inform these debates constructively, and many exchanges were highly personal and political. Discussions about whether men are battered as often as women (Steinmetz, 1977) and whether instruments such as the Conflict Tactic Scale (Straus, 1990; Straus & Hamby, 1997) are appropriate brought some violence researchers into direct confrontation with each other.

Another controversy relates to consideration of the role of other factors in men's violence against women. For example, biology, genetics, and evolution have received limited attention by researchers. For some, consideration of these factors was construed as exonerating men of their responsibility for the violence. Consideration of how partner interactions contribute to violence sometimes has been considered "off limits" because it was thought to be "blaming the victim" (Stevens, 1994). However, it is very difficult to understand how individuals are predisposed to violence and how violence is actually triggered without vigorously studying the interactional and communication patterns of couples.

In some situations, researchers, clinicians, and theoreticians have been divided along sex lines. For example, when discussing the causes of men's violence, male researchers were sometimes accused of "explaining away" or excusing men from the violence. Some men denied the violence or actually tried to justify it. This only reinforced some women's ardent views that men are unable to understand how patriarchy, sexism, and violence are all interrelated. Men's rational discussions about violence were sometimes perceived as an attempt to deflate women's anger and rage, thereby diminishing the importance of this serious problem. This only increased the polarization between some men and women and delayed the needed inter-gender dialogue that could have advanced our understanding of men's battering.

Another area of controversy concerned the use of terminology such as domestic violence, family violence, spousal abuse, battering, violent couples, relationship violence, and marital violence. For some, the use of a particular term was overly restrictive. For example, marital violence suggests that such violence occurs only within the context of traditional heterosexual marriages. In fact, statistics indicate that violence occurs in cohabiting and dating relationships just as it does within the confines of a legally "sanctioned" relationship. Violence also exists in same-sex relationships. Some argued that domestic violence includes not only violence from one relational partner to another, but also should include violence directed toward children or elderly relatives. Others objected to the term *violent couples*, which suggests that violence is bi-directional, with both partners at times being perpetrators.

We struggled with the decision whether we should, as editors, require uniform terminology across chapters, but decided that because this book was intended to be generative rather than restrictive, we would be ill-served by dictating the terminology used by the authors. In our own chapters, we generally will use the following terms: *relationship violence*, *domestic violence*, or *battering*.

Men's violence, by whatever name, is certainly an emotionally charged area, one that has generated strong feelings and much denial on a societal level. With the greater societal acknowledgment of the epidemic of battering in America, new legislation to fund victims' services, and the education of the public (Biden, 1993), there is a renewed willingness to consider even the most difficult of these emotionally charged topics.

We began our work together in the context of these personal and professional controversies. We hope that men and women now can pursue together all questions that may explain the complexity of inter-gender violence. Alliances between men and women on how violence occurs will yield more understanding than polarized positions that are based on unnecessary fear, limited scientific evidence, and outdated political agendas. Dialogues about men's violence against women need to be balanced by facts and sound reasoning from the head and compassionate emotional understanding from the heart.

LIMITATIONS OF PREVIOUS THEORIES EXPLAINING MEN'S VIOLENCE AGAINST WOMEN

It is beyond the scope of this book to extensively review the many theories proposed to explain men's violence against women. The interested reader is referred to a partial listing of the many books and articles on theories about men's violence against women (APA, 1996; Barnett, Miller-Perrin, & Perrin, 1997; Carden, 1994; Coleman, 1996; Crowell & Burgess, 1996; Dutton, 1985, 1988, 1995; Edleson & Tolman, 1992; Gelles, 1979, 1985, 1993c; Gelles & Cornell, 1985; Gelles & Straus, 1979; Giles-Sims, 1983; Hamberger & Renzetti, 1996; Kantor & Jasinski, 1997; Koss et al., 1994; Levinson, 1989a, 1989b; McCall & Shields, 1986; Okun, 1986; Steinmetz, 1987; Stordeur & Stille, 1989; Straus, 1973, 1980; Straus, Gelles, & Steinmetz, 1980; Thorne-Finch, 1992). Our preliminary review yielded dozens of separate sources that summarized theories of violence against women. Over 30 different conceptual labels were used to describe the causes of men's violence. Some of these labels overlapped, because the authors described similar concepts but renamed them. Our review convinced us, as Gelles (1993c) indicated, that theory development in this area is primitive and that specific theories on violence against women are in the very early stages of development.

The theoretical literature in this area is fragmented and confusing for a number of reasons. First, many of the theoretical analyses are limited by a specific discipline's theoretical approach. These theories have failed to capture fully the interdisciplinary and multifactored nature of violence against women. Second, individual theories of violence have been developed in reaction to the dominant paradigms of the time. The first decade of theorizing about causes of family violence was dominated by biological explanations. In reaction to single-factor biological explanations, sociocultural explanations that linked social structures to family violence were created. In reaction to these theories, feminist and sociopolitical theories emerged. Psychological theories about men's violence against women are just beginning to be created. As a result of each of these shifts in theory development, much emotion has been generated and controversies have occurred about the causes of men's violence. Coherent, interdisciplinary, and unified theories have been difficult to develop given the personal and political issues involved. Third, many of the theories are single-factor theories, limited to a single discipline, rather than more complex ones that hypothesize multiple factors explaining violence across disciplines. Furthermore, the different disciplines have used different terminology to explain men's violence against women, thereby sometimes discouraging discussion across disciplines.

From our perspective, the complexity of explaining the causes and risk factors of men's violence against women requires multidisciplinary explanations. This position is supported by Miller (1996), who indicated, "multiple levels of explanations are necessary to link developmental and biological characteristics, personalities, sub-cultural variations, and economics, social, political, and community dimensions in our model of relationship aggression. Increasingly, social science has supported the development of integrated models of human behavior that identify individual factors (such as personality) as well as socio-cultural factors" (pp. 208–209).

Based on the previously mentioned rationale, we made an early decision to explore the multiplicity of factors that contribute to violence against women and to develop a model that would consider their rather complicated interface. This book is the result of that decision.

THE PROCESS OF WRITING THE BOOK AND ITS ORGANIZATION

This book was conceived of as a dialogue between the two editors and a scholarly exchange with the chapter authors. We asked the chapter authors to read and critique our earlier manuscript that proposed 4 content areas and 13 hypotheses explaining men's violence against women (see Chapter 2 and O'Neil & Harway, 1997). We asked the authors to review the state of knowledge in one or more of the content areas. We also asked them to critique specific hypotheses we had generated in one or more of the content areas. Two of the authors were given a broader charge: to critique all 13 hypotheses across the content areas (see Marin & Russo, Chapter 3, and Gelles, Chapter 4). Each chapter represents the outcome of these critiques and new ideas generated by the authors. We believe that the resulting chapters represent a new scholarship. Some of the chapters are controversial and all of them contribute to the ongoing dialogue we started back in 1993 on the fundamental question, "What causes men's violence against women?"

When all the invited chapters were completed, we proceeded to the next step in the completion of this dialogic task. We revised and expanded our original model and hypotheses using the chapter authors' ideas and critiques. The final chapter presents a new theoretical model, 13 propositions, and 40 new hypotheses about the risk factors related to men's violence against women. We also enumerate a long list of variables that could be studied and tested through research.

PARTS AND CHAPTERS OF THE BOOK

The chapters of the book are organized into six parts. This organization allows the interested reader to consider a single part or all six parts. This first part continues with Chapter 2, which presents our preliminary model (O'Neil & Harway, 1997). Additionally, in this part there are two critiques of our model and hypotheses by two of the chapter authors. Parts II through V are organized around the four content areas that constitute our earlier model; namely, the biological factors, the gender-role socialization factors, the relational factors, and the macrosocietal factors. The sequential ordering of these content areas does not imply the relative importance of the areas in explaining men's violence. That is, the biological factor is not the most important because it comes first, nor is the macrosocietal factor the least important because it appears last. In fact, these content areas are organized around systems of increasing complexity. We begin with individual systems (the person, biological, and socialization factors) and move to the larger systems (relational and macrosocietal factors). Finally, in Part VI, we present a revised model and new propositions and hypotheses about the causes and risk factors of men's violence against women based on the chapter authors' new ideas.

The book parts are divided into individual chapters.

Part I begins with Chapters 1 and 2 and provides a context for the book. Chapter 2 presents our preliminary model explaining the causes of men's violence against women (O'Neil & Harway, 1997). In Chapter 3, Amy Marin and Nancy Felipe Russo provide a feminist critique of our model and review important issues related to men's violence against women. Richard Gelles reviews research on men's violence against women and discusses the empirical support for our multivariate model in Chapter 4. Part II, the biological factors, has two chapters. In Chapter 5, Anthony Greene evaluates the biological evidence for men's violence against women. Louise Silverstein critically reviews the evidence related to evolutionary explanations for men's violence against women in Chapter 6. In Part III, the gender-role socialization factors are discussed. In Chapter 7, Jim O'Neil and Rod Nadeau present a new model of how men's gender-role socialization and gender-role conflict predispose and trigger men's violence against women. A life-span analysis of how gender-role socialization may explain women's predisposition to relational violence is presented by Roberta Nutt in Chapter 8. The two chapters in Part IV examine the relational and systemic factors related to violence against women. Steven Anderson and Margaret Schlossberg, in Chapter 9, reconsider family systems theories and interactional explanations for men's violence against women. Sandra Rigazio-DiGilio and Steven Lanza, in Chapter 10, use cognitive developmental theory to propose an ecological perspective to understand relational violence. In Part V, Janis Sanchez-Hucles and Mary Ann Dutton's Chapter 11 focuses on the macrosocietal factors. Chapter 11 discusses how racial and cultural factors and societal violence specifically relate to violence against women of color. Finally, in Part VI, we conclude with Chapter 12, which discusses our revised model and our new propositions and hypotheses about men's risk for violence against women.

Preliminary Multivariate Model Explaining the Causes of Men's Violence Against Women

JAMES M. O'NEIL
MICHELE HARWAY

In the first chapter, we indicated that the previous literature has not fully addressed the question, "What causes men to be violent against women?" Very few multivariate models have captured the complexity of men's risks for violence against women. There is a great need for more conceptual models and theories that explain the multiplicity of factors that cause men's violence against women. The purpose of this chapter is to present a shortened version of our preliminary conceptual model that explains the multiplicity of factors that contribute to men's violence against women. A more extensive explanation of this model, with greater detail and documentation, is found in O'Neil and Harway (1997).

Multivariate approaches explaining the causes of men's violence are beginning to be discussed in a number of disciplines. Both the National Academy of Science and the American Psychological Association have convened task forces that recommended the study of the multiple factors that cause men's violence against women (Crowell & Burgess, 1996; Koss et al., 1994). The APA Task Force on Violence Against Women (Koss et al., 1994) recommended the integration of biopsychological models with sociocultural and psychological determinants of men's violence. This task force reported that few conceptualizations of men's violence have been created that consider the "... multiple levels of coinfluence—from societal to individual (which) determine the expression of violence" (p. 3). The National Academy of Science Task Force (Crowell & Burgess, 1996) stated that "the field appears to be developing toward an integrative, metatheoretical model of violence that considers multiple variables operating at different times in a probabilistic fashion" (p. 69). These two task forces advocate more complex conceptualizations that explain men's violence against women. The model proposed here responds to the task force recommendations by addressing the multiple levels and factors that explain men's violence against women (O'Neil & Harway, 1997).

PRELIMINARY MULTIVARIATE MODEL EXPLAINING MEN'S VIOLENCE AGAINST WOMEN: DEFINITIONS AND HYPOTHESES

We identified four factors or content areas in the literature that represent our initial conceptualization explaining men's violence against women. These content areas are shown in Figure 2.1 and include (1) macrosocietal factors, (2) biological factors, (3) gender-role socialization factors, and (4) relational factors. As shown in Figure 2.1, all four of these factors affect men's violence against women.

The *macrosocietal factors* are defined as those patriarchal and institutional structures that cause oppression and violence against women. The macrosocietal factors include not only the history of violence against women, but also recent changes in gender roles that may activate men's fear of power loss. As shown in Figure 2.1, the major question with the macrosocietal factors is, "How does the larger society contribute to men's violence against women?"

The *biological factors* are defined as the hormonal, neuroanatomical dimensions of men that cause violence against women. The biological factors include all men's physiological processes that may contribute to men's violence against women. The major question for this factor is, "Is men's violence against women biologically based?"

The *gender-role socialization factors* are defined as men's sexist attitudes, emotions, and behaviors learned over the life span that cause violence against women. This factor emphasizes how men are socialized restrictively to patterns of gender-role conflict, misogynistic attitudes, and negative emotions toward women. The central question with this factor is, "Do men's gender-role socialization and conflict cause men's violence against women?"

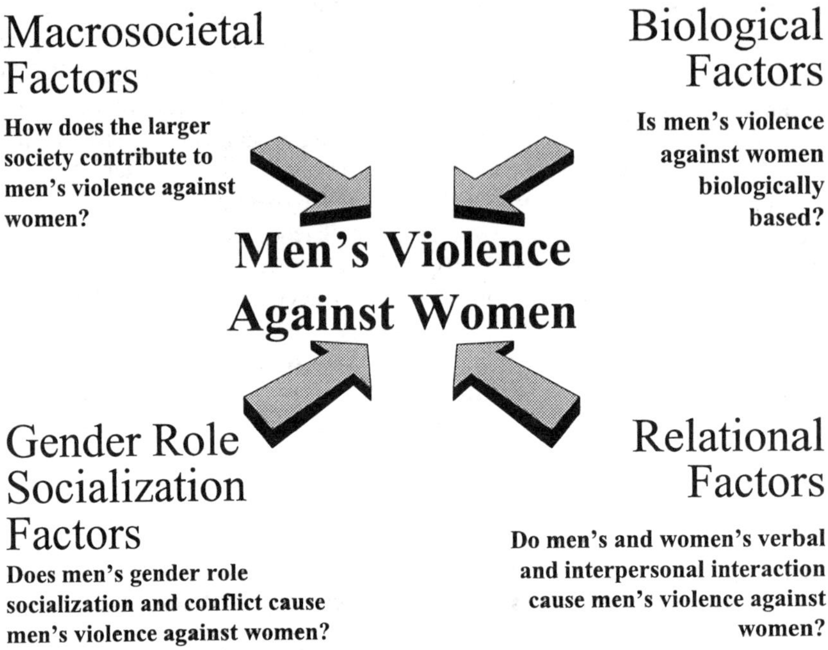

Macrosocietal Factors

How does the larger society contribute to men's violence against women?

Biological Factors

Is men's violence against women biologically based?

Men's Violence Against Women

Gender Role Socialization Factors

Does men's gender role socialization and conflict cause men's violence against women?

Relational Factors

Do men's and women's verbal and interpersonal interaction cause men's violence against women?

Figure 2.1. Preliminary Multivariate Model Explaining Men's Violence Against Women

The *relational factors* are defined as the ongoing interpersonal and verbal interactions between partners that may cause men's violence against women. This factor emphasizes the verbal and emotional communication patterns and experiences between partners that may cause men's violence against women. This factor also includes early experiences in the partner's family of origin where violence was observed or experienced. The central question of this factor is, "Do men's and women's verbal and interpersonal interactions cause men's violence against women?"

The four factors and the questions in Figure 2.1 translate to specific hypotheses about men's violence against women. In Table 2.1, we enumerate 13 hypotheses across the 4 content areas. These hypotheses represent our initial attempt to capture the multiplicity of causes of men's violence against women precisely (O'Neil & Harway, 1997). In Table 2.1, the macrosocietal factor content area enumerates three hypotheses focused on how the larger society may contribute to men's violence against women. The biological, neuroanatomical, and hormonal content area has two hypotheses focused on how men's biological processes may contribute to men's violence against women. The gender-role socialization content area has three hypotheses related to how men's socialization may contribute to men's violence against women. The relational content area has

TABLE 2.1. Content Areas, Factors, and Hypotheses Explaining Men's Violence Against Women

---

I. Macrosocietal Factors of Men's Violence Against Women: How Does the Larger Society Contribute to Men's Violence Against Women?

Hypothesis 1: Battering results from historical patterns in America that glorify men's violence, particularly violence against women (PH).

Hypothesis 2: Organizational, institutional, and patriarchal structures in society maintain unequal power relationships between men and women that tacitly or directly support domestic oppression and violence against women (PH).

Hypothesis 3: Recent changes in gender roles in American society regarding expectations and realities of women's lives have produced men's fears of power loss and have increased violence against women (PH & TH).

II. Biological, Neuroanatomical, and Hormonal Factors of Men's Violence Against Women: Is Men's Violence Against Women Biologically Based?

Hypothesis 4: Testosterone or hormonal levels in men contribute to violence against women (TH).

Hypothesis 5: Neuroanatomical differences and other biological factors in men and women produce men's tendency to be violent against women (TH).

III. Gender-Role Socialization and Conflict Factors of Men's Violence Against Women: Do Men's Gender-Role Socialization and Conflict Cause Men's Violence Against Women?

Hypothesis 6: Men's misogynistic attitudes toward women, learned during gender-role socialization, contribute to men's violence against women (PH & TH).

Hypothesis 7: Men's patterns of gender-role conflict (i.e., control, power, competition, and restrictive emotionality) contribute to patterns of violence against women (PH & TH).

Hypothesis 8: Men's unidentified and unexpressed emotions (i.e., hurt, pain, shame, guilt, powerlessness, and dependency) are expressed as anger, rage, and violence against women (PH & TH).

IV. Relational Factors of Men's Violence Against Women: Do Men's and Women's Verbal and Interpersonal Interactions Cause Men's Violence Against Women?

Hypothesis 9: Differentially socialized patterns of communication and separate gender-role cultures contribute to men's potential for violence (PH & TH).

Hypothesis 10: Psychological violence between partners can be a precursor to physical violence against women (PH & TH).

Hypothesis 11: Women's fear of men and men's fear of women contribute to the potential for psychological and physical violence in relationships (PH & TH).

Hypothesis 12: Both sexes' lack of understanding of the other's gender-role socialization experiences contributes to the potential for violence (PH).

Hypothesis 13: Viewing or experiencing domestic violence in the family of origin increases the possibility of violence against women (PH).

Notes: PH = predisposing hypothesis; TH = triggering hypothesis.

five hypotheses related to how men's and women's personal interactions, communications, and histories may explain men's violence against women.

One of the complexities in understanding men's violence against women is
differentiating between the *predisposing* factors that contribute to men's violence
and the *triggering factors*. The predisposing factors represent all the societal and
personal experiences that result in men using violence against women to solve
human conflicts. The triggering factors are the actual situational cues and interpersonal dynamics that prompt men to psychologically or physically assault
women.

Hypotheses about men's violence against women are related to predisposing
factors, triggering factors, or both sets of factors. Each of the hypotheses in Table
2.1 is categorized as a predisposing hypothesis (PH) or a triggering hypothesis
(TH). In some cases both PH and TH apply to the same hypothesis. Research on
these hypotheses can help differentiate the predisposing and triggering aspects of
men's violence against women.

Finally, the concepts and terms used in Figure 2.1, Table 2.1, require further
explanation. Terms such as *multivariate model, factors, content areas,* and
hypotheses are all interrelated. The content areas and factors are defined as the
overall areas of inquiry about men's violence against women. The content areas
and factors are operationalized through hypotheses that can be tested (see Table
2.1). The 13 hypotheses have multiple independent variables that can be tested in
research studies. The dependent variable with the 13 hypotheses is men's
violence against women. The multiple factors, hypotheses, and independent
variables in Table 2.1 and Figure 2.1 represent the multivariate nature of the
model. The term *multivariate* conveys that the model is sufficiently complex that
it captures a multiplicity of factors, hypotheses, and variables that explain men's
violence against women.

SUMMARY OF THE MULTIVARIATE MODELS
EXPLAINING MEN'S VIOLENCE AGAINST WOMEN

The presentation of the previously mentioned model is just a beginning. Our
model represents a synthesis of previous models attempting to explain men's violence (Dutton, 1985; Edleson & Tolman, 1992; Gelles & Straus, 1979; Steinmetz,
1987; Straus, 1980). In the past, some theorists acknowledged the importance of
multiple factors to explain men's predisposition to violence and the actual triggering process.

How is our model different from the earlier models and theories? First, most of
the previous theories neither have explained the multiplicity of factors in Figure
2.1 fully nor specified hypotheses that could be tested. Second, few theorists
have provided models that differentiate men's predisposition to violence against
women from the actual triggering of violence. Third, previous research has not

provided a *specific* theory of how men's and women's gender-role socialization and conflict relate to men's violence against women. Our model emphasizes both men's and women's socialization as critical factors that explain men's violence against women. Fourth, the earlier models have not discussed with very much detail how couples' interactions or relational dimensions may contribute to violence against women. Our model implies that the couple's actions and interactions are relevant to men's violence against women. Finally, many of the models of family violence have not considered fully the relationship of battering to values in the larger society. Our model implies that couples' violence is directly related to values in the larger society.

The 13 hypotheses listed in Table 2.1 are the specific hypotheses we asked the chapter authors to address. We now move on to Marin and Russo's (Chapter 3) and Gelles's (Chapter 4) critique of the model presented in Figure 2.1 and the hypotheses enumerated in Table 2.1. Later, in Chapter 12, we suggest changes in the model presented in Figure 2.1, based on our new thinking and the ideas presented by the chapter authors.

Feminist Perspectives on Male Violence Against Women

Critiquing O'Neil and Harway's Model

AMY J. MARIN
NANCY FELIPE RUSSO

A s Edwards (1991) wrote, "There is no area where androcentric bias is more visible and systematic than male violence against women" (p. 14). Ironically, it was not until the late 1980s that such violence was identified as the leading public health risk to adult women by the Surgeon General of the United States (Koop, 1985). The invisibility of partner violence is truly remarkable given it is the most common source of injury to women aged 15 to 44, more frequent than muggings, auto accidents, and cancer deaths combined (Dwyer, Smokowski, Bricout, & Wodarski, 1995). Physical assault against both married and unmarried women continues to be a widespread problem, crossing racial, sexual orientation, age, and socioeconomic lines (Goodman, Koss, & Russo, 1993; Koss, 1988; Stark & Flitcraft, 1996). Research on national probability samples suggests that 20% to 30% of *all* women will be physically assaulted by a partner or expartner at least once in their lives (Frieze & Browne,

1989), and that approximately 2 million women are physically assaulted by male intimates each year (Straus & Gelles, 1990). Considering that partner violence is a greatly underreported and underprosecuted problem, researchers have estimated that these reports may be as much as 50% lower than actual incidence and prevalence rates (Browne, 1992).

The newly found recognition of the widespread, multifaceted, and dynamic nature of partner violence is a tribute to the effect of feminism on U.S. society. Feminists have challenged researchers to develop new perspectives and alternative conceptualizations to understand, predict, and prevent male violence against women in all of its forms (Carden, 1994; Koss, Heise, & Russo, 1994; Wyatt 1994). This book focuses on one form of male violence against women: partner violence. In this chapter, after considering some feminist contributions to understanding male violence against women, we focus our lens on the multivariate model of partner violence offered by O'Neil and Harway (as described in Chapter 2) and offer some concepts and suggestions for expanding and applying it. In particular, we discuss how feminist perspectives that include biological, cognitive, and relational processes are essential to understanding partner violence.

FEMINIST CONTRIBUTIONS

Feminists have done more than simply bring attention to the problems of male violence against women. Feminists have made such violence a central issue in the women's movement around the world. They have organized shelters, developed public education programs, advocated new laws and policies, promoted change in the criminal justice and health care systems, and fostered the development of a new knowledge base that reflects the realities of diverse women's lives (Koss, Heise, & Russo, 1994).

Feminist writing and theorizing have qualitatively changed the way that researchers and scientists conceptualize and study the many forms of male violence against women (Edwards, 1991). In the 1970s, rape was a central feminist issue. Academicians during this period of time also were becoming concerned with the issues of rape and domestic violence. However, researchers generally limited their investigations to studies of either the psychological characteristics of the individual perpetrator and/or victim, or an investigation of family relationships (see Yllö, 1988, for a review). They did not emphasize gender, power, or structural dimensions of violence. Feminist writers, in contrast, emphasized such issues and began to reconstruct rape and other forms of male violence as forms of power and control (Brownmiller, 1975; Medea & Thompson, 1974; Russell, 1975).

Feminists began to look for causes of male domination in societal institutions rather than in physical strength or biological instinct. From a feminist perspective, male-perpetrated violence against women is considered to be a form of social control used to maintain a subordinate social and political status for women. In general, feminists have emphasized the social construction of male violence, not the biology or pathology of the individual (Heise, & Russo, 1994; Kelly, 1988; Koss, McHugh, Frieze, & Browne, 1993).

Another significant contribution of feminist theorizing has been a shift from viewing different forms of male violence against women as separate entities toward viewing violence against women as a unitary phenomenon and an outgrowth of male power and privilege. Feminist theorists continue to view partner violence as reflective of a larger patriarchal structure that functions to subordinate women. Major institutions (including criminal justice, health, military, athletic, and religious institutions) are seen as reflecting patriarchal values and encouraging and maintaining violence against women. A list of patriarchal values that have become institutionalized in our laws and cultural practices is found in Table 3.1.

TABLE 3.1. Patriarchal Values Related to Partner Violence

1. It is the natural, God-given right of men to have power over women.

2. The male head of a household should be in charge, hold all power, make the decisions, and be responsible for determining the actions and behaviors of those within the household.

3. Masculinity should be defined by powerful characteristics: strength, agency, independence, power, control, and domination.

4. Women pose a threat to male power and therefore need to be controlled. Femininity should be defined by weakness, passivity, dependence, powerlessness, and submissiveness.

5. Female sexuality is a particular threat to male power and therefore should be under the control of men, specifically fathers and/or husbands.

6. Sexual harassment, rape, physical violence, and any other fear-inducing tactics are legitimate and effective means to enforce male entitlements and to control women.

VIOLENCE: NAMING ITS MULTIPLE FORMS, AND IDENTIFYING COMMON ROOTS

A key contribution of feminist analyses has been the development of more complex and sophisticated conceptualizations of multiple forms of violence. In addition to partner violence, these forms include rape, sexual abuse, torture, and sexual harassment. Male violence against women is ubiquitous—found in streets, homes, schools, and workplaces around the globe (Koss, Heise, & Russo, 1994; Russo, Koss, & Goodman, 1995). It is directed also at female children, as in sexual abuse, incest, forced prostitution, and female infanticide.

Feminists have emphasized the importance of conceptualizing and naming violence in ways that reflect women's experiences (McHugh, Frieze, & Browne, 1993). Labels that do not fully encompass physical, sexual, and psychological aspects of violence and/or gay and lesbian partner abuse, dating and cohabitation violence, and intimate violence occurring outside the home have important political implications. Such labels can exclude the experiences of some women and may downplay the role of men as perpetrators. For example, use of the terms *wife battering* and *marital violence* fails to recognize the large numbers of unmarried women or lesbian women who are assaulted by their sexual partners. The terms *intimate violence* and *domestic violence* do not specifically recognize women as targets and men as perpetrators. However such violence is defined and named, women are most likely to be the victims, particularly when the violence is severe (Gelles & Cornell, 1990; Straus & Gelles, 1988, 1990). Here we speak of partner violence when referring to male violence against an intimate partner, whether married or unmarried.

In considering the experience of violence from the point of view of its victims, it must be recognized that threat of violence can be as effective as physical violence as a form of social control. Many feminists thus view acts experienced as threat, coercion, abuse, intimidation, or force used by men to control women as forms of violence (Kelly, 1988; Koss, Heise, & Russo, 1994). Thus, instances where the situation involves a threat of violence, such as stalking (Kurt, 1995) and sexual terrorism (Sheffield, 1995), are also forms of male violence against women.

Although the model here focuses on partner violence, it must be kept in mind that male violence against women can take many forms, and treating these forms as discrete categories can mask the realities of violence in women's lives. Women who experienced childhood sexual abuse report higher rates of partner violence (Russo, Denious, Keita, & Koss, in press). Furthermore, dividing battering and rape into distinct and separate categories may obscure the overlapping nature of battery and rape in women's experiences (Russo, Koss, & Goodman, 1995). Similarly, separating violence in the home from violence in the workplace may be an artificial distinction that does not reflect actual experiences. Research on violence in the workplace has indicated that relationship or partner violence accounts for a sizable proportion of women who die on the job each year (Younger, 1994). Some feminist theorists have argued that it may be more helpful to think of violence against women as a continuum rather than as discrete categories (Connors & Harway, 1995; Kelly, 1988). In this way, specific violent acts are viewed as part of a multidimensional continuum of gendered violence that acknowledges the diversity of women's experiences (Kelly, 1988; Koss, Heise, & Russo, 1994).

Regardless of the form the violence takes, some common themes emerge from the literature on male-perpetrated violence. Koss, Heise, and Russo (1994) identified several common themes in the literature on battering, rape, and sexual harassment. First, regardless of the form violence takes, it is a pervasive, tenacious, everyday event in many women's lives, an event that crosses the lines of race, ethnicity, national origin, class, religion, age, and sexual orientation. In a comprehensive review of 52 studies, Hotaling and Sugarman (1986) found that income level, education level, social status, and individual personality character- istics did not influence a woman's chances for victimization. This suggests that women from all demographic backgrounds are at risk, and studies that cross lines of ethnicity, class, and other social categories are needed.

Although feminists have emphasized the importance of understanding the experiences of diverse women, there is still an inadequate understanding of vio- lence in the lives of ethnic minority women. Fortunately, researchers are now beginning to investigate male perpetrated violence in African American (Brice- Baker, 1994; Marsh, 1993; Russo et al., in press), Native American (Chester, Robin, Koss, & Goodman, 1994; Gutierres, Russo, & Urbanski, 1994; Norton & Manson, 1995), Hispanic American (Perilla, Bakerman, & Norris, 1994), and Asian American populations (Wong, 1995; see also Sanchez-Hucles and Dutton, Chapter 11, this volume). In addition, international and cross-cultural studies are being conducted with female populations as diverse as refugees (Friedman, 1992), central American immigrants (McCloskey, Southwick, Fernandez, Eugenia, & Locke, 1995), Ghanians (Ofei-Aboagye, 1994), African Caribbeans (Brice-Baker, 1994), and women living in rural Papua, New Guinea (Morley, 1994).

Second, in all forms of violence between intimates, men are most likely to be the perpetrators and women are most likely to be the targets. This suggests that understanding gender-role constructions is key to predicting and preventing such violence. We need to know more about how these constructions vary—ethnicity, age, and region of the country are just a few examples of sources of variation in such constructions (see Nutt, Chapter 8, and O'Neil and Nadeau, Chapter 7, this volume, for expanded discussions of these issues).

Third, understanding the relationship of violence to power dynamics is another key element of the picture. The sociocultural context shapes, fosters, and encourages the use of violence to maintain inequitable power relationships in the workplace, in the home, and in the community. Fourth, the majority of women who experience violence are abused by people in their daily environment— the people with whom they live and work. Whether the act of aggression in- volves harassment, rape, or assault, the perpetrator is often known to the victim. This suggests that relational expectations and scripts also play important roles in shaping and perpetuating violence (see Rigazio-DiGilio and Lanza, Chapter 10, this volume).

Fifth, our social institutions tend to trivialize and/or ignore women's experi- ences of violence. Coaches, judges, law enforcement officials, social service workers, religious leaders, teachers, and even mental health professionals have contributed to the prevailing cultural attitudes that serve to maintain and foster male violence. Our social structures themselves often reflect inequitable gender relationships that serve to maintain the legitimacy of male violence. Relationships between female workers and male employers, wives and husbands, female patients and male doctors, female athletes and male coaches, for example, share common structural and ideological features in which women are in positions of subordination to men. These inequities reinforce the patriarchal world view that male domination over women is normal, natural, and expected.

Our health care systems, schools, workplaces, and courts exhibit systematic support for male violence against women on a daily basis. Specific to partner violence, the attitudes and practices of doctors indicate that many are failing to play a role in the prevention and treatment of men's violence against women (Easteal & Easteal, 1992). For example, partner violence often is ignored as a potential cause of problems in female patients seeking medical treatment in emergency rooms (Keller, 1996).

Our current legal and judicial systems enforce existing power relationships and thereby perpetuate partner violence (Brownmiller, 1975). Studies of police response to partner violence indicate that levels of arrests are low, protection of women is often withheld, and the attitude of the state reflects a desire to stay out of family disputes and let the family members work the problems out privately (Koss et al., 1994). Some research suggests that police officers may openly discourage women from filing formal charges against a violent spouse (George, Winfield, & Blazer, 1992). In one study of 1,870 partner violence reports over a 12-month period, less than 28% of cases ended in arrest. Although men were more likely to be identified as batterers, women identified as batterers were more likely to be charged with a serious crime. For example, black women were more likely to be arrested on felony charges (84%) than white men were (19%) for similar behavior (Bourg & Stock, 1994). Even if the male perpetrator is arrested, there are additional biases and problems in our legal system. Legal outcomes in court cases of partner violence are highly dependent on the attitudes of individual judges rather than on firm legal standards (Ford, Rompf, Faragher, & Weisenfluh, 1995). Investigations examining situations in which the justice system has failed to provide protection to female victims of partner violence have exposed several problems: the trivialization of women's experiences by law enforcement officials and judges, problems with arrest policies, and a common myth that both partners are equally responsible for the violent behavior (Busch, Robertson, & Lapsley, 1993). The inability of the criminal justice system to deal effectively with partner violence continues to be a major factor in the perpetuation of that violence.

Sixth, feminists have exposed the destructive effects of male violence—to the woman, her family, and society. Women who have been victimized suffer both immediate and long range consequences to their physical and mental well-being, and these consequences are similar for multiple forms of victimization. Although many effects are immediately apparent following the violent episode(s), other effects may last for years or may surface as intermittent problems (Goodman, Koss, & Russo, 1993; Koss & Heslet, 1992; Koss, Koss, & Woodruff, 1991).

Victims of partner violence may suffer a variety of physical wounds including bruises, cuts, broken bones, loss of hearing or vision, burns, knife wounds, and even death. The types of wounds sustained by victims of partner violence are 13 times more likely to be aimed at the breast, chest, or abdominal areas than those of accident victims (Stark & Flitcraft, 1988; Stark, Flitcraft, & Frazier, 1979). Furthermore, victims of partner violence are likely to have both old and new injuries simultaneously, in various stages of the healing process (e.g., old and new fractures, bruises, or contusions). Stark et al. (1981) reviewed the medical records of an urban area emergency room during a 1-year period and estimated that 21% of all women needing surgical services were victims of partner violence. Other research corroborates these earlier findings, suggesting that 20% to 35% of women seeking emergency room services have been assaulted by an intimate (Hamberger, Saunders, & Hovey, 1992). It is not uncommon for victims of partner violence to become "repeat visitors," presenting themselves to health-care providers repeatedly with increasingly severe injuries (Koss, Koss, & Woodruff, 1991; Stark & Flitcraft, 1988, 1996).

Effects of partner violence can extend beyond physical wounds to include a variety of psychological consequences. The aftereffects of partner violence may look very much like those experienced following any severe trauma—feelings of fearfulness, anxiety, confusion, anger, and powerlessness (Bard & Sangrey, 1986; Herman, 1992). Reactions of shock, denial, depression, and withdrawal also may occur (Dutton, 1992). In one study, as the frequency and intensity of the abuse worsened, depressive symptomatology increased and self-esteem dropped (Cascardi & O'Leary, 1992). Other studies report similar findings (e.g., Kerouac & Lescop, 1986). Long-term psychological consequences may manifest themselves in terms of post-traumatic stress disorder (PTSD). The person with PTSD may exhibit a host of specific psychological outcomes in response to a traumatic event (e.g., natural disaster, military combat, rape). Women victims of partner violence also may exhibit the symptoms of PTSD, which include dissociation, flashbacks, sleep disturbances, and irritability (Browne, 1992; Walker, 1991, 1992).

Consequences of male violence against women are not limited to immediate or short-term physical and psychological outcomes. Partner violence can have far-reaching as well as indirect effects on women's lives. Some of these consequences include high-risk sexual behavior and sexually transmitted diseases (Koss, Koss, & Woodruff, 1991; Nelson, Higginson, & Grant-Worley, 1995; Sturm Carr, Luxenberg, Swoyer & Cicero, 1990), and drug and alcohol abuse (Dutton, 1992; Kilpatrick, 1990). Partner violence also is linked to unwanted pregnancy. In one study among women who reported that their husbands or partners had "physically hurt" them during the 12 months before delivery, 70% of the women also reported that their pregnancy was unintended (Gazmararian et al., 1995).

One of the major indirect consequences of male-perpetrated violence is the effect it has on children who may witness or be involved in the abuse. Violence against women and against children is highly correlated—if one is being abused, it is likely that the other is as well. Even when children are not abused themselves, witnessing partner violence may have far-reaching consequences. Male children who have witnessed a father batter a mother are more likely to use violence in their own adult lives than are male children from nonabusive homes (Straus, Gelles, & Steinmetz, 1980). In addition, partner violence in the home is predictive of children's general psychopathology (McCloskey, Figueredo, & Koss, 1995). Even sibling and parental warmth fail to buffer the negative effects of partner violence on children's mental health.

In conclusion, feminists have emphasized that male violence against women is a complex, multifaceted phenomenon that takes multiple forms and is rooted in patriarchal social structures and cultural roles of women and men. Feminists have documented widespread and long-lasting effects of such violence to the woman, her family, and society, providing irrefutable justification for the argument that society cannot afford to define partner violence as a private issue. Understanding, predicting, and preventing such violence will require a complex and comprehensive approach that intervenes at individual, interpersonal, and structural levels. O'Neil and Harway's multivariate model is a good start in that regard.

A CRITIQUE OF O'NEIL AND HARWAY'S MULTIVARIATE MODEL

O'Neil and Harway's proposed multivariate model of male violence against women incorporates academic theorizing, scientific research findings, and feminist contributions into a working framework for understanding partner violence. The multifaceted nature of partner violence is recognized in multiple layers of analyses—ranging from patriarchal social institutions to interpersonal interactions between men and women. The proposed model can be used as a tool for generating information that ultimately may inform the prediction and prevention of partner violence. We have a number of suggestions, observations, and cautions for applying it.

Our first suggestion is to expand the model beyond predisposing and triggering hypotheses to include consideration of *inhibiting hypotheses*. That is, we need to identify the factors—ranging from fear of punishment to empathic capacity—that suppress or inhibit violent tendencies and that reduce the probability that a man will be violent toward his partner. We argue that all human beings have a potential for violence. Given exposure to so many violent models in American society, knowing how some of us learn to inhibit and redirect that potential is as important as knowing what creates and perpetuates our violent inclinations in the first place. Indeed, many antiviolence programs, such as mandatory arrest laws and programs designed to create antiviolence norms, rest on the assumption that male violence can be inhibited. Second, explanations of male violence against women must address two questions: "Why are males violent and why is it that the women closest to them are primarily the targets for violence?" Some research (e.g., research on the relationship of testosterone to aggression) is aimed more at answering the first question rather than the second, but just answering the first question is not sufficient to explain partner violence. A feminist perspective is particularly important for understanding partner violence.

MACROSOCIETAL EXPLANATIONS

In expanding O'Neil and Harway's discussion of macrosocietal explanations of male violence against women, it is important to recognize that society is a reflection of culture, a concept that encompasses every aspect of societal functioning including material artifacts, language, beliefs, values, norms, skills, and habits, as well as customs, laws, and institutions. If we are to understand how battering might result from historical patterns in America, it is important to take this broader view of the larger sociocultural context. In addition to exploring traditional beliefs and legal sanctions specifically related to violence against women, such as the "rule of thumb," other facilitating and inhibiting elements related to violence in general must be considered. For example, Nisbett's (1993) research on the legacy of the "culture of honor" in the South, as reflected in Southern students' greater likelihood to respond with anger and aggression when provoked, suggests that the links between aggression and feelings of entitlement and respect have cultural roots that need to be explored more thoroughly.

In considering macro-level strategies to inhibit violence, we have yet to see a thorough economic analysis of who benefits from violence and what tactics are used in the service of those interests. For example, who benefits from cultural beliefs that the world is threatening and that we need to purchase firearms to defend our homes? We suspect that a primary prevention strategy attempting to foster a cultural norm of nonviolence (through a media campaign or school-based interventions, for example) would be actively undermined by economic interests that depend on weapon sales. This is also an example of how an aspect of our material culture (in this case, the prevalence of weapons) can contribute to normalizing the idea of violent behavior, as well as increasing the risk of injury and death associated with partner violence.

Another hypothesis of the O'Neil and Harway model that is strongly emphasized by feminist perspectives is the focus on unequal power relationships. We need to know more about how traditional patriarchal values in our culture have become reflected in our organizational and institutional structures, which in turn legitimize and maintain male violence against women. O'Neil and Harway rightly emphasize that clergy, physicians, and others implicitly and explicitly have supported and perpetuated male violence. In fact, insofar as any institution undermines women's economic independence from men, that institution contributes to unequal power relationships between men and women, thereby aiding and abetting intimate violence directly and indirectly.

However institutional structures can perpetuate male violence in ways not obviously related to patriarchal values or gender-based inequalities in power. For example, lack of low-cost housing has forced some battered women to choose between staying in an abusive relationship or becoming homeless. Women's lack of economic resources thus makes lack of access to low-income housing a battered women's issue. In exploring how societal structures support violence against women, it is important to consider that there may be interactive effects between institutional structures and economic factors that create inadvertent support for that violence. In considering cultural supports for patriarchal values, however, it should be remembered that a culture perpetuates patriarchal values through more than its social structures and institutions. In fact, such values underlie the violence considered in all of the content areas of the O'Neil and Harway model.

O'Neil and Harway hypothesize that recent societal changes regarding expectations and realities in women's lives have produced men's fears about loss and increased violence toward women. Some authors (e.g., Kahn, 1984; Kipnis, 1976) have suggested that insofar as power over women becomes a defining quality of manhood, men will hold on to it—and even go so far as to use violence to preserve it. This hypothesis merits further exploration. However, we believe that it should be expanded beyond power to include male expectations for entitlement and privilege. We believe that power is used to enforce male entitlement and privilege. Although using power may be self-reinforcing and may itself become a part of manhood's definition, a full understanding of men's use of power requires an understanding of the patriarchal values it serves.

This hypothesis needs to be crafted with care, because if it constructs women's changing roles as a "cause" for violence, it may provide legitimization for male violence against women and lower inhibitions against that violence. Batterers already have been found to point to "unwifely behaviors" as a defense for their violent acts (Adams, 1988; Dobash & Dobash, 1979; Ptacek, 1988). Indeed, even among college students, women viewed as provoking their batterers are perceived less sympathetically than women who are perceived as not provoking their batterers (Pierce & Harris, 1993). We cannot afford to permit men to make the attribution that their violence is "caused by" women's changing roles any more than we should allow them to say "the devil made me do it." Males must take responsibility for and be accountable for their violent behavior in all its forms. It is male patriarchal values and beliefs about male dominance and entitlement, women's subordination, and the legitimacy of violence to achieve ends that make women's actions a threat—not the women's behavior in itself. Focusing on women's behavior rather than male patriarchal values and beliefs puts the male perspective at the center of the analysis and perpetuates the status quo.

Indeed, the evidence that women's changing roles play a significant role in increasing violence against women is inconsistent, and it is not clear if all relevant factors are systematically controlled. Rape and interpersonal violence are

more likely to be found in societies characterized by an ideology of male toughness and patrilocality, not equality (Otterbein, 1979; Sanday, 1981). Furthermore,
although the decade between 1975 and 1985 was a period of major social change
in women's lives, analyses of data from the National Family Violence Surveys
found that severe husband-to-wife violence declined by 21.1%. Although this
decline was not statistically significant, it is in the opposite direction of the
O'Neil and Harway hypothesis (Straus & Gelles, 1986). Furthermore, there was
a drastic decline in severe husband-to-wife violence in black couples, the couples
in which the wife's status is most likely to have increased faster than her husband's (Hampton, Gelles, & Harrop, 1989).

Although violence is a fact of life for women of all social strata, rates of severe
partner violence are lowest for upper-income white women (28 per 1,000, compared with 144 per 1,000 for lower-income black women; Hampton & Gelles,
1994). Women with unemployed husbands are at the highest risk for partner violence (Hampton & Gelles, 1994). This may be because the marital power dis-
crepancy in couples is greatest for upper-income white women, thus putting them
at the lowest risk for partner violence, although differential reporting is also an
issue. Nonetheless, the fact is that the female group with the greatest income and
education also experiences the lowest rates of violence, whereas lower-income
families experience the highest rates of violence. Although research is clearly
needed, we believe that a full understanding of the relationship between changing roles of women and partner violence will require taking into account both
facilitating and inhibiting factors associated with ethnicity and class. Finally,
interpreting any relationship between women's changing roles and their experience of violence *must take into account the changing population base of violent
families.* Insofar as the greater economic independence of women's changing
roles enables them to leave violent situations, any portrait of the relationship
between women's roles and violence that is based on the women who remain in
such relationships will be incomplete. The dynamics of violence and the psychological characteristics of women in violent relationships may be very different in
a population of battered women who have the economic resources to leave violent relationships, but nonetheless have stayed in them, compared with women
who do not have the economic resources to leave such relationships.

BIOLOGY-RELATED EXPLANATIONS

Research on the relationship of biology (including genes, hormones, and other
biological differences) to men's violence against women suffers from problems
that commonly arise whenever biological explanations of behavior are proposed
(see Greene, Chapter 5, this volume). There is a continued confusion between
correlation and causation, and failure to appreciate that behavior is a product of
the interaction between biology and environment. Further, it is important to

recognize that biology is not equivalent to heredity; it is a product of heredity interacting with environment (genotype is not phenotype). Although these are literally "truisms" of modern science, the implications of these simple facts for conceptualizing biology's contributions to behavior have yet to be fully appreciated (witness the popularity of evolutionary "explanations" of behavior that substitute labels for understanding mechanisms; see also Silverstein, Chapter 6, this volume). Correlational studies (e.g., those that correlate testosterone levels and violent behaviors) cannot distinguish cause from effect and do not explain the mechanisms involved. Until we design research that focuses on mechanisms, we will continue to be mired in controversies about the meaning of correlational findings. For example, the relationship of testosterone to activity level, temperament, response to frustration, and lack of impulse control has yet to be understood.

Research on the relationship between testosterone levels and violence, for example, is extremely controversial. Indeed, some research suggests that if the effects of testosterone are compared with those of a placebo, the placebo has a greater effect than the testosterone itself (Bjorkqvist, Nygren, Bjorklund, & Bjorkqvist, 1994). Although testosterone levels have been linked to aggressive behaviors in other mammals (Svare & Kinsley, 1987), the mechanisms that explain the links are unclear. Animal research suggests that fighting can lead to both increases and decreases in testosterone levels, depending on whether the animal wins or loses, respectively (Rose, Bernstein, & Gordon, 1975). Similar results are found in studies with humans (Booth, Shelley, Mazur, Tharp, & Kittok, 1989). In one study, college wrestlers who won their matches showed greater levels of circulating testosterone than losers (Elias, 1981). However, the same results were found in the case of winners and losers of tennis matches—a game that involves activity and competition, but certainly not violence (Mazur & Lamb, 1980). There also seems to be a correlation between testosterone and sensation-seeking (Daitzman & Zuckerman, 1980). Such findings underscore the importance of distinguishing between testosterone's links to aggression and those to activity, competition, and sensation-seeking.

Learning clearly plays a role in maintaining, if not acquiring, aggressive behaviors, even among nonhuman species. For example, whether castration leads to a reduction of aggressiveness depends on previous experience (Maruniak, Desjardins, & Bronson, 1977). Given that there is a role for learning even in "lower" animals, generalization of findings from animal studies to humans must be made with caution.

Some correlational studies report that offenders with testosterone levels higher than those in other offenders commit more violent crimes and break more prison rules (Dabbs, Carr, Frady, & Riad, 1995; Dabbs, Jurkovic, & Frady, 1991), although others have reported no relationship between blood levels of testosterone and rate of solitary confinement or breaking rules (Kreuz & Rose, 1972). Research by Dabbs and Morris (1990) suggests that a biopsychosocial approach for understanding the correlation of testosterone levels and deviant behavior is warranted. Their study of 4,462 veterans found that men in the upper 10th percentile of testosterone production were more likely to assault their wives and others. They also were more likely to use drugs, be arrested for nontraffic violations, and be absent from the military without leave. The important point here is that the relationship of testosterone to such behaviors was stronger for men of low socioeconomic status. Additional analyses based on this sample found that the relationship of testosterone to deviant behavior depended on social integration (defined by educational achievement, job stability, marriage, and participation in clubs, religious meetings, or organized groups). When previous delinquency and measures of social integration were controlled, testosterone no longer made a significant contribution to variation in adult deviance (r^2 change = 0.0004). An examination of moderating effects revealed that testosterone level had no relationship to deviant behavior among men who were socially integrated, but it did have a relationship for men who lacked social integration (Booth & Osgood, 1993).

Does testosterone cause aggression or simply amplify aggressive tendencies? Research suggests the amygdala influences aggression by communicating with the hypothalamus via the stria terminalis. What happens when you inject testosterone into that area? You get an effect only if the amygdala is already sending signals down the pathway. In that case, testosterone shortens the resting time between signals. Testosterone does not create waves of excitation down the pathway, however (for a detailed discussion on this and other related research, see Sapolsky, 1997). This, combined with the findings of Booth and Osgood (1993), suggests that testosterone heightens and maintains levels of arousal that, if not checked or channeled by the social context, can result in aggression.

Animal studies have shown that aggression is reinforcing—even the opportunity to be aggressive is sufficient to reinforce behavior in angry animals (Azrin, Hutchinson, & McLaughlin, 1965; Plotnick, Mir, & Delgado, 1971). This may be because the emotion of anger is a mediator for the translation of arousal into aggression. Researchers are beginning to explore possible physiological mechanisms that underlie such "good feelings" in response to aggression in humans. For example, researchers have found that being verbally or physically aggressive toward a source of anger can reduce blood pressure in angry subjects (Hokanson, Burgess, & Cohen, 1963). Jacobson et al. (1994) identified a subgroup of batterers who experience decreases in heart rate in conjunction with arguing, providing another example of research that explores potential physiological mechanisms that underlie aggression. Different mechanisms may apply, depending on whether the aggression is in response to frustration, threat, pain, or violation of entitlement, or is used instrumentally to achieve a goal rather than as an end in itself.

We suspect that the most promising avenue of research into the contribution of biological factors to aggressive behavior in general, and violence against women in particular, will be research that examines how biological and cognitive processes interact to influence emotion, particularly the emotion of anger. Ever since the classic study of Schachter and Singer (1962), which gave us the two-factor theory of emotion, numerous studies have documented the phenomenon of misattribution of arousal. That is, people mistakenly interpret the causes of their feelings in a wide variety of contexts (e.g., Ross & Olson, 1981; Storms & Nisbett, 1970). If some batterers have a more reactive physiology, that may provide a basis for misattribution of arousal to anger, which may in turn lead to aggression. In any case, it is the combination of arousal and context that must be considered if the emotional experience is to be understood (Lazarus, 1991a, 1991b; Reisenzein, 1983).

These theories provide a framework for considering biological, cognitive, and situational factors in interaction. For example, Lazarus (1991a, 1991b) suggested that whether anger is the emotion an aroused person responds with in a particular situation depends on the person's cognitive appraisal of the *meaning* of the situation. He proposed that anger results when a person perceives a threat to his or her ego identity or basic values (including fairness and justice), which leads to an appraisal of a personal slight or insult. Anger becomes linked to ideas of retaliation and vengeance because they offer ways to repair a damaged ego. Insofar as cultural norms lead males to expect entitlement and privilege, anger may result when those expectations are violated.

Other cognitive appraisal theories of emotion that focus on interpretation of the causes and implications of events (negative vs. positive) also hold promise in this area (e.g., Ellsworth, 1994). These theories suggest that our cognitions can not only determine our emotions in the absence of previous physiological arousal, but they also can lead to such arousal. Does arousal on the part of batterers come before or after the appraisal of an event? Only research that applies these theories to battering will answer such questions. Meanwhile, these theories provide a bridge between biological and social-role theories of male violence toward women. To these we now turn.

GENDER-ROLE-RELATED EXPLANATIONS

Gender-role socialization provides for the transmission of the cultural values of patriarchy, including male entitlement, privilege, and domination. Russo and Green (1993) argued that all gender-related behaviors, including male violence against women, can be conceptualized as reflections of gender roles rather than individual traits. The masculine gender role, which is not tied to a specific role context (e.g., home or workplace), includes agentic qualities of leadership, power, and control (Spence & Helmreich, 1978). Males are encouraged and expected to engage in inequitable power relationships with females. Violence is often viewed as a tool or a means to exert power and maintain control. These qualities sometimes have been referred to as machismo (this should not be confused with the concept of machismo as found in traditional Hispanic cultures). Machismo attitudes in the United States, as measured by subscriptions to magazines involving guns, sports cars, body building, and pornography, are strongly correlated with family homicide rates (Lee, 1995). Similarly, societies characterized by an ideology of toughness report greater degrees of rape and interpersonal violence (Sanday, 1981). These research findings suggest that strong gender-role stereotypes and attitudes are likely to contribute to male violence against women.

Although batterers have been found to hold misogynistic attitudes toward women, the relationship of such attitudes to battering behaviors is not understood. We suggest that such attitudes function as disinhibitors, legitimizing women as a target for violent behavior and paving the way for the translation of arousal into anger and aggression directed toward women if other factors are present.

As described earlier, theories of emotion that consider the interaction of biological, cognitive, and relational processes have promise for exploring how batterers interpret their experiences and develop and express their emotions. Is male violence toward women an expression of anger at the erosion of male entitlements or is it an expression of frustration in other domains (e.g., employment) redirected toward a target that has been legitimized by patriarchal values? Understanding the cognitive processes of batterers may be the key to understanding the development and transformation of their emotional experiences.

Patriarchal attitudes are also transmitted and reinforced through the mass media, a powerful socialization agent. Although there has been an increased awareness of male violence against women in the media, this awareness has not always yielded favorable outcomes. As news coverage of partner violence has increased from the 1970s to the present, so too have popular TV and Hollywood movies on the subject. Unfortunately, many of these films have served only to reinforce existing national ideologies that emphasize individual choice and free will (Kozol, 1995). Larger structural forces are often ignored in media portrayals of male violence against women. In addition, repeated exposure to violent media has been shown to desensitize participants to partner violence. Ratings of sympathy for partner violence victims and ratings of the severity of their injuries have been found to decrease after repeated exposure to such films (Mullins & Linz, 1995).

Male lack of empathy and sensitivity to others is of concern here because such feelings are important inhibitors of violence against women. For example, research suggests that whether male fantasies about sexual aggression are actually expressed in behavior depends on how sensitive they are to others' feelings (Dean & Malamuth, 1997). Indeed, empathy has been found to moderate the relationship between physiological measures of sexual arousal (penile tumescence) and aggressive behavior. Such arousal predicts aggression when empathy is low, but not when empathy is high (Malamuth, Heavey, & Linz, n.d.). Insofar as male gender-role socialization fails to instill a capacity for empathy in general, and for women in particular, it increases the likelihood of male violence.

Gender-role socialization also must be considered in the context of socialization into the larger culture, because other cultural values may have facilitating or inhibiting effects on gender-role dynamics. For example, the cultural value of individualism may result in drawing attention away from the structural factors that foster gender violence. However, it also may provide a counterforce to patriarchal values, fostering recognition of women as people with the full rights and responsibilities accorded to all citizens. A comprehensive approach should examine how specific gender-role values and expectations are reinforced and contravened by other cultural values and expectations, and how factors (e.g., individualism) may have effects in more than one direction.

INTER-GENDER RELATIONAL EXPLANATIONS

Although we agree with O'Neil and Harway that differential socialization of males and females contributes to male violence against women, we do not believe that differences in patterns of communication related to instrumentality and expressiveness are a major factor in the potential for that violence. We prefer to focus on the fact that gender-role socialization includes learning patriarchal relational scripts that can promote interpersonal violence. There is a basic heterosexual cultural script that legitimizes male dominance and eroticizes sexual inequality (Bem, 1993). The idea that women should seek out male partners who are older, taller, stronger, bigger, more educated, higher in status, more experienced, and more highly paid transforms female inequality into a romantic ideal. Male-centered objectification of women that emphasizes women's physical attractiveness and ability to satisfy men's desires provides another powerful buttress to inequality in the heterosexual script (Fredrickson & Roberts, 1997). We need to know more about how such scripts shape male–female communication and undermine the development of mutual respect and understanding between men and women.

Specifically, we need to learn more about how dating and other relationship scripts foster values, beliefs, and expectations that facilitate and inhibit violence (Pagelow, 1984). We know that destructive dating scripts can be acquired early. One study of 1,700 school children found that 57% of girls and 65% of boys reported that it was acceptable for a man to force a woman to have sex if they had been dating for more than 6 months ("Teens Express Themselves," 1988). We suspect that the idea that it is all right to use force to get a partner to do something generalizes beyond sexual intercourse. Once this concept of permissible instrumental violence becomes an acceptable part of the heterosexual script, then whether or not such violence is used probably depends on the number and the strength of the inhibiting factors present. In this context, the idea that good communication skills will play an important role in reducing partner violence seems naive.

In conceptualizing how gender-related patterns of communication might contribute to the potential for violence, it is important to distinguish between ideal gender-role socialization and the reality of men's lives. Ideally, men are socialized to be rational and to use thought and reasoning to solve problems. We argue that if all males were truly socialized in this manner, they would not be batterers, because in the long run, partner violence results only in unhappiness and disaster for all. The links to battering between lower income and less education suggest that, in fact, batterers are not good problem solvers and reasoners with regard to their battering behavior.

However, the foregoing are not the only characteristics bound up in the male gender-role package that might affect communication. Males are taught to expect entitlement and privilege, along with the respect and subservience that go along with those characteristics. These expectations may lead to patriarchal scripts for interaction that, when violated, lead to the emotion of anger, and if inhibiting factors are not present, that anger in turn may lead to violence.

Although we agree that psychological abuse is probably a precursor to physical violence, we do not believe that women's alleged superiority in verbal warfare plays a significant role in that escalation. We suspect that psychological abuse provides a means for batterers to identify women who will tolerate abuse and be unable to defend themselves. Women who avoid relationships with abusive men are thus "selected out" of the batterer's pool of targets. This may be one reason that sexually abused women are more likely to have violent partners than women who are not sexually abused (Russo et al., in press). Psychological abuse also may have a disinhibiting effect on violent behavior. We argue, however, that the idea that the verbal skills of battered women threaten their partners and that battering is a means to restore masculine identity or diminished self-esteem is a faulty construction of the dynamics. We agree that battering is a means to enforce male entitlements, manifest a batterer's sense of masculine identity, and buttress self-esteem, but the woman's behavior has little to do with it. No matter how hard a battered woman tries to please her husband, he can still find excuses for battering her. Researchers must beware of legitimizing the excuse of threatened masculinity in response to a woman's verbal attacks.

Lightdale and Prentice (1994) provided a powerful demonstration of the relationship of social-role expectations to aggression. They were interested in what would happen to gender differences in video game aggression when social role expectations were removed from the situation by a de-individuation manipulation. They found that males were more aggressive than females in the individuated condition, but that these differences were eliminated in the de-individuated condition. The gender difference (males were more aggressive than females) that was found in the individuated condition was eliminated in the de-individuated condition. Given the power of role expectations to foster as well as inhibit violence and to legitimize specific victims, gender-role dynamics is clearly a high-priority area for research and intervention.

PARTNER VIOLENCE THROUGH A FEMINIST LENS

Explaining partner violence from a feminist perspective involves an understanding of how patriarchal values become institutionalized and communicated. Many broad theories of violence fail to explain why male violence is directed at women, or why partner violence is so common compared with other forms of male violence. Some theories attempt to explain why men are more violent than women, but not why some men are more violent than others. Feminist approaches to partner violence seek to explain why women are often the victims, and men the perpetrators. They also seek to understand why the consequences of male violence become denied and trivialized, and the functions that male violence serves in the larger society. Patriarchal values serve as a starting point for understanding gendered violence dynamics.

These patriarchal values exist in a variety of forms across a variety of levels. At the macrosocietal level, our legal system, institutions, and other societal structures reflect and perpetuate these values. At the inter-generational level, these patriarchal values are passed down from generation to generation through direct instruction as well as observational learning. Many families communicate these values through actual physical force, which may explain why children from abusive homes often end up abusing their own partners and children. At a cultural level, the mass media reproduces and reinforces patriarchal values. Finally, at the individual level, patriarchal values can become incorporated into everyday thought and action as men who expect to be able to control the women in their lives resort to physical violence, sexual violence, or both when their privileged status is threatened. Eliminating male violence against women requires working at all of these levels. In the final analysis, however, striking at the core of male violence—at the androcentric assumption that males have a natural or God-given right to privilege and entitlement over women that justifies the use of force to achieve male goals—will be the key to preventing male violence against women.

Male Offenders

Our Understanding From the Data

RICHARD J. GELLES

There has been an enormous expansion of interest and study of the problem of violence toward women since the early 1970s. The main focus of research, study, and programs has been directed at the female victims of battering. Although there has been a substantial growth of programs, especially treatment groups for batterers, the fact remains that the main research questions, the majority of funding and programs, and most of the public attention have been aimed at the victims, or survivors, of battering.

There are a number of reasons why the main focus of study and programs has been directed at women and not at male offenders. First, and perhaps most obvious, victims have the most pressing needs for services and programs. Providing safety, advocacy, and appropriate criminal justice and social service intervention for victims is a main need because, until the 1970s, there were essentially no services and only minimal means of protecting female victims of violence. In addition, the feminist perspective, which is the dominant theoretical perspective used by advocates, clinicians, and many researchers in the area of violence toward women, is strong on practical programs aimed at victims of violence and abuse (Yllö, 1993).

Two major theoretical approaches to the issue of battering explain the widespread pattern of abuse as imbedded in the social context. The feminist perspective explains violence toward women using the concept "power and coercive control" (Ylö, 1993). A sociological model explains that men are violent because "they can be" (Gelles & Straus, 1988). Neither model places much emphasis on identifying or distinguishing particular factors that raise the risk of battering among some men and not among others. Both perspectives are so widely subscribed that they minimize the motivation for further study or explanation of the behavior of batterers. Finally, an important implicit assumption in the feminist and other approaches to violence is that male batterers do not change, and equally important, *all* men are capable of battering or do batter at some point in an intimate relationship. The notion that *all* men are capable of battering is built on the assumption of a continuum of violence—that violence differs by degree and not by kind or type.

These assumptions notwithstanding, there is a need for a better and more detailed understanding of male offenders, including the factors—individual, social, and cultural—that increase the risk of battering. Such an understanding is crucial for refining causal models of battering and for developing appropriate and effective intervention and prevention programs.

This chapter reviews the empirical research on men's violence toward women. The first section examines the methodological approaches used to examine men's violence toward their intimate partners. The second section reviews the research on risk factors for men's violence toward women. Finally, the chapter concludes by examining the empirical support for the 13 hypotheses proposed by O'Neil and Harway (1997; Chapter 2, this volume) for explaining men's violence toward women.

METHODOLOGICAL APPROACHES TO
THE STUDY OF BATTERERS

Because most of the research and programming has been aimed at women who were victims of battering, there has been less research on male offenders. The main data collection techniques used to study batterers have been surveys, analyses of clinical data, analyses of data collected by police departments, data collected from men in batterers' programs, and information about batterers collected from their women victims. Many research studies of batterers do not employ comparison groups, samples tend to be small, and the generalizability of the findings is questionable—especially data on batterers collected from women victims.

As noted earlier, there are three main sources of data on family violence and men's violence toward women: (1) clinical data, (2) official report data, and (3) social surveys.

Clinical studies carried out by psychiatrists, psychologists, and counselors continue to be a frequent source of data on family violence. This is primarily due to the fact that these investigators have the most direct access to cases of family violence. The clinical or agency setting (including men's treatment programs) can provide access to extensive in-depth information about particular cases of violence. Studies of violence toward women have relied heavily on samples of women who seek help at battered-women's shelters (Dobash & Dobash, 1979; Giles-Sims, 1983; Pagelow, 1981). Such samples are important because they are often the only way to obtain detailed data on the most severely battered women. Such data are also necessary to study the effect of intervention programs. However, such data, because they are based on small, nonrepresentative samples, cannot be used to estimate the incidence and prevalence of intimate violence. Clinical studies of females who were victims of battering have been used to obtain data about male offenders. Female victims are asked about the personal and social characteristics of their batterers, as well as data about the context of the battering. There are obvious reliability and validity problems that arise out of developing profiles of male offenders from data provided by their victims. One important limitation is that the female victims may not have access to, or know about, key personal or social characteristics of their male partners. It is impossible to ascertain much about the personality of male offenders if the data are collected from their partners. Clinical studies that collect data directly from male offenders tend to be limited by having small samples and no comparison groups. The obvious limitation of clinical studies of male batterers is that abusive men in treatment programs and clinical settings *are not* representative of all men who use violence against intimate partners. Other data on male offenders are collected from men participating in treatment groups. However, these studies typically focus on the effectiveness of group treatment rather than on risk markers and correlates of male battering.

Official reports constitute a second source of data on violence toward women. Although there is an abundance of official report data on child maltreatment (because of mandatory reporting laws), there has been no tradition of officially reporting domestic violence, with the exception of a handful of states that collect data on spouse abuse. The *Uniform Crime Reports* provide data on criminal family violence and family homicide, but these are limited to instances of family violence that are reported to the police, and only a small fraction of the instances of violence between marital partners are ever reported to the police (U.S. Department of Justice, 1996; Gelles & Straus, 1988). The *Uniform Crime Reports* do, however, provide reasonably reliable and valid data on fatal domestic violence. *Uniform Crime Report* data on domestic violence, including the "Supplementary Homicide Statistics," include information about the offender and the offender–victim relationship. Thus, these data can be disaggregated to examine age, race, income, and weapon used in domestic homicides. Official report homicide data from the National Center for Health Statistics are based on death certificates and thus include no information about the offender.

Social surveys are the third source of data. Such surveys are constrained by the low base rate of most forms of abuse and violence in families and the sensitive and taboo nature of the topic. Some investigators cope with the problem of low base rate by employing purposive or nonrepresentative sampling techniques to identify cases. College students are a frequently (perhaps too frequently) used population in studies of intimate violence (Cate, Henton, Christopher, & Lloyd, 1982; Henton, Cate, Koval, Lloyd, & Christopher, 1983; Laner, 1983; Makepeace, 1981, 1983). Although surveys of college students do collect data directly from male offenders, such samples are not representative of men in general, and are certainly not representative of the full range of intimate and committed relationships. A third method includes two national surveys of family violence carried out by Straus and Gelles: one in 1976, and a second in 1985. A fourth type of survey data on violence between intimates is the victimization data collected in the annual National Crime Victimization Survey (NCVS). The U.S. Justice Department has published a number of reports on intimate violence based on the data collected by the NCVS (Bachman, 1994; Bachman & Saltzman, 1995; Gaquin, 1977–1978; Langan & Innes, 1986; U.S. Department of Justice, 1980, 1984, 1994). Although victimization surveys are valuable because they are based on representative samples and have large samples, these surveys have a limited value for understanding offenders, because the data are collected from the victims and there is minimal information collected about the offenders.

Each of the major data sources has its own validity problems. Clinical data are never representative, and few investigators gathering data from clinical samples employ comparison groups. Official records suffer from variations in definitions, nonuniform reporting and recording practices, and biased samples of violent and abusive behaviors and persons (Finkelhor & Hotaling, 1984; Weis, 1989; Widom, 1988). The biases of social survey data on intimate violence include inaccurate recall, differential interpretation of questions, and intended and unintended response error (Weis, 1989).

CORRELATES OF MALE BATTERING

This section reviews the data on risk factors or correlates of men's violence against women. There has been some heated debate regarding what the risk and protective factors are for men's violence toward women. Some spokespersons argue that violence cuts across all social groups (Yllö, 1993), whereas others agree that it cuts across social groups, but not evenly (Gelles, 1993b). Some researchers and practitioners place more emphasis on psychological factors (e.g., Dutton, 1994, 1995; Dutton, Saunders, Starzomski, & Bartholomew, 1994; Hamberger & Hastings, 1986, 1988, 1991; O'Leary, 1993), whereas others locate the key risk factors among social factors (e.g., Gelles, 1993a, 1993b; Gelles & Straus, 1988; Straus, Gelles, & Steinmetz, 1980). Still a third group places the greatest emphasis on cultural factors; for example, the patriarchal social organization of societies (e.g., Dobash & Dobash, 1979, 1992; Yllö, 1988, 1993). In addition, as noted in the previous section, the source of data has an effect on the factors and variables that are identified as risk and protective factors. When basing an analysis of risk and protective factors on clinical data or official report data, risk and protective factors are confounded with factors such as labeling bias or agency or clinical setting catchment area. Researchers have long noted that certain individuals and families are more likely to be correctly and incorrectly labeled as offenders or victims of family violence. Similarly, some individuals and families are insulated from being correctly or incorrectly labeled or identified as offenders or victims. Social survey data are not immune to confounding problems either, because social or demographic factors may be related to willingness to participate in a self-report survey and tendency toward providing socially desirable responses.

The final caveat is that any listing of risk and protective factors may unintentionally convey or reinforce a notion of single-factor explanations for family violence. Clearly, no phenomenon as complex as domestic violence could possibly be explained with a single-factor model. Equally clear is the fact that almost all of the risk and protective factors discussed in this chapter and in the literature have relatively modest correlations with domestic violence. This chapter reviews risk factors for heuristic purposes, with the full knowledge that multiple factors are related to domestic violence and that there is often an interaction between and among risk and protective factors.

EXPERIENCING AND WITNESSING VIOLENCE

Drawing from research on child abuse, studies of violence against women have examined whether batterers were themselves victims of battering when they were children. The results of studies using various data collection techniques consistently find that batterers are more likely to have been abused when they were children than are men who were not abused (Caesar, 1988; Gelles, 1974; Kalmuss, 1984; Okun, 1986; Rosenbaum & O'Leary, 1981; Walker, 1979). Although the magnitude of the association varies from study to study, nearly all examinations of batterers find some association.

More important than being a victim of violence as a child is *witnessing* violence between parents. Men who witness their fathers hit and batter their mothers are more likely to batter as adults than are men who have not witnessed violence toward women (Brisson, 1981; Caesar, 1988; Gelles & Straus, 1988; Okun, 1986; Rosenbaum & O'Leary, 1981).

On occasion, some investigators and observers place too much emphasis on these findings and transform a probabilistic relationship into a single factor or deterministic explanation. Although the association between experiencing and witnessing violence during childhood and later exhibiting battering behavior tends to be consistent and strong, it is neither the only nor even the most important factor that explains or predicts battering. When the inter-generational transmission of violence occurs, it is probably the result of a complex set of social and psychological processes and is confounded with other risk markers, such as marital conflict and socioeconomic status (Hotaling & Sugarman, 1990).

INDIVIDUAL CHARACTERISTICS

A number of individual characteristics are associated with battering. Batterers tend to have a significantly lower self-esteem than nonbatterers (Goldstein & Rosenbaum, 1985). Batterers are significantly more depressed than nonbatterers (Maiuro et al., 1988). Investigators, however, caution that low self-esteem and depression may not be directly causally related to battering. Self-esteem may lead to battering or arise as a result of the battered women leaving the relationship. Similarly, depressive symptoms may arise after the abusive behavior. Because most of the studies that examine self-esteem and depression among batterers are clinical studies or entail the collection of data from men in treatment programs, it is at least plausible that lowered self-esteem and depression arise concurrently with or after the battering incident and are not precursors to violence. Most researchers, however, believe that low self-esteem *is* a precursor to battering.

A number of studies have found a high incidence of psychopathology and personality disorders—most frequently antisocial personality disorder, borderline personality organization, and post-traumatic stress disorder—among men who assault intimate partners (Dutton, 1994, 1995; Dutton & Starzomski, 1993; Dutton et al., 1994; Hamberger & Hastings, 1986, 1988, 1991; Hart, Dutton, & Newlove, 1993). Batterers appear to be a heterogeneous group, which has led some researchers to develop typologies to represent different subgroups (Dutton & Golant, 1995; Gondolf & Fisher, 1988; Holtzworth-Munroe & Stuart, 1994; Jacobson et al., 1994).

POWER AND CONTROL

There is a constellation of individual and relationship factors that supports the notion that battering arises out of men's need and desire to use power and coercive control with their partners. A number of researchers (e.g., Gelles, 1974; Hornung, McCullough, & Sugimoto, 1981; O'Brien, 1971) have found strong relationships among status inconsistency, status incompatibility, and battering. Men whose educational attainment, occupational attainment, and income are less than those of their partners (status incompatibility) are more likely to batter. Similarly, men whose occupational attainment or income is lower than would be expected due to their educational attainment (status inconsistency) are also more likely to batter. Thus, men who fail to attain the culturally expected dominant position in the family are more likely to use verbal, physical, and sexual abuse to achieve control in the absence of material and cultural sources of power and dominance.

More individually focused research on batterers finds that batterers tend to show less assertiveness toward their wives than nonabusive men (Rosenbaum & O'Leary, 1981). Abusive men are "less assertive in expressing their wants and needs in a socially appropriate and growth oriented manner" (Maiuro, Cahn, & Vitaliano, 1986, p. 285). Deficits of assertiveness or verbal expressiveness and insufficient problem-solving skills might provoke violence as a way to handle conflicts and difficulties.

Research points out that batterers have difficulties with "developing close, intimate relationships, based on mutuality" (Barnett & Hamberger, 1992, p. 34). For some men, intimacy is threatening and reinforces their dependency on their wives, thus leading to an increased use of verbal and physical force.

A review of 52 case comparison studies did not find significant differences in measures of sex-role inequality between violent and nonviolent couples (Hotaling & Sugarman, 1986). In a later analysis, the authors observe that expectations about division of labor in the household were one of the four markers associated with a risk factor they labeled *marital conflict*—the other three markers were marital conflict, frequency of husband's drinking, and educational incompatibility (Hotaling & Sugarman, 1990).

SOCIAL FACTORS

A commonly held belief in the field of family violence in general, and woman battering in particular, is that violence and abuse cut across all social classes and groups and that anyone can be an abuser. Although there is indeed much empirical support for this conventional wisdom, the data consistently indicate that although abusive behavior cuts across social groups and categories, it *does not do so evenly*. Certain social factors are risk markers of higher rates of violence and battering.

Age

As with all forms of violence and violent criminal behavior, battering is more likely to be committed by men under 30 years of age (Brisson, 1981; Fagan & Browne, 1994; Gelles & Straus, 1988; Roberts, 1987).

Employment

Unemployed men have higher rates of battering than employed men (Gelles & Straus, 1988; Howell & Pugliesi, 1988; Straus, Gelles, & Steinmetz, 1980). Blue-collar workers report higher rates of battering than workers with white-collar occupations (Bergman & Brismar, 1992; Gelles & Straus, 1988; Roberts, 1987).

Income

Given the data on employment and occupation, it is no surprise that men with a low income or who reside in low-income households have higher rates of abusive behavior toward women (Gelles & Straus, 1988; Hotaling & Sugarman, 1990).

Stress and Marital Conflict

The mechanism through which unemployment, low income, and other factors seem to work to produce battering is likely to be stress. The greater the number of individual, familial, and social stressors individuals encounter, the greater the likelihood of battering behavior. Straus and his colleagues (1980) found a direct relationship between stress and battering only for those men between the poverty line and the highest-income group. It seems that those in the top-income group can use economic resources to insulate themselves from the stress of stressor events. For those below the poverty line, the effects of poverty may be so pervasive that additional stressors have little important effect on the likelihood of violent behavior.

Hotaling and Sugarman's (1990) meta-analysis of factors related to male violent offenses found that high levels of marital conflict and low socioeconomic status emerged as the primary predictors of an increased likelihood and severity of wife assault. However, the relationship among stressful life events, the personalities of the people affected by them, and the role of stress as a factor in marital conflict and family violence remains poorly understood. It is not clear whether violent men lack conflict management skills or whether the sources of marital conflict in seriously or frequently violent relationships are different from those that characterize relationships that are nonviolent or infrequently violent (Hotaling & Sugarman, 1990).

Social Isolation

Researchers have found an association between social isolation and abusive behavior (Straus, Gelles, & Steinmetz, 1980). It is not entirely clear whether the social isolation is a causal factor or a symptom of a more pervasive pattern of controlling behavior exhibited by the batterer. In other words, isolation might be a causal factor—perhaps because the lack of social networks increases the influence of stressor events—or batterers may deliberately isolate themselves and, more important, their wives or partners, as part of an overall pattern of coercive control.

Alcohol and Drugs

The "demon rum" explanation for violence and abuse in the home is one of the most pervasive and widely believed explanations for all forms of violence. Addictive and illicit drugs, such as cocaine, crack, heroin, marijuana, and LSD, are also considered causal agents in child abuse, wife abuse, and other forms of abuse and violence. The relationship among alcohol, drugs, and battering is not as simple as the explanation provided in the "demon rum" mode—that alcohol and other illicit drugs reduce inhibitions and, thus, increase the likelihood of violence. Coleman and Straus (1983) and Kaufman-Kantor and Straus (1987) found that men who drank the most did not have the highest rates of battering. Drinking frequency or drinking amount is not directly related to the likelihood of violence. The highest rates of battering were among binge drinkers. Research on drugs other than alcohol does find correlations between drug use and violence, but the causal mechanisms are much more complex than the simple "disinhibition" explanation (Gelles, 1993a).

EVALUATING EMPIRICAL AND THEORETICAL SUPPORT FOR THE 13 HYPOTHESES IN THE O'NEIL AND HARWAY MODEL

Although research on male violent offenders has lagged behind empirical investigations of female victims, a sufficient body of knowledge on the correlates of male offending has been amassed to yield both hypotheses and theoretical and conceptual models about the causes of violence against women. Gelles and Straus (1979), for example, reviewed 19 theories of family violence, and O'Neil and Harway (1997; Chapter 2, this volume) enumerated 13 hypotheses related to men's violence toward women.

This section summarizes the empirical and theoretical support for the 13 hypotheses, grouped under the 4 categories proposed by O'Neil and Harway: (1) macrosocietal explanations; (2) biological, neuroanatomical, and hormonal explanations; (3) men's restrictive and sexist gender-role socialization and specific patterns of gender-role conflict, and (4) inter-gender relational explanations.

MACROSOCIETAL EXPLANATIONS

The three macrosocietal hypotheses are all derived from feminist theories of violence toward women (Dobash & Dobash, 1979; Pagelow, 1984; Smith, 1991a,

1991b; Yllö, 1983, 1988, 1993). The three hypotheses are these:

1. Battering results from historical patterns in America that glorify men's violence, particularly violence toward women.

2. Organizational, institutional, and patriarchal structures in society maintain unequal power relationships between men and women that tacitly or directly support domestic oppression and violence against women.

3. Recent changes in gender roles in American society regarding expectations and realities of women's lives have produced men's fears of power loss and increased violence toward women.

The three hypotheses are based on the assumption that the historical pattern of patriarchal social organization of societies supports violence toward women. This occurs because women are structurally subordinate to men and because men's control of women is socially approved and glorified. Changes in society that challenge men's dominant social position result in more violence as men attempt to retain their dominant position.

These three hypotheses are the most difficult to test. The historical hypothesis is generally supported by selected historical data, as well as by data that support the assumption that all known societies are patriarchal. Beyond the anecdotal historical data, there are no consistent cross-cultural or historical data with which to actually test the first two hypotheses in this category. Because patriarchy is found in all societies, the key independent variable in Hypothesis 2 is essentially invariable and thus the hypothesis is not testable as stated.

The third hypothesis could be tested; however, as noted in an earlier section of this chapter, there are few consistently reliable incidence or prevalence data that can be used to assess the claim that change in gender roles produces men's fear of loss of power and thus increases violence toward women. Although advocates claim that violence toward women is increasing, survey data (Gelles & Straus, 1988; Straus & Kaufman-Kantor, 1992) and official report data on homicide (Craven, 1996) indicate that violence toward women actually has decreased in the last few years. Thus, the data that do exist do not support the hypothesis that increased violence occurs as a result of changes in gender roles in the United States. However, it could be that changing gender roles affect only a certain segment of the population—unemployed men, men with a low level of education, men with few verbal skills, or men who have few of the resources with which to claim the socially defined dominant role for men in families. We have not yet tested whether domestic violence rates have increased for these subpopulations of men.

BIOLOGICAL, NEUROANATOMICAL, AND
HORMONAL EXPLANATIONS

Explanations of violence against women that are based on biological, neuroanatomical, or hormonal factors are, to a certain extent, antithetical to macrosocietal explanations. Macrosocietal explanations see violence toward women as a gendered behavior, which results from the social organization of society. Biologically based theories see violence as the result of intra-individual factors, which are theoretically independent of culture or social organization.

Biological hypotheses are promising, largely because they have not yet been tested. Research on biological factors is often based on studies that obtain subjects from incarcerated populations. Although this is an accessible population, such sampling confounds the factors that led the men to be "caught" with the factors that caused their violent behavior. There are few general population surveys that examine the relationship between biological factors and violence. Although such studies would be difficult to carry out (due to the low base rate of severe violence in the general population and ethical/informed consent issues), they would be valuable.

To date, the only suggestive empirical support for biological hypotheses of violence toward women is the Jacobson et al. (1994) research that identified a small group of violent men who were labeled *vagal reactors*. This group experienced a drop in heart rate during a laboratory situation that involved a marital argument. The men whose heart rate dropped were more violent than the men whose heart rate increased during the argument. This finding suggests a biological or hormonal basis of severe violent behavior toward women.

MEN'S RESTRICTIVE AND SEXIST GENDER-ROLE
SOCIALIZATION AND SPECIFIC PATTERNS
OF GENDER-ROLE CONFLICT

These three hypotheses focus on male attitudes toward women and patterns of male–female conflict as the basis of violence toward women. The attitude hypothesis (Hypothesis 6) rests on social learning theory. Patterns of gender conflict draw from feminist theory, whereas the hypotheses about men's unidentified and unexpressed emotions are less theoretically based than the other two hypotheses in this group.

Hypothesis 6, which states that men's misogynistic attitudes toward women learned during gender-role socialization contribute to men's violence toward women, is a social–psychological derivative of the macrosocial hypothesis that relates patriarchy to violence toward women. Research, however, does not generally find that attitudes toward sex roles are risk factors for violence toward women (Hotaling & Sugarman, 1986). Research has found that hypermasculinity correlates with attitudes supportive of marital rape (Mosher & Tompkins,

1988) and that men whose attitudes favor patriarchy were more violent toward their female partners in the previous year (Smith, 1991a). Such attitudes also were correlated with low income, low education, and lower-status jobs.

As noted earlier, marital conflict in general and expectations about division of labor in the household specifically are risk markers for violence against women (Hotaling & Sugarman, 1990). This provides some empirical support for Hypothesis 7, which states that men's pattern of gender-role conflict contributes to patterns of violence toward women.

There have been no specific tests of Hypothesis 8, that men's unidentified experiences and expressed emotions are expressed as anger, rage, and violence toward women. However, this hypothesis is consistent with Gilligan's (1996) theory that shame is the major underlying causal factor in acts of severe violence and Berkowitz's (1993) proposition that angry feelings are the key causal mechanism that leads to aggression and violence.

INTER-GENDER RELATIONAL EXPLANATION OF VIOLENCE TOWARD WOMEN

The last five hypotheses explain violence toward women as arising out of the relationships between men and women. These hypotheses focus on communication patterns, the relationship between psychological and physical violence, fear of the other partner, lack of understanding of the other's gender role, and the act of witnessing domestic violence as a precursor to current violence.

With the exception of the hypothesis on witnessing violence, which is based on learning theory, the other four hypotheses are not based on developed theories of violence and aggression.

As noted in the review of risk markers, there is empirical support for Hypothesis 13, that viewing domestic violence in the family of origin increases the probability of violence toward women in adulthood. This correlation is quite consistent. What remains to be explained is the mechanism through which witnessing works to produce the increased risk of adult domestic violence.

There is also abundant empirical support for the relationship between psychological violence and physical violence (Stets, 1990). However, as Stets (1990) explained, psychological and physical aggression are manifestations of two different underlying phenomena, and what explains the relationship is a two-step process that starts with verbal aggression and moves on to physical aggression.

There is less direct empirical support for the other three hypotheses in this group. Although clinical insights suggest that socialized patterns of communication and separate gender-role cultures, women's fear of men and men's fear of women, and a lack of understanding of the other's gender-role socialization experiences contribute to an increased risk of intimate violence, little has been done in the way of quality empirical research to test these hypotheses.

CONCLUSION

Although research on male offenders lags behind domestic violence research that examines female victims, one conclusion about the correlates and causes of men's violence toward women is inescapable. No one factor can explain the presence or absence of men's violence in intimate relationships. Characteristics of the individual, family, social situation, community, and society are related to which men are violent and under what conditions. Individual and emotional characteristics, psychological characteristics, and community factors, such as cultural attitudes regarding violence, are moderated and influenced by family structure and family situations. In addition, power and control are common features of nearly all forms of family and intimate violence. Thus, if family and intimate violence is to be effectively treated and prevented, interventions and preventive efforts need to be aimed at the importance of power and control and the functions of the family system.

Biological, Neuroanatomical, Hormonal, and Evolutionary Factors Explaining Men's Violence Against Women

Introduction

In this part, biological factors are examined from two different perspectives. Anthony Greene, in Chapter 5, considers the research evidence that supports biological explanations of men's violence. These include theories about genetic, endocrine, neurotransmitter, brain dysfunction factors, and other related research. He indicates that there is limited evidence for explaining men's violence against women from biological, genetic, and neuroanatomical perspectives.

In Chapter 6, Louise Silverstein reviews the evidence that supports an evolutionary explanation for men's violence against women. Using a feminist evolutionary approach, Silverstein argues against an essentialist evolutionary approach because it does not consider the importance of culture in constructing behavior. She presents sociobiology as a more scientifically rigorous approach to examining evolutionary explanations of men's violence. She explains that the interaction of biological and environmental factors is critical to explaining men's violence. Using primate literature as a model, Silverstein presents substantial evidence on the effect of the ecological context on shaping human behavior and, specifically, men's violence against women.

5

Biological Perspectives on Violence Against Women

ANTHONY F. GREENE

Aggressive behavior has been shown to be stable across time, situations, and generations within the same family (Huesmann, Eron, Lefkowitz, & Walder, 1984). Huesmann et al. found early aggressive behavior to be predictive of later aggressive acts, including spouse abuse, child abuse, criminal behavior, and other types of physical aggression. Geffner and Rosenbaum (1992) discussed the tentative evidence in support of a cyclical process of child abuse that leads to abuse as an adult, which leads in turn to abuse of the next generation of victims. This association of aggression and violence and its stability across time and generations suggests that there are intra-individual factors that contribute to interpersonal violence.

Research has suggested that personality characteristics that reflect high levels of anger expression are common among domestic violence offenders (Greene, Coles, & Johnson, 1994; Lohr, Hamberger, & Bonge, 1988; Maiuro, Cahn, Vitaliano, Wagner, & Zegree, 1988). Trait anger is defined as the disposition to perceive a variety of situations as unfair or threatening and thus anger-provoking (Deffenbacher, 1992; Spielberger et al., 1985). Trait anger refers to relatively stable individual differences in the proclivity to experience anger states (Johnson & Greene, 1992), and it often precedes violent or aggressive acts.

Concurrently, there are many angry people who do not have a significant psychological pathology. Hamberger and Hastings (1986) found that 15% of their sample of domestic violence offenders showed no evidence of psychopathology. Approximately 25% of the Greene, Coles, and Johnson (1994) sample had subclinical scores on their measures of pathology. Interpersonal violence is obviously multidetermined and occurs in individuals with and without significant psychopathology.

Although a host of theories exists regarding the underlying dynamics of family violence (see Feldman & Ridley, 1995, for a review), integrative explanatory characterization of the full range of psychobiological theories of violence is only beginning to emerge. Rosenbaum, Geffner, and Benjamin (in press) have proposed a biopsychosocial model of relationship aggression, which includes arousal, threshold, and high habit strength factors as contributors to aggression. Risking oversimplication, Greene, Lynch, Decker, and Coles (1997) have suggested that personality features and psychobiology may be predictably related in domestic violence. O'Neil and Harway (1997) proposed several content areas and hypotheses related to domestic violence that need to be explored. They organized their content areas into macrosocietal; biological, neuroanatomical, and hormonal; gender-role socialization and gender-role conflict; and inter-gender relational explanations. They further differentiated their hypotheses within each content area into predisposing and actual triggering hypotheses.

The purpose of this chapter is to describe current research regarding psychobiological intra-individual determinants of battery, aggression, and violence. Specifically, O'Neil and Harway's (1997) biological, neuroanatomical, and hormonal content area hypotheses will be addressed in this chapter. The two hypotheses are these:

> **Hypothesis 4:** Testosterone or hormonal levels in men contribute to violence toward women.

> **Hypothesis 5:** Neuroanatomical differences or other biological factors in men produce men's tendency to be violent toward women.

There is little support for the hypothesis that hormones predispose men to batter, although other endocrine functions may contribute to violence. In contrast, the data are somewhat convincing that for a certain percentage of cases, abnormal brain functioning is the predisposing factor, not the actual triggering event. This review will be organized into five sections: (1) genetic theories, (2) endocrine theories, (3) neurotransmitter theories, (4) brain dysfunction theories, and (5) summary.

GENETIC THEORIES

Research into the genetic origins of violent behavior includes studies of the heritability of violent traits and the effect of genetic anomalies. The primary methodologies used in the first category include family of origin studies, adoption studies, and twin studies. Family of origin and twin studies are used because of the genetic similarities between individuals, whereas the adoption studies provide a control for the effects of the developmental environment.

Although "about 50% of measured personality diversity can be attributed to genetic diversity" (Tellegen et al., 1988, p. 1035), research has been inconsistent in demonstrating a link between genetic factors and violent behavior. In their review on studies of twins using self-report methods to determine aggressiveness, Tedeschi and Felson (1994) concluded that aggressive behavior is not caused directly by genetic factors, but that these factors indirectly influence or modify aggressive behavior.

Walters (1992) performed a meta-analysis of 38 family, twin, and adoption studies to examine the connection between genetics and criminal behavior. He reported that the studies published after 1975 were better designed than earlier studies and provided less support for a gene–crime relationship. Additionally, the adoptive studies were less indicative of a gene–crime link than were the family and twin studies. He concluded that there was only a weak gene–crime correlation.

The correlation may be even weaker for violence as a subset of crime. Mednick, Gabrielli, and Hutchings (1984) found that adopted children of criminal biological parents were likely to engage in criminal behavior. However, this apparent genetic link was true only for criminal activity, and not specifically for violent crimes. Volavka (1995) also reviewed the literature and concluded that twin studies support a genetic influence on criminal behavior, but that the association with violent behavior is not as clear because most studies were not designed to study violence. He concluded that there is emerging evidence that "suggests a propensity towards violent criminal behavior which results from an interaction between genetic, prenatal, and perinatal factors" (p. 153).

It is generally believed that human males are more aggressive than females; one implication is that aggressive behavior may be associated with the Y chromosome. Adams (1991) argued to the contrary and suggested that it is an erroneous assumption to conclude that males are more aggressive. He argued that human and animal research studies have indicated no differences in aggression between males and females. Although his primary focus was on including female aggression in the study of aggression, he suggested that anger in humans is an offense-motivational system. It is not sufficient to isolate one factor that may contribute, because many factors are involved.

In support of there being some kind of genetic anomaly that is responsible, Tedeschi and Felson (1994) provided a succinct review of studies of prison populations in which there was a higher percentage of males with extra chromosomes (XYY and XXY) than is found in the general population. This sample also was found to score lower on intelligence and achievement tests, which probably contributed to a greater likelihood of being apprehended. The interpretation of the effect of the chromosomal anomalies on the potential for violence is thus confounded.

The evidence for a definitive link between genetics and violent behavior is weak. The literature supports that there is heritability of criminal, but not necessarily violent, tendencies. This may be interpreted to mean that genetic factors alone do not explain or determine violent behavior. Although genetic mapping of generations of batterers eventually may help us to predict an individual's violence potential, because all men and mixed genetic phenotypes do not batter, this genetic link is considered mostly a myth.

ENDOCRINE THEORIES

Endocrine theories of violent behavior have emerged similarly from the assumption that the males of most species are more aggressive. Exceptions notwithstanding (Adams, 1992), the differences between the sexes are enough to implicate hormones as potentiators of aggression (Tedeschi & Felson, 1994). Kreuz and Rose (1972) reviewed the histories of aggressive behavior in a sample of incarcerated individuals and found no relationship overall between their testosterone levels and aggression. However, they did find a higher level of testosterone in the 10 male prisoners who had committed the most violent crimes.

Virkkunen et al. (1994) reported an association among high cerebrospinal fluid, testosterone concentrations, and aggression or interpersonal violence in male alcoholic prison inmates. They found that the violent male prisoners had a higher testosterone level than did the healthy volunteers used as a control group. This finding is open to multiple interpretations. The effects of alcoholism and the prison environment are confounds in this study.

The investigation of the relationship between testosterone and violent behavior is complicated by the influence of social variables. It has been observed that testosterone levels rise and fall as a result of competition (Archer, 1991; Elias, 1981; Mazur & Lamb, 1980). In males who win or dominate, testosterone levels are higher than in those who are dominated. Whether this reflects an activating or a facilitating effect of testosterone is not clearly understood. The presence of testosterone may permit aggression, which is modified by the environment and previous learning experience of the individual (Tedeschi & Felson, 1994).

To complicate the picture further, the findings are not exclusive to males. Saliva testosterone levels of female prisoners also have been found to be related to criminal violence (Dabbs, Ruback, Frady, Hooper, & Sgoutas, 1988). These investigators found that saliva testosterone concentrations were lower in females who had committed defensive violence to protect themselves, whereas higher levels were found in females who had committed unprovoked violence. Interestingly, the mean testosterone concentration for the female prison inmates was not significantly different from that for a sample of female college students.

Violent behavior associated with premenstrual syndrome (referred to as premenstrual dysphoric disorder in the current clinical terminology) includes increased suicide attempts, more successful suicide attempts, the necessity of increased restraint on violent female criminals, and a greater likelihood of violent crimes (Tedeschi & Felson, 1994). Initially, it was believed that the hormone associated with female aggression was estrogen. However, subsequent research has suggested that multiple androgens are important. There is no consistent evidence in the research to support an explanation of the physiology and etiology of premenstrual syndrome and its associated psychopathology (Gitlin & Pasnau, 1989). The available literature indicates that women who participate in crimes are more likely to do so during the premenstrual period and are more likely to be apprehended (Volavka, 1995). However, the fact that behaviors experienced by some women before menstruation are not universal is sufficient to refute the simplistic interpretation of this data (Carlson, 1994). Hence, the relationship of violence and aggression to premenstrual syndrome is unclear, lending little additional support to the hormonal theory of aggression.

Hypoglycemia, or low blood sugar, also has been associated with irritability and aggression (Volavka, 1995). During hypoglycemic states, individuals can be extremely negative in their attitude and reject helpful suggestions (Moyer, 1987). The deficiency of glucose renders the brain incapable of efficiently utilizing oxygen, resulting in the loss of neural function. When the hypoglycemia is severe, violence may be one of the outcomes (Moyer, 1987).

A low blood glucose level following a glucose tolerance test has been reported in alcoholic offenders with intermittent explosive disorders (Virkkunen et al., 1994), and the presence of hypoglycemia also significantly predicted recidivism in 57 violent offenders and arsonists (Virkkunen, De Jong, Bartko, Goodwin, & Linnoila, 1989). However, the correlations and behaviors were not consistent across subjects. De Jong, Virkkunen, and Linnoila (1992) failed to confirm that hypoglycemia was related to recidivism. The best conclusion seems to be that endocrinological factors are related to aggressive and violent behavior, such as battery, perhaps by indirectly potentiating impulsive acts or perhaps by their role in adaptation to the demands of a stressful environment.

NEUROTRANSMITTER THEORIES

The neurochemicals (neurotransmitters) most examined in the research on violent behavior include serotonin, norepinephrine, dopamine, and monoamine oxidase (MAO). Human pharmacological research has suggested that "serotonin plays an inhibitory role while norepinephrine and dopamine each play a facilitating role" (Raine, 1993, p. 85). Serotonin and norepinephrine are believed to be involved with the sleep and arousal system, whereas dopamine is involved in learning, memory, and voluntary movement (Raine, 1993). However, the measurements of these chemicals are necessarily indirect and may not accurately represent the actual levels in the brain.

Although there seems to be an association between the dysfunction of the serotonergic system and impulsive behavior, a relationship with aggression has not been consistently confirmed (Volavka, 1995). Pharmacological evaluation of serotonin levels has suggested that impulsivity and serotonin levels are inversely related. Lower levels of the serotonin metabolite cerebrospinal fluid 5-hydroxy-indoleacetic acid (CSF 5-HIAA) were associated with a lifetime history of aggressive behavior and suicide attempts in one study (Brown et al., 1982). Linnoila et al. (1983) found relatively low concentrations of 5-HIAA in the cerebrospinal fluid (CSF) of impulsive violent offenders; the lowest levels were found in those who had attempted suicide. They concluded that "low CSF 5-HIAA concentration seems to be associated with a tendency towards repeated, impulsive violent behavior which can be directed both towards oneself (suicide attempts) as well as towards others (attempts of murder) and with early onset alcohol abuse" (p. 2611). Thus, these authors demonstrated a trivariate relationship among low concentrations of 5-HIAA, suicide attempts, and impulsive aggression.

Following up on this idea, Virkkunen et al. (1994) found a significantly lower CSF 5-HIAA concentration in their alcoholic, impulsive inmates compared with that of alcoholic, nonimpulsive inmates. They concluded that it is impulsivity that is associated with lower CSF 5-HIAA concentrations. In their study, the unincarcerated healthy volunteers also had comparably low levels of CSF 5-HIAA. They explained these findings as probably being due to seasonal variations in serotonin levels. Regardless of this questionable interpretation, the volunteers were not reported to be impulsive or violent. Again, it is clear that there is an interaction among the determinants that lead to violence.

In a meta-analysis of the recent research on antisocial groups and violent behavior reported by Raine (1993), there were significantly lower serotonin levels in violent antisocial individuals, antisocial men with borderline personality disorder, suicidal antisocial men, and those without a history of alcohol abuse when compared with those antisocial individuals who did not demonstrate these characteristics. Overall, the CSF levels of serotonin in violent antisocial personalities were lower when compared with those who were nonviolent.

However, these studies predominantly reflect incarcerated samples, so the interpretation of these relationships may not be generalized to unincarcerated individuals.

Research on norepinephrine and violence in humans is less extensive than that on serotonin, but that two are often conducted jointly (Volavka, 1995). Correlations between violent behaviors and a metabolite of norepinephrine, CSF 3-methoxy-4-hydroxyphenylglycol (MHPG), have been inconsistent. Brown et al. (1982) were not able to replicate the results of an earlier study in which elevated MHPG levels were positively related to a history of aggression. In the meta-analysis by Raine (1993), 32 norepinephrine-effect reports were examined. The CSF measures revealed that antisocial individuals with alcohol abuse, borderline personality disorder, and depression had significantly lower levels than those without such histories. Violent offenders had lower levels of urinary norepinephrine. Antisocial persons with a history of alcohol abuse and depression had significantly higher urinary epinephrine values than those without such a history. These results present an inconsistent picture and suggest that norepinephrine's role is not as direct as serotonin's (Raine, 1993), or perhaps that norepinephrine exerts a moderating effect on the relationship between serotonin and violence (Volavka, 1995).

Two other neurochemicals that have been examined in relation to violent behavior are the neurotransmitter dopamine and the metabolic enzyme monoamine oxidase (MAO), which is involved in the metabolic degradation of serotonin, norepinephrine, dopamine, and other neurotransmitters (Volavka, 1995). In the meta-analysis reported by Raine (1993), the mean effect size for dopamine was nonsignificant in the antisocial population. In one study, low MAO activity was associated with "victimful criminal behavior" (Ellis, 1991, p. 233). However, in persons convicted of violent crimes, the MAO activity was no lower than in those convicted of nonviolent crimes. Ellis concluded that evidence indicated a link between MAO activity and crime, but that no causal connection could be implicated from his research.

There are several problems with the research on neurotransmitters. In addition to sample selection issues, impulsive aggression has not been clearly operationalized and the origins of neurotransmitter dysfunction remain unknown (Volavka, 1995). Additionally, many of the violent crimes were committed by alcoholics, which precludes both generalization to other populations as well as creates additional questions regarding chemical interactions. To examine the role of neurotransmitters more accurately, it would be necessary to do a spinal tap to obtain CSF. This is virtually impractical and unethical to do on human subjects under most circumstances for research purposes. This area of research may hold promise, but the ethical and methodological constraints preclude firm conclusions.

BRAIN DYSFUNCTION THEORIES

An underlying premise of neuropsychology is that the brain has specific areas that correlate to behavioral and physiological functioning. According to a review of the clinical literature relating to neuropsychological correlates of violence and aggression, "the neuronal network controlling aggressive tendencies is reported to begin in the bilateral prefrontal cortex and be centralized in the organs of the limbic system, including the septum, hippocampus, caudate nucleus, thalamus, and amygdala. The posterior regions . . . lie in the anterior lobe of the cerebellum." (Golden, Jackson, Peterson-Rohne, & Gontkovsky, 1996, p. 3). These authors reviewed several mechanisms by which damage may occur and the supporting evidence for each.

Studies examining the effects of damage to the frontal cortex have shown a "pattern of behavior changes including argumentativeness, lack of concern for consequences of behavior, loss of social graces, impulsivity, distractibility, shallowness, lability, violence, and a reduced ability to utilize symbols" (Raine, 1993, p. 109). It is believed that the frontal lobes, especially the orbitomedial areas, are involved with the inhibition of inappropriate behaviors (Volavka, 1995). Frontal lobe dysfunction has been found in criminal and violent subjects in a direct positive relationship with severity and frequency of violence. However, violent crime has not significantly emerged for nonviolent individuals who incurred a lesion in the frontal lobe (Volavka, 1995). Thus, frontal lobe dysfunction may be a moderator of violence rather than a cause.

Epileptic seizures have been observed in a high proportion of the prison population (Whitman et al., 1984). However, the relationship between violence and epilepsy is apparent only in specific groups, such as temporal lobe epileptics (Volavka, Martell, & Convit, 1992) and homicidal juveniles (Lewis et al., 1985). Volavka (1995) suggests that aggressive behavior may be more related to brain dysfunction and social prejudice than to seizure activity.

Dysfunction of the dominant lateral hemisphere has been associated also with violence in psychopathic subjects (Volavka, 1995). Some evidence suggests that left fronto-temporal-limbic structure dysfunction is disproportionately represented in criminal and violent populations (Raine, 1993). Some data suggest that violent individuals have less lateralization for speech and demonstrate greater linguistic processing in the right hemisphere (Raine, 1993). Whether this reduced language lateralization is a marker of some neuroanatomical cause of violent behavior or whether violence is a manifestation of the frustration of living with brain dysfunction remains unclear.

In a study by Rosenbaum et al. (1994), strong evidence was presented that head injury could have been an etiological factor in over 50% of their sample of 53 batterers, compared with 25% of maritally discordant nonbatterers and only 16% of a maritally satisfied control group. They concluded that having a head injury was the best predictor of being a batterer and that a significant head injury increased the chances of marital aggression sixfold. Even though in this study the brain dysfunction theory does not account for all the variance in battering, it becomes fairly undeniable that any kind of brain dysfunction may become a pre-disposing or actual triggering event.

SUMMARY OF BIOLOGICAL THEORIES

The foregoing review of the available information regarding genetic, endocrine, neurotransmitter, and brain dysfunction theories of aggression and violence suggests the following conclusions:

1. There is modest support for the heritability of criminal behavior, but there is much less support for a purely genetic basis for violent behavior. Genetic constitution is subsequently not considered to play a significant role in men's violence toward women.

2. Testosterone is apparently related to aggression in some manner for men and women, and multiple androgens appear to be involved for women who commit violent acts. However, because the hormones appear to influence both sexes equally with respect to aggression, hormones are not thought to differentially explain the higher prevalence of battering among men.

3. Serotonin levels and impulsive acts seem to be inversely related, and norepinephrine may moderate the relationship of serotonin to impulsivity. Although there are both impulsive and methodical batterings, these data suggest that pharmacotherapy may indeed be beneficial with the impulsive types of batterers.

4. Frontal lobe function, especially left fronto-temporal-limbic, appears to modulate violent or aggressive behavior. Lateralization to the right hemisphere for language has been posited to be related to criminal or violent behavior. A history of head injury is a strong positive prognosticator for relationship aggression.

Clearly, biological influences may be strongly implicated in any act of violence. The foregoing review seems to suggest that the hypotheses offered by O'Neil and Harway (1997; Chapter 2, this volume) were partially supported. There was very little indication that genetics or hormones that are functioning in normal ranges have any significant differential effect that might explain men's battery of women. Therefore, Hypothesis 4, that testosterone and other hormones explain men's violence toward women, is not supported by this review. Conversely, the data suggest that abnormal brain functioning is often a factor in violent and impulsive acts, and one could then speculate that this would apply to batterers as well. According to one study, as many as half of the batterers may be suffering the sequelae of a childhood head injury (Rosenbaum et al., 1994). Therefore, Hypothesis 5, that neuroanatomical differences or other biological factors explain men's violence toward women, seems to be partially supported. It remains unclear whether males suffer head injury disproportionately more than females, which is the implication of these findings.

Because much of this research has not been focused on domestic violence or wife battering, many of these conclusions and inferences are speculative. More studies are needed that include the adequate assessment and documentation of the biological factors that may contribute to the response to treatment. I agree with O'Neil and Harway's (1997; Chapter 2, this volume) emphasis on prevention as the most effective level of intervention. However, there is much room for secondary and tertiary intervention studies as well, in which all dimensions of the phenomenon can be studied in a comprehensive, integrated manner. Perhaps now that we are beginning to develop multidimensional models of domestic violence, the field can grow.

It has become much less societally acceptable for men to batter their partners. It is also better understood that there is a myriad of dynamics that determine this behavior, and effective intervention will require consideration of multiple etiological, predisposing, triggering, and actualizing factors. Several researchers and theorists have begun to provide heuristic models that allow examination of those dynamics in a more multidimensional, biopsychosocial perspective (Greene et al., 1997; O'Neil & Harway, 1997; Chapter 2, this volume; Rosenbaum, Geffner, & Benjamin, in press). This approach is likely to yield a more realistic conceptualization of men's violence against women.

The Evolutionary Origins of Male Violence Against Women

LOUISE B. SILVERSTEIN

An evolutionary analysis of the origins of male violence does not fit neatly into the O'Neil–Harway (Chapter 2, this volume) multivariate model, because an evolutionary explanation is, in itself, a multivariate model. Although evolutionary theory is commonly viewed as a strictly biological frame of reference, evolutionary explanations are actually based on a complex array of both biological and ecological factors. In terms of the O'Neil–Harway model, an evolutionary analysis spans the four content areas: macrosocietal; biological, neuroanatomical, and hormonal; gender-role socialization; and inter-gender relationships. Within the O'Neil–Harway typology, an evolutionary perspective on male violence represents a predisposing, rather than a triggering, hypothesis. This chapter presents an evolutionary framework for viewing the complex interaction of biological and environmental factors in understanding male violence.

Given the pervasive influence of culture and learning, many social scientists question the relevance of evolutionary theory to the origins of complex human behaviors. I believe that an evolutionary perspective is essential if one aspires to tease out the relative effect of biology versus culture, especially in terms of gender differences in behavior. In my view, cross-cultural comparisons are inadequate because all human cultures are variants of a single gender-based cultural organization (i.e., patriarchy). Thus, what may appear to be similar patterns of behavior across cultures are actually constructed by the same culture of male dominance. Within this context, a cross-species, rather than a cross-cultural, comparative analysis can speak more directly to the effect of biological versus cultural factors. I believe that evolutionary processes set the macrosystemic context within which individual behavior, societal trends, and cultural processes unfold.

However, not all evolutionary theories are equal. Some evolutionary biologists continue to focus on a "strict constructionist" approach to explaining human behavior that focuses on the gene and natural selection (e.g., Dawkins, 1982). A new genre of psychological theory based on this "strict constructionist" approach has gained prominence within the discipline of psychology (e.g., Archer, 1996; Buss, 1988, 1995; Daly & Wilson, 1994). Evolutionary psychologists attempt to identify evolved psychological mechanisms that underlie observable behaviors. These theorists propose that certain behaviors are universal, species-typical, and sex-specific evolutionary adaptations caused by natural selection. This focus on universal sex differences has intensified the historical tendency of feminists and other social scientists to reject all attempts to trace the evolutionary origins of human behavior.

At the same time that evolutionary psychology has presented a "strict constructionist" interpretation of the evolutionary origins of complex human behaviors, a contrasting trend has emerged within evolutionary biology. This new point of view moves away from an emphasis on the primacy of the gene and natural selection, and toward a focus on the plurality of evolutionary processes (e.g., Gould, 1997; Gray, 1997; Oyama, 1989).

As a part of this new approach to understanding evolutionary processes, a trend toward integrating feminist theory and evolutionary explanations of behavior has emerged (e.g., Gowaty, 1997; Hrdy, 1997; Smuts, 1995; Sork, 1997; Zihlman, 1997). These feminist scholars have focused on the complex interplay of genetic, developmental, and environmental variables in the construction of human behavior. They have compiled an extensive body of empirical data based on fossil evidence, comparative animal studies, archeological artifacts, and cross-cultural data. In contrast to the evolutionary psychological emphasis on universal sex differences and the relative fixity of behaviors across evolutionary history, this body of knowledge points to the overlap of behaviors between the sexes and the relative flexibility of complex human behaviors.

In this chapter, I contrast these two approaches to understanding the evolutionary origins of male violence against women. I critique the rape adaptation hypothesis, the evolutionary psychological position that violent male behaviors, such as rape, represent sex-specific, species-typical evolutionary adaptations (Thornhill & Thornhill, 1992). I argue that this approach is not scientifically rigorous because it presents hypotheses that are virtually untestable: It ignores relevant cross-species and cross-cultural data and it selectively includes data that support its hypotheses and ignores data that do not.

I argue that sociobiology, the use of cross-species data to examine the social and biological origins of behavior, is more scientifically rigorous because it is based on a body of data on nonhuman animals that can be empirically verified. This approach focuses on the interaction of a wide array of biological and environmental variables. In contrast to the historical tendency of evolutionary explanations to focus on genetic determinism, feminist sociobiology generates hypotheses about manipulating environmental variables to promote progressive social change (see Hrdy, 1997; Smuts, 1995).

I endorse Smuts's (1995) sociobiological position that violent male behaviors are neither sex-specific nor species-typical adaptations. Rather, rates of male violence vary significantly, depending on the complex interplay of biological and ecological variables. I argue, in agreement with Smuts, that the macrosocietal context of patriarchy (i.e., male dominance over women) is the primary variable that creates and maintains the necessary conditions for high rates of male violence, in general, and male violence against women, in particular. This point of view is illustrated by a comparative, cross-species analysis of rates of male violence within human, chimpanzee, and bonobo societies.

This cross-species analysis indicates that one societal variable, female–female cooperation, is closely linked to differences in rates of male violence. When female–female cooperation is high (e.g., within bonobo culture), male violence toward both females and other males is low. When female–female cooperation is low, as it is among chimpanzees and human primates, rates of male violence are significantly higher.

The cross-species analysis points to the importance of institutionalized male dominance as the crucial factor in the perpetuation of gendered violence, rather than biological, psychological, or sociological characteristics of individual men or the specific context of relationship patterns. Thus, I argue that it is not as effective to ask, "Which men are likely to become rapists or batterers?" or "Under which social conditions is intimate violence likely to occur?," as it is to inquire, "What are the macrosystemic conditions that contribute to male dominance and how can we change those conditions?" The chapter ends with a consideration of social policy initiatives that contribute to equalizing the power balance between men and women and to encouraging female–female cooperation. From my perspective, a focus on manipulating the macroenvironmental context in terms of dismantling patriarchy is the most effective way to decrease male violence.

To summarize my hypotheses:

1. Institutionalized male dominance (i.e., patriarchy) is the crucial factor in the perpetuation of male violence.

2. Decreasing male dominance through a variety of social policies (e.g., equal pay for equal work; increasing the number of women in higher-paid jobs and professions; family policy that allows both men and women to participate in the care of young children.) reduces male violence.

3. Increasing female–female cooperation is effective in lessening male violence against both women and other men.

EVOLUTIONARY PSYCHOLOGY: THE THORNHILLS' RAPE ADAPTATION HYPOTHESIS

Although I am arguing that an evolutionary framework is important for understanding complex human behaviors, such as violence, I am not endorsing all evolutionary explanations. Rather, I want to educate the reader to evaluate which evolutionary explanations are based on "good science" and which evolutionary arguments are based on less rigorous science. Therefore, I am including two contrasting evolutionary approaches: sociobiology (which in my view is "good science") and evolutionary psychology (which in my view is less rigorous).

The rape adaptation hypothesis is an example of evolutionary psychology. It states that the behavioral tendency to rape has evolved in the male psyche because rape was an adaptive reproductive strategy for men in earlier periods in our evolutionary history. Evolutionary psychology is a relatively new discipline that attempts to identify evolved psychological mechanisms that underlie current observable behaviors (Archer, 1996; Buss, 1988, 1989, 1995; Daly & Wilson, 1994; Gangestad, 1993; Wilson, Daly, & Scheib, 1997). Evolutionary psychologists emphasize that "psychological adaptation must somehow causally underlie all human feelings, cognition, and emotions" (Thornhill & Thornhill, 1992, p. 363). The key word here is *somehow*.

To claim that behaviors such as sexual coercion or rape are adaptations, *in the Darwinian sense*, one must show that the specific behavior is the product of natural selection (i.e., that it is inherited and has contributed to reproductive success in the past). Given the many other possible sources for current behaviors (i.e., randomness and the ubiquitous effects of learning), it is extremely difficult to provide a scientifically rigorous argument that complex human behaviors are the result of natural selection. Proposing that behaviors are related to evolution in a vague and unrelated way is insufficient to claim that they represent an evolutionary adaptation. It is precisely this specific linkage to natural selection that evolutionary psychology has been unsuccessful in establishing.

The Thornhills (Thornhill & Thornhill, 1992) hypothesized that "men have certain psychological traits which evolved by natural selection, specifically in the context of coercive sex and made rape adaptive during human evolution" (p. 364). They considered briefly and then dismissed alternative explanatory paradigms. These included social learning theory, comparative data on nonhuman animals, and an analysis of whether rape contributes to reproductive success in current cultures. The cursory nature of their consideration of alternative hypotheses is problematic, because ignoring data that disconfirm their hypotheses decreases the scientific rigor of their approach.

The Thornhills proposed that there were selection pressures on men throughout evolutionary history that favored the development of psychological traits that favored forcing a reluctant partner to have sex. To support their hypothesis, they cited as "strong evidence" (p. 366) claims by others that observed sex differences in human attitudes and behavior are the result of natural selection (e.g., Buss, 1988, 1989; Symons, 1979). Whereas the authors cited are evolutionary psychologists and used the same speculative theory-building techniques to support their claims, it is questionable to cite their work as "evidence."

A more rigorous method would be to present the work of theorists who do *not* agree with the Thornhills' point of view (e.g., social learning theorists or feminist sociobiologists) and to provide relevant data to indicate why these contrasting theories are wrong. To do this, the Thornhills would have to present a strong argument that the psychological mechanisms underlying these "masculine" and "feminine" behaviors are adaptations caused by natural selection and are not the product of cultural learning.

The Environment of Evolutionary Adaptation

To buttress their hypothesis about the adaptiveness of sexually coercive behavior, the Thornhills presented speculations about the environment of evolutionary adaptation (EEA). The EEA refers to the ecological context (desert, savannas, etc.) within which evolution took place. The Thornhills proposed that "sexually attractive human females who were sexually uninterested and resisted the sexual advances of males are likely to have been a consistent feature of the human evolutionary environment" (p. 366).

Whenever we search for evolutionary origins, informed speculation is often necessary, especially in terms of complex human behaviors. The process of evolution is so slow that its effects cannot be observed directly. However, speculating about the EEA must be done carefully, because it is difficult to provide scientific data to support claims about a specific environmental context that no longer exists. In this regard, it is problematic to speak vaguely of a single EEA. *Homo erectus* left Africa more than 2 million years ago and settled in every ecological context throughout the world. Foley (1995–1996) has pointed out that there is so much diversity among the ecological environments of current hunter–gatherers (e.g., the San people of the Kalahari desert and the Inuit of the Arctic Circle) that it is impossible to speak about a uniform EEA.

Other scientists use the African rainforests and savannas as models for the EEA, which are the environments that contain the oldest specimens of fossil evidence from our hominid ancestors (e.g., Smuts, 1995; Zihlman, 1997). The Thornhills, in contrast, characterize as irrelevant comparative animal studies and current cultural practices of modern hunter–gatherers, arguing that these data do not address the "*specific* (italics added) selection pressures of past human populations" (Thornhill & Thornhill, 1992, p. 365).

The reader is at a loss in terms of how to think critically about whether sexual coercion was once adaptive, because the Thornhills are not specific about the social and economic context of the hypothetical EEA. Were our ancestors living under conditions of abundant or scarce resources? Do males or females leave the group they were born in when they reach adolescence? Are human females living in one-male groups like gorillas, multimale groups like chimpanzees and bonobos, or in solitude and isolation like orangutans? Are females bonded with each other, or socially isolated? We know that these variables dramatically affect the willingness of females to engage in sex and the frequency with which males use aggression to force "reluctant partners" among our closest genetic relatives (Hrdy, 1997; Smuts, 1995). Yet the Thornhills reject the relevance of these comparisons.

The Thornhills explained their rejection of comparative animal studies "because the selective environments that produced human psychological adaptations were unique to our species" (p. 365). This is an odd claim. We share 98.6% of our DNA with chimpanzees and bonobos, and slightly less with gorillas. We all evolved originally in the context of the African rainforest and savannas mosaic. From my perspective, it is difficult to see why our original EEA would have been unique.

The Thornhills also failed to specify the economic system of their hypothesized EEA. Cross-cultural data have indicated a positive correlation between women's economic dependence on men and male violence against women. In cultures where women are separated from direct production and control of resources, rape increases significantly (Schlegel & Barry, 1986). Similarly, Levinson (1989a) reported a significantly higher rate of wife-beating in cultures where the degree of male control over the products of family labor was higher. The Thornhills fail to address these cross-cultural data.

Another major problem with the Thornhills' analysis is that it considers adaptation (i.e., reproductive success) only from the perspective of the male. Because adaptation is also the goal of females, one must consider what selective pressures must have been operating to ensure that females would not be impregnated by an inappropriate mate. Two types of countertactics exist: avoiding rape or minimizing the possibility of conception if a rape does occur. The Thornhills do not consider relevant cross-species or cross-cultural data. For example, do forced copulations actually result in successful conceptions and what percentage of conceptions originating from force end in spontaneous abortions (e.g., Baker & Bellis, 1993)? Unless the Thornhills can demonstrate that rape actually improves an individual's reproductive success, they cannot assert that rape is an evolutionary adaptation.

A Priori Predictions

In addition to speculating about the EEA, evolutionary psychologists generate a priori predictions and then look for behavioral data that are consistent with those predictions. If they can identify behaviors that are consistent with their predictions, evolutionary psychologists consider this correlational consistency sufficient evidence that the behaviors are adaptive and, therefore, the product of natural selection. I find this process circular, rather than scientifically rigorous. Whereas the "predictions" are often based on existing research, the outcome of the "prediction" is known in advance.

The Thornhills followed this hypothesis-testing approach. They generated a series of predictions in an attempt to determine whether rape was a specific evolutionary adaptation or simply a by-product of other evolved behaviors; for example, a general desire for sexual intercourse or a general tendency to use force to attain any reward. Examples of their predictions include: men will exhibit high levels of sexual motivation and performance in both coercive and noncoercive mating situations; gaining physical control by force should be sexually arousing to men because it facilitates forced copulation.

In my view, neither their predictions nor the research that the Thornhills cited to support their predictions presents evidence relevant to their claim that rape is an evolved adaptation. Given the power and speed of cultural evolution in contrast to natural selection, strong data are needed to suggest that natural selection is at work, especially when one is claiming sex-specific, species-typical adaptations. As Smuts (1992) concluded in a commentary on the Thornhills article, it seems more plausible to hypothesize that both men and women have underlying psychological mechanisms for identifying the costs and benefits of various behavioral strategies. Given the observation that the coercive behavior of other men is not met with negative consequences, it is more parsimonious to hypothesize that boys and young men are socialized to find the use of sexual coercion acceptable. The absence of rape in less patriarchal cultures, like Tahiti (Gilmore, 1990) or the Aka pygmies of Central Africa (Hewlett, 1992), further suggests that sexual coercion is culturally specific, rather than species-typical.

My criticisms of this evolutionary psychological analysis of rape can be summarized as follows: it does not address the primary criteria that are necessary to argue that a behavior is the product of natural selection (i.e., that it is inherited and that it has contributed to reproductive success in the past); it ignores important, relevant cross-species and cross-cultural data; the analysis presents a speculative account of an environment of evolutionary adaptation that does not conform to what is known either about our evolutionary past or about the diversity of current hunter–gatherer cultures; and it selectively includes social science research that confirms a priori predictions and excludes research that would disconfirm them.

The most impressive element of our evolutionary heritage is a brain that can respond flexibly to wide variations in environmental contexts. The evolutionary psychological approach, which proposes fixed and invariant species-typical and sex-specific behaviors, does not correspond to what we know about the flexibility of underlying brain mechanisms.

THE SOCIOBIOLOGICAL APPROACH

The sociobiological approach analyzes cross-species research and generates hypotheses about human primate behavior based on nonhuman primate behavioral patterns (Hrdy, 1990, 1995, 1997; Smuts, 1995; Smuts & Gubernick, 1992; Wrangham, 1987; Wrangham & Peterson, 1996; Zihlman, 1997). To contrast the approach of evolutionary psychologists, I present an article by Smuts (1995) that explored the evolutionary origins of patriarchy.

Smuts's theoretical question was, "Why have all human societies been male dominant throughout evolutionary history?" Like the Thornhills, Smuts proposed that male control of female reproduction through sexual coercion is an important part in understanding human relationships. However, in contrast to the Thornhills' focus on sexually coercive behavior as a species-typical evolutionary adaptation, Smuts attempted to identify environmental conditions that increase or decrease the probability that male violence against women will occur. Using the comparative, cross-species approach, Smuts analyzed how the sexual power balance varies under different environmental circumstances.

THE RELEVANCE OF NONHUMAN ANIMAL DATA

Before turning to the animal data, I want to address the question of whether nonhuman animal behavior is relevant to understanding complex human (animal) behaviors. Since Darwin created the concept of evolution, humankind has had difficulty accepting its similarity to nonhuman animals. Darwin was the first to point out that if any species other than human were creating the phylogenetic classification system, human beings simply would be listed as another species of ape (Darwin, 1871). We now know that by every index typically used to categorize species (i.e., anatomical characteristics, blood chemistry and DNA), human beings are more closely related to chimpanzees and bonobos than are gorillas (see Wrangham & Peterson, 1996, for a discussion of the evidence). We also know that all the cognitive traits that previously were thought to make humans unique have proven to be myths. Chimpanzees and bonobos use tools, can learn language, and can produce art (Diamond, 1992). Bipedalism, the ability to walk upright, is now thought to be the primary characteristic that differentiated our hominid ancestors from the other apes.

Primatologists now estimate that we diverged from the chimpanzee–bonobo lineage about 5 million years ago. Why did our species change so much over the last 5 million years, while our chimpanzee and bonobo relatives changed so little? Wrangham and Peterson (1996) proposed that chimpanzees and bonobos have remained the same because they stayed in an unchanging habitat, the tropical rainforest. The essential forest structure is the same as it was when bonobos and chimpanzees originally evolved from our common ancestor. Thus, the apes living within that habitat have remained essentially the same. Hominids, in contrast, continued to evolve as they adapted to varied and changing habitats.

The fossil evidence suggests that, using their bipedal adaptation to move farther and faster, our ancestors immigrated into northern Africa during a period when rainforests covered most of the continent. During a subsequent period of drought, the rainforests in the North dwindled, while those in the South remained more or less intact. Our hominid ancestors were forced to adapt to woodlands and savannas. One line of hominids began to develop a much larger brain about 2 million years ago. These early ancestors also began to shape stone tools and rely on meat to supplement their diet. They also discovered how to use fire (about 1.5 million years ago) and developed spoken language. About 10,000 years ago, they invented agriculture. These cultural innovations represent dramatic departures from the rainforest lifestyle of our ape relatives.

However, many continuities in behavior have remained across the space of evolutionary time. Affiliative and aggressive relationship patterns, extensive nonverbal communication, mating strategies, maternal–infant relationships, variations in male–infant involvement, male dominance displays, political alliances, gender politics, and warfare are all part of the social scene among both human and nonhuman apes. Readers have to decide for themselves whether the differences or continuities are more salient. My bias is that ape behavior and social relationships have much to teach us about ourselves.

Cross-Species Analysis

In contrast to evolutionary psychology, which proposes that behavior is more or less consistent across evolutionary history, Smuts's approach to understanding male violence against women is to emphasize behavioral variations. She noted that in some primate species (e.g., hamadryas baboons), males try to control females all the time, whereas in others (e.g., olive baboons and chimpanzees), females are subjected to male aggression primarily when they are in estrus. In still other species (e.g., tamarins and marmosets or bonobos), male attempts at sexual coercion are virtually nonexistent.

Male violence against females is low in two main environmental contexts: where there is little sexual dimorphism (i.e., a small difference in size and strength between males and females, seen in siamangs, gibbons, marmosets, and tamarins) or where females live in kin-bonded groups where female relatives establish supportive social relationships with one another (e.g., olive baboons). Male violence is high when sexual dimorphism is great and/or social support for females is lacking. For example, coercive sex is common among orangutans, where females almost always live alone and males are significantly larger than females.

Sexual dimorphism is also high among baboons. However, rates of male violence vary, depending on the social organization of the subspecies (Smuts, 1995). Male violence is high among hamadryas baboons, where females leave the troop they were born in and migrate to a new troop. Migrating to a new troop means that an individual gives up family and social supports. Hamadryas baboons live in one-male troops, where every female is constantly herded and harassed by the male as he tries to protect his harem from the advances of stranger males, who continually challenge his hegemony. Within this context, females have very little power.

Among olive baboons, in contrast, it is the males who leave their natal troop. The females remain, enjoy the social support of female kin, and benefit from their mothers' place in the dominance hierarchy. Within this context, alliances with high-ranking females are necessary for males to attain and maintain their positions within the male dominance hierarchy. Thus, olive baboon females have a much more equal power position relative to males than do hamadryas females. Correspondingly, they are also subject to much less male aggression.

Smuts (1995) pointed out, however, that when olive females were introduced into a hamadryas troop, their more liberated behavior lasted about half an hour. At first, when the male tried to "herd" them with bites and blows, the females ran away. However, after several serious bites, each female began to follow the male. This experiment was striking in how quickly females became submissive in response to serious aggression and the lack of social supports.

It is interesting to note that Smuts does not make a point of arguing that either the "liberated" behavior of the olive baboons or the submissive behavior of the hamadryas baboons is adaptive in the Darwinian sense. This example illustrates how the issue of adaptation varies, because a behavior can be adaptive only within a *specific* environmental context. When environmental conditions change, a previously adaptive behavior may be rendered nonadaptive. When the context changes, behavioral repertoires change and nonadaptive behaviors tend to decrease or disappear. Thus, the "liberated" behavior of the female olive baboons was adaptive within their natal context, but it became radically nonadaptive and rapidly changed within the new environmental conditions of the hamadryas culture.

The same phenomenon of change would be true of the behavior of the hamadryas male if he were transplanted into an olive baboon culture. The olive baboon culture values long-term, affiliative relationships between males and females. Thus, his aggressive herding behavior would be nonadaptive in that it would decrease his mating opportunities. Either he would change tactics rapidly or he would be extruded from the group and enjoy little reproductive success.

Three Ape Cultures

Smuts compared and contrasted the sexual balance of power within three ape cultures: chimpanzees, bonobos, and human beings. In all three, sexual dimorphism is minimal, so high levels of male aggression would not necessarily be predicted. However, in all three species, females typically leave their natal group and migrate into a new group, a context within which male aggression is generally high. Among these three species, it is the *power balance between the sexes* that accurately predicts the rate of *male aggression* against females. Among chimpanzees and human beings, the incidence of male aggression is high. In contrast, among bonobos, male aggression against females is virtually absent.

Given the similarity of DNA among these three species, I argue that to understand these between-group differences the relevant question to ask is, "What are the environmental conditions within the bonobo culture that work to lessen male aggression?" Smuts reviewed the empirical research on bonobos and chimpanzees (e.g., Idani, 1991; Kano, 1992; Wrangham, 1987). All observers of these animals agree that it is the high level of female cooperation and social cohesion that provides individual females with a high degree of power and freedom from sexual coercion. (There is no consensus among primatologists about whether the bonobo culture is best characterized as female-dominant, co-dominant, or female-influenced. See de Waal & Lanting, 1997; Parish, 1996; and Wrangham, 1987, for discussions of this controversy.)

Unlike chimpanzees and human beings, bonobo females band together to increase their power relative to males and, especially, to inhibit male violence. How is it that bonobo females have been able to establish and maintain this high level of female cooperation, whereas chimpanzee and human females have not? Wrangham (1987) proposed that it is the ecological context of resource abundance that is central to the establishment of female alliances. Female bonobos do not have to compete with one another for limited resources. They are free to spend time feeding together, thereby establishing social relationships and alliances. The mechanism for establishing these cohesive female–female social relationships and political alliances is same-sex sexual interactions among bonobo females. Chimpanzees, in contrast, live among gorillas who compete with them for certain kinds of food. Thus, chimpanzee females live in a context of limited resources. To decrease conflict over limited food sources, chimpanzee females feed alone and do not have the opportunity to establish close social relationships with one another.

Another aspect of bonobo society that is closely related to the social power of females is the absence of strong male coalitions. Smuts notes that male–male coalitions, even among chimpanzees and humans, are always shaky because males are always competing with one another for food and for access to females. Male–male cooperation must provide significant benefits for males to overcome their natural competitive antipathy and form cooperative alliances. These benefits are lacking in the bonobo society. The ecological context of abundant resources decreases the competitive pressure for food. Most individuals have enough food, so allying with some males against others to control limited food sources is not necessary.

Similarly, the social fabric of bonobos provides abundant sexual resources. Sex occurs more frequently and among more combinations of individuals than in other primate societies. Because of the frequency of sexual interactions, males do not need to compete with one another for access to females. In addition, the core feeding areas of bonobo females are very large, geographically. This makes it difficult for males to cooperate in defending access to more than one female. Under these ecological conditions, male alliances provide few benefits.

A Speculative Account of the Evolution of Patriarchy

Like the Thornhills, Smuts speculated about the evolution of social behaviors during the course of evolutionary history. In contrast to the Thornhills, however, Smuts generated hypotheses informed by cross-species research. She hypothesized that among ancestral hominids, like all of our ape sisters, females tended to leave their natal groups. Thus, women were deprived of the social support networks of female kinship systems. Their ability to resist male aggression was compromised by reduced social support from kin and female allies.

Among chimpanzees, male–male alliances are rudimentary. Smuts speculated that over the course of evolutionary history, through the use of language and writing, the male–male alliances already present among chimpanzees became more effective and were used to increase male power over women. Ultimately, men were successful in generating cultural norms that legitimized the use of force to control female sexuality (e.g., the widespread cultural acceptance of acquaintance rape and wife-beating in response to adultery).

In all other primate cultures, females feed themselves (have direct access to resources). Although there is some food sharing among apes and some monkeys, nonhuman primate females do not rely on others for most of their food. Because of the increased protein necessary to produce significantly larger-brained infants, meat became more central in the diet of our hominid ancestors than it was in the diet of any other primate. Smuts speculated that once the shift to meat eating occurred, the importance of hunting further enhanced male power.

Since the development of agriculture, men historically have gained control of resources that women need to survive and reproduce. Smuts proposed that male–male alliances and male control over resources produced a positive feedback loop. The possibility of controlling resources increased the benefits of male cooperation, so that the tendency toward male–male alliances grew stronger over time. In a nomadic, foraging lifestyle characteristic of nonhuman primates and hunter–gatherer cultures, women continued to produce and control resources. However, the sedentary lifestyle of agricultural production made it easier for men to control the resource base that women depended on for both survival and reproduction, and, ultimately, the women themselves.

Smuts also emphasized that, in pursuing their material and reproductive interests, women often have engaged in behaviors that reinforce male control of resources and female sexuality. Thus, women also have contributed to the perpetuation of patriarchy. For example, in stratified, polygynous societies, women benefit from marrying rich men. Rich men can demand behaviors that increase paternity certainty. Within this context, women in these societies often require that their daughters comply with customs that control female sexuality, such as purdah or cliterodectomy.

In a fashion similar to the Thornhills, Smuts generated hypotheses about the evolution of human behaviors over the course of evolutionary history. However, the sociobiological approach to hypothesizing about the evolutionary origins of current human behaviors is more effective than the evolutionary psychological approach for a number of reasons. Throughout her discussion, Smuts emphasized how each new hypothesized evolutionary adaptation built on previous behaviors is currently observable among our primate relatives. For example, although institutionalized male dominance is a relatively recent cultural construction, the presence of male interest in controlling females can be seen in both monkeys and apes. The human harem, characteristic of some agricultural societies, is seen in a rudimentary form among other primate species (e.g., hamadryas baboons and gorillas). This approach, which links human behavior to currently observable nonhuman primate behavior, allows hypotheses to be tested using empirical data.

MEN'S VIOLENCE AGAINST WOMEN

What can an evolutionary perspective contribute to the development of a multivariate model of the etiology of men's violence against women? I have described each of these approaches to the evolutionary origins of male violence against women in great detail to emphasize that evolutionary theory can be helpful, neutral, or destructive to feminist goals.

From my perspective, the Thornhills' focus on rape as a species-typical, sex-specific adaptation does not make a significant contribution to a discussion of the etiology and treatment of male violence. Their recommendations for future laboratory research to explore the specific combination of sexual and violent stimuli that men find sexually arousing does not seem a particularly effective way to address the systemic problem of male violence. Although the Thornhills stated that they were interested in identifying the social contexts that decrease the probability of rape, their discussion actually emphasized the fixed nature of sexual coercion across varying social contexts.

Smuts's (1995) analysis was more effective in suggesting directions for change. Her analysis pointed out the importance of social context in determining the frequency and intensity of sexual coercion and violence against women. Smuts demonstrated that the social context of strong male–male coalitions and weak female–female cooperation increased violence against nonhuman female primates. These data point to the importance of female cooperation, particularly in terms of economic and political solidarity. Her analysis also demonstrated the importance of achieving economic independence for women, reducing inequality among men, refusing to comply with patriarchal practices, and deconstructing ideologies that justify gender inequality.

Many of these recommendations have long been part of the feminist agenda. In my view, the most powerful new message that emerged from this cross-species analysis was the central role of female cooperation in creating a context that limited male abuse of power. In the next section, I discuss in detail the ways that female cooperation enhances the power of females in the bonobo society.

A Counter-Strategy to Male Violence: Female Cooperation Within the Bonobo Society

Before beginning this analysis, I want to emphasize that there is still much about apes that we do not understand. Tracking animals in the wild is incredibly difficult. Many behaviors have been inferred, but never directly observed (e.g., cannibalism of other apes, voluntary matings of female chimpanzees with extra-group males, and certain kinds of violent encounters, including intergroup murder and warfare). New data continually emerge that challenge many of our inferences (e.g., see Gagneux, Woodruff, & Boesch, 1997, for a reassessment of the relation between male dominance rank and reproductive success).

Comprehending the bonobo social organization may be even more problematic than understanding chimpanzees, because they have been studied less extensively. Bonobos are found exclusively in a small section of an inaccessible rainforest in the Republic of Congo (formerly Zaire). These animals have been studied (primarily by Japanese researchers) only for the last 20 years and only at two primary sites: Wamba, where the animals are provided with food, and

Lomako, where the animals are not provisioned. Parish (1996) has studied captive bonobos at three zoos worldwide. Thus, the knowledge base on these animals is very limited. Many aspects of their social behavior are imperfectly understood. Undoubtedly, much of what we think we know now will prove to be incorrect in the future. With that caveat in mind, I review the data on the bonobo culture.

There is currently a consensus among researchers that bonobo females, both in the wild and in captivity, enjoy a much more equal power status relative to males than do most primate females (de Waal & Lanting, 1997; Furuichi & Ihobe, 1994; Hashimoto, 1997; Parish, 1996; White, 1996; Wrangham & Peterson, 1996). Female cooperation, expressed through influential political coalitions, is thought to be the social glue that has transformed their power and influence. The extent of that influence can be seen in all aspects of life.

At all research sites, females have been observed to have feeding priority (White, 1996). Males often arrive first at a feeding site to feed before the females arrive, because once the females are present, they monopolize access to food. Bonobo females, in contrast to chimpanzees, can even retain ownership of meat, the most prized food source, despite pressure from males. Although individual females in the wild do not outrank males, coalitions of females can elicit submissive behavior from males.

Female influence also dramatically affects the incidence and expression of violence in the bonobo culture (Kano, 1992). Bonobo males do not cooperate to attack a female as they do among chimpanzees; rather the opposite occurs. Although bonobo females in the wild are relatively nonaggressive, they will band together to counterattack if a male is harassing a female. Males seem to be involved in more frequent violent encounters; however, female–female fights are reported to be the most vicious. Despite the intensity of female–female aggression when it does occur, female dominance rank is not contested through violence. Instead, rankings seem to be determined by seniority, rather than by fierceness. The older females, who have resided in the community longest, are higher ranking than younger females, who are more recent immigrants.

Female influence also extends to the male dominance hierarchy (de Waal & Lanting, 1997). The closest, and most enduring, social bond among bonobos is between mother and son, whereas in chimpanzees, the closest bonds are between males, often among brothers. At Wamba, bonobo mothers are very important in determining their son's rank within the male dominance hierarchy. Typically, when a mother's rank declines, so does her son's, and vice versa. At Lomako, the importance of mothers in determining male dominance is less clear. Among chimpanzees, male dominance is most frequently achieved and maintained by soliciting male allies who back up an individual male's dominance threats. At Wamba, it is the mothers who provide the political backup for their sons.

Sexual relationships are central to bonobo social organization and the absence of violence. Again, there is consensus among researchers (de Waal & Lanting,

1997; Hashimoto, 1997; White, 1996; Wrangham, 1993) that sex is used to serve a variety of goals: to establish heterosexual and homosexual friendships and political coalitions; to prevent violence; to beg for food; to appease the loser of a dominance struggle; and to provide pleasure. Sexual interactions are observed more frequently and in more combinations among bonobos than among any other species of ape. Even infants and juveniles are initiated into the culture of sexual politics (Hashimoto, 1997).

Face-to-face clitoral–clitoral interaction (called GG rubbing; Kano, 1992) between females is thought to be an important method for establishing female coalitions. Males seem to be aware of the power implications of this behavior. Parish (in de Waal & Lanting, 1997, p. 114) reported that among one group of captive bonobos, the male dramatically and repeatedly objected to GG rubbing between the two adult females in his group. In this instance, the female composition of the group had been changed. After the shift, the new female members of the group were not bonded and began to use every opportunity to engage in clitoral–clitoral sexual interactions. The resident male objected to these interactions, continually mounting an intimidating display. Despite his objections, the females continued their interactions, although more furtively. Parish speculated that the male may have wanted to inhibit the formation of this bond because bonobo females typically use these close relationships to control food and attack males.

Studying the bonobo society also has much to teach us about abuses of power. In captive communities, Parish (1996) found that more than 40% of aggressive encounters were initiated by one or more females attacking and often severely wounding males. Most of the observed instances were of several females holding down a male while biting him. These attacks occurred in a variety of contexts: when a new zookeeper was introduced; when a new infant was born; or when a male was annoying a female. However, some of the aggression occurred in the absence of any stimulus. Parish speculated that the females might have been using violence solely for intimidation. de Waal and Lanting (1997) reported, in an interview with Parish, an incident in the Stuttgart Zoo, where the lone male in the group was discovered with his penis cut in two and hanging by a shred of skin. Because the alpha female customarily harassed him, the researchers assumed that she had bitten it off. These observations suggest that, at least in captivity, the power balance in favor of females creates a context that supports female abuse of males. These data on female violence contradict Thornhills' hypothesis that violent behavior in males is an evolved, sex-specific behavior.

The Evolutionary Perspective as a Model for Change

How does an evolutionary perspective relate to other explanations of male violence? Given the prevalence of male violence against women across many different societies, it is tempting to conclude that there are genetic or biological factors that predispose men toward violent behavior. Evolutionary explanations have often focused on this attempt to identify genetic and/or biological variables as predisposing factors in determining behavior. Thus, it is somewhat paradoxical that an evolutionary framework based on a sociobiological analysis of cross-species behavior points to the importance of systemic and contextual, rather than biological, variables.

Chimpanzees, bonobos, and human beings share 98.6% of their DNA in common. Many natural scientists, including Darwin, have argued that these three groups are not different species, but rather three subspecies of apes. Yet, bonobos differ significantly in terms of the low incidence of violent male behavior. The genetic similarity between bonobos and the other two groups makes it difficult to argue that the high rates of male violence in both chimpanzee and human cultures are biologically based. Instead, the biological uniformity across groups suggests that behavioral differences in male violence must be attributable to variations in environmental variables. Three macrosystemic factors emerged as significant differences in the bonobo society: the abundance of resources; the absence of strong male–male coalitions; and the presence of strong levels of female cooperation.

In terms of hypotheses from the O'Neil–Harway model (Chapter 2, this volume), the evolutionary perspective dismisses Hypotheses 4 and 5, that male violence is caused by differences in hormonal levels or neuroanatomical structures, either among men or between men and women. Whereas male bonobos share a virtually identical genetic heritage with male human beings and chimpanzees, but are generally not violent toward females, biological factors cannot be seen as causative. Turner (1994) reached a similar conclusion in her review of human and animal (mostly rats) research on genetic and hormonal influences on male violence. She concluded that, although the research is limited and fraught with methodological problems, there is some evidence that personality traits (such as emotionality and impulsiveness) may be inherited, and these may in turn affect aggressive and antisocial behavior. However, the influence of genetic and hormonal factors on aggression appears to be "sparse and inconclusive" (p. 247).

An evolutionary explanation does agree with the macrosocietal hypotheses (1–3) that male violence is caused by historical patterns in America that glorify men's violence, patriarchal organizational structures that maintain unequal power relationships between men and women, and recent gender-role changes that have decreased male power, generated anxiety, and increased battering. However, an evolutionary framework proposes that these three levels *derive from* the macrosystemic factors identified in the cross-species analysis (i.e., effective male–male political coalitions and low female–female cooperation). Thus, if the macrosystemic factors were changed, these lower-level systemic variables (institutionalized patriarchy, historical glorification of violence, etc.) would automatically change as well.

An evolutionary framework also subsumes the hypotheses relating to gender-role socialization and inter-gender relationship patterns (6–8), because norms defining these cultural practices have developed within the context of high male dominance. If a more equal power balance between men and women at a societal level were legitimized by a new cultural ideology and codified by reforms in the legal system, then parenting and socialization practices also would change. Similarly, the ways in which men and women relate to each other in intimate relationships are constructed by cultural ideology and socialization practices (Hypotheses 9–13). Thus, if the ideology of male dominance were changed to one of gender equality, we could expect intimate relationship patterns to change as well.

Thus, an evolutionary perspective is an overarching framework, which proposes that the roots of male dominance were established long before social relationships were formally organized into a patriarchal structure. From a biological perspective, females are the limiting sex in primate reproduction (i.e., females can bear and nurse only a limited number of offspring), whereas males can potentially sire a much larger number. Therefore, males are predisposed to compete with one another for mating opportunities with available females. Within these biological constraints, an evolutionary perspective points to the importance of ecological factors in supporting or discouraging male–male and female–female coalitions. Under conditions of scarce resources, females must compete with one another for food, and thus the possibility of establishing and maintaining female–female coalitions is diminished. Scarce resources similarly enhance the benefits of male–male coalitions (i.e., males can band together to control access to both food resources and females). In the presence of strong male–male alliances and weak female–female coalitions, the power imbalance between males and females generates a society organized by male dominance, and high rates of male violence emerge.

Cross-species data further illustrated how, when the power balance shifted, the direction of violence and abuse also shifted. Thus, just as male dominance in chimpanzee and human cultures generated violence against females, in the female-centric bonobo culture, the potential was present for violent abuse of males by females. In my view, this evidence that documents the shift in the direction of abuse, further underlines the power of a macrosystemic approach to the understanding and treatment of violence.

Many other theorists have examined contextual factors that support male violence. Daly and Wilson (1994) presented an extensive discussion of the evolutionary psychological perspective. They discussed the incidence of male violence within multiple relationship contexts: among same-sex rivals; within opposite-sex relationships; and between parents and offspring. For example, they identified several contexts within which domestic violence increases: when a wife is sexually unfaithful; when she unilaterally terminates a relationship; and when she is "too independent, and in response to other factors that activate male sexual jealousy mechanisms" (p. 269).

The authors pointed out that all the contexts within which violence increased represented contexts in which the man's reproductive success was threatened. In a manner similar to the Thornhills, Daly and Wilson concluded that these contextual variations provided evidence of the adaptive origins of domestic violence. This analysis suffers from the same problem that characterized Thornhills' explanatory framework in that the authors do not provide evidence to support their claim that male violence is a product of natural selection.

A behavior can be adaptive in the evolutionary sense (i.e., contribute to future reproductive success) and yet be environmentally determined, and thus not a product of natural selection. For example, Hrdy (1990) demonstrated that female mammals can bias the sex of their offspring, depending on a combination of the mother's rank in the dominance hierarchy and whether sons or daughters emigrate from their natal group. In olive baboons, daughters remain in their natal group; sons emigrate. Thus, higher-ranking olive baboon mothers tend to give birth to a significantly greater number of daughters than sons. Because daughters remain in their natal group, they can benefit from the mother's high dominance rank. Similarly, lower-ranking mothers give birth to a significantly greater number of sons. Sons have a chance to increase their dominance in the new community above their mother's low rank, thereby improving their reproductive success. Thus, a behavior can be adaptive and *not* represent an evolved species-typical trait; it may vary depending only on the environmental context.

Archer (1994b) also looked at contextual variables in his analysis of the origins of male violence. He identified three different levels of power: structural, organizational, and relationship. A structural context represents an entire society (e.g., in male dominant cultures, male power is legitimized through an ideology of male superiority). Organizational power is used to justify the use of violence against women through codified laws and the court system. The context of personal relationships is the final level of power analysis.

Goodwin (1994) presented a similar typology, which examined contextual factors at both the societal and the relationship level. She argued that the level of male dominance within a given culture affected the rates of violence expressed at a relationship level. In addition, she noted that environmental factors external to society (e.g., war or economic depression) could exacerbate the frequency with which men managed their anxiety through battering women. Goodwin further advocated a careful examination of the phenomenological world of the couple to determine specific environmental factors such as physical setting (e.g., fraternity party and the presence of alcohol) or a multigenerational tradition of using violence to settle intimate conflict. Goodwin's analysis examined both macrosocietal factors (i.e., level of male dominance) and the microcontext (i.e., a couple's cycle of emotional interactions) within which male violence against women occurs.

Smuts's sociobiological analysis differs from both Archer and Goodwin in that it does not see different contextual levels as independent. It views the issue of male dominance as the single organizing construct for all contextual levels. Thus, if power relationships were reordered at the macrocultural level, then relationship patterns would be transformed correspondingly within every social context. The bonobo research also pointed out that the context of high female power limited male violence, not only toward females and between males within a community, but also between communities. Thus, the evolutionary framework hypothesized that the power balance between males and females constructs cross-cultural violence as well as intracultural violence.

Recommendations for Change

How can we use the insights gained from an evolutionary analysis to think about specific social policy changes? Before suggesting new social policy initiatives, I want to outline the existing policy that could be seen as an expression of female–female cooperation. The entire feminist movement, which has insisted on making male violence against women visible, could be understood as a societal mechanism of female cooperation. Similarly, interventions that exist for women who are victims of male violence (battered women's shelters, support groups, rape hot lines, etc.) traditionally have been initiated by women, and they could be interpreted as examples of female cooperation.

Unfortunately, feminist ideology (i.e., achieving equality for all women) has not been embraced by the majority of women within U.S. society. Many women who have achieved positions of power have not reached out to other women to share that power. When the feminist movement has been successful, it often has been to help women as victims. Too rarely has the movement routinely adopted a proactive stance to enhance women's power and status.

The bonobo society points to female cooperation as one crucial variable in limiting male dominance and improving the quality of life for women (and men). I believe that this emphasis on female cooperation is particularly relevant to dismantling male dominance within human society. The cross-species data indicated specific contexts within which female cooperation (and thus power) declined: the absence of abundant resources; and the custom of females leaving their natal group and thus being deprived of the support of their relatives. These observations suggest the importance of women attaining economic security (i.e., sufficient resources) and establishing emotional, social, and political support networks. Based on these data, three social change initiatives can be immediately identified. The need: to transform the socialization of girls to emphasize female cooperation; to generate cooperative economic ventures among women to increase their economic independence and stability; and to create a cultural gender ideology that legitimizes the advantages of female cooperation and economic independence.

It is not enough to be theoretically convinced that it is in women's long-term best interests to cooperate. Grass roots organizations are needed that make cooperation economically beneficial to women (e.g., stock market clubs, cottage industries, food co-ops, day-care cooperatives, group housing). If cooperating with other women does not offer economic benefits, women will be unlikely to change their behavior.

To achieve widespread economic change, we must also systematically increase political power for women. One might argue that women have had the vote for 70 years, but have yet to learn how to use it. To use it effectively, women must use it cooperatively. We must learn to see our common interests as being greater than our differences. The feminist movement historically has been guilty of being too white, too middle class, too heterosexist, and, correspondingly, too insensitive toward the different needs of lesbians, poor women, and women of color. In the past decade, significant efforts have been made to improve the inclusiveness of feminist organizations. This trend toward inclusion of all women within the movement must be maintained and enhanced.

Given the importance of early socialization in the transference of social norms, we must transform the socialization of girls. How can we dramatically alter the way that girls view other girls? How can we generate a sense of solidarity and collaboration among girls to transform institutions of male dominance, rather than to comply with them? It is likely that societal institutions must change before socialization practices. Parents will not socialize girls to behave in a way that is disadvantageous to them in the short run. Therefore, we must institutionalize the benefits of female–female cooperation before we can expect widespread changes in the socialization of girls.

I have focused here on women changing the power imbalance between the sexes because I assume that the majority of men, like all dominant groups, are unlikely to relinquish power and privilege voluntarily. However, it is important to acknowledge that there are some men who realize the price men pay for dominance (O'Neil, Good, & Holmes, 1995; Pleck, 1981; Levant & Pollack, 1995). These men are already working to acknowledge and relinquish male privilege and to share power with women and with less powerful men. They are thus available as partners in this effort to reorganize the power imbalance within patriarchy.

The participation of pro-feminist men is particularly important in changing the way that we socialize young boys, so that boys do not automatically assume male privilege and work to maintain male dominance. Miedzian (1991) has made several suggestions about how the socialization of boys must change: decrease the misogyny that is endemic to the practice of organized sports and provide boys with early experiences of taking care of infants and young children. I add the following: valuing the expression of feelings by boys, especially feelings of vulnerability, and decreasing the homophobia that is endemic to boy culture, specifically through social tolerance for cross-gender behavior in boys.

New socialization practices and new economic and political institutions require a specific gender ideology that legitimizes gender equality, the advantages of female cooperation, and the relinquishing of male privilege. Behavioral change and ideological change are reciprocal and reinforce each other. If we want to raise boys who do not fight for dominance, we have to generate a cultural ideology that underlines the negative effects (e.g., "the dark side") of traditional masculinity (Brooks & Silverstein, 1995). Similarly, if we want to establish female–female cooperation as a cultural norm, we have to prescribe for women the advantages of cooperating, rather than competing, with one another.

Until recently, it was often necessary to comply with aspects of patriarchy that were disadvantageous to women because women lacked the power to create alternatives for themselves. This continues to be true in many developing nations. With the widespread entrance of women into the workforce in the industrialized West, more women now have economic and political power. Thus, they have more benefits to exchange among themselves. However, in many, if not most, milieux, men continue to have the preponderance of economic and political power. This continuing context of male dominance reinforces the continuing competition among women for access to dominant men. Without a clear ideology that argues for the long-term benefits of female–female cooperation, the short-term exigencies of female–female competition may continue to construct relationships among women.

In my view, the bonobo research can be used to begin to construct such an ideology. This research suggests that high levels of female cooperation significantly change the power balance between males and females. This change in the balance of power has a number of advantageous effects: it decreases male violence against females, against other males, and between different communities. I hope that this chapter will contribute to the creation of this ideology.

CONCLUSION

I have described why I think that a feminist sociobiological analysis is effective in contributing to an understanding of the evolutionary origins of complex human behaviors such as male violence. Sociobiology examines the interplay of biology and the environmental context in a way that can be used to identify systemic variables that can point the way to social change.

I have argued that the evolutionary psychological approach is not effective for a number of reasons: it presents hypotheses that are not testable empirically; it ignores relevant cross-species and cross-cultural data; and it focuses on intra-psychic, rather than systemic, variables.

I have argued that male violence against women is one consequence of male dominance within a patriarchal culture. I have presented cross-species data suggesting that female cooperation is one important variable in decreasing male dominance. I have made specific recommendations for social change: creating new economic and political organizations that support female cooperation; transforming the socialization of girls; and generating a new gender ideology that legitimizes female cooperation. I am hopeful that this chapter will contribute to that process of social change.

Men's and Women's Gender-Role Socialization and Gender-Role Conflict Factors Explaining Men's Violence Against Women

Introduction

T he two chapters included in this part review the literature on men's and women's gender-role socialization. Jim O'Neil and Rod Nadeau (in Chapter 7) present a conceptual model and 10 hypotheses to explain how gender-role socialization predisposes men to violence against women. They also make hypotheses about how men's violence against women is actually triggered. They hypothesize that the formation of a sexist masculine gender-role identity can lead to distorted gender-role schemas that produce fears of femininity and fears about being emasculated. The gender-role conflict that men experience with women can be emasculating to them and produces fear, anger, shame, embarrassment, humiliation, defensiveness, and feelings of loss of power and control. From their perspective, men develop three self-protective, defensive patterns of gender-role conflict, including power and control, restricted emotionality, and homophobia and heterosexism. They theorize that these patterns are activated when men experience threats to their masculine gender-role identity from women. O'Neil and Nadeau hypothesize that when these self-protective defense mechanisms break down, men's violence can be triggered.

In Chapter 8, Roberta Nutt considers how women's gender-role socialization across life stages predisposes women to men's violence. Gender-role devaluation, gender-role restriction, and gender-role violation are defined as patterns of gender-role conflict with preferences for things that are typically male and devaluation of things that are typically female. Nutt argues that these patterns make it difficult for women to enter into equitable heterosexual relationships with men and set appropriate boundaries to prevent violence. She reviews the literature about women's development within each life stage and gives examples of the gender-role conflict patterns that women experience. Nutt's analysis provides a greater understanding of the gender-role factors that make women particularly vulnerable to domestic violence.

7

Men's Gender-Role Conflict, Defense Mechanisms, and Self-Protective Defensive Strategies

Explaining Men's Violence Against Women From a Gender-Role Socialization Perspective

JAMES M. O'NEIL
RODNEY A. NADEAU

In this chapter, we theorize how men's gender-role socialization contributes to violence against women. We hypothesize that gender-role socialization, distorted gender-role schemas, gender-role conflicts, defense mechanisms, and self-protective defense strategies are primary factors that predispose men to be violent against women. We also discuss the triggering dynamics that cause violence against women. We hypothesize that power conflicts and abuses, psychological violence, situational events, threats to a man's gender-role identity, and a breakdown of defenses all contribute to the triggering of men's violence against women. Our goal is to expand on previous conceptualizations that point to men's gender roles as primary factors in explaining men's violence toward women.

Ten hypotheses provide the foundation for the major points in this chapter. These hypotheses indicate that many men in general, and violent men in particular, experience the following:

1. Are socialized in sexist ways by our patriarchal society into restrictive values of the Masculine Mystique and Value System.

2. Develop a masculine gender-role identity based on restrictive and sexist gender-role stereotypes.

3. Learn distorted gender-role schemas of masculinity and femininity during their gender-role socialization.

4. Learn distorted gender-role schemas that produce fears of femininity, fears of emasculation, and gender-role conflict.

5. Experience negative emotions from their gender-role conflict including anger, fear, anxiety, shame, guilt, loss, sadness, self-hatred, and hurt.

6. Develop self-protective defensive strategies and use defense mechanisms to protect their masculine gender-role identity when coping with gender-role conflict and negative emotions.

7. Are predisposed to be dysfunctional and abusive, and are sometimes violent with women because of their gender-role conflict and learned defensiveness.

8. Abuse power and become defensive during power conflicts with women, particularly when loss of power or control is at stake and when their masculine gender-role identity is threatened.

9. Use psychological violence and threats against women when the self-protective defensive strategies begin to break down and traditional defenses no longer work.

10. Use violence against women when triggering events occur, when defense strategies no longer work, and when defense mechanisms break down.

Our goal is to expand on these hypotheses and offer new ways to understand the causes of men's violence.

This chapter is arranged in the following way. First, we review the previous literature that has explained how men's gender roles have contributed to violence against women. Second, using the earlier literature and our own concepts, we present a theoretical model that explains how men's gender-role socialization, gender-role conflict, and self-protective defense strategies predispose men to violence against women. Third, we review the relevant literature and explain our theoretical model. Fourth, the triggering dynamics of men's violence toward women are explained using the following concepts: power conflicts, abuses of power, psychological violence, threats to the man's gender-role identity, and triggering events. Given the complexity of the topic and the past problems with other authors' terminologies, we provide our own operational definitions throughout the chapter. Finally, we make recommendations for the future and discuss some of the limitations of our own theory.

MEN'S GENDER ROLES AS PREDICTORS OF VIOLENCE AGAINST WOMEN: VAGUE CONCEPTS AND LIMITED RESEARCH

The relationship between men's gender roles and violence against women has been discussed in the previous literature (APA, 1994; Archer, 1994a, 1994b; Brooks & Silverstein, 1995; Crowell & Burgess, 1996; Koss et al., 1994). Factors identified as contributing to men's violence against women have not specifically explained how men's gender roles contribute to violence against women. Furthermore, very few empirical studies have directly assessed how gender-role factors contribute to men's battering. The few and inconclusive studies completed have related men's violence against women to traditional gender-role expectancies (Crossman, Stith, & Bender, 1990; Finn, 1986; Hotaling & Sugarman, 1986), hostile masculinity (Malamuth, Sockoskie, Koss, & Tanaka, 1991), adversarial relationships between the sexes (Pleck, Sonenstein, & Ku, 1991), and masculine ideology (Good, Heppner, Hillenbrand-Gunn, & Wang, 1995). How men's gender roles contribute to violence against women has a very limited theoretical or empirical foundation and, consequently, remains in its earliest stage of understanding.

A more comprehensive gender-role model of the multiple, gender-related factors that explain men's violence toward women is needed. In this chapter, we introduce such a conceptual model. We provide a greater specificity on how men's gender-role socialization and gender-role conflict can predispose men to use violence and how these gender-related factors may actually trigger the violence.

CONCEPTUAL MODEL EXPLAINING MEN'S VIOLENCE AGAINST WOMEN FROM A GENDER-ROLE CONFLICT AND GENDER-ROLE SOCIALIZATION PERSPECTIVE

Figure 7.1 presents a conceptual model that explains how the larger patriarchal society, men's gender-role socialization, gender-role conflict, self-protective defense strategies, and traditional defense mechanisms contribute to men's violence against women.

Figure 7.1 depicts both the predisposing and triggering dynamics of men's violence against women. The predisposing dynamics are defined as the gender-role-related factors and processes that render men vulnerable to using violence against women. The triggering dynamics are the actual situational cues and interpersonal processes that prompt men to psychologically or physically assault women.

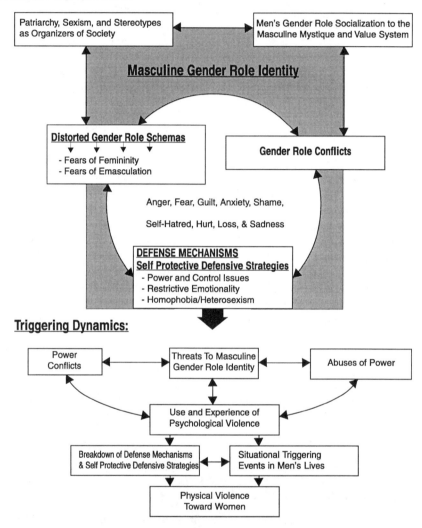

Figure 7.1. Predisposing and Triggering Dynamics of Men's Gender-Role Socialization and Gender-Role Conflict Resulting in Violence Against Women

At the top of Figure 7.1, on the left, the predisposing dynamics show the larger patriarchal society as the spawning ground for men's sexism and violence toward women. The larger patriarchal society, sexism, and gender-role stereotypes are shown as organizers of our society. Patriarchy instills sexist values and stereotypes that influence how men relate to women, to other men, and to themselves. In the top-right corner of Figure 7.1, men's gender-role socialization and, specifically, the Masculine Mystique and Value System are shown. The Masculine Mystique is a complex set of sexist values and beliefs that define optimal masculinity in society and in men's lives. Masculine gender-role identity is formed by the overall patriarchy and men's sexist socialization to the values of the Masculine Mystique. This identity is continually shaped by the four interacting and socializing dynamics shown in the middle circle of Figure 7.1. First, distorted gender-role schemas are learned during a boy's gender-role socialization. These distorted gender-role schemas produce fears of femininity and fears about being emasculated. Second, gender-role conflicts that occur in boys's and men's lives may potentially be emasculating for them. Third, as shown in the middle of the circle of Figure 7.1, men experience a spectrum of negative emotions, such as anger, fear, guilt, anxiety, shame, self-hatred, hurt, loss, and sadness, during their gender-role socialization. They respond to these emotions by experiencing fears of femininity and fears of being emasculated that threaten their masculine gender-role identity. Fourth, men develop traditional defense mechanisms and three self-protective defense strategies to cope with their negative emotions. The self-protective defense strategies operate to mediate men's negative feelings and increase their ability to cope with gender-role conflict. These self-protective strategies include (a) power and control, (b) restricted emotionality, and (c) homophobia/heterosexism. In short, these self-protective defense strategies keep men temporarily safe, but do not effectively resolve the gender-role conflict and negative emotions about their masculine gender-role identity.

The bidirectional and circular arrows at the top and in the middle of Figure 7.1 depict the complex relationships between the concepts and processes that predispose men to use violence. The multiple arrows show how the macrosocietal aspects of sexism and patriarchy interact in complex ways with the man's masculine gender-role identity and his psychological sense of self. The large, bold-faced arrow at the bottom of the defense mechanism and strategies depicts how the entire set of predisposing dynamics affects the triggering dynamics at the bottom of Figure 7.1.

Men's psychological and physical violence toward women is triggered when their defenses and self-protective defense strategies break down. As shown in the bottom half of Figure 7.1, power conflicts, abuses of power, and psychological violence can increasingly pose threats to a man's gender-role identity. Over time, the man's defenses become less effective in protecting his masculine gender-role identity. When couples have power conflicts, abuses of power may occur. Couples may use and experience psychological violence as conflicts go unresolved, thereby increasing the interpersonal tension and potential for violence. Situational triggering events in men's lives or the family situation (unemployment, health problems, extramarital affairs, parenting dilemmas, money problems) may serve as the stimulus for greater and greater threats to the man's gender-role identity. When men's self-protective defense strategies and defense mechanisms no longer work (i.e., they partially or completely break down), the potential for psychological and physical violence is hypothesized to be high.

The bidirectional arrows at the bottom of Figure 7.1 show the complex relationships between the factors that trigger violence. Power conflicts, abuses of power, psychological violence, and threats to a man's gender-role identity are the interrelated factors that contribute to triggering men's violence. How these factors operate in a man's life is quite idiosyncratic and interacts with the overall dynamics of the couple's relationship (see Chapters 9 and 10 by Anderson and Schlossberg and by Rigazio-DiGilio and Lanza, respectively, in this volume).

In summary, the conceptual model explains how men might learn to be violent toward their partners from a gender-role socialization perspective. The model relates directly to Hypotheses 6–8 in the second chapter of this book (see O'Neil and Harway, Chapter 2). These hypotheses stated that men's sexist gender-role socialization, misogynistic attitudes toward women, patterns of gender-role conflict, and unresolved and unexpressed emotions contribute to men's violence against women. In this chapter, we expand on these hypotheses and use Figure 7.1 as the overall chapter organizer.

PATRIARCHY, SEXISM, AND GENDER-ROLE STEREOTYPES AS ORGANIZERS OF SOCIETY

Patriarchy, sexism, and gender-role stereotypes are contextual factors that help to explain how men's gender-role socialization contributes to violence against women. Patriarchy is classically defined as the supremacy of the father over his family members and the domination of men over women and children in every aspect of life and culture. Patriarchy oppresses women because it condones abuses of power and violates women's basic human rights. Patriarchy is also responsible for the overt and covert discrimination against women in careers, religion, politics, families, and civic life. Sexism is the social, political, and personal expression of patriarchy. The patriarchal value system enforces sexism as "the norm," when really it is psychologically destructive and many times a form of psychopathology (Albee, 1981). Simply put, sexism is incongruent with democratic principles and basic human rights because it violates fundamental concepts of equality, justice, and human freedom. Sexism maintains the patriarchal status quo through restrictive gender-role stereotypes. These stereotypes of masculinity and femininity are a direct expression of patriarchy and sexism in men's and women's lives. These stereotypes are learned very early in life and predispose men and women to use different power bases dictated by sex. From our perspective, these power bases and sexist stereotypes are promoted by our capitalist economic system, because they shape public and political opinion and are used to sell consumer products. Negative gender-role stereotypes exert great power in people's lives and produce ongoing conflict between the sexes. In the next section, we discuss how gender-role stereotypes influence men's gender-role socialization through the Masculine Mystique and Value System.

THE MASCULINE MYSTIQUE AND VALUE SYSTEM: THE CRADLE OF VIOLENCE TOWARD WOMEN

As shown in Figure 7.1, the larger patriarchal society reinforces sexism and rigid gender-role stereotypes of masculinity and femininity for men and women. Through these stereotypes, separate and polarized gender-role identities for men and women are internalized, with masculinity being perceived to be superior to femininity. Masculine gender-role identity is shaped by these stereotypes of masculinity and femininity through the values of the Masculine Mystique.

The Masculine Mystique and Value System consists of a complex set of values and beliefs that define optimal masculinity in society (O'Neil, 1981a, 1981b, 1982, 1990). The Mystique is based on numerous assumptions, expectancies, and attitudes about what "manhood" really means. The Masculine Mystique is a form of masculine ideology (Pleck, 1995; Thompson & Pleck, 1995) and implies (a) that men are superior to women and masculinity is superior to femininity; (b) that power, control, competition, and dominance are essential to prove one's masculinity; (c) that emotions, feelings, vulnerability, and intimacy are to be avoided because they are considered feminine and weak; and (d) that career successes and heterosexual potency are measures of one's masculinity. These values and beliefs are based on rigid gender-role stereotypes and imply the implicit inferiority of femininity compared with masculinity.

Many parents support the Masculine Mystique and socialize boys into these sexist values. Consequently, boys experience great pressure to demonstrate their masculinity in their early years. Proving one's masculinity is an early task for boys and it extends into early and middle adulthood. Some men compulsively need to prove their masculinity over and over to maintain their masculine gender-role identity. How the values of the Masculine Mystique predispose men to conflict with women is more apparent in the context of men's gender-role identity.

MASCULINE GENDER-ROLE IDENTITY: CONSCIOUS AND UNCONSCIOUS ASPECTS OF MASCULINITY AND FEMININITY

Masculine gender-role identity is defined as an individual man's total conception of his masculine roles, values, functions, expectations, and belief systems. This includes how biological sex and the stereotypes of masculinity and femininity shape the man's sense of self over the life span. Masculine gender-role identity is everything that the man says and does that communicates his masculine and feminine dimensions. Men's public gender-role identity is experienced through masculine and feminine values, attitudes, and behaviors in his varied work, family, and leisure roles. The private experience of masculine gender-role identity is the man's deep, internal experience of self as male, including all of his conscious and unconscious feelings, fears, and ambivalences about his gender role.

Men have both conscious and unconscious aspects to their masculine gender-role identity (Geis, 1993; Pollack, 1995). Unconscious feelings, fears, anxieties, and ambivalences about one's gender-role identity are beyond men's total awareness, but they still can shape his behavior and feelings about self. Analyses of men's unconscious and internal dynamics of masculine gender-role identity have been theoretically discussed (Jung, 1953; Levinson, Darrow, Klein, Levinson, & McKee, 1978). During early cognitive development, a boy's masculine gender-role identity is primarily a dualistic, categorical, classification process whereby masculine and feminine dimensions emerge as bipolar opposites. For many boys and men, developing a masculine gender-role identity means repudiating all feminine attitudes, roles, and behaviors and endorsing the Masculine Mystique and Value System. For many men, a polarized way of viewing masculinity and femininity becomes a part of adulthood. Many men have gender-role identities that reflect the sexist stereotypes of the Masculine Mystique and Value System. As man's gender-role identity develops, cognitive distortions about gender roles and intense fears can result from narrow and polarized views of masculinity and femininity.

PREDISPOSING DYNAMICS OF MASCULINE GENDER-ROLE IDENTITY: DISTORTED GENDER-ROLE SCHEMAS, FEARS OF FEMININITY, AND FEARS OF EMASCULATION

Men's masculine gender-role identity can be shaped by learning distorted gender-role schemas and by having two types of volatile fears that can predispose them to use psychological and physical violence against women. As shown by the arrows in Figure 7.1, men's distorted gender-role schemas can produce both the fear of femininity and the fear of being emasculated. Fears of femininity and emasculation can be experienced both consciously and unconsciously, and play a significant role in males' interpersonal relationships with both men and women.

Distorted Gender-Role Schemas

The role of cognition in learning gender-role attributes and behaviors has been discussed in the literature (Bem, 1981, 1983; Cross & Markus, 1993; Eisler, 1995; Geis, 1993). Gender-role schema conceptualizations have been defined by

Bem (1981, 1983) and are relevant to how men internalize a masculine gender-role identity. Bem's notion of gender-role schema proposes that (1) individuals learn cultural definitions of femaleness and maleness through gender-role schemas, (2) schemas include networks of associations that organize and guide an individual's perception of masculinity and femininity based on sex, and (3) schemas become part of the self-concept and are used to evaluate one's personal adequacy as a male or a female. Gender-role schemas are employed to make judgements that direct both a person's thought and a person's behavior (Cross & Markus, 1993; Koss et al., 1994). Bem's schema theory provides a conceptual framework of how men think about masculinity and femininity and how they perceive their gender-role attributes and identities.

Distorted gender-role schemas are exaggerated thoughts and feelings about the role of masculinity and femininity in a person's life. Boys and men internalize these distortions when they learn the stereotypes of the Masculine Mystique from the larger patriarchal society, from the media and peers, and in families and schools. Distortions occur when a man experiences intense pressure to meet stereotypic notions of masculinity, resulting in fears and anxieties about not measuring up to traditional gender-role expectancies.

Mahalik and Cournoyer (1997) hypothesized that men's gender-role conflicts include cognitive distortions about masculinity and femininity. Extending Mahalik and Cournoyer's work, we hypothesize that boys and men internalize distorted gender-role schemas of femininity and masculinity that are highly sex typed, rigid, restrictive, sexist, homophobic, hypermasculine, and what commonly has been called macho ways of thinking. Distorted gender-role schemas operate in men's relationships with both sexes. Many boys and men struggle with distorted gender-role schemas when they are creating their masculine gender-role identities. There can be confusion and stress as they cognitively compare themselves to very high standards of manhood established by the larger patriarchal society. Unexpressed emotions, confusion, and fear foster the development of distorted gender-role schemas. These exaggerated views of masculinity and femininity ultimately can result in gender-role conflict, dysfunctional behavior, and serious conflicts with women.

Distorted gender-role schemas are related to the Masculine Mystique and Value System and can predispose men to be violent and actually trigger assaults. Examples of distorted gender-role schemas include: (1) believing that men and masculinity are superior to women and femininity; (2) thinking that power and control are essential to prove one's masculinity; (3) believing that feelings, intimacy, and emotions are only feminine, rather than human; and (4) judging one's masculinity and personal value based on heterosexual potency and career success. These and other distortions of gender roles can produce fears and anxieties.

Fear of Femininity

One of the primary outcomes of distorted gender-role schemas is the fear of femininity, which has been defined as a strong, negative emotion in the self or others associated with feminine values, attitudes, and behaviors (David & Brannon, 1976; O'Neil, 1981a, 1982; O'Neil, Good, & Holmes, 1995). The fear of femininity occurs because boys learn to subordinate and devalue feminine values during childhood and early adulthood. To subordinate feminine values implies that (a) femininity is inferior to masculinity and (b) people who display feminine characteristics are inferior, inappropriate, and/or immature. The subordination and devaluation of feminine values is central to understanding the conflict between the sexes in many areas of life, specifically in men's violence toward women.

Consciously or unconsciously, men usually have difficulty integrating the feminine sides of their personality. Many men are socialized to avoid anything feminine to solidify their masculine gender-role identities. During certain periods of development, they learn to devalue and distance themselves from anything feminine. Avoiding or suppressing a fundamental aspect of oneself, such as femininity, is difficult. Consequently, there is much ambivalence and conflict with men's femininity. The dynamics of fearing one's femininity are not well understood and many times are unconscious to the man (Jung, 1953). When a man fears his feminine side, he really fears that others will see him as stereotypically and negatively feminine (e.g., weak, dependent, submissive) rather than as positively masculine. The cost of showing stereotypic feminine qualities could result in being devalued, ridiculed, or emasculated. These are high costs to a man seeking to fulfill the Masculine Mystique.

Because masculinity and femininity become stereotyped and dichotomized in the man's psyche, men seek to identify with masculinity to establish their gender-role identities. There are usually fears and anxieties about how to fully meet the stereotypes of masculinity. There are also questions about how to avoid appearing feminine. The man may exaggerate masculine qualities through hypermasculine activities to compensate for the naturally occurring need to express his feminine side.

Fears of Emasculation

Another result of distorted gender-role schemas is fear of emasculation. Whereas the fear of femininity was defined as a strong negative emotion about femininity, emasculation is the fear of losing masculine status and power in the eyes of others. One of men's greatest fears is to be emasculated. To be emasculated means to be deprived of virility or procreative powers; to be castrated; to be deprived of masculine energy, vigor, or spirit; to be weakened; to be unnerved by others in terms of your masculine gender-role identity. In short, emasculation means losing one's masculine identity and energy. Being emasculated is part of almost every boy's and man's gender-role identity development. He may feel emasculated by devaluing comments, failures, sexual dysfunctions, and perceived losses of control and power. Being emasculated is very painful for men and can activate very primitive impulses including regression, aggression, and violence. Emasculation threatens a man's gender-role identity and can produce conflict. When this threat occurs, the man may decide to restore his masculinity through aggressive words or actions. Being emasculated or fearing that it will happen can produce defensiveness and gender-role conflict, which are defined in subsequent sections.

GENDER-ROLE CONFLICT: PREDISPOSING MEN TO DEFENSIVENESS, NEGATIVE PSYCHOLOGICAL HEALTH, AND DEEP EMOTIONS

As shown in Figure 7.1, we hypothesize that men's distorted gender-role schemas elicit fears of femininity and of being emasculated, and can, consequently, cause gender-role conflict (O'Neil, 1981a, 1981b, 1982, 1990, 1998; O'Neil & Good, 1997; O'Neil, Good, & Holmes, 1995). Gender-role conflict is defined as a psychological state in which socialized gender roles have negative consequences on the person or others. Gender-role conflict occurs when rigid, sexist, or restricted gender roles result in restriction, devaluation, or violation of others or self (O'Neil, 1990; O'Neil, Good, & Holmes, 1995; O'Neil, Helms, Gable, David, & Wrightsman, 1986). Gender-role conflict implies cognitive, emotional, unconscious, or behavioral problems caused by socialized gender roles learned in sexist and patriarchal societies (O'Neil et al., 1986).

Most males experience a gender-role conflict when their masculinity is questioned by others. For example, a seven-year-old boy who is called a sissy for expressing his feelings is experiencing a form of early emasculation and gender-role conflict. Parents who criticize their son's intellectual, physical, or personal development may activate the young man's fears about becoming a masculine success. Being called a "queer," "fag," or "homo" for deviating from the Masculine Mystique is a common experience in middle school and throughout early adulthood. Crude and critical comments from girls about one's masculine physique, intelligence, or personality (usually called heterosexual antagonism) can stimulate gender-role conflict. Women who critically comment on a man's lack of strength, sexual potency, or skill can threaten a man's gender-role identity and stimulate gender-role conflict.

A man's personal experience with gender-role conflict can be psychologically painful. Dynamically, men may personally devalue, restrict, or violate themselves when they do not meet the expected gender-role stereotypes or their own gender-role expectancies. Men may be unconscious to gender-role conflict and unaware of their gender-role fears, anxieties, and distortions related to gender. Whether gender-role conflict is unconscious or conscious, there may be many difficult questions such as, "How am I perceived as a man?", "Do I appear masculine?", "Am I living up to masculine standards?", "Am I going to look bad?", "Am I going to fail?", "Am I a loser?", "Am I inadequate?" Under these conditions, the man may experience fears of failure as a man and be vulnerable to depression, anxiety, and self-abuse. He may medicate himself through alcohol, drugs, compulsive exercise, or overeating. His unresolved emotions also can be expressed through verbal or physical abuse of others.

Empirical research on men's gender-role conflict has been associated with poor psychological health, including low self-esteem, anxiety, personal stress, anger, depression, problems with intimacy, and negative attitudes toward seeking help (O'Neil et al., 1986; O'Neil, Good, & Holmes, 1995). No study to date has assessed the relationship between gender-role conflict and men's battering, but other aggressive attitudes toward women and homosexuals have been documented (O'Neil, 1998; O'Neil & Good, 1997; O'Neil, Good, & Holmes, 1995). For example, gender-role conflicts have been associated with hostility toward women (Chartier, Graff, & Arnold, 1986), with negative attitudes toward homosexuals (Ducat, 1994; Rounds, 1994), with sexual aggression (Kaplan, O'Neil, & Owen, 1993; Rando, Brittan, & Pannu, 1994), and with sexual harrassment (Jacobs, 1996). These initial studies indicate that gender-role conflict can be hazardous to men's health and relates to negative or hostile attitudes toward women and gay men.

As the foregoing research suggests and as is graphically shown in the middle of Figure 7.1, negative emotions, such as anger, fear, guilt, anxiety, shame, self-hatred, hurt, loss, and sadness, can result from men's sexist gender-role socialization, gender-role conflict, distorted gender-role schemas, and fears of femininity and emasculation. The documented relationship between men's gender-role conflict and men's negative emotions has implications for understanding men's gender-role identity and their potential for violence. Deep emotions caused by gender-role conflict are potentially experienced as threats to many men's gender-role identities. These threats can cause defense mechanisms to operate and activate self-protective defensive strategies to cope with gender-role conflict. In this way, deep emotions that are unprocessed are replaced with a "defensive masculinity" that can predispose men to insecurities, emotional turmoil, and violence against others. As subsequent sections elaborate, it is hypothesized that defense mechanisms and self-protective defensive strategies are developed to protect men's gender-role identities and to help them cope with negative emotions related to gender-role conflict.

MEN'S DEFENSE MECHANISMS AND SELF-PROTECTIVE STRATEGIES DEFINED

How do boys and men respond to the emotions related to fears of femininity and emasculation and gender-role conflict? We hypothesize that gender-role conflicted males use defense mechanisms and develop self-protective defense strategies when their gender-role identities are threatened. This defensiveness and these self-protective strategies can predispose men to greater personal restrictions that can lead to problems, including psychological and physical abuse of women. Only a few authors have discussed how defense mechanisms operate in relationships and how these unconscious dynamics relate to men's violence against women (Goldberg, 1982, 1993; Stordeur & Still, 1989). For example, men's defensive autonomy with women has been discussed by Goldberg (1982, 1993). He theorizes that men's gender-role socialization is largely an unconscious and defensive process of externalizing masculine gender roles while repressing femininity. We expand on Goldberg's defensive autonomy concept by describing men's traditional and self-protective defense strategies.

Defense mechanisms are cognitive and unconscious processes that protect individuals from excessive anxiety by denying, falsifying, or distorting reality. Mahalik, Cournoyer, DeFranc, Cherry, and Napolitano (1998) indicated that men's ego defense mechanisms ". . . maintain homeostasis by preventing painful ideas, emotions, and drives from forcing their way into consciousness" (p. 249). Some of the traditional defense mechanisms include repression, denial, projection, reaction formation, displacement, rationalization, isolation, and compensation.

Self-protective defense strategies are defined as both conscious and unconscious thoughts, attitudes, and behaviors that are used in relationships to protect a man's gender-role identity. These strategies develop from unresolved gender-role conflict experienced during a man's gender-role socialization. Furthermore, self-protective defense strategies operate to manage intense emotions that emanate from gender-role conflicts and are used to manage threatening interpersonal interactions, particularly with women. Self-protective defense strategies are activated by conscious and unconscious reactions to (1) perceived threats to one's masculine gender-role identity, (2) fears of not meeting the values of the Masculine Mystique, (3) fears of being labeled feminine, (4) fears of being emasculated, (5) distorted gender-role schemas, and (6) overall gender-role conflict.

In our analysis, defense mechanisms and the self-protective strategies serve three psychological defensive functions. First, they defend men against losses of power and control in interpersonal relationships. Second, they protect men from labeling and from experiencing or expressing strong emotions in interpersonal exchanges. Third, they defend men against threats to their heterosexuality, and against fears about their own homosexual inclinations and the homosexual orientations of others. The psychological outcomes of this defensiveness may include personal restriction and rigidities in thought and behavior; restriction of others; emotional distortions, over-reactions, and cognitive blind spots; and increased potential for self-destruction or abuse of others.

When men encounter the feminine through women and simultaneously experience their own femininity, the potential for gender-role defensiveness and interpersonal conflict is increased. Three self-protective defense strategies may be activated to cope with the internal and external conflicts. In the next section, we theorize that the self-protective defense strategies of power and control, restrictive emotionality, and homophobia and heterosexism predispose men to be personally and interpersonally dysfunctional and potentially abusive and violent toward women. This predisposition means that we believe that these unconscious and conscious defenses are the early, formative basis for men's potential abuse and violence against women. In each of the following sections, these self-protective defensive strategies are defined and then related to the traditional defense mechanisms.

CONTROL AND POWER AS SELF-PROTECTIVE DEFENSIVE STRATEGIES

Men's problems with power and control have been discussed in the men's literature for many decades (David & Brannon, 1976; Doyle, 1995; O'Neil, 1981a, 1981b, 1982). Previous definitions of power and control have not explained how gender roles mediate power and control dynamics between men and women (O'Neil & Egan, 1993). Furthermore, power and control have not been defined as a masculine defensive process that protects men's gender-role identity.

For the purposes of this chapter, power and control are conceptualized as defensive processes learned during men's gender-role socialization. Power is operationally defined as the need to influence and control others to express gender-role values and establish (or maintain) one's masculine gender-role identity (O'Neil & Egan, 1993). From this perspective, the use of power solidifies a man's self- and personal identity based on gender-role values and attitudes. Control is a means to obtain and keep power. It involves regulating and restraining others and having individuals or situations under one's command.

Furthermore, men's uses of power and control are potentially defensive and self-protective in a number of ways. First, power and control can be used defensively if the man believes that they protect him from threats to his masculine gender-role identity. Masculine gender-role identity for many men is predominantly defined by power and control. A threat to a man's power frequently is a threat to his masculine gender-role identity. Second, when men fear their femininity or fear being emasculated, power and control can be used to demonstrate their strength and manhood. Third, power and control serve defensive functions related to emotions and fears by enforcing restrictive emotionality in others and the self. Fourth, power and control are used to resolve gender-role conflicts and restore men's positive sense of masculinity.

Masculine defensiveness can emanate from distorted gender-role schema related to power and control. One distorted schema is that to be masculine, one must have power and control over others and the overall environment. Men also may believe that demonstrating power and control is part of proving their masculinity to others. For these men, proving their masculinity is not a one-time thing; it must be done over and over again. Another distorted belief is that a limited supply of power exists, and that power is always external to the self. Many men deny the sources of their internal, personal power. They may be continuously pitted against others in competitive "power plays" that can result in dysfunctional and abusive relationships. Some men also may believe that power should be possessed only by men or that men should have more or total power over women. Another distorted gender-role schema relates to the consequences of loss of power and control. Men may view loss of power and control to women as a threat to their masculine gender-role identity. Loss of power and control may imply loss of masculinity, thereby stimulating defensiveness, and deep emotions. When men lose power and control, they often feel emasculated. They may attempt to compensate for the loss through manipulations, aggressiveness, abuse, and even violence (Kahn, 1984).

How do power and control predispose men to possible violence against women? Frequently, men's conflicts with women are a result of unresolved power and control conflicts (Gelles, 1993c). Kahn (1984) discussed the "power wars" between men and women. Many couples "walk on the edges" of their power dynamics in their daily lives without facing the central themes that produce conflict. Men learn to manage their relationships with women by having control and power over them. For some men, having control of their partners is a way to validate their masculine gender-role identity. When men use power and control to manage relationships with women, women can become objects to be manipulated. This approach is dehumanizing to women and can set the stage for abuse and coercive actions. Some men have difficulty giving up power and control during interpersonal exchanges or conflicts. Giving up power and control would appear unmanly, feminine, and pose threats to their masculine gender-role identity. Some men irrationally equate loss of power and control with a loss of masculinity. It is well known that when men lose their power, they are more likely to use abuse and violence (coercive power) to compensate for the loss (Kahn, 1984). The tragedy of the power-oriented, controlling man is that he forfeits interpersonal and emotional flexibility and rarely gets his deeper emotional needs met.

When there is a threat to a man's power or control from a woman, specific defense mechanisms may be activated. These defenses are used to protect the man's gender-role identity and help him with his feelings of loss, vulnerability, shame, anger, and/or inadequacy as a man. These defense mechanisms help relieve men of their fears about loss of power and control, and they usually deny, falsify, or distort gender-role schemas related to power.

Repression operates when a man is unconscious of his needs for power and control. He may have no awareness of his obvious power struggles. He may deny that power and control issues or abuses are really operating, but demand that he control all major decisions. Projection operates when men blame women for their excessive need to control or have all the power. Therefore, women may be blamed for causing relationship problems and conflicts. Reaction formation may produce a disregard for power and control, and the man may hide behind weakness and vulnerability. He may temporarily withdraw from power conflicts and regress to earlier stages of development. He may displace his feelings of power or powerlessness to safer objects that are weak or vulnerable (i.e., the poor or racial minorities). Men may intellectualize or rationalize power conflicts by using logical reasoning to explain why the conflict exists. Finally, isolation, as a defense, may produce no emotions, only thoughts about power dynamics.

RESTRICTIVE EMOTIONALITY AS A SELF-PROTECTIVE DEFENSIVE STRATEGY

Restrictive emotionality is defined as men's fears about expressing feelings, difficulty finding words to express basic emotions, and a need to restrict others' emotional expressions. Restrictive emotionality implies that men have difficulty verbalizing feelings, giving up emotional control, and being vulnerable to self or others. Restrictive emotionality implies having difficulties in self-disclosure, recognizing feelings, and processing the emotional complexity of interpersonal exchanges.

Restrictive emotionality, as a self-protective defense strategy, functions to inhibit men's own feelings or works to restrict other people's feelings. Stereotypic masculinity is threatened by emotions, because feelings (except for anger) are considered to be stereotypically feminine. Consequently, restrictive emotionality is a defensive process that keeps a man distanced from his femininity and from those people who express feelings. Restricting and devaluing others' emotional expressions is a way for men to be in control and to assert their power.

As a defense strategy, restrictive emotionality prohibits the experience of deep feelings and results from at least four distorted gender-role schemas about emotions. The first schema is that emotions, feelings, and vulnerabilities are signs of being feminine and should be avoided. The second is the distortion that emotional men are weak, immature, dependent, and out of control. The third is the belief that emotional communications are dangerous because one's inner fears could be exposed, thereby resulting in loss of control and power. A man who expresses emotions may be judged as inappropriate, a liability, weak, unreasonable, or gay. The fourth notion is that the expression of vulnerable emotions always results in being taken advantage of by others. These distorted schemas are the basis for men's fears about emotions and can result in self-protective defensive strategies when emotions enter interpersonal relationships.

How does restrictive emotionality, as a self-protective defense mechanism, predispose men to be violent with women? During gender-role socialization, many men and women learn different approaches to human communication, particularly with respect to expressing emotions. Women learn to focus more on the emotional, intuitive, and interpersonal part of human exchanges, whereas men learn to emphasize rational, intellectual, and problem-solving approaches. For some men, emotional communication is threatening. This threat can result in men attempting to control the relationship by restricting women's emotions and permitting only one emotion: anger. Many times this anger is used to enforce the norm of restrictive emotionality in the home. These dynamics can cause stress, resentment, and miscommunication that lead to serious conflicts. Women's emotionality may threaten a man's gender-role identity, generate fears of emasculation, and generate fears about losing control of the relationship. The couple's unexpressed emotions and negative thoughts may build up and funnel into anger, hostility, and rage. Explosions of anger can sometimes result in aggressive and out of control behavior. Psychological violence and battering may be an extreme consequence of restrictive emotionality.

Numerous defense mechanisms may operate when a man experiences his deep emotions or women's emotions that threaten his masculine gender-role identity. Repression may operate by driving out all emotions from consciousness to avoid the meaning and importance of the affect. Through denial, women's emotions may not be heard or remembered if they are threatening to the man's masculine gender-role identity. Projection may occur when the man's own negative emotions threaten his masculinity and he blames others for having the feelings he cannot accept in himself. With reaction formation, the man may express emotions that are the opposite of his real feelings to protect his masculine identity. A reversion to earlier ways of processing emotions occurs when a man regresses to an early stage of development. He may use immature emotional processes to act out the feelings (i.e., temper tantrums, withdrawal, pouting, and physical force). Displacement may occur by directing personally threatening emotions toward some other person or object. For example, fear, anger, jealousy, guilt, shame, and rage may be expressed at women, children, pets, gay men, or even objects, such as walls. Emotions that threaten the man's gender-role identity may be rationalized or isolated completely into intellectual thought to protect him. When a man has no feelings, he is usually experiencing denial of affect. Therefore, he is not able to experience, label, or express emotions. Finally, with compensation, the man who feels inadequate and embarrassed by his emotionality may exaggerate stereotypic masculine qualities to overcome his feelings of inferiority. This kind of man may be highly rational, closed, and hypermasculine in his interpersonal exchanges.

HOMOPHOBIA AND HETEROSEXISM AS SELF-PROTECTIVE DEFENSIVE STRATEGIES

The relationship among homophobia, heterosexism, and men's violence toward women is not as obvious, and it is more indirect than with the defensive processes of control, power, and restrictive emotionality. Numerous definitions and complex conceptual connections need to be presented to explain how homophobia and hetereosexism predispose men to be violent against women.

Heterosexism is the belief system that heterosexuality is superior to and more natural than gay, lesbian, and bisexual orientations (Morin & Garfinkle, 1978). Homophobia is hostility or prejudice toward gay men and lesbians, persistent fears and dread of homosexuals (Herek, 1986; MacDonald, 1976), and negative attitudes and feelings toward homosexuality in others and toward "homosexual features" in oneself (Shidlo, 1994).

Homophobia and heterosexism are self-protective strategies that men use to develop and sustain their masculine and heterosexual gender-role identities. These defense strategies represent deep insecurities, fears, rigidities, restrictions, and distortions that cause men much stress and strain. We hypothesize that homophobia and heterosexism, as self-protective strategies, severely restrict men and serve the following seven functions:

1. falsely reinforce men's confidence in demonstrating the Masculine Mystique and Value System;

2. falsely protect men from threats to their masculine gender-role identity;

3. falsely protect men from their fears of femininity and fears of emasculation;

4. produce distorted gender-role schemas related to femininity, gay men, and the homosexual lifestyle;

5. keep men from labeling, expressing, and experiencing deep emotions;

6. falsely mediate men's fears of homosexuals and their insecurities about their own sexual orientations;

7. falsely compensate men when they feel powerless and out of control.

These seven defensive functions of homophobia and heterosexism have a direct relevance to predisposing men to be violent toward women.

How do men become predisposed to developing homophobia and heterosexism as a self-protective defensive strategy? They learn distorted gender-role schemas about men, women, and human sexuality that produce defensive homophobia and heterosexism. First, men erroneously learn to equate femininity with homosexuality and masculinity with heterosexuality. This distortion mixes up sexual and erotic orientations with the gender-role attributes of masculinity and femininity. Second, there is the distortion that "normal" sexuality is exclusively heterosexual. Only heterosexuality is considered as a healthy form of sexual expression by these men. All other forms of sexuality are considered deviant and abnormal. A final distortion is that gay men are obsessively interested in sex with many men. When this distortion is personalized for the individual man, it turns into the fear that gay men will "want to do it with me too." For many heterosexual men, the most emasculating experience possible is to be forced to have sex with another man.

Men's fear about femininity is directly related to their fears about homosexuality, their distorted gender-role schemas, and the etiology of homophobic defensiveness. Levinson et al.'s (1978) case studies revealed that men's aversion to femininity is in part related to their fears of homosexuality. Fears about one's own femininity become translated into fears about one's sexual identity, specifically whether one is a homosexual, bisexual, or heterosexual. Men's fear of appearing feminine, and therefore gay, is a heavy burden for a man striving to fulfill the Masculine Mystique. Not only is there a fear of homosexuals but also a fear of being labeled gay if you express stereotypical feminine values, attitudes, and behaviors. When femininity is confused with homosexuality, it breeds homophobia, heterosexism, and threatens men and their masculine gender-role identities.

Homosexuality is personally and politically threatening to men because it alters the sexual and power dynamics between men and women. Gay sexuality is not based on the typical male–female power dynamics. Gay men deviate from masculine stereotypes because they have sex with each other. Furthermore, gay men deviate from the sexist Masculine Mystique because they do not seek power and control over women through interpersonal and sexual conquests. Some heterosexual men feel losses of power and control when homosexuality is sanctioned. Men's overall power is based on heterosexual and patriarchal dominance of women. Homosexuality weakens the traditional heterosexual way of having power and control over women. Heterosexuality protects the patriarchy because it promotes sexist stereotypes and maintains unequal power bases between men and women. However, homosexuality threatens and changes these sexist power bases because masculine and feminine stereotypes are violated. Many men have built their masculine gender-role identities on this "dominance dynamic" and unconsciously feel losses of power and control when homosexuality is sanctioned. Homophobia and heterosexism are defensive strategies for dealing with perceived losses of power and control, particularly during conflicts with women.

How does this homophobic and heterosexist dynamic predispose men to be violent toward women? From our analysis, men's homophobic, heterosexist, and angry emotions can be expressed in two ways. First, these homophobic emotions can be directly expressed at gay men and lesbian women who are devalued, despised, feared, and sometimes harrassed or killed by heterosexual men. There is both a conscious and unconscious rage and fear of homosexuals who violate the masculine code and who simultaneously represent the feminine.

The second, more indirect and usually unconscious, outlet for men's angry homophobia is when they interact with women. For threatened men, the result of inner homophobic turmoil can be to validate their masculinity through hetero-sexual activity. Heterosexuality and relationships with women can help men dis-tance themselves from their femininity and homosexual anxiety. Men know that being a man is to be sexually and personally powerful with women; this means attracting females and being sexually active with them. Sex with women is one way for men to prove their masculinity and to validate their heterosexuality. Supposedly, heterosexual activity validates a man's gender-role identity, dimin-ishes his fears about homosexuality, and distances him from his femininity.

Yet heterosexuality does not usually distance the man from his femininity and fears about his masculine gender-role identity. Instead, it brings him closer to his own femininity through direct contact with women. When men experience women intimately, they can consciously or unconsciously encounter the feminine within the women and simultaneously within themselves. Many times these encounters include emotional exchanges where feelings and vulnerabilities are expressed. Men's fear of femininity and fears about being emasculated may be activated during emotional and conflictual encounters with women. During these conflicts, the man may face femininity that he fears in the women and himself.

Furthermore, men can experience their homophobia and heterosexism in their intimate relationships with women. If the man equates women's femininity with male homosexuality, the negative emotions expressed toward the woman can be intense. Negative and fearful femininity, which the man erroneously connects to homosexuals, can be mixed up in his heterosexual encounters. When a man con-fuses a woman's femininity with his rageful feelings about "feminine" homosex-uality, the relationship can be very turbulent. His heterosexual encounter with the feminine can activate homophobic anxiety, fears, and rage that can be expressed toward women. Encountering the feminine in this way, the man may experience serious threats to his masculine self-identity, fears of femininity, and fears about losing power and control. These reactions may be in the form of hypermasculine, aggressive behavior to mediate both fears of femininity and fears about homosexuality. Aggressiveness and potential violence therefore serve as a means to ensure that the man is not gay, feminine, or losing power to women or homosexuals.

Numerous defenses may operate when the man's homophobic feelings threat-en his masculine gender-role identity. When a man experiences femininity as a homosexual attribute, he can project these emotions by stating that homosexuals are immoral, sick, deviant, and abnormal. These feelings may be expressed as a fear of homosexuals or hatred toward them and their lifestyle. Women who chal-lenge male dominance and control may be categorized as lesbians or "dykes." The man also can repress his feelings about homosexuals by pushing them out of consciousness, only to have them surface when he least expects it (i.e., during conflicts with women). With reaction formation, the man may express positive feelings toward gays, when in fact he really harbors deep-seated fears and hostilities toward them. Homophobic reactions may produce regression to earlier immature states, where the man uses homophobic language or harrassing behaviors toward gays. Words such as *queer, fag,* or *dyke,* and *gay bashing* represent hatred and negative emotions toward gays, femininity, and, sometimes, women. Homophobic feelings may be transferred to other individuals who represent femininity, particularly women. Fear, anger, and rage at gays becomes mixed up with unexpressed emotions toward women. Logical, rational thinking (rationalization) may cover up homophobic feelings. The man logically justifies his homophobia by reasoning that all gays are feminine, immature, unfriendly, and pathological. Homophobic feelings may be separated from thought through isolation of all affect. There may be a complete denial of homophobic and heterosexist attitudes. Through identification and introjection, the man may identify with the perceived negative femininity of gay men and feel negative about his own feminine characteristics. Through compensation, the man feels his own femininity ("homosexuality") is a personal failure and shows exaggerated and hypermasculine qualities.

SUMMARY OF PREDISPOSING DYNAMICS OF MEN'S VIOLENCE AGAINST WOMEN

The concepts discussed earlier imply that men's gender-role identity can become threatened by gender-role conflict; based on distorted gender-role schemas and fears about femininity and emasculation that activate three self-protective defensive strategies. These defensive strategies (control and power, restrictive emotionality, and heterosexism and homophobia) function ineffectively and protect men only temporarily from their gender-role conflict and fears of emasculation. As shown in the middle of Figure 7.1, men nonetheless experience negative and intense emotions as a part of their gender-role socialization, including anger, fear, guilt, shame, self-hatred, hurt, loss, and sadness. These intense and predisposing emotions set the stage for the triggering dynamics of men's violence against women, as given in the following section.

THE TRIGGERING DYNAMICS OF MEN'S VIOLENCE AGAINST WOMEN

The lower part of Figure 7.1 described earlier in the chapter depicts the triggering dynamics of violence against women from a gender-role socialization perspective. The predisposing dynamics of men's violence described earlier all affect the triggering dynamics, as shown by the large arrow in Figure 7.1. Triggering dynamics are defined as the situational cues and interpersonal processes that prompt men to psychologically or physically assault women.

The seven boxes shown at the bottom of Figure 7.1 provide an overall paradigm to understand the triggering of men's violence against women (see Figure 7.1). Power conflicts with women may activate threats to the man's overall masculine gender-role identity. These power conflicts can lead to abuses of power and the use of psychological violence against women (O'Neil & Egan, 1993). Psychological violence is an outcome of abuses of power and it interacts with the situational and triggering events in the man's and couple's lives.

We propose four hypotheses about the actual triggering of men's violence. First, we hypothesize that men's power conflicts, abuses of power, and psychological violence are usually precursors to most physical assaults against women. Second, we hypothesize that physical violence against women is most likely to occur when men feel that their masculine gender-role identity is threatened. Third, we hypothesize that violence against women is most likely to occur when men's defenses and self-protective defense strategies completely or partially break down. Fourth, we hypothesize that there are specific, situational triggering events in the couple's life that can cause violence against women. We later discuss these hypotheses about men's violence toward women, as shown at the bottom of Figure 7.1.

POWER CONFLICTS, ABUSES OF POWER, AND PSYCHOLOGICAL VIOLENCE TRIGGERING MEN'S VIOLENCE AGAINST WOMEN

Most acts of violence against women relate to unresolved power dynamics and power conflicts in the couple's life (Koss et al., 1994). Power dynamics refer to the flow of power between individuals and how it affects attitudes, behaviors, and decisions. Power conflicts occur when there are disagreements over goals, decisions, or choices (O'Neil & Egan, 1993). Serious power conflicts may occur when the power of one partner is perceived as decreasing the power of the other. Power conflicts are inevitable in life and can be functional or dysfunctional. In functional power conflicts, power issues are discussed and aspects of compromise, negotiation, fairness, and conflict resolution are employed. In dysfunctional power conflicts, power dynamics hinder the effective interpersonal functioning, and abuses of power can occur.

Abuses of power are situations where power is used to devalue, restrict, or violate another person (O'Neil & Egan, 1993). In these situations, individuals' self-determination, freedom, dignity, and safety are compromised because of the abusers' need to validate themselves or have their own way. Furthermore, men's abuse of power may be expressed by using psychological violence against women. Men who are defensive or use self-protective defensive strategies especially may feel the threats to masculine gender-role identity as power conflicts go unresolved and psychological violence increases.

Psychological violence exists when power is used and abused by one person to dehumanize and treat another person as an object (O'Neil & Egan, 1993). Acts of psychological violence are abuses of power in which one person attempts to devalue, restrict, or violate another person to maintain control, power, advantage, or position. Power is used to willfully destroy or impair a person's competence, respect, self-esteem, happiness, and dignity as a human being. Psychological violence can be conscious or unconscious, intentional or unintentional, overt or covert, continuous or sporadic (O'Neil & Egan, 1993).

Table 7.1 lists the operational dimensions and definitions of psychological violence. The 18 dimensions of psychological violence can be categorized according to the 3 outcomes of power abuse: devaluations, restrictions, and violations (O'Neil & Egan, 1993). Dimensions 1 through 5 are primarily related to devaluation and negation of another person. Dimensions 6 through 9 reflect attempts at personal restriction and control of another person. Dimensions 10 through 18 reflect direct violation or victimization of a person.

It is not just the single act of psychological violence that triggers battering, but the cumulative effects of these violations over time. Many of the dimensions of psychological violence listed in Table 7.1 can cause gender-role conflicts and deep emotions. They also can activate men's defenses and self-protective defensive strategies when men interact with women. The man who uses psychological violence also may feel losses of power and control and severe threats to his masculine gender-role identity. When men use psychological violence, they initially may feel degrees of power and control, but ultimately feelings of powerlessness and shame may be experienced. Men's psychological violence against women is used to recover from perceived or real losses of power, fears of emasculation, and threats to their masculine gender-role identity. We hypothesize that in most dyadic situations, these psychologically violent dimensions are precursors to an actual triggering act of violence between partners.

SITUATIONAL TRIGGERING EVENTS OF MEN'S VIOLENCE AGAINST WOMEN

A number of situational triggering events in a couple's life can escalate power conflicts to the point where power abuses and psychological and physical violence can occur. Typical triggering situations that stimulate power conflicts and abuses of power in heterosexual relationships include the use of money, jealousy, flirting, affairs, in-laws, parenting, division of labor, sexual problems, friends, career transitions, religious and moral dilemmas, unemployment, relocation, the use of alcohol, and threatened or actual divorce and separation. The more intense the conflicts are, the greater the possibility is for psychological violence. Personal devaluations, restrictions, and violations are more likely to occur under these circumstances. When the man perceives he is losing power

TABLE 7.1. Operational Dimensions and Definitions of Psychological Violence

Dimensions	Definitions
1. Put-downs	To disparage, belittle, criticize, disapprove of a person; to make that person ineffective.
2. Name calling	The use of offensive names to win an arguement or to induce rejection or condemnation without objective consideration of the facts.
3. Humiliations	To reduce to a lower position in one's eyes or others' eyes; to mortify, or abuse; to be extremely destructive to one's self-respect or dignity.
4. Diminishing self-esteem	Intentionally lowering another person's self-satisfaction and self-respect.
5. Gossip	Rumor or report of an intimate nature; chatty talk that is destructive to a person.
6. Emotional and intellectual manipulations	To control or play upon by artful, unfair means so as to serve one's purpose.
7. Fear-inducing techniques	Using an unpleasant, often strong emotion caused by anticipation or awareness of danger to a person.
8. Threats and intimidation	An expression of intention to inflict evil, injury, or damage on another person.
9. Coercion	To restrain or dominate another person; nullifying an individual's will; to compel to an act or choice; to enforce or bring about by force or threat.
10. Rejections	To refuse to accept or consider a person.
11. Scapegoating	When a person bears the blame for others.
12. Lying	Marked by or given to falsehood; likely or calulated to mislead another person.
13. Dishonesty	Lack of honesty or integrity; disposition to defraud or deceive; characterized by lack of truth, honesty, or trustworthiness with a person.
14. Person neglect	To give little attention or respect; to disregard; to leave undone or unattended through carelessness.
15. Abandonment	Desert, forsake, to give up completely; disinterest in the fate of another person.
16. Seductive behaviors	Using sexual actions that have alluring or tempting qualities.
17. Harrassment	To worry and impede another person by repeated raids; to exhaust or fatigue; to annoy persistently another person (worry).
18. Sexual harrassment	Unwanted sexual overtures or actions that victimize a person.

Source: Reprinted from Abuses of Power Against Women: Sexism, Gender Role Conflict, and Psychological Violence, by J. M. O'Neil, & J. Egan. In E. Cook (Ed.), *Women, Relationships and Power: Implication for Counseling* (p. 77). © ACA. Reprinted with permission. No further reproduction authorized without written permission of the American Counseling Association.

and control in the relationship, feelings of emasculation, deep, negative emotions, and threats to masculine gender-role identity can become quite intolerable. Under these conditions, the possibility for distorted gender-role schemas is high. Furthermore, the defenses and self-protective defense strategies that once worked become less effective, leaving the man feeling out of control with his raw emotions of fear, anger, self-hatred, and rage toward women, femininity, and usually himself.

BREAKDOWN OF DEFENSES AND SELF-PROTECTIVE DEFENSIVE STRATEGIES TRIGGERING MEN'S VIOLENCE AGAINST WOMEN

Some men reach a psychic breaking point. The defenses and self-protective defensive strategies that once mediated gender-role conflict and potential emasculation partially or fully break down. The threats to the man's gender-role identity are directly and intensely felt. When a man's use of psychological violence appears to be ineffective in maintaining power and control over his partner, the use or threat of physical violence is more likely. He perceives that there is no other option but to use force to regain the power, stop the threats, and reestablish his masculine gender-role identity. The breakdown of the defenses and three self-protective defensive strategies of power and control, restrictive emotionality, homophobia and heterosexism are described next.

The breakdown of the man's defenses and the power and control self-protective defensive strategies can result in violence against women. The man feels powerless and is desperate to regain his power and his masculine self-image. He feels emasculated and knows no other effective method to even the score than the use of aggressive force. Psychological violence becomes ineffective in manipulating and controlling his partner. His partner has the upper hand in the power conflicts, or he perceives it that way. Personally, the man recognizes that she is winning and that he is losing. When this becomes obvious to others outside the relationship, there is even more pressure on the man to use physical threat and assault to regain his masculine dominance.

The defense strategies related to power and control become less effective in keeping the man safe. His lack of power and control cannot be denied. He can no longer rationalize his power loss and his being out of control. Consciously or unconsciously, he knows that he has failed to meet the values of the Masculine Mystique. He fears appearing feminine. Regressive methods of restoring his old masculine gender-role identity only make him feel weaker and more powerless. Projecting and blaming his power and control loss on his partner do not provide real safety from feeling emasculated. Regressing to childhood ways of resolving conflict, he knows force and threat to be one way to disrupt the process. Projection of his rage reinforces that his partner is the one who needs to be disciplined and punished. The only perceived option for regaining power and control to reinstate a positive masculine gender-role identity is physical assault and battering.

When the defenses and the self-protective defensive strategies related to restrictive emotionality break down, the man can no longer contain his anger, fear, shame, and rage. Vulnerability, pain, expression of emotions, and shame are still prohibited because of the values of the Masculine Mystique. Yet, repressed, negative, and raw emotions, such as anger and rage, can become explosive and direct. The anger, fear, and rage can no longer be denied, displaced, or rationalized. Emotional regression may occur by venting pent-up hostile feelings in physically assaultive ways. Women's emotionality may be perceived as emasculating or threatening and may trigger the violence. For the emasculated man, the solution, or the unconscious dynamic, may be reduced to this thought and action: I must silence her and stop the flow of emotions directed at me in any way I can.

The breakdown of defenses and strategies related to homophobia and heterosexism is usually unconscious to the man, but can trigger men's violence toward women. When these defenses collapse, the man's gender-role identity is so threatened he can no longer hold in his rageful feelings toward homosexual (feminine) men and women. Both represent a threatening femininity that can activate deep, rageful fears and anger. Under these threatening circumstances, the man may feel that homosexual men and women are gaining too much power and interpersonal control. This leaves the man powerless, but determined to regain control, even by using threat and force. Rageful homophobic and heterosexist feelings can no longer be repressed. Rationalization and denial about his lost power and control can no longer work to reassure him of his manhood. His masculinity and heterosexuality have been invalidated. He may imagine or insinuate that his partner is a lesbian, because she rejects and invalidates his masculinity. The man's homophobic rage turns to violence to validate his heterosexuality. The intense threats and emasculation by gay men and feminine women have reduced him to a single and irrational question: "Am I still heterosexual, and do I appear heterosexual to others if I have feelings and cannot control my women?" Getting in touch with his inner feelings makes him feel that his heterosexuality is in doubt, meaning that he is, or may be seen as, gay. This is an emasculating possibility. These threats to the man's heterosexuality by gays and women together result in homophobic rage that must be discharged. Without the defenses and self-protective defensive strategies operating, violence is the only way to regain one's masculine and heterosexual identity.

IMPLICATIONS OF THE CONCEPTUAL MODEL FOR UNDERSTANDING MEN'S VIOLENCE AGAINST WOMEN

The model in Figure 7.1 should stimulate further discussion on the role of men's gender-role socialization in violent acts against women. Multiple sources of variance need to be considered to explain men's violence against women. This chapter specifies additional concepts that explain how socialized gender roles can predispose and trigger men's violence against women. We believe that some portion of the variance, explaining violence against women, emanates from men's gender-role conflict and sexist gender-role socialization. What that portion of the variance is, is an empirical question for researchers to vigorously pursue. Enough empirical research exists that indicates that gender-role conflict predicts negative views of women to recommend additional research on men's battering from a gender-role socialization perspective. The model also may provide useful concepts to understand other male problems including rape, child abuse, suicide, crime, gang violence, and men's violence against men.

Numerous limitations to the model presented need to be addressed. Our model shows how the larger macrosocietal system (patriarchy, institutional sexism, and stereotypes) contributes to men's abusive behavior with women. Future analyses should discuss critically how the larger patriarchal and sexist system continually interacts with a man's predisposition to gender-role conflict and violence. Figure 7.1 shows this connection through a series of arrows. The relationship between the larger macrosocietal system and men's specific behaviors is not fully addressed in each section of the chapter. Furthermore, the model does not address how men's socialization interacts with women's socialization and defense mechanisms to predispose and trigger men's violence. Therefore, Nutt's analysis of women's gender-role conflict (Chapter 9, this volume) needs to be integrated with our model.

Additionally, our model does not address the important issues of how age, class, race, ethnicity, nationality, and sexual orientation may differentially affect the predisposition to the use of violence. Specifically, the model needs to be expanded to explain gay and lesbian battering dynamics. Future revisions of the model need to consider these diversity variables to explain violence across diverse groups (see Sanchez-Hucles & Dutton, Chapter 11, this volume). The model also needs to be extended to evolutionary explanations of masculinity that are currently emerging (see Archer, 1994a, 1994b; Daley & Wilson, 1994; Silverstein, Chapter 6, this volume). Furthermore, because of the lack of attention given to this topic, some of our premises lack empirical evidence and are speculative in nature. Finally, the model does not indict all men as violent or intend to pathologize men in any way. The predisposing and triggering dynamics presented in Figure 7.1 were conceptualized to better understand how men's sexist gender-role socialization may contribute to men's potential for violence.

The hypothesis that the etiology of men's violence is learned, defensive, and potentially unconscious raises controversial questions, such as, "How responsible are men for their learned or unconscious violence?" We take the position that men are totally responsible for both conscious and unconscious motivations to victimize women. A promising area of clinical intervention and research is how to help men become aware of their gender-role socialization and personality defenses that make them dysfunctional and potentially violent.

One of the future challenges for practitioners and researchers is how to translate Figure 7.1 into preventative and remedial programs for men. We believe that a gender role conflict and gender role socialization curriculum for men is essential to explain the complexity of factors that can potentially contribute to violence against women. Besides completing research on the model, effective ways need to be created to translate the chapter concepts to pragmatic and relevant programs that help men assess their own risk factors for victimizing women. Lectures, printed information, media, music, self assessment exercises, group experiences, autobiographies, and readings could be used to make the ideas in this chapter directly useful to men.

Finally, trying to explain what causes men to victimize women from a gender-role socialization perspective, should not be construed as trying to "explain away," "subtly excuse," or condone men's violence against women. We are attempting to do the opposite: to shed some new light on how men's gender-role conflict and socialization contribute to the victimization of women. Our analysis does not absolve men from their responsibility for their violent behavior. The goal of this chapter was to focus on men's gender-role conflict and socialization as one way to help men become responsible for their violence and to end it. Furthermore, ending men's violence requires new and positive paradigms of masculinity that do not emphasize masculine power, control, domination, and heterosexuality. This new paradigm of masculinity is just beginning to emerge in psychology and other disciplines, and holds promise for decreasing the great amount of violence that numbs us all.

NOTES

The authors want to thank many friends and colleagues who provided valuable feedback and critique on earlier versions of this chapter. Dr. James Mahalik of Boston College provided valuable assistance with the chapter, particularly his suggestions regarding how to label self-protective defense stategies. The following people also provided helpful feedback: Dr. Ann Fischer, Department of Psychology, University of Akron; Dr. Steve Anderson; Dr. Sandra Rigazio-DiGilio; Mary Alice Neubeck, School of Family Studies, University of Connecticut; Julie Goldberg, CAPS Program, University of Maryland; Dr. Michele Harway, Phillips Graduate Institute; and Marina Chebotayev O'Neil, University of Connecticut. Students in the class HDFR 259, Men and Masculinity: Psychosocial Perspectives, during the Fall of 1996 at the University of Connecticut, provided excellent feedback on the homophobia and heterosexism section of the chapter.

Women's Gender-Role Socialization, Gender-Role Conflict, and Abuse

A Review of Predisposing Factors

ROBERTA L. NUTT

This chapter considers women's gender-role socialization and the ensuing gender-role conflict as a major predisposing factor for women's domestic violence victimization. Most cultures, including ours, teach women that they are of lesser value than men. Women are not taught self-respect, personal confidence, and assertiveness skills, which are all necessary preventive traits against domestic violence. It is not surprising, therefore, that their gender-role socialization does not protect women from domestic violence; in fact, it may set them up to be recipients of abuse.

This chapter reviews women's gender-role socialization through a chronology of life stages and demonstrates gender-role conflict through common patterns of preferences for things male and the devaluation of things female. The life stages include infancy, childhood, adolescence, early adulthood, and middle and later adulthood, through which will be traced gender-role socialization expectations such as discouraged achievement, restricted identity development, depression and low self-esteem, overemphasis on appearance and beauty, dependency and submissiveness, caretaking and nurturing of others, emphasis on and overvaluation of relationships, feelings of inferiority, learned helplessness, pressure toward marriage and motherhood, and exaggerated femininity. These patterns provide examples of *gender-role devaluation, gender-role restriction,* and *gender-role violation,* which make it difficult for many women to develop heterosexual relationships based on equal power and to assert appropriate boundaries against domestic violence. The chapter concludes with recommendations for the future, including needed changes in institutional structure and policy and therapeutic implications.

Women's gender-role socialization leads to a variety of conflicting (O'Neil & Egan, 1992a) or paradoxical (Halas & Matteson, 1978) messages regarding gender appropriate attitudes and behavior. The concept of gender-role conflict is particularly useful in explaining women's vulnerability to domestic violence. "Gender-role conflict occurs when rigid, sexist, or restrictive gender roles, learned during socialization, result in the personal restriction, devaluation, or violation of others or self. The ultimate outcome of this conflict is the restriction of the person's human potential or of someone else's potential" (O'Neil & Egan, 1992a, p. 61). According to O'Neil (1992), women's gender-role conflict is characterized by "emotionality, noncompetitiveness, guilt, powerlessness, loss of control, lack of confidence, fear of failure, role conflict, fear of success, lack of assertiveness, sexualized behavior, dependency, homophobia, and health care problems" (p. 90). Women's restrictive gender-role socialization and the resulting gender-role conflict that devalues, restricts, and violates women, both lead them into violent relationships and prevent them from leaving.

Table 8.1 illustrates O'Neil and Egan's (1992a) notion of gender-role conflict with examples, which includes three categories of abuse of power: *gender-role devaluation, gender-role restriction,* and *gender-role violation.* These are further divided into two directional types, defined by whether the woman is being acted upon by others (or the culture) or by self (internalized oppression). The specific (and often overlapping) gender-role conflicts listed in the table will be reviewed as patterns cutting across all life stages. "*Gender-role devaluations* are experienced when women either deviate from or conform to feminine gender-role norms. This devaluation can occur because women actually exhibit power in stereotypically masculine ways or because they express powerlessness that is traditionally associated with the feminine stereotype" (O'Neil & Egan, 1992a, p. 61). Examples of gender-role devaluations from Table 8.1 are criticalness of appearance, discrimination in the classroom, and math and science anxiety. "*Gender-role restrictions* occur when women confine themselves or are confined by others to traditional gender-role norms related to power. This confinement causes violation of personal freedom and human rights . . . . Restrictions limit options, deny needs, and often represent manipulative control and abusive uses of power" (O'Neil & Egan, 1992a, pp. 61, 64). Some examples of gender-role

TABLE 8.1. Gender-Role Conflict Examples for Women

	Devaluation	Restriction	Violation

By self	Feelings of inferiority
	Low self-esteem
	Critical of appearance
	Lack confidence in
	  academic ability
	Not deserving of respect
	Math and science anxiety
		Restricted identity
		Emphasize appearance
		  and relationships over
		  achievement
		Lower risk taking
		Lower career aspirations
		  and expectations
		Learned helplessness
		Lack of autonomy
		Dependence
		Lack of assertiveness
		Waiting for men
		Caretaking and nurturing in
		  families
			Victim of violence
			Eating disorders
			Depression
			Misogyny
			Passivity
			Submissiveness and
			  subordination
			Overvaluation of
			  love relationships
			Inability to set boundaries
			Sacrificing personal needs
			  for others

By others	Discrimination in
	  classroom
	Society's preference
	  for boys
	Low achievement
	  expectations
	Sexist advertising
	Not listening to women's
	  opinions
	Double standard of aging
	Inattention to women's
	  health issues
		Protectiveness by adults
		  during play
		Restriction of identity
		  development
		Pressure to marry
		Lower career expectations
		Motherhood mandate
		Appropriate toys, books,
		  and so on
		Emphasis on appearance
		  and popularity
			Battering
			Psychological
			  violence
			Physical violence
			Backlash
			Elder abuse
			Misogyny
			Lower income

restrictions from Table 8.1 include restricted identity development, lower career aspirations and expectations, dependence, and learned helplessness. *"Gender-role violations* occur when women harm themselves, are harmed by others, or harm others because of destructive power dynamics. To be violated is to be abused, hurt, and victimized because of power and gender-role conflict" (O'Neil & Egan, 1992a, p. 64). This includes depression, overvaluation of love relationships, and physical and psychological violence. As summarized by O'Neil and Egan, "Men can devalue, restrict, and violate women to maintain their sexist advantage. Women may also react to their own powerlessness by asserting their power in abusive ways or by devaluing, restricting, or violating themselves. . . . Psychological as well as physical violence can be the consequence" (p. 52). Gender-role conflict and violence are both interrelated examples of abuses of power. "Gender roles mediate power relations" as "men and women learn different perspectives on power that affect their interpersonal dynamics" (p. 55).

The power differentials between men and women and the gender-role conflicts that ensue are closely related to five hypotheses that O'Neil and Harway
describe in Chapter 2 of this volume. Specifically, Hypothesis 2 states that
"organizational, institutional, and patriarchal structures in society maintain
unequal power relationships between men and women that tacitly or directly
support domestic oppression and violence against women." Gender-role messages received in every life stage reinforce the unequal power between men and
women through a variety of organized structures. Thus, gender-role messages
described in this chapter and summarized in Table 8.1 support Hypothesis 2.
Hypothesis 6 states that "men's misogynistic attitudes toward women learned
during gender-role socialization contribute to men's violence toward women."
This chapter presents evidence that women are also socialized to misogyny,
which contributes to men's violence toward women. Different social roles, patterns of communication, fears, and lack of understanding also may contribute to
violence in relationships. These variables all relate to Hypothesis 9, which concludes that "differentially socialized patterns of communication and separate
gender-role cultures contribute to the potential for violence." The premise is also
related to the propositions in Hypotheses 11 and 12, respectively, that "women's
fear of men and men's fear of women contribute to the potential for psychological and physical violence" and "both sexes' lack of understanding of the other's
gender-role socialization experiences contributes to the potential for violence in
the relationship." Recent authors have postulated that men and women seem to
lack understanding of the other sex and appear to be living "in two separate cultures because of the gender messages they receive throughout a lifetime that
reinforce and reward different value systems, different personality characteristics, different communication styles, different problem-solving techniques, dif-
ferent perspectives on sexuality, assign different roles, and hold different expectations for relationships. Clearly, the roots for conflict between the genders are
extant in this gender-socialization process" (Philpot, Brooks, Lusterman, & Nutt,
1997, p. 65).

Although a variety of changes have occurred in the last decade or two regarding expectations and roles of women and men in American culture, most writers
and researchers still report different, and sometimes opposite, gender-role developmental patterns for girls and boys that lead to significant socialized differences
in adult women and men. Parents still tend to dress girl babies in pink and boy
babies in blue and accept or expect different behaviors based upon gender
throughout their growing years. These differences have been well documented
and have significant implications for a variety of conflicts between men and
women, including men's violation of women through violence, women's predisposition toward or tolerance of that violence, and the difficulty many women
have in leaving abusive relationships.

INFANCY

As mentioned earlier, parents still tend to dress girl and boy babies differently, in both color and style (Matlin, 1996). A baby girl's clothing tends toward dresses, ruffles, bows, flowers, frills, and the color pink and other pastels. These clothes and colors suggest delicacy and fragility and *restrict* the behavior of baby girls. Many parents even tie a bow around a baby girl's head to make it clear that she is a girl. The bow is tied around the head because the baby does not have enough hair to attach it any other way. By contrast, clothing for boys is either blue or bright primary colors and often sports oriented. These clothes lend themselves more to action and rough-and-tumble activity. Gender differences are also reflected in the choice of decoration in children's bedrooms (Matlin, 1996). Girls' rooms are more likely to be decorated with flowers, ruffles, and lace, whereas boys' rooms are typically blue and have animal themes (Pomerleau, Bolduc, Malcuit, & Cossette, 1990). Decor and clothing choices emphasize that girls are more fragile and need protection, which demonstrates a *gender-role restriction* and, possibly, a *gender-role devaluation*. The message about fragility communicates to girls that they cannot protect themselves and therefore are marks for male aggression.

Adults play with girl and boy babies in different ways (Huston, 1983). Boy babies are often handled more roughly and played with more aggressively. Boy babies are typically seen as stronger, better coordinated, firmer, hardier, and more alert, whereas girls are described as weak, delicate, little, and beautiful (Rubin, Provenzano, & Luria, 1974). Girl babies are usually treated more gently, even though biological evidence demonstrates that girl babies are actually tougher and hardier (Lerner, 1968). The most important variable related to how adults treat children is the child's gender (Delk, Madden, Livingston, & Ryan, 1986; Stern & Karraker, 1989). This differential treatment again conveys to girls that they seem to be fragile, delicate, and breakable. These messages in turn *restrict* girls' feelings of personal power. Internalization of such messages and the subsequent *gender-role conflict* later leads to women's own *devaluation* of self, making them predisposed to being easier targets for male aggression and more resigned victims.

Finally, there is evidence that in this culture and many others, boy babies are preferred over girl babies, especially for a firstborn child (Arnold & Kuo, 1984; Hamilton, 1991). This preference for males has an often subtle but vast effect on all girls, damaging their feelings of worth. It leads them to *devalue* themselves and other women and girls, and to accept that domination by and violence from men is just and proper. It is no surprise then, that many more girls express a desire to be male than boys express a wish to be female (Brown, 1958; Unger & Crawford, 1992).

CHILDHOOD

In childhood, the differential treatment of girls and boys increases. Research by Gilligan (1982) and Chodorow (1978) indicated that girls are kept closer to their mothers and are more likely to be *restricted* from activities and protected by their parents, whereas boys are expected to separate from their mothers and learn independence. The close connection between girls and their mothers leads to the development of good relationship skills and interests, but the lack of experience in autonomous functioning and independence seeking and self-esteem building *restricts* the development of girls and women in public arenas. In reverse fashion, boys easily develop skills related to autonomy and independence (Lewis, 1972), but do not easily develop skills for maintaining good interpersonal connections in work, social life, and family. When women lack sufficient autonomy, independence, and self-esteem, they will have more difficulty setting boundaries against inappropriate behavior (e.g., violence from men). These *gender-role restrictions* also make leaving an abusive situation difficult.

Children's books, toys, and messages from the media communicate society's expectations of their appropriate gender role (Bordelon, 1985; Clark, Lennon & Morris, 1993; Kortenhaus & Demarest, 1993; O'Brien & Huston, 1985a, 1985b; Robinson & Morris, 1986; Roopnarine, 1986; Signorielli & Lears, 1992). Girls' toys are more often related to home, nurturing, or appearance (cooking utensils, kitchen appliances, doll babies, makeup, etc.), whereas boys' toys tend toward vehicles, sports, weapons, science, or building (cars, balls, guns, chemistry sets, Legos, etc.). These toys are often seen as a means of preparing children for their future roles as adults. Moreover, traditional fairy tales and modern stories for girls usually portray women as passive victims or decorative figures (Dworkin, 1974). In these stories, events happen to women and they are often rescued by male figures (Purcell & Stewart, 1990). These stories also communicate that beautiful women increase the value of the male figure to whom they are attached. Consequently, girls are taught to look good and to rely on men to take care of them. Even television commercials generally depict women in roles of service to others and not in charge of their own lives (Lovdal, 1989). These messages that women and girls are primarily valued for their appearance and not their competence (an instance of *gender-role devaluation*) begin in childhood and are lifelong (Freedman, 1986; Wolf, 1991). These messages, women's eventual feelings of lack of competence to take care of themselves, and the belief that they need the care and protection of a man, *restrict* women's options when they are confronted by a violent relationship. This gender-role socialization may help explain the difficulty some women have in leaving violent relationships.

In school and at home, girls are encouraged to learn homemaking and caretaking skills. In contrast, boys are encouraged to be active, play sports, be aggressive, and to solve problems (Lytton & Romney, 1991). These differences translate into biased expectations regarding the type of jobs children consider to be appropriate by gender (Archer, 1984; Betz, 1993), with boys being steered into careers that provide greater power and autonomy.

Boys are more often called upon in the classroom and are given more encouragement to speak up in public. Boys are more often called by name, and their answers are given more careful attention and time (AAUW Educational Foundation, 1992; Sadker & Sadker, 1994). The Association of American Colleges (Hall & Sandler, 1982) described this *gender-role restriction* from others as a chilly classroom climate for women, and it extends from elementary school through college and graduate school. In addition, the process by which males and females learn and perform in the classroon differs, and the male style is favored (Belenky, Clinchy, Goldberger, & Tarule, 1986). This leaves girls feeling less valued in the classroom (an example of *gender-role devaluation*) and, as a consequence, they participate less. This process, in turn, takes a toll on feelings of self-worth. During the elementary years, the two sexes also resist involvement in the activities of the other sex (Feiring & Lewis, 1987; La Freniere, Strayer, & Gauthier, 1984), marking the beginning of feelings of dividedness and lack of understanding between the genders. As reported earlier, more girls express feelings of wishing they were boys, than the reverse. Consider the negative connotation of "sissy" versus "tomboy" (Martin, 1990; Unger & Crawford, 1992). Many consider being a tomboy a normal part of female development (Plumb & Cowan, 1984), and tomboys are more likely to be viewed as creative (Lott, 1978) and leaders (Hemmer & Kleiber, 1981), whereas, sissies are viewed as deviant. Our culture's preference for masculine over feminine activities and characteristics and the greater latitude and flexibility in gendered behavior and attire that women and girls are allowed is a result of the higher status of masculine characteristics and behavior (Feinman, 1981; Urberg, 1982). Thus, it is more readily understandable that a girl or woman would prefer a more highly valued masculine trait or activity (a tomboy activity), whereas a boy or man who engages in feminine behavior or activities (a sissy) is behaving not only inappropriately, but is also choosing lower-status behavior and activities (Unger & Crawford, 1992). The higher value of masculine traits later leads to the higher status of men over women in heterosexual relationships and the willingness of the woman to submit to that greater power in her *devalued* status. A direct consequence for our understanding of violence is that the man may have internalized permission to abuse his power through violence, and because the woman feels powerless, it predisposes her toward difficulty in resisting or escaping that violence.

ADOLESCENCE

Gender differences are even further accentuated at adolescence. Pipher (1994) considered adolescence the most critical period of *gender-role conflict* and change. She stated, "Something dramatic happens to girls in early adolescence.

Just as planes and ships disappear mysteriously into the Bermuda Triangle, so do the selves of girls go down in droves" (p. 19). Girls, who have performed well in elementary school, at adolescence often pull back from academic achievement. Those who continue to perform well academically are often criticized and made to feel different, inappropriate, and unfeminine, causing *gender-role devaluation* (Unger & Crawford, 1992). High academic performance is considered a masculine trait. At adolescence, girls often demonstrate a decreased interest in science and mathematics (Bush & Simmons, 1987), and they lose confidence in their academic abilities (Freiberg, 1991; Walker, Reis, & Leonard, 1992), unrelated to their capability. High school guidance counselors and others still tend to direct adolescents toward gender-appropriate majors and career choices (Alexander & Cook, 1982; Harway & Astin, 1977). Boys are given a wider diversity of choices, whereas girls are often *restricted* and directed toward traditionally "feminine" careers such as nursing, teaching, library work, child-care work, and secretarial work. These careers are lower paying, and this creates a dual trap for women: their lower pay contributes to a lowered self-esteem and a belief that they are not worthy of being treated well (either in the workforce or at home—a kind of *gender-role devaluation*). The low pay also traps the woman into staying in abusive heterosexual relationships because the man has greater earning potential. Guidance counselors tend to view girls (and boys) with nontraditional interests and career plans as disturbed and less emotionally and mentally healthy than their peers (Abramowitz et al., 1975; Betz & Fitzgerald, 1987). The social costs of academic achievement (loss of popularity), the movement toward objective analytical ways of learning (considered to be masculine) rather than toward intuitive and experiential learning (considered to be more feminine) in the classroom, and the shift in focus toward dating, appearance, domestic skills, and eventual family life also have been blamed for adolescent girls' change in performance (Unger & Crawford, 1992).

As dating interests increase, girls tend to pay more attention to appearance and social popularity. Large amounts of money are spent on makeup, clothing, and fashion magazines. Although it is biologically appropriate for teenage girls to increase their fatty tissue to maintain normal reproductive functioning, an increase in weight at adolescence becomes problematic for girls whose culture values a lean "masculine" body and *devalues* a more feminine round body (Martz, Handley, & Eisler, 1995; McKinley & Hyde, 1996; Mintz & Betz, 1988). This overemphasis on appearance and the stringent dieting that many adolescent girls submit themselves to have taken a serious toll on female health and have led to increasingly prevalent eating disorders in females of all ages, but especially adolescents (Frederick & Grow, 1996). Kaschak (1992) described this *violation* of the female body as a combat zone in that "women become the enemies of their bodies in a struggle to mold them as society wishes, to mediate and embody conflicts between the physical and the demands of society" (p. 193). She elaborated that "conflicts surrounding women's desires and appetites, about taking up space, and about adult sexuality are expressed elegantly and painfully in eating disorders in women" (Kaschak, 1992, p. 195). Fredrickson and Roberts (1997) described the consequences of a culture that objectifies the female body as creating shame, anxiety, and serious mental health problems. Women's guilt about not being physically perfect and taking up more than their share of space (a share that is defined as small and is thereby an example of *self-devaluation*) makes them particularly predisposed toward and vulnerable to violence.

YOUNG ADULTHOOD

In young adulthood, the emphasis on relationships in women's lives and external achievement in men's lives continues to grow. In describing the developmental stage of "Identity versus Role Confusion," Erikson (1964, 1968) indicated that a young woman cannot fully form an identity until she knows the man she will marry. Hence, he assumes that she cannot independently define her own identity and that she must satisfy her relational needs before all other needs. He often equates womanhood with motherhood. Although Erikson has responded to feminist criticisms of the *restrictions* on women in his theoretical work, and newer theories and accounts of female development promote the strengths and necessity of connection (Jordan, Kaplan, Miller, Stiver, & Surrey, 1991) and female power (Cantor, Bernay, & Stoess, 1992; Miller, 1991), many professionals and the public still follow his original writings. The assumption that a woman cannot develop a separate identity and is defined by the men in her life (father, husband, male children—leading to a *restriction* of her self-concept, affect, and needs) makes it difficult for her to express her wants and needs in a relationship and to set boundaries against abuse. In saying no to abuse, a woman risks not only loss of relationship, but also loss of identity.

Kolbenschlag (1981), in her aptly titled book, *Kiss Sleeping Beauty Goodbye*, described young women as continually waiting: waiting for the completion of something missing and waiting for some young man to bring fulfillment to their lives. During this waiting time, young women are *restricted* from living fully and from developing their own lives, when life is actually passing them by. She concluded that, "The 'tomboy' phase, which often precedes puberty, is, for many young girls, the last eruption of individuated personality before the fall into 'beauty' and the inevitable 'sleep' of the female psyche (p. 8). The second persona in the . . . girl's repertoire is that of the desire to live for another. This role will school her in self-forgetfulness, service and sacrifice, in nurturing rather than initiating behaviors. . . . She will give up everything when the expected one comes, even the right of creating her own self" (p. 10). At the same time, Miller (1986) noted "in our culture serving others is for losers, it is low level stuff. Yet serving others is a basic principle around which women's lives are organized; it is far from such for men" (p. 61). Kolbenschlag (1981) concluded that "giving advice to women [about who they should be] has been one of the most constant industries in Western civilization" (p. 11). Telling women who they should be *devalues* women as inferior creatures who need help and who must accept the role that God and Nature (and often men) have intended. Some women become passive and submissive, depend on others for protection and identity, and suffer from many fears, such as that of being alone, of new events, and of the environment in which they live. These women are predisposed to be "perfect" victims for domestic violence because they may feel that they do not have the resources to make it on their own or to demand better treatment. Fears of the outside world from which they need protection may also keep them from leaving. The *self-devaluation* is sufficiently serious that some women are so convinced that they are inferior and unworthy that they believe they deserve the violence.

In *The Cinderella Complex*, Dowling (1982) suggested that women are kept in a somewhat childlike state of dependence. They do not feel free to make their own choices and feel that they need direction from another, usually a male. They are not confident in their own abilities to care for and support themselves. Sometimes this dependence is not obvious in the individual woman's behavior. However, it exists at the emotional level and affects what the young woman will allow herself to become and how she will relate to others. It may create internal barriers to or *restrictions* on her educational and occupational success and achievement, thereby limiting the development of healthy feelings of autonomy and self-confidence. It may cause her to invest in heterosexual relationships that are not in her best interest. Although many couples are fairly well matched on general characteristics and values, when there is a difference, the man is expected to be older, better educated, and make more money (Hare-Mustin, 1978; Peplau & Gordon, 1985). This tendency has been termed *marry up* for women and *marry down* for men (Unger & Crawford, 1992), with obvious implications for power differentials in the marital relationship. Research in the 1980s scared young women by telling them that if they were single at 30, they were more likely to be killed by a terrorist than to get married (Bennett, 1986). These messages create a paradox by communicating that women are not okay unless they get married, but if they do get married, they must give up their self, their value, and their autonomy (a type of *gender-role devaluation*).

Even though American women are waiting later in their lives to marry, the expected lifestyle for adults, especially women, is heterosexual marriage, traditional gender roles, and the rearing of children (Chaffin & Winston, 1991). In 1960, the median age for first marriage was 20.3 years; in 1970, it was 20.8 years; by 1983, it was 22.8 years; and in 1985, it was 23.3 years (Norton & Moorman, 1987). Extended families begin to ask very pointed and intrusive questions of a young woman who has reached the age of 28 or 30 and has not married. Others begin to assume that no man wants her and, therefore, that there is something wrong with her (she is *devalued*).

A woman who does not have children is also looked at askance. "The motherhood mystique asserts that being a mother is the ultimate fulfillment for a woman. (In contrast, men are viewed as being fulfilled not merely by becoming fathers but by having varied, unique lives full of experiences and achievements.)" (Unger & Crawford, 1992, p. 431). Russo (1979) termed this societal pressure the *motherhood mandate*. Hoffnung (1984) pointed out that although motherhood is widely praised, it is actually *devalued* with low prestige and status.

During young adulthood, young women get little encouragement for developing independence, problem solving, abstract thinking, risk taking, and career maturity (a *gender-role devaluation*). In fact, much vocational research demonstrates that the career aspirations of young women are typically significantly lower than their abilities (Betz & Fitzgerald, 1987; Fitzgerald & Crites, 1980). These lowered aspirations serve as *restrictions* that disempower young women in the classroom, in interpersonal relationships, in the work force, and in the larger culture. Even though helpful new resources in women's careers have been developed (Betz & Fitzgerald, 1987; Walsh & Osipow, 1994), women are often steered into teaching or homemaking careers and kept from acquiring important skills, such as working with computers (Arch & Cummins, 1989). This situation makes it more difficult for a woman to develop the self-esteem necessary for truly healthy living and sets her up or predisposes her to become involved in a violent relationship that she may feel she cannot leave. Through lowered self-esteem and other kinds of *gender-role devaluations,* she may feel that she does not deserve more in a relationship and does not deserve to leave. Other factors that may keep her in an abusive relationship may include her husband's higher prestige and her feelings that she does not have the skills to survive on her own.

MIDDLE AND LATER ADULTHOOD

In middle and later adulthood, the earlier established patterns continue. Women are primarily valued for their appearance and their caretaking abilities (a form of *gender-role devaluation* and *gender-role restriction*). In her book, *The Beauty Myth*, Wolf (1991) described in great detail how images of beauty are detrimental to women. Women sacrifice much in terms of money, time, and esteem in the pursuit of beauty (which is a *restriction of self*). "Since the Industrial Revolution, middle-class Western women have been controlled by ideals and stereotypes as much as by material constraints" (p. 15). The pursuit of beauty is one of the strongest ideals and stereotypes. Women must want to embody the quality of beauty, "and men must want to possess women who embody it. . . . Strong men battle for beautiful women" (p. 12). In addition to advantages in relationships with men, beauty has become a currency in the work place. Three myths about beauty have arisen that hide how appearance is used to discriminate against women. These myths are (1) "'Beauty' . . . [is] a legitimate and necessary qualification for a woman's rise in power. (2) . . . 'Beauty' can be earned by any woman through hard work and enterprise. . . . (3) The working woman was told she had to think about 'beauty' in a way that undermined, step for step, the way she had begun to think as a result of the successes of the women's movement. . . . For every feminist action there is an equal and opposite beauty myth reaction. . . . The closer women come to power, the more physical self-consciousness and sacrifice are asked of them. . . . You are now too rich. Therefore, you cannot be too thin" (p. 28).

Complicating this search for beauty is the evidence that the current standard for beauty is one that no woman can achieve. In the United States and western Europe, the standard of beauty with its criterion of extreme thinness has become for most women an impossible goal (Kilbourne, 1994). As stated earlier, Heyn (1989) has suggested that the current ideal female figure is that of an adolescent male. This impossible goal *devalues* women and results in distorted body image, chronic personal dissatisfaction, depression, eating disorders (a *gender-role restriction*), excessive cosmetic surgery, and a lack of self-esteem (Bruch, 1985; Dunn, 1994; Saltzberg & Chrisler, 1995). Brownmiller (1984) considered dieting the new equivalent of footbinding or corseting for women. The concerns about weight and the obsession with dieting today (another *self-imposed restriction*) are so prevalent that Rodin, Silberstein, and Striegel-Moore (1984) have labeled the phenomenon *normative discontent*. Even normal-weight women consider themselves too fat (Fodor & Thai, 1984). Such discontent, dissatisfaction, and *self-devaluation* make it difficult for a woman to stand up for herself in unhealthy, particularly violent, situations and to set appropriate boundaries. In fact, Brown (1987) has suggested that women's distortion of body image and fear of fat have resulted from male standards that value smallness, weakness, and the absence of overt power in women. This absence of power and weakness make women predisposed and vulnerable to involvement in abusive relationships.

As one might expect, the socialization messages discussed earlier have consequences for women's mental health. Particularly harmful are messages that women are not in charge of their own identity and that they are primarily valued for their appearance and as objects (Fredrickson & Roberts, 1997). Hare-Mustin (1983) also observed the harmfulness of gender-role socialization and *gender-role conflict* and suggested that "the demands of traditional sex roles lead to more problems for women than for men. Certain aspects of women's sex roles may influence the development of mental illness, such as holding in negative feelings, behaving to satisfy a male partner, passivity, learned helplessness, exaggerated femininity, and other-directedness" (p. 595). Pittman (1985) recommended seeing "both men and women as victims of their own gender roles" (p. 32) and considered rigid gender roles as pathological. Women, who are socialized to attend to and feel responsible for the emotional needs of others, can easily fall into service as emotional conduits in their relationships. Because of their socialized need to meet the emotional needs of others, many women feel unable to set emotional and physical limits when relating to someone they perceive as having greater power or value than themselves (a *restriction* in setting boundaries). Setting limits is also problematic for women when they feel a strong emotional connection to someone, for example, a romantic partner. Gender-role socialization can have a seriously detrimental effect on female–male relationships when women give power to men to act on their behalf (Pittman, 1985). The caretaking role leads women to overvalue love relationships (*devaluing* their selves in the process) and to invest too much of their self-worth in their connections and relationships (Hare-Mustin, 1983; Horney, 1973). Pittman (1985) expressed particular concern over violent relationships. He suggested that women stay in such relationships because "a dictate of femininity is that women should put up with anything to maintain the public image of a Happy Marriage, whatever be the reality" (p. 31). They *restrict* their options because of *self-devaluation*, which results in interpersonal *violation*.

At midlife, some women "wake up" to the socialization messages (Kolbenschlag, 1981) and begin to make changes. At this time, many women who have raised their families are entering the work force, sometimes for the first time, or are continuing their education (Alington & Troll, 1984). They are enjoying their new lifestyles and accomplishments (Mitchell & Helson, 1990), but many are angry about the time they feel they have lost and at the internal and external barriers they experience on the way to their new goals. The changes these women make may also negatively affect heterosexual relationships because just as a woman may be developing her career and work life, her male partner may be nearing, or preparing for, retirement. It is also a time when many high-level male executives are being laid off or outplaced. This puts partners' interests and growth out of synchrony, at best, and in conflict, at worst. When traditional role norms are violated, increased *gender-role conflict* results (Good, Dell, & Mintz, 1989; O'Neil, Fishman, & Kinsella-Shaw, 1987). This kind of *gender-role conflict* and differences in life path can lead to resentment and violence. There are growing suggestions that the changes in balance of power as women leave traditional roles might also lead to male violence (Coleman & Straus, 1986; Kahn, 1984; Yllo, 1984). The assumption is that male violence may increase because of the threat to his dominance in the relationship and in the culture (an example of *gender-role restriction* and *gender-role devaluation*). He may attempt to recapture power through violence. This assumption fits Hypothesis 3 in Chapter 2, which states that "recent changes in gender roles in American society regarding expectations and realities of women's lives have produced men's fears about loss and have increased violence toward women." There has certainly been growing attention in the media to "angry white men" who have lost influence in the workplace to women and people of color and to growing groups of antigovernment white male militia. This resentment toward women has been described in detail by

Faludi (1991) in what she has termed *Backlash: The Undeclared War Against American Women.* Although Faludi has focused on a broad cultural movement against women in the workplace, politics, health care, media, and so on, she did not address possible changes in individual relationships. This hypothesis about change in the power balance bears ongoing attention. However, although more women are in the workforce ("an increase from 20% of women in paid jobs in 1900 to 55% in 1986," Hochschild, 1989, p. 12), women are still concentrated in (*restricted* to) lower status and lower-paying jobs (U.S. Department of Labor, 1994). Women still hold a minority of high-status jobs and suffer discrimination on the career ladder (Kaufman, 1995). Given the small size of the change in power differential between men and women in this country, it may be too soon to accurately evaluate the effect of these changes on domestic violence.

THE SENIOR YEARS

There is evidence that in later years, there is some tendency toward role reversal between women and men (Sinnott, 1984). Women tend to become more independent and in charge of their lives, and men tend to become more relationally oriented and may grieve the connections that they missed. Unfortunately, however, in a culture that values women primarily for their appearance, appearance is not perceived as a commodity that improves with age (Healey, 1986). Men's attractiveness is enhanced by career achievement, increased financial and social status, and grey hair; women's is not. Wrinkles on a man's face are considered marks of maturity and character, whereas women's faces are expected to remain youthful and unlined (Matlin, 1996), a physical impossibility. Sontag (1972) labeled this phenomenon, which *devalues* women, the *double standard of aging.* For example, it is much more socially acceptable for a man to marry a woman 20 years his junior than the reverse (Cowan, 1984; Sontag, 1972). Older women are often referred to in demeaning slang as witch, old hag, crone, old bag—all of which connote ugliness, evil powers, and repulsiveness (Covey, 1988; Grambs, 1989). Older women in fairy tales often appear as wicked stepmothers and evil witches (Lesnoff-Caravaglia, 1984). Only recently have feminist authors (Friedan, 1993; Jong, 1994) begun to challenge stereotypes of older women.

Related to the particular *devaluation* of older women is the culture's long-standing silence about menopause (Unger & Crawford, 1992). The normal changes of midlife have been medicalized (Cowan, Warren, & Young, 1985; Rostosky & Travis, 1996), couched in negative terms of loss (Chrisler, Johnson, Champagne, & Preston, 1994), and considered embarrassing. These attitudes have caused many women to fear growing older and to attempt to hold onto youth at all cost. This *devaluation,* added to women's lack of confidence and self-esteem, have made older women more likely to become involved in or to stay in a bad or violent relationship. Only recently have feminist authors (Greer, 1992; Sheehy, 1992) begun to encourage women to make their own decisions about how to cope with menopausal changes and bring discussion of these issues into the open.

Due to gender differences in life expectancy and the tendency for women to marry older men, there are many more widows than widowers in this country (Hess & Waring, 1983). Widowhood for many women has traditionally been described as a time of loneliness, social isolation, depression, anxiety, and poverty (Lopata, 1979; Matlin, 1996). Women's better skills in interpersonal relationships do give them some advantages for building quality into their later lives, but there are many subgroups of culture that shun and reject older people (Whitbourne & Hulicka, 1990), particularly single women (a *gender-role devaluation* and *gender-role restriction*). Widows' fears of being alone may predispose or lead women to being in abusive relationships or may keep them from leaving bad relationships.

There is also a growing concern about elder abuse (Harway, Hansen, Rossman, Geffner, & Deitch, 1996). Elder abuse is more likely to be perpetrated by a spouse than by adult children (New York City Department for the Aging, 1990; Pillemer & Finkelhor, 1988), with wives being more often the target than husbands (National Aging Resource Center on Elder Abuse, 1990). These facts are not surprising, given that gender-role socialization issues continue throughout the life span. Previously cited research has suggested that abuse may increase as power differentials between men and women narrow. With retirement and increasing loss of health and mobility, power differentials between older men and women may narrow, and violence, as a consequence, may increase. With fewer options, older women may thus feel trapped in poor relationships.

SUMMARY AND CONCLUSIONS

Although this chapter does not intend to suggest that women are in any way responsible for men's violence toward them, it reviews specific issues in women's gender-role socialization that increase the likelihood that women will become involved in violent relationships or find it difficult to leave them. It does not review external barriers such as financial problems, lack of education or job training, problems with child care, difficulties with the police or courts, general lack of resources, and so on.

Consistent patterns of *gender-role devaluation, gender-role restriction*, and *gender-role violation* have been reviewed (see Table 8.1). These include

1. being valued primarily for appearance and the inherent impossibility of ever looking good enough;

2. the expectation of living through others and sacrificing personal needs for others;

3. society's higher valuing of males than females;

4. the lower academic and career expectations of women;

5. feelings of passivity and learned helplessness; and

6. general disempowerment and loss of self-esteem.

All of these patterns predispose many women to have difficulty setting appropriate personal boundaries in relationships or to leave violent situations. Walker (1989) suggested that the abused woman does not feel that she is truly a separate individual who can function without her violent partner. Other factors mitigating against her leaving include the intermittent reinforcement of the "good times," the concept of learned helplessness, and the lack of police intervention and protection (Walker, 1989). Added to these constraints is the widespread societal view in which "the recipient is perceived as someone who must have done something to deserve the abuse. This view affects the type of help that a battered woman can expect from others; family members are likely to urge her to 'try harder,' friends and clergy may tell her it is her duty to make her marriage work, police and legal representatives are likely to underplay and discount the danger she is in, and psychotherapists may attribute to her at least partial blame for the violence" (Harway, Hansen, Rossman, Geffner, & Deitch, 1996, p. 164).

Her vulnerability in each of these issues is compounded by her *devalued* status because of her gender-role socialization to passivity, feeling inadequate, controlled emotion, self-blame, and low self-esteem (Okun, 1986; Walker, 1981). Hoff (1990) reminded us that in addition to the socialization issues that create problems with self-esteem for many women, the actual battering or violence itself further acts to decrease the woman's self-esteem and self-acceptance. Hoff (1990) further described women's accounts of why they got involved or stayed with batterers as being due to the following reason: "They loved their partners, tended to excuse negative behavior, and acted on their commitment to making marriage work" (p. 40). They also expressed "their lack of confidence in their ability to 'make it' without a man" (p. 40). These reasons fit well with the *devalued* socialized role of women as nurturers who need relationships for personal identity, as those responsible for making relationships work at any personal cost, as people who live through and for others, and as individuals who do not have confidence in themselves and their abilities. Hoff placed strong weight on the "cultural values regarding women, marriage, and the family, and how these values and beliefs influence the action of individual women entrapped in violent relationships" (p. 47). All of these descriptions counter the popular myths that battered women are masochists, ask to be beaten, and easily could leave if they really wanted to (McHugh, Frieze, & Browne, 1993). These myths serve to blame the victim and keep her from receiving necessary help.

The effect on women of *gender-role conflict, gender-role devaluation, gender-role restriction*, and *gender-role violation* also bears a striking resemblance to descriptions of lack of power as a loss of voice (Belenky et al., 1986) and therefore loss of the concept of self. Belenky et al. saw voice as a metaphor for a variety of aspects of women's development and experience. Common descriptions used by women they interviewed included "being silenced," "not being heard," "feeling deaf and dumb," and "having no words" (p. 18). In fact, women do "talk less in mixed groups and are interrupted more often" (pp. 17–18) than men. This lack of voice or lack of personal power in society leads women to feel passive, dependent, dumb, subdued, subordinate, reactive, incompetent, and overpowered. This silence so robs women of voice and personal, subjective knowing, that most women even find it difficult to describe themselves, a difficulty clearly related to the earlier described problems in developing an independent identity. Belenky et al., listed many instances of violence that result from this powerlessness or lack of voice.

That some researchers have found little difference between battered and non-battered women, except a family history of violence (Hotaling & Sugarman, 1986; Walker, 1984; Walker & Browne, 1985), suggests that more women may be at risk for violence than is suspected. Whereas all women share similar gender-role socialization and some level of conflict characterized by *gender-role devaluation, gender-role restriction,* and *gender-role violation,* socialization itself may increase the risk to all women to be involved in a violent relationship.

There is also no sufficient information available as yet to fully understand racial and ethnic differences in female response to violence. There is certainly evidence of gender-role socialization messages that vary by culture (Cervantes & Cervantes, 1993), some examples being messages regarding careers and achievement among white, African American, and Asian American women (Hyde, 1991), body weight (Thompson, 1994), and aging (Brown & Kerns, 1985; Grambs, 1989). However, most cultures do teach similar values regarding women as nurturers and mothers (Cervantes & Cervantes, 1993; Ramirez, 1991) and valuing women primarily for appearance. Issues of acculturation level are also important. In understanding the gender socialization processes that affect a woman and her dealing with violence, one must take special care to consider her own personal socialization messages, how similar they are to the general culture, and how much they are influenced by variables of race, ethnicity, SES, geography, and so on. (See Chapter 11, this volume, by Sanchez-Hucles and Dutton, for a fuller description of the effect of race and culture on violence.)

The gender-role socialization messages that women receive throughout their lifetimes predispose them to involvement in violent relationships. Being taught that they are less important than men (*devalued*), less powerful than men (*restricted*), and worthy only for their appearance and nurturing abilities programs women to expect less and demand less than equitable treatment in relationships. Such socialization also creates misogyny (*violation*) in both women and men.

Significant improvement will come not through individual efforts, but through changes in organizational and institutional structures that foster women's *devaluation* and powerlessness. Changes in educational curricula, resources, and instructional styles, portrayal of women and men in the media, and child-rearing practices are necessary. Women and girls must be valued for their character, intelligence, and strength, and not for their appearance. Female assertiveness, competence, and achievement must be encouraged and rewarded individually and publicly. Women must be given equal status with men in the political, corporate, educational, and family realms of daily life. Only then will women not allow themselves to be victimized, and men will not feel entitled to victimize them.

Individual women can be helped by personal empowerment and understanding the consequences of gender-role socialization and conflict. Therapists must be trained to accomplish this work. This training must include understanding the effect of gender-role socialization and conflict on all their clients. They must particularly understand *gender-role devaluation, gender-role restrictions*, and *gender-role violations* inherent in the current culture. Therapists must examine their own gender-role journey (O'Neil & Egan, 1992b) and its effect on their feelings and biases. Psychotherapy training should include coverage of gender bias in research, theory, and practice, with the goal of encouraging the learner to adopt nonsexist models. Gender issues, related power differentials, and issues of violence must be included in all basic coursework, including personality theory, development, psychopathology, assessment, theory and practice of psychotherapy, multicultural psychology, family psychology, ethics, research, and practicum (Nutt & Gottlieb, 1993). Practitioners must understand the inherent difficulties for both women and men in changing gender-role patterns, particularly female passivity and male entitlement. Training in the basic precepts of feminist or gender fair therapy (Fitzgerald & Nutt, 1986; Nutt, 1991; Philpot et al., 1997) that includes empowerment of the client, analysis of the gender-role journey, equality in the therapist–client relationship, validation of female experience, validation of male emotions, encouragement of self-nurturance, examination of gender rules in communication patterns, and valuing of both autonomy and connection for all clients would be especially useful.

PART **IV**

Relational
and Interactional
Factors Explaining
Men's Violence
Against Women

Introduction

T he relational explanations for men's violence against women
are considered from two different perspectives in this part. Steven
Anderson and Margaret Schlossberg, in Chapter 9, reexamine family systems
theories as a way to explain domestic violence. Although these theories have
been critiqued harshly in the past, these authors argue that family systems theories have much to offer in understanding battering. They indicate that the importance of relational context and patterns of interaction over time has not been
emphasized in the literature pertaining to battering. In addition to assessing
strengths and limitations of systems perspectives, Anderson and Schlossberg
examine the relational hypotheses of the O'Neil and Harway model and present
two additional relational hypotheses.

In Chapter 10, Sandra Rigazio-DiGilio and Steven Lanza propose an ecological perspective to understand men's violence against women. The Systemic
Cognitive-Developmental Theory (SCDT) model presented organizes the
interface of individual, interpersonal, and sociological factors that contribute to
domestic violence. A basic premise of this model is that the interface among individuals, partnerships, families, and larger systems is fundamentally a cultural
exchange process. The SCDT provides a useful method to identify worldviews
that couples use to express feelings, thoughts, and behaviors related to violence
and to examine the adaptiveness of the relational system. Rigazio-DiGilio and
Lanza indicate that the model is helpful in making appropriate therapeutic interventions. They present research questions that could be tested using SCDT.

Systems Perspectives on Battering

The Importance of Context and Pattern

STEPHEN A. ANDERSON
MARGARET C. SCHLOSSBERG

The problem of men battering women is a complex issue, and no one perspective has yet been able to explain the phenomenon fully. Much of the available literature has emphasized individual or societal perspectives. Individual perspectives, such as social learning, psychodynamic, or psychiatric models, emphasize the characteristics, personality traits, and level of psychopathology of the individual batterer. Sociological and feminist perspectives highlight the sanctions that society fails to place upon men's use of violence or the sociopolitical climate that reinforces an unequal, patriarchal power structure that favors men's dominance over women and supports male aggression and violence as acceptable norms. Systems theories, in contrast, emphasize an interpersonal perspective that focuses upon the social and relational contexts and the unique patterns of interaction that recur within relationships. Systems perspectives highlight the unique histories of each partner and the situational factors that characterize a given relationship.

In our view, family systems approaches to understanding the problem of battering remain undeveloped. Perhaps this is because, as some have suggested, family systems theorists have denied or minimized the problem of battering (Avis, 1992; Bograd, 1984; Kaufman, 1992). Perhaps Gelles, Lackner, and Wolfner (1993) are correct in their assessment that feminist and sociological perspectives are so widely endorsed that the study of other explanations for battering have been deterred. Whatever the reason, we contend that systems perspectives have a great deal to offer the study of battering. Available research consistently has pointed to the importance of the relational context and the patterns of interaction that occur over time in violent relationships. We further contend that attention to family systems formulations can raise additional questions for empirical study that heretofore have remained relatively unaddressed.

In this chapter, we provide our definition of male-to-female violence, assess the strengths and limitations of the systems perspectives in conceptualizing male-to-female violence, review relevant empirical research as it applies, and propose questions for further study that emerge when systems perspectives are closely scrutinized. Our analysis deals with Part IV of O'Neil and Harway's (Chapter 2) multivariate framework. In particular, we address the role of men's and women's socialization as it pertains to differences in their communication styles (Hypothesis 9), the role of psychological violence or verbal abuse as a precursor to physical battering (Hypothesis 10), and the relationship between one's earlier family-of-origin experiences and the likelihood of becoming a batterer or battered in one's adult relationships (Hypothesis 13). Two of our own hypotheses provide the overall organization of this chapter: (1) Men's violence toward women can be understood only by examining the social and relational contexts within which it occurs and (2) understanding male-to-female violence requires an examination of the patterns of interaction that characterize battering relationships.

DEFINITION

We use the term *battering* to describe male-to-female violence. Battering is more than physical aggression. It is the systematic use of physical aggression or the threat of physical aggression to intimidate, subjugate, and control another human being (Jacobson, Gottman, & Short, 1995; Kaufman, 1992). We use this definition for several reasons. First, it incorporates forms of psychological or emotional abuse when these behaviors involve strategies intended to coerce or regulate the woman's freedom. Second, it distinguishes the kinds of physical aggressions enacted by women toward men from those enacted by men toward women. Even though national surveys have found that as many women are violent toward their husbands as husbands are toward their wives (Gelles & Straus, 1989; Straus & Gelles, 1990), rarely do women systematically use physical aggression to subjugate or control men (Jacobson, Gottman, & Short, 1995). Husbands' physical aggression results in more physical injury, health problems, stress, depression, and psychosomatic symptoms than does wives' aggression (Cantos, Neidig, & O'Leary, 1993; Carden, 1994). Wives' physical aggression is often in self-defense (Gelles & Straus, 1989; Straus & Gelles, 1990). Third, this definition emphasizes that abuse is a pattern that occurs within a relationship over time.

A CRITICAL ASSESSMENT OF SYSTEMS THEORY

The systems approach to understanding battering has been severely criticized, particularly by feminist writers who charge that it obscures the seriousness of the physical abuse suffered by women. Furthermore, by assuming a nonlinear, or nonblaming stance toward all members of the system, the batterer is absolved of full responsibility and the wife is viewed as "co-responsible" for the battering (Bograd, 1984, 1987; Harway & Hansen, 1993). In addition, feminist writers point out that gender roles are central to the functioning of the family and are inseparable from the broader social, political, and cultural contexts (Goldner, 1985a). Family systems theories have failed to attend to the power and status differentials that exist between men and women, both within the broader culture and within the family system (Avis, 1992; Bograd, 1984; Goldner, 1985b). These power and status differentials promote male privilege and dictate unequal patterns of interaction between couples. From this perspective, it is the prevailing cultural norms and differences in gender socialization that account for battering (Avis, 1992; Bograd, 1987; Hansen, 1993; Kaufman, 1992).

These criticisms have made an important contribution to our understanding of battering. For instance, most family theorists and therapists now hold the view that men must be held fully responsible for their violent behaviors (Sprenkle, 1994). Additionally, most family therapists now advocate gender-specific treatments for male batterers and their partners, especially in cases of severe violence where the safety and security of the woman cannot be assured. Family therapy approaches are typically recommended in cases of mild-to-moderate violence (Gelles & Maynard, 1995; O'Leary & Murphy, 1992) or only when the threat of further violence has been eliminated (Gondolf, 1993; Lawson, 1989; Mones & Panitz, 1994).

However, the following research findings support our view of the importance of systems perspectives in understanding battering. First, in a recent review, Whitchurch and Pace (1993) concluded that men are indeed able to control their violence, because the majority of batterers are not violent against others outside their families. This, combined with the fact that violence is usually perpetrated against the batterer's own children and wife, suggests that the locus of violence is in the relational context, rather than within the individual.

Second, although it is important to consider the cultural and political contexts within which violence occurs, these dimensions are not sufficient to explain violence, because as Jacobson, Gottman, and Short (1995) pointed out, batterers are not violent 24 hours a day, 7 days a week.

Third, there is no consistent psychological or sociocultural profile of the battered woman. As Hotaling and Sugarman (1990) noted after reviewing 400 empirical studies and the reanalysis of some earlier national data, "there is no evidence that the statuses a woman occupies, the roles she performs, her demographic profile, or her personality characteristics consistently influence her chances of becoming a victim of wife assault" (p. 393). Instead, what appear to be more predictive of the woman's risk for repeated assault are situational variables such as a woman's financial dependence upon her partner, fear of threats of retaliation toward her or her children, hope based upon his promises that he will change, shame associated with reporting the violence, and avoidance or victim-blaming by helping professionals or significant others (Carden, 1994). Such situational factors point to the relational and broader social contexts as critical factors in understanding the woman's participation in a battering relationship.

Fourth, despite consistent findings of significant correlations between male violence and individual variables, such as drug and alcohol problems, low self-esteem, inexpressiveness, dependency, jealousy, and rigid and traditional attitudes toward women, there is growing consensus that no conclusive single batterer profile exists (Gondolf, 1993; Hotaling & Sugarman, 1986; Saunders, 1992). This also suggests that the relational context may be a critical factor in understanding differences in the types of batterers.

Fifth, studies have shown that physically aggressive and nonaggressive marriages can be differentiated on the basis of interactional variables. For example, violent couples clearly differ from nonviolent couples in their level of positive communication skills and problem-solving styles (Cordova, Jacobson, Gottman, Rushe, & Cox, 1993; Lloyd, 1996; Margolin & Burman, 1993; Sabourin, Infante, & Rudd, 1993). Several studies have found that the behaviors of physically aggressive spouses were highly contingent upon the behaviors of their partners. When one spouse exhibited angry or contemptuous affect, the partner was likely to reciprocate that behavior (Burman, John, & Margolin, 1992; Cordova et al., 1993). This pattern was more consistent and lasted longer for violent couples than for nonviolent and nondistressed couples (Burman, John, & Margolin, 1992). The interactional patterns and styles of communication that couples enact to deal with interpersonal problems and situational stresses are central issues in systems perspectives.

Sixth, research suggests that the majority of violent couples stay together (Gondolf, 1993; Lloyd, 1996; Mones & Pantiz, 1994). Placing full responsibility for the abuse upon the man does not alter the need to understand the dynamics that operate in these systems. This information is essential if we are to develop more effective treatments to alter repeating interactional cycles that serve as the context for abuse (Margolin & Burman, 1993).

Seventh, as Hansen and Goldenberg (1993) pointed out, assigning blame for the violence to the perpetrator may, in fact, perpetuate the woman's perception of her own ineffectiveness and victimization, based on research that has found that most battered women attribute responsibility for the violence at least partly to themselves, especially in the early stages of a violent relationship (Cantos, Neidig, & O'Leary, 1993; Holtzworth-Munroe & Hutchinson, 1993). Assigning blame to one or both partners fails to focus on the issue of both people having "inadequate skills to solve the original problem" (Hansen & Goldenberg, 1993, p. 85).

A systemic view of female battering must take into account the actions of the batterer, the responses of both partners, and the unique context within which the violence occurs. We agree with Hansen and Goldenberg (1993) that neither partner must be seen as a victim. Both are active individuals capable of changing their behavior. The woman can learn how to protect herself and her children, and the batterer can learn to control his violent behavior.

STRENGTHS AND LIMITATIONS OF SYSTEMS PERSPECTIVES

The previously mentioned points are not intended to suggest that systems perspectives are without limitations. However, in our view, some of the criticisms leveled against systems perspectives are valid, whereas others are not. For instance, systems perspectives *describe* violent interactions and emphasize questions such as "how?" or "what?" Such questions include, "How do violent men relate to their wives?" and "How do wives respond when their husbands become violent?" "What kinds of communication patterns or problem-solving styles are associated with battering episodes?" Systems theories do not provide causal explanations for the frequently asked question, "Why do men batter their wives?" It is inconsistent to use the systems theories to *explain the cause* of family violence because, by definition, systems theories do not address the linear notion of cause and effect. Thus, it is inconsistent to use systems theory to assert that violence *results* from the partners' need to maintain a homeostatic pattern or that violence is the *product* of an interaction between an "over-adequate woman" and an "under-adequate man" who uses violence to reestablish the equilibrium in the relationship. Such interpretations use interactional concepts to explain in a manner that is inconsistent with systems perspectives.

A common criticism of systems perspectives is that they implicitly blame the victim and absolve (not blame) the batterer by seeing the relationship, rather than the batterer, as the focus of study. Drawing a blaming/nonblaming distinction is again inconsistent with systems perspectives, which are more concerned with "how persons are involved in a battering relationship" than with "who is to blame." A systems perspective does not absolve batterers of responsibility for their violence nor does it blame the victim (Sprenkle, 1994). However, it does take into account the complex set of influences that define each interpersonal encounter and holds each partner responsible for any actions that contribute to abusive interactions.

Systems theorists have been criticized for ignoring the social, political, and cultural contexts that reinforce a patriarchal social system, protect men's dominance, maintain women in subordinate positions, and ignore women's victimization. Although this is a valid point, it should be stressed that systems perspectives always have espoused the importance of multiple levels of context in understanding family dynamics and individual behavior. These include the biological, psychological, societal, and even the broader ecological levels.

Finally, perhaps the most compelling argument against systems theories has been their inability to address the power politics of traditional gender roles, the family's division of labor, and the status of women in society and in the family. By emphasizing pattern, context, and circular interaction, systems perspectives are said to be unable to address linear concepts such as power. Although there is some merit to these arguments, it is not entirely the case that systems perspectives are unable to address the concept of power.

One way to conceptualize power is in terms of an interpersonal bargaining process by which one achieves intended effects over another (Scanzoni, 1979). This process is governed by a myriad of factors including prevailing societal norms (e.g., the gender roles of men and women), a couple's established communication patterns, the level of trust in the relationship, and each partner's assessment of the costs and rewards associated with a given course of action. Power is not static and does not reside within one person or another, but rather it is distributed. That is, partners share, or take control over, different spheres of the relationship (e.g., income generation, housework, home repairs, and parental discipline).

Power is considered *legitimate* when the authority of a partner over a given sphere is negotiated within the relationship and agreed upon by both parties. Such a process leads to perceptions of fairness, equity, and trust that the relationship will produce future rewards. However, power is *nonlegitimate* when it involves efforts to control the other partner or aspects of the relationship without the authority to do so having been agreed upon by both partners. The partner's response to efforts to coerce, dominate, or exploit may be to refuse to submit, passively submit, submit while constantly communicating dissatisfaction, or continually seeking to renegotiate to remove the injustice. The exercise of legitimate power serves to *resolve* interpersonal conflict, whereas nonlegitimate power merely *regulates* conflict, leaving a residue of hostility, distrust, inequality, and a sense of devaluation. Couples vary along a continuum, with those at one end demonstrating legitimate power (negotiated authority) in most spheres of the relationship. At the other extreme are couples in whose relationships negotiation is limited and nonlegitimate power (domination) prevails in most spheres of the relationship (Anderson & Sabatelli, 1995; Scanzoni, 1979).

From a systems perspective, power is not a property of a person nor is it the inevitable by-product of a particular social or cultural context. Rather, power is determined by a variety of contextual variables (e.g., societal norms, public policies, availability of economic resources, family-of-origin experiences, and outcomes of the couple's previous interactions) and by the ongoing process of negotiation that has been established between the partners. It is these factors that explain the individual batterer's violent actions and the partner's responses. Both participants are viewed as exerting interpersonal power (influencing or attempting to influence the other) and both are, at the same time, influenced by external forces over which they have limited or no control. As Dell (1989) noted, this is perhaps both the strength and limitation of systems perspectives. They provide us with an important conceptual tool, but they provide no help in defining the *causes* of oppression, status inequality, gender discrimination, or family violence (Goldner, 1985a, 1985b; Bograd, 1984).

It should be clear from the foregoing discussion that the two most important contributions of systems perspectives are in understanding the context within which battering occurs and in understanding the interactional patterns that occur within battering relationships. We now examine these two dimensions in more detail.

CONTEXTUAL FACTORS RELATED TO BATTERING

Research on battering has identified a number of factors that may compose the context within which battering occurs. At the outset, we must register the caution that the unique context within which battering occurs undoubtedly differs for each relational system. No two relationships or family systems are exactly alike. Each is the product of unique individuals, with distinct personal traits, abilities, histories, and past relationship experiences. We review the factors that have been associated with battering to highlight critical variables and to emphasize the complexity involved in understanding battering. This includes socioeconomic variables, alcohol and drug use, stress, isolation and the absence of social support, societal norms, earlier family-of-origin experiences, and marital conflict and distress.

Socioeconomic factors, such as the batterer's level of education, occupational prestige, and income, are thought to be one element of the context of battering (Hoffman, Demo, & Edwards, 1994; Hotaling & Sugarman, 1986; Steinmetz, 1987; Straus, Gelles, & Steinmetz, 1980). Violence is more likely to occur when the husband has fewer perceived or actual resources than his wife, because he may feel threatened by his wife's status relative to his own (Yllö & Bograd, 1988). The context of battering frequently involves the use of *alcohol or other drugs* on the part of the batterer (Hotaling & Sugarman, 1986; Steinmetz, 1987). Drugs and alcohol have the potential to exacerbate an individual's emotional instability or to intensify interpersonal conflicts. The substance may act as a dis-inhibitor for those prone to violence or provide a justification or excuse for vio-lence (Hayes & Emshoff, 1993). Sometimes the substance abuse becomes a topic of contention between the batterer and his wife. Battering is more likely to occur within systems and among individuals experiencing higher levels of *stress* (Gelles, 1974; Straus, Gelles, & Steinmetz, 1980). Stress, defined as a demand-capability imbalance, results when the demands upon the individual or family system are beyond the system's resources for coping. Violence is one response or strategy for coping with stress and frustration. For instance, if a husband cannot meet his family responsibilities and role expectations because of inadequate edu-cation, a low status job, or low income, the level of stress is enhanced and the likelihood of violence increases (Gelles, 1974). *Isolation* from community, extended family, and other social supports exacerbates the effects of stress and marital conflict by removing potential coping resources, such as emotional sup-port, information, and legal and professional assistance, from the woman. Batterers often attempt to limit the wife's outside contacts (Walker, 1984), and such isolation diminishes the likelihood that societal sanctions will be imposed upon the batterer and the likelihood that interventions will be sought to teach him more effective coping strategies to replace the violence. *Societal norms*, such as rigid sex-role stereotypes that support men as rational, aggressive, and dominant, and women as emotionally expressive, irrational, accommodating, and depen-dent, constitute another contextual factor. Such sex-role differences reinforce societal tolerance of battering and the use of violence as a viable solution to con-flict and other problems (Carden, 1994; Harway & Hansen, 1993).

The context within which violence occurs also includes the experiences of partners in their own *families of origin* (Carden, 1994; Tolman & Bennett, 1990). One of the most common research findings in the family violence literature is that adults who were abused as children, or who witnessed marital abuse as children, are more likely to be abusive with their intimate partners as adults (cf. Barnett & Hamberger, 1992; Doumas, Margolin, & John, 1994; Gelles & Straus, 1989). The strongest relationship appears to be between battering as an adult and witnessing violence in one's family of origin (Barnett & Hamberger, 1992; Gelles & Straus, 1989; Hotaling & Sugarman, 1986). One's family-of-origin experiences establish a legacy that affects identity development, one's attitudes and beliefs about women, and the interpersonal strategies one develops to deal with significant others.

However, consistent with systems perspectives, a number of researchers have concluded that violence in one's family of origin is neither a sufficient nor a necessary condition for violence in one's current intimate relationship (Carden, 1994; Pagelow, 1992; Straus, Gelles, & Steinmetz, 1980). For example, Pagelow (1992) suggests that although an intergenerational cycle must be considered, "there is sufficient reason to question the blanket assumption of a cycle of violence, and to consider the family history of violence as only one factor out of many that may be associated with a greater probability of adult violence" (p. 111). Similarly, Cappell and Heiner (1990) concluded that "a full explanation of spousal aggression will have to address factors in addition to the presence or absence of spousal violence in the family of origin" (p. 150).

A *high level of conflict* and *marital distress* are additional contextual factors that are significantly related to battering (Edwards, Fuller, Vorakitphokatorn, & Sermsi, 1992; Stets, 1990; Straus, Gelles, & Steinmetz, 1980). Distressed couples experience higher levels of stress than satisfied couples, and they tend to blame problems upon each other, complain, criticize, and put each other down (Anderson & Sabatelli, 1995). Hotaling and Sugarman (1990) reported that conflicts in violent marriages often involved disagreements over division of labor, frequent drinking by the husband, and the wife having a higher educational attainment than the husband. However, it is important to keep in mind that not all conflicted or distressed relationships experience violence.

Furthermore, not all violent relationships are characterized by marital distress. For example, Lloyd (1990, 1996) found that a group of nondistressed couples also reported battering episodes, although not as frequently as a group of distressed couples. This was especially true for couples in the early stages of marriage and where a reserve of positive exchanges still existed in the relationship.

From a systems perspective, all the previously mentioned contextual factors, representing social, cultural, extended family, and individual levels, are thought to be moderated by the patterns and dynamics that operate within the family system (Anderson & Sabatelli, 1995). Although it must accommodate its cultural environment, the family and its members also actively screen, interpret, and modify cultural standards to fit with the family's unique identity; that is, their system and rules for relating (Bagarozzi & Anderson, 1989). The family's relationship rules and role expectations are further defined by the unique qualities, traits, and abilities (and disabilities) of its individual members. The context influences the strategies the family develops to manage its daily tasks; regulates the emotional environment; establishes the identity of each member and the family as a whole; and regulates the boundaries between individual members and subsystems, and between the family and the outside world (Anderson & Sabatelli, 1995). Socioeconomic factors, alcohol or drug abuse, stress, social isolation, societal norms, one's family-of-origin experiences, or marital conflict are not thought to *cause* battering. Rather, they enhance the likelihood that men will use violence and that the family will organize around the battering as a strategy for relating to significant others. Data presented by Hoffman, Demo, and Edwards (1994) support this view by finding that the negative effects of stress, alcohol abuse, and socioeconomic status on wife abuse were indirect, rather than direct. That is, they were mediated by marital interactions. Stress, alcohol abuse, and socioeconomic factors affected the level of marital conflict and dissatisfaction, which in turn predicted physical wife abuse.

INTERACTION PATTERNS ASSOCIATED WITH BATTERING

The two primary questions addressed in this section are (1) "What are the inter-actional dynamics that operate during the immediacy of the battering episode?" and (2) "How do violent patterns of interaction develop in relationships over time?" On the whole, we know very little about the actual interactions that occur during battering episodes. Much of our knowledge comes from retrospective self-reports of those engaged in battering episodes. Observational studies with couples who have acknowledged battering have shown that batterers engage in higher levels of threat, blame, criticism, and other negative behaviors than do husbands in nonviolent marriages. Both husbands and wives in violent marriages enacted fewer positive behaviors (approval, accepting responsibility, smiling, and paraphrasing) and greater levels of disagreement, criticism, and put downs than did partners in nonviolent marriages. They also were more likely to exhibit rigid patterns of interaction in which hostile, angry behaviors by one partner would trigger hostile responses by the other spouse (Burman, John, & Margolin, 1992; Cordova et al., 1993; Jacobson et al., 1994). Violent couples also have been found to differ from nonviolent couples in their level of communication and problem-solving skills (Infante, Sabourin, Rudd, & Shannon, 1990; Sabourin, Infante, & Rudd, 1993). When husband and wife are both deficient in communication abil-ity and the husband is in a less powerful position, there is a greater risk of bat-tering (Babcock, Waltz, Jacobson, & Gottman, 1993). Overt verbal hostility and passive aggression are also precursors to battering (Murphy & O'Leary, 1989; O'Leary, Malone, & Tyree, 1994).

Those who have examined the question of how battering evolves over time have approached it from several different perspectives. Some have described battering as falling along a continuum starting early in the rela-tionship and escalating in severity over time, with psychological aggression (humiliation, degradation, threats of harm, property damage, economic deprivation, and isolation and restriction) preceding and then later co-occur-ring with physical aggression (Murphy & O'Leary, 1989; Stets, 1990). Yet, as many as one half of battering relationships have been found to cease to be violent over a 1- to 3-year period. This was particularly likely to occur in less severe cases (Feld & Straus, 1989; Woffordt, Mihalic, & Menard, 1994). Thus, for some, but not all, cases, violence appears to follow a developmen-tal pattern that begins early in the relationship and becomes more serious and dangerous over time.

The most extensive writing on an interactional cycle of violence over time has come from Walker (1984). She described three characteristic phases that occur in abusive relationships. The *tension building* phase is characterized by mounting incidents of conflict, anger, threats, and minor physical assaults. During this phase, women in Walker's study described common elements of fear, anger, denial, and rationalization for the abuse, as well efforts to please or placate their abusers. The second phase is one of acute *violence*, which varies in duration from one couple to another. During this phase, women typically experience feelings of helplessness and futility, and often excuse their partners from taking responsibility for the violence and blame themselves for the abuse. In the subsequent *honeymoon* phase, the abuser apologizes, expresses guilt and shame, and becomes very loving and promises that the battering will never happen again. According to Walker, many women believe this promise and deny the severity of their abuse and the likelihood that it will recur. The pattern becomes rigid and continues because the honeymoon period is highly reinforcing for the wife, and the use of violence to control his wife is highly reinforcing for the husband. According to Woffordt, Mihalic, and Menard (1994), the battering cycle becomes "an habitual strategy" for resolving conflicts.

However, we must point out that research has not consistently supported Walker's cycle of violence. Some men turn from apologizing to blaming the spouse for the battering (Walker, 1984); some rarely apologize, but instead continue to control and abuse (Gondolf, 1988; Saunders, 1992). Thus, the model appears to describe the interactional pattern of some, but not all, couples over time.

On the basis of the available data, the following points can be summarized that are consistent with a systems perspective. It is not the presence of conflict that distinguishes the battering relationship from others. Conflict is inevitable in any intimate relationship. The myriad of tasks that must be managed (parenting, work, household, and financial) and the differences in spousal expectations provide ample opportunities for misunderstandings, disagreements, and conflicts to occur. The critical factor is how conflict is negotiated within the relationship. Couples differ in the degree to which their strategies are effective or ineffective in managing conflict. Positive strategies promote mutual understanding, resolve differences, and foster intimacy. Destructive strategies are oriented toward "winning at all costs" or exerting nonlegitimate control over another (Anderson & Sabatelli, 1995). Systems perspectives assume that partners in a battering relationship lack the necessary skills for constructively handling conflict. This, combined with contextual factors (e.g., family-of-origin experiences, attitudes toward violence as acceptable, and substance abuse), increases the risk of battering. Violence escalates as a result of failed attempts to resolve conflicts through less negative strategies.

Some may read this assessment as holding the battered woman responsible for the battering and minimizing the responsibility of the batterer. A counterargument could be raised that women do nothing to provoke their partners (Bograd, 1992) and have been found to demonstrate effective social and interpersonal skills in intimate relationships with other men after being separated from the batterer (Walker, 1984). However, more recent research has not supported this latter view, finding instead that both men and women reenact similar roles (batterer, battered) and relational strategies in subsequent relationships (Kalmuss & Seltzer, 1986; Woffordt, Mihalic, & Menard, 1994). Furthermore, many women do respond in ways that escalate or reinforce the pattern of violence, in both pre-marital and marital relationships (Flynn, 1990; Steinmetz, 1987; Straus & Gelles, 1990). We address this issue further in the final section of this chapter, in which we raise questions that have received little or no attention in the literature, but which are highlighted by systems perspectives.

FUTURE RESEARCH QUESTIONS DERIVED FROM SYSTEMS PERSPECTIVES

In our view, systems perspectives offer considerable promise in helping to unravel the complex processes that occur within battering relationships. In this section, we list a number of questions that we believe warrant further empirical examination.

1. *Can relational typologies be developed to describe previous research on battering relationships more accurately?* In a review of the various typologies developed to describe male batterers, Holtzworth-Munroe and Stuart (1994) hypothesize three subtypes of batterers that were consistent with previous research. *Family-only* batterers, the most common type, were described as the least violent and were violent only with family members. They were the least likely to have psychological, legal, or substance abuse problems, or to have wit-nessed violence in their own families of origin. Family-only batterers also were described as having more satisfying and less conflictual marriages. They were the group most likely to feel remorse and shame over the battering. *Dysphoric/borderline* batterers were described as more emotionally unstable and violent primarily within the family, but also sometimes outside the family. They were described as engaging in more severe violence that included physical, psycho-logical, and sexual violence. They were further described as having extreme pre-occupation with, and dependency upon, their wives and showing high levels of jealousy, marital dissatisfaction, and ambivalence about their relationships. The *generally violent* batterers were described as the most violent, the most likely to treat their wives as objects, the least likely to show remorse, and the most likely to blame their partners for the battering. They also were most likely to have anti-social personality disorders, be criminally violent outside the home, have alcohol or drug abuse problems, and to have witnessed violence in their own families of origin. We propose that such batterer typologies might be a useful starting point for developing relational typologies that describe different relationship dynamics within each group. For instance, couples in the *family-only* group may be more likely, because of poor communication and problem-solving skills, to engage in escalating cycles of verbal conflict and physical aggression. Wives in such

relationships may be more likely to "fight back," given the less severe nature of the marital problems and the generally lower level of physical danger. Relational themes of intense possessiveness, jealousy, loyalty, control, rejection, abandonment, enmeshment, and poor individuation that have been identified in the literature may be more likely to occur in the *dysphoric/borderline* typology (Bartle & Rosen, 1994; Ferraro, 1988; Lloyd, 1996; Mones & Panitz, 1994). Such relationships also may be the most dangerous for wives to leave and the most likely to include patterns of stalking or other forms of intense surveillance and control of the woman's behavior. In contrast, themes of impulsivity, unpredictability, volatility, extreme oppression, and depersonalization may characterize the *generally violent* group. Wives in these relationships may be the most likely to report unprovoked assaults and to feel the most terrorized, traumatized, and fearful of fighting back (Walker, 1984). Of course, our hypotheses are speculative and intended only to illustrate an avenue for future research.

2. *What are the characteristics of the interaction patterns in couples who successfully terminate the violence in their relationship?* Research has suggested that as many as one half of battering relationships cease to be violent over time (Feld & Straus, 1989; Woffordt, Mihalic, & Menard, 1994). Yet we know little about the couples who succeed in maintaining their relationship and successfully terminate the battering (Goldner, 1992; Hansen & Goldenberg, 1993). For instance, do couples who overcome violence differ significantly from those who do not in the types or severity of contextual variables influencing their relationship (e.g., severity of alcohol use, stress, isolation from the community or extended family, and earlier family-of-origin experiences)? Do they differ in their level of communication, conflict-resolution, or problem-solving skills, or in their strategies for negotiating power issues within the relationship? Answers to such questions should assist in the development of more effective prevention and treatment strategies (Holtzworth-Munroe, Markman, O'Leary, Neidig, Leber, Heyman, Hulbert, & Smutzler, 1995).

3. *What are the interactional dynamics that occur within early family-of-origin experiences that may account for the intergenerational cycle of violence?* Are there particular patterns of interaction that occur within the family of origin that can help explain how some individuals who are exposed to family violence during childhood perpetuate this pattern into their adult relationships and some do not? As we noted earlier, there appears to be a greater likelihood of becoming involved in a violent relationship in adulthood, either as a batterer or as a spouse, when one witnesses violence between significant others as opposed to experiencing it directly, but, what are the mechanisms by which this occurs? Caesar (1988) presented some anecdotal evidence to suggest that batterers were more likely to become caught up in their parents' marital conflicts and to be enlisted by one parent or the other as an ally or a mediator. In contrast, those who did not become batterers as adults were more likely to remain disengaged from the

family conflicts. These same patterns of overinvolvement and disengagement have been observed even in children who witness marital conflicts between their parents that do not involve physical violence (Anderson & Sabatelli, 1995; Cummings & Davies, 1994). We still know very little about family processes in earlier childhood and their relationship to adult family violence.

4. *What is the relationship between violence in the marital relationship and the functioning of other subsystems in the family, such as the parenting subsystem?* Systems perspectives assume that stress or conflict in one part of the family affects functioning in other parts of the system as well. Studies have begun to address the question of whether the impact of battering on children is the direct result of witnessing traumatic events or an indirect result, affecting parents' ability to parent their children effectively in a hostile environment. Results suggest that battering is related to children's adjustment indirectly through impaired parenting strategies that involve a complex set of variables, including the parents' and child's gender, the responses of the child to each parent, and the responses of each parent to the other parent's actions toward the child (Margolin, John, Ghosh, & Gordis, 1996). Additional research is needed to unravel relationships between battering and different subsystems within the family.

5. *What role do current family-of-origin relationships play in perpetuating or ending the battering?* Research on the family of origin has generally examined the relationship between childhood experiences as a victim or witness of family violence and men's and women's tendency to use, or be victimized by, violence in their adult relationships. We know of no research that has examined the role of parents, siblings, and other extended family members in encouraging or discouraging the current battering relationship. For instance, Serra (1993) presented a case study in which the wife's parents encouraged the daughter to stay with her husband, despite the danger, because the husband had convinced the parents that he could not live without his wife. In another case, the woman's mother and sister gave the batterer some Valium to help calm him down after he put a gun to his wife's head, but they did nothing to ensure their loved one's safety (Serra, 1993).

6. *Do battering relationships follow a developmental course?* Studies have shown that at least some battering relationships follow a pattern of progressively more frequent and severe episodes of battering over time (Murphy & O'Leary, 1989; O'Leary, Malone, & Tyree, 1994; Stets, 1990; Walker, 1984). We also know that partners can overlook, ignore, or forgive the verbal and physical abuse early in the relationship, but that over time, the abuse tends to erode the quality of the relationship (Lloyd, 1991). Cantos, Neidig, and O'Leary (1993) found that mutual aggression that was not in self-defense was most common in young married couples who generally used lower levels of aggression and reported less dissatisfaction with the relationship. However, women in more severely violent relationships often reported high levels of marital discord and reported that their

physical aggression was often in self-defense. Early on, wives are more likely to attribute blame or responsibility for the battering to themselves, but as the severity increases, they are more likely to hold their partners responsible (Cantos, Neidig, & O'Leary, 1993; Holtzworth-Munroe & Hutchinson, 1993). These findings suggest a pattern of systematic changes in the relationship over time. However, we do not know yet whether specific stages of development of a battering relationship can be identified, whether specific patterns of interaction characterize each stage of relationship development, or whether different typologies of battering relationships follow different developmental paths.

7. *What are the characteristics of marriages in which violence is directed toward husbands from wives?* Although not directly related to the current discussion, systems perspectives also raise the question of violence enacted toward men by women. In their review of available research, Hotaling and Sugarman (1986) identified only seven case-comparison studies that addressed this question, and five of them were from the same data set. Are the interactions in these relationships qualitatively different from those in which battering occurs or do they share some common characteristics?

CONCLUSION

It is extremely difficult to specify the situations in which battering will occur, because the meaning of the specific situation is known only to the participants in the interaction. The particular cues, or trigger events, to which each batterer responds are subjective and may vary from time to time (Bagarozzi & Anderson, 1989; Ferraro, 1988; O'Neil & Harway, Chapter 2, this volume). These triggers are undoubtedly a product of past experiences in the family of origin, cultural messages about the roles of men and women and the acceptance of violence, the couple's unique relationship history, level of earlier unresolved conflict in the relationship, the previously established strategies for resolving conflict, and the outcomes of previous battering episodes.

For instance, what is the focus of the man's attention at the moment he decides to become violent? Is he responding to the hurtfulness of his wife's previous comment or anticipating greater pain from her next comment (Margolin, Gordis, Oliver, & Raine, 1995)? Does he respond to what would appear to an outsider to be an apparently insignificant event, such as the evening meal not being prepared on time, because he experiences this as a loss of control over his environment? Does he associate the current situation with others in which he has felt vulnerable, inadequate, or threatened (Ferraro, 1988)?

What is the focus of the woman's attention at the moment of attack? Is she primarily concerned with keeping her children safe even at personal cost to herself? Has she come to accept that she has, in fact, done something to warrant the kind of attack she receives? Have her earlier family-of-origin experiences consistently exposed her to violence so that she now accepts battering as an unavoidable, expected occurrence (Hotaling & Sugarman, 1986)? Has she determined that she will not tolerate this kind of abuse and respond with psychological abuse or physical violence in turn? Has she decided that she has had enough and that she must leave this relationship?

We have argued here that systems perspectives have much to offer in understanding the variability and complexity that characterize battering relationships. Some couples are able to negotiate differences in their relationship successfully by allocating legitimate power and authority to each partner in different spheres of their relationship, whereas others are characterized by strategies that rely upon the use of nonlegitimate power, domination, and control. It has been suggested that no single profile of the male batterer exists and that some men are violent only within their families, whereas others evidence a more generalized pattern of aggression. Some couples manage to eliminate violence from their relationship on their own, whereas others follow a pattern of increasing severity from verbal to physical abuse. These and other findings point to the importance of systems perspectives' emphasis on context and pattern in helping to explain male-to-female violence.

Inter-Gender Relational Dimensions of Violence Toward Women

A Co-Constructive-Developmental Perspective

SANDRA RIGAZIO-DIGILIO
A. STEPHEN LANZA

W hat are the origins of relationship violence? Why do some male perpetrators resort to using only physical or psychological means of intimidation, whereas others employ both forms of relationship oppression? How do family-of-origin, sociocultural, and sociopolitical influences affect the frequency, intent, severity, and duration of relationship violence? How can questions such as these be answered in ways that assist theoreticians, researchers, and clinicians to comprehend, as best as possible, each partner's experience in context?

Historically, social scientists have examined the inter-gender relational dimensions of violence from discrete individual, systemic, and sociologic perspectives. Commonly accepted ecological views—fully incorporating all three frames of reference—have yet to be sufficiently articulated or developed. It is our contention that the field would benefit from ecological frameworks that advance the integration of factors, such as biology (cf. Elliot, 1976; Greene, Chapter 5, this volume; Money & Ehrhardt, 1972), interpersonal communication and power discrepancies (cf. Babcock, Waltz, Jacobson, & Gottman, 1993; Lloyd, 1990), gender socialization (cf. Birns, Cascardi, & Meyer, 1994; Nutt, Chapter 8, this volume; O'Neil & Nadeau, Chapter 7, this volume), sociocultural factors (cf. Sanchez-Hucles & Dutton, Chapter 11, this volume) and historical determinants (cf. Bograd, 1984, 1988; Dobash & Dobash, 1977, 1979; Lesse, 1979), because these are understood to contribute to relational violence.

In this chapter we share one such ecological perspective. It is a *co-construc-tive-developmental framework* for human and systemic growth and adaptation that can be used to organize interrelated individual, interpersonal, and sociologic variables that predispose or trigger the use of relational violence. Basic to this framework is the idea that the interface among individuals, partnerships, families, and larger systems is fundamentally a *cultural exchange process*. That is, individuals are simultaneously influenced by and influence the partnerships, families, and larger systems of which they are a part. The recursive and interdependent nature of this process suggests that individuals construct an understanding of themselves and others vis-à-vis their positions within relational and wider systems over time. Based on these positions, individuals come to understand themselves and their relationships through the selective prescription (suggesting imposition) or ascription (suggesting choice) of family and cultural themes that occur throughout the life span. These views, in turn, affect the ways in which individuals operate and influence partnerships, families, and wider systems. It is our contention that a more comprehensive understanding of the inter-gender relational dimensions of violence toward women can be advanced by taking this entire cultural exchange process into account.

Although ecological theories are helpful in conceptualizing the multiple levels of reality that affect a particular target population, oftentimes these theories fall short when applied to empirical research or clinical practice. Many of these theories fail to provide adequate substance for researchers to determine primary focal points or to design satisfactory methodological tools that will advance theory construction. Additionally, many such theories overwhelm practitioners by providing too broad a terrain of analysis and too many reference points to consider for clinical intervention. For example, consider relational violence in which the current status of ecological positions suggest that relationships where men are violent toward their female partners do not exist in isolation from the intrapersonal factors that each person brings to the partnership (i.e., biology, personality, family of origin, and developmental history), of the interpersonal dynamics generated by the relationship (i.e., balance of power and control, patterns of interaction, and collective meaning-making), or of the wider contextual issues influencing each individual and the partnership (i.e., patriarchy, gender socialization, and status of women). Such factors have been implicated as contributory to the development of relational systems that exhibit physical and psychological violence (cf. Berliner, 1990; Bograd, 1984; Connors & Harway, 1995; Dutton, 1988, 1994; Edleson & Tolman, 1992; Edleson, Eisikovits, Guttmann, & Sela-Amit, 1991; Gardiner & McGrath, 1995; Gutsche & Murray, 1991; Magill, 1989; Weitzman & Dreen, 1982). However, the unique ways individuals and couples experience, interpret, and behave within these relational systems have not yet been explored sufficiently to provide substance to researchers or clinicians (Rigazio-DiGilio, Lanza, & Kunkler, 1994).

The co-constructive-developmental perspective provided in this chapter incorporates the influences of intrapersonal, interpersonal, and wider contextual factors in the development of the relational system. Additionally, the constructs derived from this perspective offer linguistically based, conceptual tools that can be used to explore the beliefs, experiences, and actions of individuals, couples, and wider systems that propel some men to use violence against their female partners. For example, unequal distributions of power, oppressive images of women, and the normative nature of violence in our Western, male-dominated society can be examined within the social relationships that absorb and communicate these ideals and ideas through linguistic channels. As such, we can examine how the oppression of power and violence can take place within the context of these social relationships (cf. Foucault 1988a, 1988b) by understanding and questioning how this absorption and interpersonal communication takes place for partners during the cultural exchange process. In effect, the model provides theoretical constructs that can be used by researchers, theoreticians, and practitioners to describe and intervene at the multiple levels through which relational communication patterns are formed, maintained, or transformed.

This chapter has four objectives. First we provide a brief description of the central tenets undergirding the co-constructive-developmental framework. Second, we demonstrate how the conceptual tools derived from these tenets can be used to operationalize those hypotheses proffered by O'Neil and Harway (Chapter 2, this volume) concerning the inter-gender relational dimensions of partnership violence. Our third objective is to highlight some specific conceptual and empirical tools that can be used to provide alternative perspectives regarding the inter-gender relational dimensions of partnership violence. We do this to demonstrate how one overarching theory—while addressing a broad range of variables associated with relational violence—can be used to examine a particular segment of the cultural exchange process in ways that might stimulate future research. Finally, we offer some possibilities to continue the theoretical and empirical advancement of this co-constructive-developmental perspective on relational violence.

SYSTEMIC COGNITIVE-DEVELOPMENTAL THEORY

Developmental Counseling and Therapy (DCT) (Ivey, 1986, 1991) represents a co-constructive view of individual growth, adaptation, and change. *Systemic Cognitive-Developmental Theory* (SCDT; Rigazio-DiGilio 1993, 1994a, in press a; Rigazio-DiGilio & Ivey 1991, 1993) extends this perspective to relational (i.e., couples and families) and wider contextual (i.e., networks, community, organization, society, and culture) systems. SCDT has demonstrated utility in theory building, research designing, and treatment planning for issues such as systemic therapy (Kunkler & Rigazio-DiGilio, 1994; Rigazio-DiGilio & Ivey, 1997), clinical supervision (Anderson, Rigazio-DiGilio, & Kunkler, 1995; Rigazio-DiGilio & Anderson, 1991, 1994; Rigazio-DiGilio, Daniels, & Ivey, in press), theories of human and systemic development (Ivey & Rigazio-DiGilio, 1991; Kunkler & Rigazio-DiGilio, 1994), multiculturalism (Cheatham et al., 1997; Rigazio-DiGilio & Ivey, 1995), organizational, sociocultural, and sociopolitical evolution (Rigazio-DiGilio, in press b; Rigazio-DiGilio, Anderson, & Kunkler, 1995; Rigazio-DiGilio, Ivey, & Locke, in press), and integrative psychotherapy (Rigazio-DiGilio, 1994a, 1994b; Rigazio-DiGilio, Goncalves, & Ivey, 1996). In this section, the basic assumptions and theoretical constructs derived from SCDT are described and applied to the inter-gender relational hypotheses generated by O'Neil and Harway (Chapter 2, this volume).

The Foundational Assumptions Undergirding SCDT

The developmental theory undergirding SCDT synthesizes linear and hierarchical (Haley, 1973; Kohlberg, 1976; Piaget, 1954), cyclical and relational (Carter & McGoldrick, 1989; Gilligan, 1982), and spiraling (Combrinck-Graham, 1985) theories of human and systemic development within a broad, holistic, and co-constructive framework. It is theorized that, throughout our development, the recursive interaction that occurs between person and environment continually promotes the co-construction of worldviews that, in turn, influence how we approach our world, our life tasks, and our relationships. These worldviews represent a construction of reality (Larner, 1994) and influence the ways individuals and relational systems experience, understand, and function in the world. In the cultural exchange process that occurs over the life span, these worldviews are constantly being modified as we face new developmental tasks and circumstances. We will always face flaws in our ideas of reality, and we need to move to alternative perspectives if we are to continue to grow and adapt.

Four key assumptions provide the foundation upon which SCDT is built.

1. Individual worldviews

2. Collective worldviews

3. Holistic, co-constructive development

4. Nonpathological growth adaptation

Assumption 1: Individuals possess a unique *worldview* that is a natural and logical consequence of their developmental history. This worldview has been forged by genetic and environmental forces. That is, individual worldviews are co-constructed, modified, deconstructed, and reconstructed as individuals interact within particular environments (i.e., the family of origin, the wider community and culture) over their life spans. An individual's worldview can be likened to the primary perceptual filter through which feelings, thoughts, actions, and reactions to physical and social environments are interpreted and expressed. In terms of relational violence, it is postulated that an individual's worldview incorporates a position regarding the use of violence in interaction as a form of communication and power. An examination of the origins and manifestations of this position is a crucial step in understanding how and why violence becomes an acceptable form of expression for particular individuals in relationships.

Assumption 2: As individuals come together to develop a partnership, the resultant system co-constructs a *collective worldview* that influences the partners' behaviors, thoughts, and feelings with each other and with the wider environment. The recursive nature of influence between the partners and between the partners and the outside world generates guiding rules that come to govern what is acceptable and tolerable within the relationship. This collective worldview evolves over time and can be influenced directly, to varying degrees, by either person and by the wider context. Based on this assumption, it is suggested that the level of acceptability and tolerance within this collective worldview for how, when, and by whom violence is expressed must be considered in a systemic examination of relational violence.

Assumption 3: SCDT is based on a *holistic, co-constructive* perspective of human and systemic development. That is, individuals and systems deal with multiple tasks simultaneously (holistic) and in a socially negotiated fashion (co-constructive). In this regard, development occurs within affectual, cognitive, and behavioral domains as we remain involved in dynamic interactions with various environments over time. SCDT does not posit that adaptation happens in an isolated fashion or in a specified, hierarchical sequence. Rather, individuals, systems, and wider networks repeat some or all of their previous developmental phases as they uniquely respond to internal and external demands for change. This assumption leads to the conjecture that individuals and systems that are able to acknowledge various developmental tasks and access multiple resources to navigate their life course will be less likely to experience the use of violence in their relationship.

Assumption 4: Finally, SCDT advocates a *nonpathological* perspective of human and systemic growth and adaptation. This perspective presupposes that individuals and relational systems are logically reacting to their biological and social environments. The utility of labeling individuals, couples, or families as pathological is, therefore, rejected. Under this assumption, couples who manifest violent interactions are reclassified from a pathogenic or deficit perspective to a salutogenic or developmental perspective. They are recognized to be experiencing developmental impasses or delays. These delays are considered to reflect various pathogenic dimensions of an oppressive culture or to reflect the couples' reaction to their position within a dominant societal frame.

Integrating the Four Assumptions

These four assumptions can be used to understand how individuals, relational systems, and wider contexts co-construct worldviews within which violence can occur. Throughout life, demands are placed on individuals and relational systems to adapt to new situations and experiences. The nature, flexibility, and compatibility of individual, relational, and wider contextual worldviews determines the degree to which physical and psychological violence may be used in an attempt to meet these demands. To test this conjecture, the SCDT assumptions are now integrated with the inter-gender relational hypotheses established by O'Neil and Harway (Chapter 2, this volume).

LINKING SCDT ASSUMPTIONS TO THE INTER-GENDER RELATIONAL HYPOTHESES

O'Neil and Harway (1997) have advanced a series of 13 hypotheses that focus on the ecological aspects of relational violence. This section begins to bridge the four SCDT assumptions with the five inter-gender relational hypotheses contained in their overall series. Broad areas for future research focused on the co-constructive-developmental aspects of partnership violence are indicated.

> **Hypothesis 9:** This hypothesis proposes that differentially socialized patterns of communication and separate gender-role cultures contribute to the potential for violence.

It is generally accepted that men and women have been socialized differently (cf. Nutt, Chapter 8, this volume; O'Neil & Nadeau, Chapter 7, this volume). As such, their developmental histories have led them to naturally and logically co-construct significantly different communication patterns in their movement toward growth and adaptation. Communication differences, such as content, focus, methods of disclosure, and concern for product-oriented versus relational-oriented results, are grounded in the socialization processes that both genders experience over time—in their families of origin, families of procreation, and wider sociocultural and sociopolitical environments.

The communication that occurs between partners is clearly a cultural exchange process. SCDT suggests that when these multiple cultures are accounted for within individual and collective worldviews, there is a greater tolerance, flexibility, and resource pool that can be counted on to solve the day-to-day and long-term issues and to learn about and from one another. For example, individuals and partners who know and accept the validity of different gender-based perspectives, resources, and environments—beyond those prescribed by their own cultural and gender mores—will be able to synthesize multiple perspectives along their developmental journey. Conversely, SCDT suggests that individuals in partnerships that are separated by the parameters of each person's cultural and gender-specific dictates may resort to methods of control or submission when attempting to generate a collective worldview. For example, controlling individuals may use psychological or physical violence to modify their partners' worldview to fit their own, to reposition their partners' worldview to a lesser status of importance, or to discount their partners' views altogether. In contrast, submissive individuals may sacrifice their own worldviews to comply with the real or inferred expectations of their partners. In effect, when two individuals cannot understand, enter, and use the world of the other, more frustration and less adaptive communication patterns emerge. Lloyd (1990) empirically substantiated this point, concluding that distressed couples evidence greater levels of anger and verbal attacks and use less negotiation than nondistressed couples do.

> **Hypothesis 10:** This hypothesis proposes that psychological violence between partners can be precursors to physical violence toward women.

SCDT postulates that those who can access a wide range of cognitive, affective, and behavioral resources within their individual or collective worldviews have more options to draw upon when adapting to internal and external demands for development and change. Conversely, those who have limited access to such resources—either because these have been underdeveloped or underused—have less ability to work through these demands for change and manifest more signs of distress. Clinical (Lanza & Kunkler, 1994; Lanza, Rigazio-DiGilio, & Kunkler, 1993, in press; Rigazio-DiGilio, Lanza, & Kunkler, 1994) and empirical (Rigazio-DiGilio & Ivey, 1990) evidence supports these claims.

To begin with, SCDT suggests that individuals or couples who rely on worldviews that promote psychological forms of intimidation and control to maintain a sense of equilibrium demonstrate a propensity toward physical violence during times of stress. Accordingly, SCDT predicts that the potential for moving from psychological to physical violence is higher in the early phases of relationship development or as established couples face significantly different demands for change. In these situations, stress is high and the guidelines of acceptability and tolerability for physical manifestations of violence have not yet been fully articulated. This would be true for individuals in newly developing couples, because they are attempting to integrate the worldview of the other while at the same time maintaining the integrity of their own unique perspective. This also would be true for established couples facing significant normative or non-normative stressors who have not fully developed a broad range of acceptable, nonviolent communication patterns. They too are attempting to integrate alternative perspectives and demands for change while maintaining the integrity of their own previous individual and collective worldviews. In either situation, these couples have yet to form safe and predictable ways to address fears and to negotiate and resolve differences. Their inability to do so leads to an increase in frustration and overwhelms their limited range of expression, oftentimes propelling movement from psychological intimidation to physical violence in an attempt to regain a sense of equilibrium.

Additionally, SCDT hypothesizes that individuals or couples with previously co-constructed worldviews predicated on the belief that control—or submission to control—was a necessary form of adaptation and survival, would move from psychological to physical forms of violence over time. These individuals and couples may begin by relying on a set of repetitive patterns involving negative psychological interactions to direct and influence the relationship. As such, their available range of alternative, nonviolent cognitions and behaviors does not sufficiently develop or is underused. This increases the likelihood that intensified forms of intimidation and submission will be co-constructed, leading toward a propensity for physical forms of control.

> **Hypothesis 11:** This hypothesis proposes that women's fear of men and men's fear of women contribute to the potential for psychological and physical violence in relationships.

It is our contention that fear has the potential to restrict both men's and women's attempts to search for and experiment with underdeveloped or underused resources. Therefore, when fear is a primary force in a relationship, the likelihood of overusing a narrow range of perspectives and options increases. To the extent that this narrow range of options is already based on intimidation, control, or submission, the reaction to the fear may include physical and psychological forms of violence.

The cultural exchange process associated with SCDT suggests that the predominant themes inherent in our patriarchal society have a definite influence on the collective meaning-making processes that occur in couples experiencing psychological and physical violence. Accordingly, these couples tend to adopt co-constructive processes parallel to those used in the dominant sociocultural and sociopolitical contexts. In this regard, the views of the "privileged and powerful male" tend to dominate collective meaning-making. In these situations, men oftentimes resort to controlling actions to minimize feelings of ambiguity, of being overwhelmed, or of losing their sense of self. Their fear of feeling less powerful or powerless in relationships may be a precursor to violence (Finkelhor, 1983), in that they more forcefully impose their views on their partners. On the other hand, women in these situations tend to sacrifice individual views for the sake of the relationship—because they fear both the potential for harm and the loss of the relationship. In this regard, they tend to accommodate to the worldview of their partner. These couples are not able to successfully create a safe environment in which they can practice or master a more mutually negotiated collective worldview.

Clinical investigations using DCT and SCDT (Lanza & Kunkler, 1994; Lanza, Rigazio-DiGilio, & Kunkler, 1993; Rigazio-DiGilio, Lanza, & Kunkler, 1994), have found that—for couples experiencing relational violence—the man's worldview tends to dominate the relationship, predisposing him to use threats and other fear-inducing tactics to maintain a control that may, to him, seem tentative. Partners of such men tend to maintain a silent verbal posture or attempt to finesse, usually unsuccessfully, an extended vision. Although what is observed is an interaction where the woman's voice is silenced, it is often the case that the woman moves through an intrapersonal developmental journey wherein she begins to question her position in the relationship (Wolf-Smith & LaRossa, 1992).

Hypothesis 12: This hypothesis proposes that both sexes' lack of understanding of the other's gender-role socialization experiences contributes to the potential for violence in the relationship.

SCDT suggests that relational violence is more likely to occur for couples whose collective worldview fails to provide options to enter the gender world of the other. In other words, when individuals in a couple lead separate and incompatible lives with different significant others, tasks, roles, rules, and positions, the gap between individual worldviews increases, and the bridge to understanding these worldviews becomes less effective. As such, individual worldviews may become reified and competitive. This decreases the couple's ability to incorporate new, more adaptive cognitions, emotions, and behaviors, and increases the potential for communications based on power, control, and intimidation. The *right perspective*, versus a *shared perspective*, becomes the primary objective for these couples, oftentimes silencing one voice for the sake of the other and for the sake of couple unity. SCDT suggests that the power of socialized differences, increased traditionalization of roles, and the failure to find shared points of connection between individual worldviews increases the likelihood for violence to occur.

Hypothesis 13: The final hypothesis proposes that viewing relational violence in the family of origin increases the possibility of violence toward women in adulthood.

SCDT suggests that individual contributions to a collective worldview are influenced by family-of-origin experiences, which can constrain and govern the range of potential cognitions, emotions, and behaviors available to the couple. For many individuals, images of psychological and physical violence toward women or weaker family members (e.g., children, elderly, and disabled individuals) are salient factors that influence the predominant assumptions that support their individual worldview. These assumptions exert tremendous influence regarding their understanding of physical and psychological violence as an acceptable and tolerable means of control, adaptation, and survival in their relationships. Should these individuals enter a relational environment that does not successfully challenge or confront the basic assumptions underlying their co-constructed individual worldview, they will continue to garner evidence of the appropriateness of physical and psychological violence. As a collective worldview that promotes the continuation of these assumptions is co-constructed, a replication of family-of-origin experiences is possible.

In summary, these five hypotheses provide a broad vista to observe and analyze the effects of socialized gender differences as they relate to the incidence of relational violence. SCDT provides one avenue to operationalize key variables within an integrated, ecological perspective. In the next section, we operationalize these initial thoughts about inter-gender violence using analytic tools basic to SCDT.

OPERATIONALIZING INTER-GENDER-RELATIONAL DIMENSIONS OF VIOLENCE

SCDT provides a set of research and conceptual tools that can be used to explain individual and collective development and meaning-making. We have been using these tools in theory construction (Lanza, Rigazio-DiGilio, & Kunkler, in press; Rigazio-DiGilio, Lanza, & Kunkler, 1994), clinical practice (Lanza & Kunkler, 1994; Lanza, Rigazio-DiGilio, & Kunkler, 1993, 1995), and research (Lanza, Cramer, Kunkler, & Rigazio-DiGilio, 1994) aimed at examining how relationship violence is expressed, maintained, accepted, and extinguished. The SCDT constructs that offer the most explanatory power in terms of relational violence include

1. individual and collective cognitive-developmental orientations;

2. phases of relational development;

3. cognitive-developmental structures;

4. adaption and change processes; and

5. co-constructive transactions.

In describing each of these constructs, specific research areas regarding relational violence are formulated.

Cognitive-Developmental Orientations

The companion models of DCT and SCDT theorize that individuals, human systems, and wider social networks use various *cognitive-developmental orientations* to make meaning along their developmental journey. These orientations are the constituent factors that compose a holistic worldview—that is, we tend to experience, understand, and operate in the world using elements of several different orientations to formulate our worldviews. Based on a metaphorical reinterpretation of neo-Piagetian constructs (*sensorimotor/elemental, concrete/situational, formal/reflective, dialectic/systemic*), these orientations represent different frames of reference that can be accessed to construct multiple perspectives and options for adaptation and change.

Clinical (e.g., Rigazio-DiGilio & Ivey, 1990) and empirical (e.g., Heesacker, Rigazio-DiGilio, Prichard, & Ivey, 1997) evidence shows that cognitive-developmental orientations can be identified reliably in the natural language used by individuals and relational systems, and additionally support two basic DCT/SCDT hypotheses. The first is that adaptive individuals and systems have the ability to receive and experience sensory information (*sensorimotor/elemental*), act predictably in their world (*concrete/situational*), reflect on and analyze self and situations (*formal/reflective*), and critically examine the origins, processes, and outcomes of their interactions (*dialectic/systemic*). The second is that DCT/SCDT questioning strategies can be used to elicit responses within each of these orientations, thereby facilitating broader conceptualizations and options. The first concept is critical in explaining the predisposing and triggering factors of partnership violence. The second highlights the notion that wider contexts do promote individuals and systems to co-construct, deconstruct, and reconstruct their perspectives on issues such as violence.

Using DCT to Categorize Individual Orientations

Each cognitive-developmental orientation offers valuable and alternative ways to navigate through the life span. As such, individuals who can effectively access resources in several orientations have multiple points of reference to draw upon when working through developmental issues. Conversely, individuals who rigidly adhere to one orientation or haphazardly access several orientations have limited access to multiple perspectives and options. This implies a "broader is better" assumption. When individuals access several orientations, they have many adaptive possibilities. However, when they cannot, they are constrained within a narrow range of possibilities.

Although any orientation may have potential influence at any given time or in response to particular situations, it has been found that individuals primarily operate within one predominant orientation in response to specific circumstances (e.g., Rigazio-DiGilio & Ivey, 1990; Rigazio-DiGilio, Lanza, & Kunkler, 1994). If this *predominant orientation* is used in conjunction with other ancillary orientations, then *adaptive resources* are accessed and development is enhanced. However, when this orientation is exclusively used, at the sacrifice of all others, then *constraining resources* are accessed and development is inhibited. Although each orientation offers both adaptive and constraining resources, it is often the case that men who are violent primarily access the constraining resources associated with their predominant orientation. With this in mind, the constraining factors of each orientation (see Table 10.1) are used to define and illustrate how men who rely on violence experience and operate in their worlds.

Using the construct of individual orientations, researchers and practitioners can distinguish among the various worldviews used by people when expressing feelings, thoughts, and behaviors related to violence. For example, both Bill and Jim were remanded to counseling for hitting and pushing their spouses. DCT techniques were used to quickly distinguish critical differences about the worldviews used by Bill and Jim. Note that, although on the surface, both men use the same violent methods of control, the internal experiences and conceptual understandings of each man are radically different.

Bill (operating predominantly from a sensorimotor/elemental orientation) became visibly anxious during conflicts with his partner. He experienced rapid and shallow breathing, felt his heart rate increase, and felt his face redden and his muscles tense. Under increasing stress, he experienced feeling overwhelmed and unable to make sense of the myriad of emotions the situation initiated in him. After hitting his wife and pushing her down, he felt overcome by guilt and remorse.

Jim (operating exclusively within a concrete/situational orientation) did not directly experience his emotions during conflicts with his partner. He viewed his violence as a result of her behavior. "She backed me into a corner. What else could I do? She gave me no choice. She pushed my buttons." Jim experienced his violent "reactions" as justified. His abusive behavior and rationale for that behavior were predictable, linear, and limited. After hitting his wife and pushing her down, he felt no guilt or remorse and had a customary way to minimize his violence and blame his wife.

Research Implications Related to Individual
Cognitive-Developmental Orientations

Individual orientations have been verified empirically as measurable constructs (Rigazio-DiGilio & Ivey, 1990), but their application to relational violence has, thus far, been studied solely from a clinical perspective. Researchers could use the already established methodology to determine if men primarily operating within similar orientations view the buildup and release of aggression in comparable fashions. Such research could advance our understanding of the various ways men who rely on violence understand and operate in their worlds, and could assist us to formulate prevention and treatment options tailored to the differing meaning-making systems of these men. Similarly, the individual orientations of

TABLE 10.1. The Four Individual Cognitive-Developmental Orientations

Sensorimotor/elemental

Individuals who predominantly rely on the *sensorimotor/elemental orientation* tend to be overwhelmed by their sensory experience and affect, and have a limited capacity to distinguish between environmental stimuli and their own emotions. These individuals are prone to impulsive behavior and irrational, disorganized thoughts. Men who exhibit violent tendencies exhibit tangential and circumstantial speech and appear emotionally reactive, highly anxious, and unable to act safely on their feelings. They often report low frustration tolerance, intense levels of anger, profound feelings of guilt, and feelings of inadequacy, inferiority, insecurity, or helplessness. Clinically, they may exhibit depression, delusional jealousy, and paranoia.

"When I get this uptight, the only way to calm down is to break something."

Concrete/situational

Individuals relying predominantly on the *concrete/situational orientation* usually have the capacity to act predictably. However, their behaviors are confined to a narrow range and their linear explanations of the world are limited and inflexible—often seeing issues as either right or wrong. Men who are predisposed toward violence perceive physical and psychological harm as the quickest and only alternative available to them to exert power in a relationship. They appear separate from their emotions and offer only situational descriptions of their feelings. They usually see only one causal explanation for their violence, which most often involves blaming their partner and negating their own responsibility for their actions.

"She knew wearing that would make me jealous, but she still wore it."

Formal/reflective

At a more abstract level, individuals primarily operating within the *formal/reflective orientation* are able to reflect on and analyze their thoughts, feelings, and actions, yet they cannot see or act on the flaws in their reasoning and patterns. Abusive men rely on rationalization, intellectualization, and depersonalization to justify their acts of violence. They seem detached and emotionally unaffected by the consequences of their abuse and lack the ability to translate insight into actions that might illuminate their violent behavior. The patterns that they are aware of often include justifications for the violence, a sense of entitlement, and a view of the world as a struggle for survival.

"I know drinking affects my ability to tolerate her nagging, but I deserve time to unwind with friends."

Dialectic/systemic

Individuals operating primarily within the *dialectic/systemic orientation* are aware of the historical and contextual factors that influence their thoughts, feelings, and actions. They are able to conceive of multiple perspectives and are aware of their beliefs, yet they are unable to alter these beliefs to allow for more adaptive constructions of self and others. Men who are violent use complex and sophisticated reasoning, well embedded in traditional gender roles and power differences, to support the logic justifying their abuse. Their views, which are resistant to change and devoid of emotion, reflect messages of a society that justifies the use of violence against women as being out of their control. These men are far removed from the reality of their abusive actions and from any means to alter their behavior. They may detect flaws in their reasoning, yet they cannot translate these complex thoughts into actions to stop the abuse.

"Men have been reacting this way for centuries. Men in my family have acted this way as far back as I can remember. How can you expect that I can be the one to change all that."

women in abusive relationships could be categorized and correlated to coping styles and communication patterns. These data could assist us in developing treatment options geared to various information processing styles. Another line of research could explore the communication processes that occur between partners with widely discrepant or similar worldviews or who rely on relational violence as a form of expression. Understanding the subtleties of these processes could assist systemic therapists to facilitate more productive lines of communication that lead to common understandings within the couple. Finally, the relationship between individual orientations and the wider culture could identify predisposing environmental influences that mediate the expression of aggression. Similar analyses can be conducted by classifying and analyzing the relationship of collective orientations and relational violence.

Using SCDT to Categorize Collective Cognitive-Developmental Orientations

Relational systems construct *collective cognitive-developmental orientations* as their worlds merge over time. Additionally, they have the potential to access a variety of orientations throughout their developmental journey and in response to specific life tasks. Like individuals, relational systems also approach specific issues from predominant collective orientations. These collective orientations operate at the level of the relationship system, governing couple interactions. This collective orientation may be an amalgamation of each individual's predominant orientation or a representation of the primary orientation of one dominant individual. In most cases of male violence toward female partners, the men's predominant orientation tends to dominate the collective orientation (Lanza & Kunkler, 1994). In some cases, the female's orientation does set the frame for the couple, but men still may engage in violent acts as a way to neutralize the woman's influence over the relational system (Babcock et al., 1993).

Table 10.2 provides descriptions and illustrations of the collective orientations that tend to be present in relational systems experiencing violence. As with Table 10.1, the descriptions portray couples who rely rigidly on one orientation, at the expense of all others.

Using the construct of collective orientations, researchers and practitioners can distinguish among the various worldviews used by couples when expressing feelings, thoughts, and behaviors related to violence. For example, after their arrest, Cynthia and Pat (a couple who rely on the sensorimotor/elemental orientation) could not come to a consensus about how their relationship had gotten out of control. They knew physical abuse had intensified, but could not explain why this was occurring. They were not clear about how to handle economic and parental stresses, making their life seem overwhelming and unpredictable. Both wanted to depend on each other, but neither appeared to have an adaptive way to navigate in their environment. Cynthia wanted reassurance that she would not get

TABLE 10.2. The Four Collective Cognitive-Developmental Orientations

Sensorimotor/elemental

Couples who rely on this orientation are prone to chaotic and impulsive behaviors. Violence often occurs during negative emotional exchanges and tends to be reactive. The concept "hot headed thoughts" (Burns, 1980) typifies the thoughts and emotions that lead to male violence. Conflicts are dominated by emotion at the exclusion of reason and adaptive action. Issues remain unresolved, keeping couples overwhelmed and stuck in their emotions. Couples are incapable of predictable, organized thoughts and behaviors that might interrupt the abusive spiral. After abusive situations, men tend to exhibit remorse and guilt, which women, feeling frightened and isolated, may accept anxiously. Communication lacks clarity and directness, and unresolved ambivalence predominates. Partners feel controlled by stressors and by the behavior of the other.

"We were just trying to figure out what to do is all. And all of a sudden there was a knife and blood. Right in front of the kids! It just got so out of hand."

Concrete/situational

Couples restricted within this orientation rigidly adhere to a predictable range of thoughts, feelings, and actions. Their collective worldview is unyielding and inflexible. Control and violence come to be expected. The findings of Geffner, Mantooth, Franks, and Rao (1989) that violent couples use more "shoulds" and "oughts" are indicative of couples operating within this orientation. Conflicts tend to be resolved through the use of covert, controlling behaviors. Although partners can recount each violent episode, they see each situation as separate, with its own unique cause-and-effect explanation. They do not see the patterns that connect these episodes. After abusive situations, men offer dismissals and excuses, which women may not fully accept or reject.

"When we got in the door, the fighting began. This time, drinking was involved. So, even though we had resolved this issue of jealousy in the past, this time it turned into pushing and shoving."

Formal/reflective

Couples relying on this orientation exhibit an intellectual distance from abusive episodes. Although they can reflect on and recognize the flaws in their interactional patterns, they lack the capacity to challenge the beliefs that permit abuse or to act in meaningful ways to stop violence. They are unable to access resources, implement adaptive behaviors, or co-construct a relationship free of violence. Subsequent to abusive situations, men tend to offer sophisticated justifications, which women tend to accept in their partner's presence, yet may question outside the relationship. The rationalizations used to justify, excuse, or deny violent behavior reported by Wolf-Smith and LaRossa (1992) are suggestive of couples primarily operating within this orientation.

"No matter how hard we try to change the way we discuss our most pressing issues, we always end up in a situation where intimidating comments put an end to the conversation."

Dialectic/systemic

These couples have elaborate understandings of the complex factors undergirding their relational system. Their ability to identify, challenge, and reconstruct their beliefs, along with their capacity to maintain multiple frames of reference, often leaves them confused and unable to act on insight. This can lead to violence due to fears of femininity, and the potential loss of a man's masculinity, control, and power can be overwhelming. Furthermore, messages in the wider environment or in each individual's history may support the use of violence. In effect, even though these couples may have the ability to understand wider historical and contextual influences, they may be caught in an oppressive environment that does not offer effective alternatives for violent behavior. After abusive episodes, men may express a responsibility for and understanding of their violence. Women may voice disapproval and suggestions. The couple tend to be unable to initiate actions based on these discussions.

"Even though this happened in both our families, we were surprised when it erupted in our relationship. The cut-throat nature of our business seems to have entered into the privacy of our home."

hurt, but feared being on her own and, therefore, was comforted by Pat's pleas for support while he tried to change. After their arrest, Richard and Donna (a couple who rely on the concrete/situational orientation) minimized the episode of abuse and blamed the neighbors and the police for adding to their stress by overreacting. Both were calm and apologetic, and asked the caseworker what to say to the judge so that this situation could be put behind them. When asked about other episodes, they reported separate reasons for each incident and did not recognize a pattern of abuse.

Research Implications Related to Collective Cognitive-Developmental Orientations

The construct of collective cognitive-developmental orientations is another dimension that can be useful in explaining how violence manifests itself in couples who operate within different orientations. The implications of the correlations between violent types and categories and collective cognitive-developmental orientations could influence the efficacy of preventive and treatment services.

Phases of Relational Development

Partners co-construct a collective orientation through a recursive and developmental process (Rigazio-DiGilio & Ivey, 1993; Rigazio-DiGilio, Lanza, & Kunkler, 1994). The four phases of relational development are

1. system exploration;

2. system consolidation;

3. system enhancement; and

4. system transformation.

These phases are not limited to a duration of time. In fact, some couples, although they have been together for over 30 years or more, never move beyond the system exploration stage.

1. System Exploration. In this phase, the sensory worlds of individuals merge, as each shares perspectives, emotions, and behaviors. The newly forming relational system is influenced primarily by a unidirectional, diffuse external boundary. That is, at this phase, individuals are quite susceptible to the outside influences of family, friends, and the wider environment. Both individuals are additionally affected by the historical, developmental, and contextual factors each brings to the relationship. Both try to determine the degree to which their own unique historical worldviews (e.g., values, assumptions, predispositions, and beliefs) will survive, as well as the degree to which they will integrate the "world of the other" (Whitaker, 1976). Couples tend to repeat this phase at critical transitional junctures over their life course.

2. System Consolidation. Over time, a couple's repeating experiences evolve into a collective view of the relationship that begins to organize predictable ways of thinking, feeling, and acting. During this phase, the external boundary of the relational system becomes more impermeable so that a collective worldview can begin to crystallize. This worldview then regulates the interactional patterns that have formed around predominant habits, routines, themes, and episodes that emerge during the history of the relationship.

3. System Enhancement. As relational development evolves, partners are able to reflect on and modify their sense of themselves in an open fashion that allows for greater flexibility, but does not disrupt the stability achieved in the system consolidation phase. The relational system's external boundary becomes increasingly permeable and bidirectional as information begins to move more freely in and out of the system. At this point, the relational system is exercising as much, if not more, influence on others (i.e., family, friends, and co-workers), yet is responsive to internal and external demands for change. As this process continues, the players in relational systems may develop an awareness of how their conception of themselves is influenced by historic and sociocultural factors.

4. System Transformation. The ability to challenge historical and contextual influences that allow for novel options in thinking, feeling, and acting is an indication of this phase. During system transformation, the external boundary of the relational system becomes more open to new information from the world outside the couple system. The relational system is able to redefine its rules based on individual, collective, and situational factors. These new data are incorporated into alternative and, hopefully, more adaptive worldviews.

The Relationship Between Developmental Phases and Partnership Violence

The holistic assumption undergirding SCDT suggests that adaptive relational systems repeatedly move through all four phases as they encounter and work through each developmental milestone (e.g., moving in together, getting married, having children, illness, and divorce) and nonnormative event (e.g., the loss of a child, unemployment, and war). Less adaptive systems may become arrested within one phase, and it will be difficult to move through other phases so that the couple can master the tasks related to normative and nonnormative stressors.

Clinical evidence suggests that most couples dealing with relational violence are arrested in either system exploration or system consolidation (Rigazio-DiGilio, Lanza, & Kunkler, 1994). This speculation is consistent with the findings that more violence occurs in relationships that exhibit low marital adjustment, as defined by the individual's perceptions of satisfaction in the marital relationship and the degree of matching between the partner's perceptions (Edelson et al., 1991).

Within the SCDT paradigm, relational violence may be manifested in relationships at the system exploration phase because these couples have not developed strong enough internal bonds to exclude constraining or otherwise damaging influences. These influences may be from their families of origin, significant others, stressful events, or wider environments. Furthermore, these partners have not developed safe, predictable ways to discuss differences and negotiate conflict. Psychological and physical violence may be used as a form of manipulation and control, especially to prevent the intrusion of unfamiliar or threatening worldviews and to regulate patterns of closeness and distance. Because the external boundary of such couples is not firm and the patterns of interaction are not clear, increasing levels of violence may result and be endured. This pattern of expanding violence in exploratory couples is consistent with the findings of O'Leary, Malone, and Tyree (1994), who noted that violence decreases as couples move from dating (system exploration) to marriage (system consolidation). It additionally parallels the work of Lehr and Fitzsimmons (1991), who reported that, contrary to traditional beliefs, violent couples are significantly more disengaged than nonviolent couples. Emphasizing the permeability of boundaries in the system exploration phase is the finding that stressful life events lead to male violence (Kishur, 1989; MacEwen & Barling, 1988; van der Kolk, 1988).

Couples at the system consolidation phase tend to experience violent encounters as part of a predictable pattern involving escalation, blowup, and contrition (cf. Walker, 1984). In these relationships the violent act may be kept secret from the outside world and the reasons for the violence are sometimes kept secret from each partner. The fears that men and women have about loss of self-esteem, increasing levels of alienation, images of abuse in their families of origin, and lack of alternative communication patterns create an envelop around these partnerships that insulates each individual from outside sources of influence and help. Additionally, this enveloping process takes place within the relational system, in that each partner constructs a wall around the self, thereby diminishing the level of adaptive communication within the partnership. Often in these relationships, violence increases in intensity and frequency over time as the pattern becomes more anticipated (Walker, 1979).

Evolving into system enhancement, continued relational development is marked by public acts. These acts can occur outside the relationship (e.g., seeking assistance at a shelter, calling the police, friends, or family, and going for therapy) and between the partners themselves (e.g., refusing to honor the batterer's justifications for violence, striking back in self-defense) (Wolf-Smith & LaRossa, 1992). As outside resources come to bear and couples seek to alter their abusive patterns, the system enhancement phase is fully entered. This is an extremely risky stage, because the violence may increase in an attempt to prevent the woman from "going public" both within and outside the relationship.

During the system transformation phase, the couple may commit to cease the violent behavior or to dissolve the partnership. Although couples in this phase are able to identify and challenge the rules, roles, and assumptions supporting the violence, they may be unable to construct new ways to interact that do not sustain the use of physical or psychological abuse.

Research Implications Related to the Phases of Relational Development

To move research further in this area, the speculation of where, in the developmental process, the more extreme and frequent expressions of violence emanate needs to be corroborated. Similarly, the patterns of violence associated with each phase need to be elaborated. By using the conceptualization of relational development presented here, researchers can explore the relationship between the frequency and intent of psychological and physical violence and the level of relational development achieved by distressed and nondistressed couples. Such research could lead to a clearer definition of couples at risk for violence.

Additionally, social scientists could examine the phase of relational development and the permeability of the boundary between the couple and the wider social milieu. This might help to further understand the connection between acts of violence by men in their relationships and the dispositions toward the use of violence as a form of power in the wider culture.

Categorizing Cognitive-Developmental Structures

According to the developmental theory undergirding DCT and SCDT, individual and collective worldviews are composed of multiple perspectives emanating from some combination of the four cognitive-developmental orientations. That is, individuals and relational systems tend to access various orientations in unique ways to formulate their own distinctive worldview. How individuals and relational systems access particular orientations is operationalized through the construct of *cognitive-developmental structures*. This structure can be categorized by examining two dimensions: (1) the degree of internal organization and (2) the range of movement within and across the four orientations.

SCDT defines four types of cognitive-developmental structures. These are

1. flexible and varied;
2. rigid;
3. diffuse; and
4. underdeveloped.

1. Flexible and Varied Structures. These structures allow access to the resources inherent within all or most of the cognitive-developmental orientations.

This results in individuals being able to access a wide range of thoughts, feelings, and behaviors to meet the demands of internal and external stressors. It is usually the case that the predominant orientation serves as the base and as the point of departure for moving within and among the various orientations. For example, a female whose primary orientation is concrete/situational initially may approach leaving her violent partner by learning new ways to function predictably as a single parent in a new neighborhood, with less money, and with new demands for child care. As she became more adept at day-to-day tasks and routines, she might grieve the loss of her former identity as a wife in an intact family system (sensorimotor/elemental), while also learning to generalize her adaptive behaviors to map out job or career options (formal/reflective). Finally, she may move toward a reconstruction of her own identity based on the transformation that has occurred (dialectic/systemic) in her life and in her position as a single parent within the wider environment.

   2. *Rigid Structures*. These structures represent an overreliance on one orientation, at the sacrifice of accessing resources in any of the others. Individuals and relational systems with rigid structures are limited to the narrow range of thoughts, feelings, and behaviors found within their predominant orientation. For example, although a female who relies exclusively on the sensorimotor/elemental orientation might be able to experience and express distress in a shelter, she may be too overwhelmed by the dramatic changes she would need to make by leaving the relationship to actually begin such steps.

   3. *Diffuse and Underdeveloped Structures*. These types of structures represent weak connections within and among the various orientations. Individuals and relational systems with diffuse or underdeveloped structures respond to the world by moving chaotically within and across less-established orientations, leaving them unable to effectively access competencies in any one orientation. *Diffuse structures* are represented by individuals and relational systems who, by virtue of haphazardly accessing a small subset of resources within several orientations, never fully develop any one orientation. For example, a female leaving her abusive relationship might learn an insufficient set of coping skills (concrete/structural); begin, but not complete the grieving process (sensorimotor/elemental); learn ways to access social service resources in the service of her children, but not in the service of herself (formal/reflective); and successfully transform her identity as a single parent, but not as a single adult, in a wider social environment (dialectic/systemic). *Underdeveloped structures* are represented by individuals and relational systems that have not yet had the opportunity to establish strong foundations in any of the available orientations. For example, when a female first leaves an abusive situation, she needs time to establish foundations in each environment. If she is called upon to access resources not yet developed (i.e., use the legal system as a resource for protection), she may be unable to do so effectively without structured guidance.

The Relationship Between Cognitive-Developmental Structures and Partnership Violence

It is speculated that the flexibility of an individual's or couple's cognitive-developmental structure influences the degree to which violence may be used as a method of social control, relational control, or personal expression. SCDT posits that *rigid* and *diffuse or underdeveloped structures* lead to greater reliance on violent behavior to settle disagreements and to reaffirm differentiated power positions. Several subhypotheses can be derived from this conjecture.

In terms of individuals, men who have *rigid cognitive-developmental structures* that are built upon a justification of violence toward women hold to and generalize this belief with great intensity, tending toward a reification of the assumption. To them, the belief is "reality," and, as such, it is extremely difficult to alter. Gottman et al.'s (1995) research on men whose heart rate decreased during violent episodes suggests the intractability of a rigid cognitive-developmental structure. For such men, violence is seen as a justifiable and routine form of control. For these men, violence is more systematic and deliberate, and is perceived as the only avenue available to express negative experience. In contrast, men who rely on *diffuse* and *underdeveloped structures* are predicted to demonstrate more sporadic violent eruptions. The violence is more reactive and haphazard, and is not perceived as being under their control. Finally, in couples where both partners exhibit highly rigid structures and violence is used, the violent episodes tend to increase in both severity and frequency (Lehr & Fitzsimmons, 1991). Alternatively, when partners in a violent relationship rely on *diffuse* or *underdeveloped* structures, the haphazard and chaotic nature of their lives and communications patterns suggests that the precursors to violence are difficult to predict.

In terms of collective cognitive-developmental structures, couples who manifest *diffuse* or *underdeveloped structures* may lend themselves to greater treatment possibilities because the couple's belief system is not so reified (Rigazio-DiGilio, Lanza, & Kunkler, 1994). Alternatively, couples who operate within a *rigid* collective structure have a narrow and reified range of thoughts, feelings, and behaviors that are more difficult to challenge and alter. Once challenged, these couples have difficulty learning alternative nonviolent behaviors and generalizing new learnings to novel situations.

Research Implications Related to Cognitive-Developmental Structures

Understanding the intensity and potency of individual and collective cognitive-developmental structures that permit violence against women could help differentiate the types of batterers as well as the types of relational systems where violence occurs. This research could lead to alternative typologies of individuals and couples who experience relational violence based on the flexibility and range of movement across the four orientations. The nature of the cognitive-developmental structure addresses how a person or couple might react to the need for adaptation and change. In the next section, we describe how change is viewed from a co-constructive-developmental perspective and how this relates to relational violence.

Adaption and Change Processes

Growth and adaptation are inhibited by or stimulated through the twin processes of *assimilation* and *accommodation*. SCDT postulates that effective adaption and change result from the interaction between assimilation (i.e., how individuals and systems incorporate the environment using preexisting frames of reference) and accommodation (i.e., how individuals and systems alter preexisting frames of reference to incorporate new data; Piaget, 1963). Through the process of *assimilation*, individuals and relational systems incorporate new data from their experience into their extant cognitive-developmental structures. Alternatively, the cognitive-developmental structures of individuals and relational systems are challenged and altered to meet the demands of their circumstances through the process of *accommodation*. A central SCDT hypothesis is that individuals and relational systems capable of balancing the dynamic processes of assimilation and accommodation are better able to negotiate stability and change.

The Relationship Between Adaptation and Change Processes and Partnership Violence

Overreliance on assimilation or accommodation results in developmental impasses or delays. With respect to men's violence toward women, these developmental delays result in individual and collective worldviews that are limited by previous and current experience that reinforces stereotypical beliefs regarding violence, power, and control.

For example, men who are overassimilators distort new information to fit their existing worldview, and use power and control to impose these constructions of reality on their partners (cf. Avis, 1992; Gerber, 1991; Kaufman, 1992). Conversely, men who are overaccommodators experience little difference between themselves and their environment. They are unable to establish a sense of stability in their world. They may be seeking approval or may be overly dependent on their partner for unconditional love (cf. Elbow, 1977). As a result, these men might use violence as an attempt to organize otherwise chaotic experiences (Finkelhor, 1983; Hotaling & Sugarman, 1986).

SCDT speculates that violent symmetrical couples (where both partners are overassimilators or overaccommodators) will exhibit higher levels of violence than violent complimentary couples (overassimilators matched with overaccommodators). This is supported by the work of Cordova, Jacobson, Gottman, Rushe, and Cox (1993), who differentiated distressed partnerships in which men used violence from those in which violence was not perpetrated against women, based on the reciprocal nature of their communication patterns. These researchers found that partners whose communication patterns paralleled each other entered into a negative reciprocal relationship that could tend toward violence.

Research Implications Related to Adaptation and Change Processes

The concepts of assimilation and accommodation can be used to examine the communication patterns within relationships where violence is experienced. This classification scheme can shed new light on the relationship between relational violence and how couples process information during the cultural exchange process that occurs between individuals, relational systems, and wider social networks. The transactional nature of this interaction is explored within the SCDT concept of the co-constructive process.

Co-Constructive Transactions

SCDT posits that the development, maintenance, modification, and transformation of individual and collective worldviews are the result of the co-constructive transactional process that occurs between individuals, relational systems, and wider social networks over time. Individual and collective worldviews are both enhanced and restricted by the intrapersonal, relational, contextual, and developmental factors involved in the ever-present cultural exchange process.

The Relationship Between Co-Constructive
Transactions and Partnership Violence

In relationships where men are violent toward their female partners, the collective worldview can be limited by contextual factors such as the feminization of poverty (Avis, 1988; James & McIntyre, 1983; Lerner, 1987), gender socialization of women (Imber-Black, 1986) and men (Kaufman, 1992), and witnessing or being victim to family-of-origin abuse (Gelles & Straus, 1988; Murphy, Meyers, & O'Leary, 1993; Sonkin, Martin, & Walker, 1985). Langhinrichsen-Rohling, Neidig, and Thorn (1995) found that, in military couples labeled as severely violent, both husbands and wives did not differ in the prevalence of witnessing parental aggression, but that wives were more likely than husbands to report being beaten during childhood. The perpetrator of the violent acts and the severity of these acts within the family of origin also were implicated in the presence of violence in marital relationships. Observation of abuse in the family of origin is a powerful indicator of future relational violence (cf. Hotaling & Sugarman, 1986). Harsh treatment as a child (Simons, Wu, & Conger, 1995) and anxious attachment in childhood (Wallace & Nosko, 1993) also have been implicated.

Economic and competitive issues between men and women within the larger culture also are related to relational violence. Lack of adequate contextual resources (e.g., available, effective, legal, and psychotherapeutic sanctions for men, accessible services and proactive legal responses for women) maintain these restricted worldviews regarding the place and acceptability of violence in relationships (Bograd, 1992). Even when men feel inferior to their partners in terms of economics, decision-making, and communication power, they are more likely to use violence to regain a sense of superiority (Babcock et al., 1993). Levinson's (1989) cross-cultural investigations suggest that "wife beating" is systematically related to aspects of culture, such as a strong cultural emphasis on the use of violence to resolve interpersonal disputes and gender-based economic inequities. In a comprehensive ecological model, these cultural antecedents are not seen as the sole explanation for relational violence (cf. Breines & Gordon, 1983), but rather are considered a necessary, but not a sufficient, factor in predisposing some men to use violence against women.

Research Implications Related to Co-Constructive Transactions

The concept of co-constructive transactions suggests that we attend to issues beyond the individual and the relationship. That is, illogical worldviews that promote the use of violence do not occur solely within an individual or within a relational system. As such, it is incumbent upon researchers and clinicians alike to determine the origins and location of these oppressive worldviews when working in the field of relational violence. Researchers could assist in the operationalization of the ecological variables that support such oppressive behaviors.

USING A CO-CONSTRUCTIVE-DEVELOPMENTAL FRAMEWORK TO ADVANCE THEORY AND RESEARCH

SCDT constructs offer practical tools that can be used to describe the personal, relational, and cultural factors implicated in the expression of aggression toward women in our society. Integrating these constructs with the hypotheses proffered by O'Neil and Harway (Chapter 2, this volume) can begin to advance a comprehensive theory of the inter-gender dimensions of relational violence.

Table 10.3 poses implementing questions, based on SCDT constructs, for each of the five inter-gender relational hypotheses. These questions may be valuable in researching the targeted variables identified in each specific hypothesis. This table is not intended to be exhaustive, but rather to stimulate further ideas about

TABLE 10.3. SCDT Implementing Questions for Research on Inter-Gender Relational Violence

Hypothesis 9: Differentially socialized patterns of communication and separate gender-role cultures contribute to the potential for violence.

Implementing Questions

1. To what degree does the compatibility of the *individual cognitive-developmental orientations* affect the expression of violence in couples? For example, does the frequency or intensity of violence vary with the distance between predominant orientations of the partners?

2. What role does the expression of violence have in the *collective cognitive-developmental orientation* of the couple?

3. How is the image of a man and the image of a women expressed in *individual and collective orientations* different in violent and nonviolent couples?

4. To what degree do the socialized patterns of communication and separate gender-role cultures influence the use of violence at particular *phases of relational development*?

5. Does the use of violence as a form of communication and a manifestation of gender identity differ for perpetrators who have flexible, rigid, diffuse, or underdeveloped *cognitive-developmental structures*?

6. Are overaccommodators or overassimilators more prone to use violence?

7. How closely aligned are individual, collective, and societal worldviews about the use of violence and communication differences between the genders in violent couples?

Hypothesis 10: Psychological violence between partners can be precursors to physical violence toward women.

Implementing Questions

1. Do men who predominantly operate within the *sensorimotor and concrete orientations* manifest more physical forms of violence than men who operate within other orientations?

2. Do men who predominantly operate within the *formal and dialectic orientations* rely on more psychological forms of violence than men who operate within other orientations?

3. Do manifestations of psychological or physical violence correlate with the male's *cognitive developmental structure*?

4. Do manifestations of psychological or physical violence correlate with the *collective orientation* or the phase of *relational development* in couples?

5. Does the expression of physical and psychological violence differ for *overaccommodators* or *overassimilators*?

6. In what ways do men who rely on psychological violence find justification for the subjugation of women in our society?

Hypothesis 11: Women's fear of men and men's fear of women contribute to the potential for psychological and physical violence in relationships

Implementing Questions

1. How is fear of the other gender evident in the formation of *individual and collective predominant orientations*?

2. Does fear of the other gender influence the *structure of individual and collective orientations*? For example, does a person who rigidly fears the other gender demonstrate a greater use or expectancy of violence in the relationship?

TABLE 10.3. *(Continued)*

3. Does fear of the other gender affect the level of *accommodation/assimilation* evident in the partnership?

4. In what ways does the wider social milieu reinforce the notion that fear of the other gender is a valuable coping style?

Hypothesis 12: Both sexes' lack of understanding of the other's gender-role socialization experiences contributes to the potential for violence.

Implementing Questions

1. Does the power of socialized differences and failure to find common points of connection between *worldviews* increase the couple's likelihood toward violence?

2. Are couples who become blocked at *system exploration or system consolidation* more prone to manifest violent behavior?

3. Do *rigid and diffuse cognitive-developmental structures* based on a lack of understanding of the other's gender-role socialization experiences increase the propensity for conflict and violence to occur?

4. Do *overassimilators or overaccommodators* demonstrate more lack of understanding of the other's socialization experiences, and is either associated with the expression of violence?

5. To what extent do men's *rigid worldviews* and the wider sociopolitical context establish an environment that precludes the understanding of women's socialization experiences?

Hypothesis 13: Viewing domestic violence in the family of origin increases the possibility of violence toward women in adulthood.

Implementing Questions

1. How does the effect of viewing relational violence in the family of origin affect the formation (e.g., *orientation and structure*) of *predominant individual and collective worldviews*?

2. In what ways does witnessing or experiencing relational violence as a child place developmental inhibitors on the processes of *relational development*?

3. What coping style, *overaccommodating or overassimilating*, was used by the individual who witnessed or experienced violence in his or her family of origin? How is this coping style still evident in the current relationship?

4. What influence do family-of-origin issues exert on a couple's *individual and collective interpretation* of relational violence?

---

how we can investigate the ecological dimensions of relational violence within a co-constructive-developmental framework.

By using the constructs of cognitive-developmental orientations and structures, researchers and clinicians can explore how each member of the couple experiences, interprets, and reacts to the potential and real use of psychological and physical violence. From a relational perspective, constructs that describe collective cognitive-developmental orientations, structures, and phases of system development can be used to elucidate the aspects of a couple's communication and relational patterns that are prone to rely on violence as a part of their interactional process. Examining the style of assimilation and accommodation that each member of a partnership uses to address new environmental and developmental demands also may shed light on situations in which men have a higher propensity to use violence and control as a coping strategy. Finally, the concepts embedded within the co-constructive transaction process could equip researchers with tools that isolate and define how contextual and intergenerational influences trigger the use of violence by some men and not others. Structured interviews and inventories based on the SCDT framework can add a new dimension to the instrumentation used to explore relational violence. Quantitative instruments such as the Conflict Tactics Scale (Straus, 1979), the Sex Role Egalitarianism Scales (Beere, King, Beere, & King, 1984), the Approval of Marital Violence Scale (Saunders, 1980), and the Psychological Violence Scale (Owen & O'Neil, 1992) can be complemented by devices based on SCDT constructs to bring out the historical and current contextual factors that are associated with relational violence.

CONCLUSION

SCDT has been offered as a means to qualitatively explain how violence becomes part of relational systems. This chapter outlines a co-constructive-developmental perspective that provides an alternative explanation for how violence develops and is reinforced within and among individual, relational, and contextual domains. By operationalizing SCDT constructs, researchers can identify, track, and elucidate the dimensions of violence within relational systems. Once operationalized, these models can be translated into policy decisions and treatment programs targeted at intrapersonal, interpersonal, and societal domains. Only by clearly defining the major contributory factors of men's violence toward women, will we be able to decrease the psychological and physical harm to current and future generations.

Macrosocietal, Racial, and Cultural Explanations of Violence Against Women

Introduction

T he overall theories that consider men's violence from a macrosocietal perspective were partially critiqued in Part I. Chapter 11, in
Part V, considers more specifically how macrosocietal, racial, and cultural factors
explain men's violence against women. Janis Sanchez-Hucles and Mary Ann
Dutton address how racial and cultural factors are linked to societal and domestic violence. They suggest that an understanding of men's violence must consider societal, cultural, and individual levels of analysis as well as the interaction of
these three. Sanchez-Hucles and Dutton acknowledge that the use of violence in
our country has historical roots and institutional support through racism, sexism,
and classism. They hypothesize that institutional support for violence sends a
message to everyone that violence is an acceptable part of our society. They indicate that acts of cultural violence are committed by those with power against
those with lesser power. In turn, our society has learned to devalue those with less
power, including women, people of color, and particularly women of color. This
devaluation has made violence toward these groups acceptable. Moreover,
this chapter considers cultural pressures, operant within a variety of ethnic
groups, that relate to men's expression of violence. They also examine how
unemployment, poverty, and undocumented immigration status can affect domestic violence. The authors posit that the interaction of these forces contributes to
the existence of domestic violence. They argue that social, cultural, and racial
factors put ethnic minorities at high risk for both societal and family violence.
Finally, they describe resilience factors that may help protect people of color from
violence.

The Interaction Between Societal Violence and Domestic Violence

Racial and Cultural Factors

JANIS SANCHEZ-HUCLES
MARY ANN DUTTON

The feminist movement of the 1960s has been largely responsible for highlighting the scope and severity of men's violence toward women in the United States (Kanuha, 1994). Although the study of family violence has been adopted across disciplines, to date, little attention has been directed to understanding the racial and cultural dynamics that mediate men's violence toward women for people of color (Asbury, 1987). This omission has occurred for a variety of reasons. First, early analyses of domestic violence relied on individual mental health pathology that ignored or minimized sociopolitical (Ho, 1990) and cultural contexts (Bograd, 1984); second, national survey data, crime statistics, and revictimization statistics do not routinely include data on racial groups ("Report of the Task Force," 1996); and third, even when racial and ethnic minority groups are studied, these groups are usually compared with Eurocentric models of family violence and are pathologized as a consequence.

In addition, Burns (1986) has indicated that in every society, both permissible and impermissible violence exists. In the United States, the most impermissible violence is acted out against European American men, followed by European American women, when the violence is perpetrated by men of color. In this society, violence against people of color is definitely permissible and is most permissible with respect to women of color. Women of color reside at the lowest levels of status in United States society, and as a result, they are more likely to be objectified and marginalized (Sandoval, 1990). As a result of the permissibility of violence toward women of color, there is less of an outcry when these women are victimized, fewer resources to help, and huge gaps and silences with respect to research and practice about how to advance the understanding and prevention of violence against women of color. As an example, many individuals strongly believe that if O. J. Simpson had been accused of battering and murdering an African American rather than a European American female, his case would have received very different attention. In addition, many communities of color have long commented on how rarely violent crimes against people of color are given the same attention in the media or accorded the same consequences by the criminal justice system as crimes against majority members.

This chapter is designed to illuminate the racial and cultural factors that link societal and domestic violence. To accomplish this objective, the factors that mediate men's violence toward women of color are explored. It is hypothesized that men's violence toward women of color can be explained by examining factors at the societal, cultural, and individual levels of analyses, as well as by the interaction of these three levels.

Figure 11.1 shows the individual, societal, and cultural factors that interact to cause both societal and domestic violence. The societal factors are defined as the historical and ongoing patterns of racism, sexism, and classism that have exposed all American families to societywide violence. These include slavery, the attempted genocide of Native Americans, and the brutal treatment of immigrant groups. The pervasive use of violence in this society and its use at the highest levels of authority send a clear signal to the population that violence is an acceptable and integral part of this society and provides the foundation for understanding the tolerance of men's violence toward women.

The violence associated with societal factors is typically practiced by those with power against those with lesser power. As a consequence, norms have developed that devalue women, people of color generally, and women of color specifically, and make violence toward these individuals permissible or without significant consequences. Norms of unequal gender roles, traditions of patriarchy, and the practices of chauvinism and misogyny in societal institutions have served to increase the acceptability of domestic and societal violence in families of color, as well as in majority families.

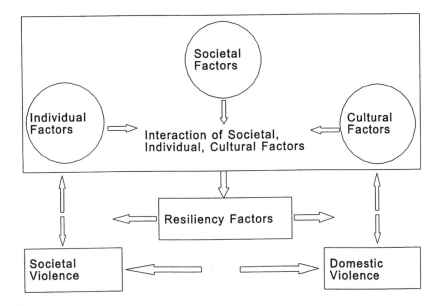

Figure 11.1. A model depicting the factors affecting societal and domestic violence.

A third area of societal factors involves sociocultural and structural barriers. These barriers include prejudice, discrimination, poverty, underemployment and unemployment, inadequate resources, language obstacles, and fear of authority figures, which may intersect to promote family violence.

It is also hypothesized and depicted in Figure 11.1 that cultural factors operate within each ethnic minority group to mediate the expression of violence. Cultural factors are defined as the traditions, norms, philosophies, values, expectations, and behaviors that characterize racial and ethnic groups. These cultural factors relate to a group versus an individual orientation, religious values, gender-role expectations, tensions and strains, cultural stereotypes, and practices in which violence is denied, minimized, or tolerated in ethnic minority communities.

At the individual level, it is hypothesized that the broad array of individual differences in areas such as personality, education, income, employment status, level of acculturation, family dynamics, legal status with respect to citizenship, and the criminal justice system also mediate the expression of domestic and societal violence.

Finally, the interaction of forces at societal, cultural, and individual levels creates a nexus of forces that can precipitate domestic violence. These influences include gender-role tensions and role strain, limited resources and opportunities that can engender poverty and inadequate education, isolation and unsafe neighborhoods, and greater usage of public versus private resources that all too frequently result in insensitive, inadequate, and discriminatory services.

As illustrated in Figure 11.1, many of the factors that expose families of color to domestic violence also place them at high risk for societal violence. Consequently, this discussion also explores the similarities and differences in the social characteristics and sequelae of both domestic and societal violence. Analyses will demonstrate that despite myths to the contrary, the costs of domestic violence rival those of societal violence. An understanding of the interaction between societal and domestic violence is essential to design and implement effective violence prevention programs.

A final consideration is to review the resiliency factors among ethnic minority families that combat the multiple influences that support violence. Resiliency factors are those resources that typically stem from individual differences or cultural traditions that are practiced within racial and ethnic groups. Some of these mediating variables include an emphasis on communal values and extended families, flexible gender roles, religion, and cultural traditions of valuing women.

Figure 11.1 represents the overall scope of the chapter, and each factor is discussed individually and in interaction with the other factors. Three hypotheses are made with respect to domestic and societal violence as follows.

1. Individual, societal, and cultural factors interact to cause both societal and domestic violence toward women of color.

2. The interaction of these factors puts women of color at high risk for both domestic and societal violence.

3. For women of color, domestic and societal violence share common social characteristics with each other, but are also dissimilar from each other.

This chapter addresses the macrosocietal hypotheses mentioned in Chapter 2 (O'Neil & Harway, this volume). Specifically, we address Hypothesis 1, that indicates that battering results from historical patterns in America that glorify men's violence toward women, and Hypothesis 2, that organizational, institutional, and patriarchal structures in society maintain unequal power relationships between men and women that tacitly or directly support domestic oppression and violence against women.

SOCIETAL FACTORS

Current and Historical Patterns of Cultural Violence

Historical analyses of ethnic group families demonstrate that their adaption to this country often was marred by widespread violence. It is hypothesized that the violence that these family members experienced has, in turn, led to internalization and acting out of violence within these families.

Native Americans endured the theft of their land, forced relocations, the murder and rape of their people, and ongoing attempts to replace tribal and cultural traditions with government control. Studies of Native Americans suggest that, historically, women in this culture held major positions of respect equal to men. Domestic violence was virtually absent until Native culture intersected with Western and Christian patriarchal beliefs about women and alcohol, which then resulted in high rates of domestic violence, suicide, and unemployment (Allen, 1986). Berlin (1987) noted that across the 400 different tribes or Indian nations found in the United States, there is a breakdown in families' abilities to transmit traditions, values, and activities. Children often must cope with boarding schools and being far apart from their families.

Theorists assert that the long-term and systemic practices of cultural violence against Native people have led to the internalization of anger and hatred and the acting out of these emotions in the form of violence against each other. Cultural violence refers to the practices of institutional racism, discrimination, subjugation, emotional abuse, and physical violence that is practiced by people of a majority group against those in minority groups. This cultural violence against Native Americans has been directly linked to substandard living conditions, poor housing, government dependency, low life expectancy, malnutrition, alcoholism, and family violence (Asbury, 1993).

Researchers have noted that Native and Aboriginal people often recreate the same control in their families that the government has exercised against them. Specifically, these men often practice the following against their spouses: isolation, economic restrictions, travel limitations, brainwashing, legal sanctions, and manipulation (Pressman, 1994). Meanwhile, women may react to the controls imposed on them by abusing and neglecting their children or by psychological problems including alcoholism, high suicide rates, and depression and anxiety disorders (La Fromboise, Choney, James, & Running Wolf, 1995).

African Americans' historical legacy involves the kidnapping of Africans; the horrors of the transatlantic passage; the attempts to eradicate families, language, and culture; and the rape, violence, and brutality that existed in slavery and continues in the present. As has been the case with Native Americans, it has been hypothesized that the dehumanizing treatment that African Americans have experienced in the wider culture has led to feelings of anger, frustration, and helplessness that can be acted out through acts of violence within the African American community by both men and women (Bulhan, 1985; Fanon, 1963).

Traditional African culture, which is the foundation for today's African American experience, cherished women as strong, independent leaders whose significance was demonstrated by the Asante proverb that reminds us that women give birth to chiefs (Sudarkasa, 1981a, 1981b; Young, 1986). African men held a heritage as providers and protectors of the family who shared decision making with women and elders. This African legacy is still seen in the socialization of

African Americans who exhibit respect toward elders, flexible gender roles, and a strong reliance on extended kin networks (Boyd-Franklin, 1989; Hill, 1972).

Asian Americans are often considered a "model minority" group because of their high educational achievements. This stereotyping minimizes the legacy of violence that many Asian Americans experienced both as they immigrated to the United States and in the internment of Japanese Americans during World War II. The stereotype also overlooks the fact that they are often underemployed and underpaid given their educational credentials (Asbury, 1993).

The "model minority" stereotype disguises the fact that although some subgroups of Asian Americans, such as the Japanese, show high educational attainment, other subgroups do not (Sue & Okazaki, 1990). The majority of Asian Americans are in the lower to middle categories of employment and are not in skilled and supervisory positions (Lai, 1986). In addition, although Asian Americans often show relatively high levels of family income, this is often because large families reside together and several family members contribute to the economic resources (Chen & True, 1995). It is also true that poverty rates are high for many Asian refugee and immigrant families, whereas families who have had several generations of acculturation to U.S. society may enjoy higher incomes.

Asian Americans often experienced the violence of rape and sexual abuse during the process of immigrating to the United States (Mollica, Wyshak, & La Velle, 1987). Many Malaysian, Filipino, and Japanese women came to the United States by way of mail order businesses, which advertised that these women would be subservient and dependent on their husbands. Some Asian American women were abducted and forced into prostitution in the United States (Ho, 1990; Yung, 1991).

It has been theorized that those who have recently immigrated to this country may have internalized the violent and repressive practices of control that they witnessed or experienced in their country of origin (Freire, 1991; Pressman, 1994). These experiences and attitudes are then further shaped by the patriarchal structure in this country that promotes the idea that women should be controlled. If immigrant males feel powerless and unable to fulfill their masculine roles or are confronted with unemployment or underemployment, changing gender roles and an inability to protect their families, the battering of women may result (Pressman, 1994).

It is less clear how Asian American women process the violence and control to which they have been subjected. Due to the strong cultural prohibitions and controls surrounding the lives of Asian American women, perhaps depression is a manifestation of their complex reactions in response to how they are treated and what they have experienced. It is clear that immigrant and refugee women face the triple burden of discrimination due to gender, race, and often their undocumented status (Jang, Lee, & Morello-Frosch, 1991).

Another group of immigrant women that is vulnerable to domestic violence comprises those women who are married to military spouses. These women often suffer from racism, sexism, isolation, frequent moves, limited resources, and language barriers, as well as the anger that is directed at them when they achieve some success in negotiating the educational and economic systems of this country (Ho, 1990). For example, research has suggested that many men find Asian American women attractive as spouses because they expect these women to be docile, submissive, and to remain in their homes. When these women gain educational credentials and income from work outside their homes, these changes are perceived to upset and threaten the balance of control that is held by the men.

Immigrant women are often reluctant to report violence due to fears of deportation, language barriers, and confidentiality issues. When violence is reported by immigrant women, it is often in life-threatening and crisis situations that overcome their resistance to ask for assistance (Lai, 1986). The battered immigrant women provisions of the Violence Against Women Act enacted by the Congress have begun to provide some remedies for these concerns.

Historically, researchers have attempted to explain domestic violence in Hispanic families by noting characteristics such as close-knit families, submissive females, and dominant males. Contemporary research reveals that these families are less rigid and male dominated than has been previously reported and that there is more mutuality in household decision making and responsibilities than was previously believed (Vasquez, 1994).

Hispanics in the United States come from more than 32 countries (Torres, 1991). These families, like Asian American families, reflect a vast diversity of immigration experiences. Although some families were able to immigrate and retain their educational and socioeconomic status, Hispanics as a group, like African Americans and Native Americans, have a high percentage of families in poverty who have not achieved the same life expectancy and educational attainment as European Americans.

Sociocultural and Structural Barriers

Culture can be understood as the way a group meets basic psychological and biological needs and includes values, norms, beliefs, attitudes, and traditions (Hill, Soriano, Chen, & La Framboise, 1995; Pinderhughes, 1989). Sociocultural barriers and inequities, such as prejudice and discrimination, underemployment and unemployment, poverty, poor resources and access to services, all may interact to promote family violence. Specifically, sociocultural barriers combine to prevent families of color from achieving their basic psychological and biological needs and predispose men of color to express their rage and frustration against the safe targets of women, rather than toward societal representatives of prejudice and oppression. Structural barriers such as language and fear of authority figures in turn may exacerbate violence when it prevents ethnic minorities from seeking and receiving adequate assistance ("Report of the Task Force," 1996).

Although domestic violence is found across all income levels and racial ethnic groups, poverty has been indicated as a risk factor for violence. When higher rates of violence are found for ethnic minorities, it appears that it is social and economic inequalities, not ethnicity, that makes these ethnic minority families more prone to violence ("Violence and Youth Report," 1993). Rates of poverty are high in all ethnic minority groups, with 15% of nonminority children living in poverty as compared with 38% Hispanic, 44% Asian and Pacific Islander, 45% African American, and 90% Native American.

It is important to note, however, that ethnic minorities and lower-income individuals are overreported in the violence data because they are more likely to seek assistance from public versus private resources. Public assistance sources are more likely to report violence than are private caregivers, who have more difficulty believing and reporting that their higher-income clientele may be involved in violence and who may have a greater investment in protecting them from disclosure of this information (Lockhart, 1985; Staples, 1976; Strauss, Gelles, & Steinmetz, 1980). Root (1996) reflected that socioeconomic status relegates domestic violence in communities of color to mythical proportions, whereas it renders violence to near invisibility in majority families with greater financial and other tangible resources.

Ethnic minority women are disproportionately found in poverty (White, 1990) and are at high risk for being battered, as well as for being victimized by all types of violence. These families are vulnerable to violence because they often live in high-crime areas and are without the economic resources that would allow them to live in safer environments. In addition, ethnic minority families have disproportionate numbers of single-mother homes where the annual household incomes are from $12,000 to $15,000, which is less than that found in Anglo American families (Asbury, 1993).

Specific data on the battering of ethnic minority women are sparse, with more information available on African American women than on other groups (Root, 1996). An ethnographic examination of battering in African American families has revealed that fewer upper-class women experience abuse than lower-income women, but those upper-income women who were abused experienced a higher number of incidents of abuse. African American women who witnessed their fathers' violence toward their mothers proved to be at higher risk for abuse than those who did not (Lockhart & White, 1989).

Sorensen and Telles (1991) found that Mexican-born Mexican Americans had lower rates of battering than did other Mexican Americans. When compared with European Americans and African Americans, Hispanic women report longer time periods for their abuse. This may be related to the finding that Hispanic women marry at a younger age than do women of other groups, have more children, fewer financial resources, and less education, and, due to their financial dependence, they are less likely to leave relationships than are African American and European American women (Koss et al., 1994). Strauss and Smith (1980) also cited economic deprivation, youthfulness, and urban residence as risk factors for Latinas with respect to battering.

Perhaps less is known about the incidence and prevalence of battering in Native American women than in other ethnic minority groups. In addition to problems of underreporting, there are problems with classifying race accurately, collecting data systematically on a national scale, and including both on- and off- reservation information (Yung & Hammond, 1994). Allen (1986) has asserted that domestic violence is rapidly growing based on informal data from tribes. LaFromboise et al. (1995) reported that in 1982, 38% of Native American women sought assistance due to violence. A particularly frightening finding in one study showed that 80% of Native American women across a five-state area had experienced sexual assault (Old Dog Cross as cited by Allen, 1986).

Ho (1990) indicated that little is known about Asian American violence because women of this group seek assistance from public services only rarely. Despite their diversity, many Asian American women share an unwillingness to disgrace their families by admitting that they have been abused or by seeking a divorce, because by engaging in these behaviors they risk social ostracism. Recent studies document that battering does occur in Asian American communities and is often related to immigration and acculturation issues (Rimonte, 1989; Song, 1986).

The Lack of Significant Consequences for Domestic Violence

The literature on abuse suggests that one factor that perpetuates men's violence toward women across racial groups is the lack of significant negative consequences. With respect to women of color, it has been further hypothesized that the severity and lethality of violence toward these women

1. is an expression of the anger and frustration men of color feel as a result of racism and discrimination;

2. reflects the limited resources women of color have in protecting themselves; and

3. illustrates the perception of men of color that they particularly have little to lose by engaging in violence because they a priori enjoy so little status in society (Koss et al., 1994).

CULTURAL FACTORS

Group Versus Individual Orientation

Family violence has flourished in part due to the widespread beliefs that what happens in the family is private, that outsiders should not intervene, and that wives and children are the domain of males (Martin, 1983; "Report of the Task Force," 1996). This public versus private distinction is exacerbated in families of color, who show strong cultural traditions that focus on the welfare of the group rather than on the individual. Ethnic minority cultures often have been described as "face-oriented"; that is, appearance and status with respect to the outside world are important. The extended family, not individual members, is the primary unit to be preserved. "Dirty laundry," such as domestic violence, is something that should be dealt with within the family or tolerated, but it should not be discussed with outsiders.

A significant factor in this turning within to solve problems is the valid suspicion and fear that many ethnic minority families feel with respect to receiving help from societal institutions. Ethnic minority members know that when reports of battering are made to the criminal justice system, ethnic minorities are at risk for incarceration at disproportionate levels, for police maltreatment, and for further victimization from the criminal justice system or helping professions. As a result of police maltreatment toward men, females in ethnic minority communities often tolerate abuse rather than risk a long-term incarceration for the men who batter them or only report the most severe and life-threatening incidents to the criminal justice system (Asbury, 1993).

Ethnic minority women often attribute the abuse they receive to the larger society and not to the men who batter them (Asbury, 1987; "Report of the Task Force," 1996). These women feel that it is their duty to sacrifice themselves to violence and possibly death, rather than to risk losing the financial, emotional, and role support of the male in the family and thereby diminish the family unit. Ethnic minority women also may prefer silence to reporting lest their experience of violence confirm violent stereotypes about their group in society (Allen, 1986). Stereotypes that people of color are violent also serve to perpetuate violence by making service providers less receptive and helpful to victims in need.

The Role of Religion

Many ethnic minority women are taught to have a strong allegiance to their church and religion. This valuing of religious teaching has been adaptive, because, historically, religious institutions have been places for people to show leadership and control and to receive reinforcement for the family unit. Unfortunately, many of these religions have a strong patriarchal foundation, and women receive clear messages that the welfare of the family is more important than their individual well-being (Torres, 1991). They are, therefore, implicitly and explicitly told to tolerate abuse and violence rather than to disrupt the family unit or undermine the authority of men as the "head of the household." Hence, the abuse of women of color continues in many cases because of the tolerance and passivity of religious leaders who fail to use their influence to halt this violence (Ho, 1990; Lai, 1986).

Gender-Role Expectations, Tensions, and Strain

Gelles and Strauss (1988) have profiled one group of male batterers as poor, young, economically unstable, and disappointed with their current standards of living. Males in uncertain economic straits can become threatened if their partners attain higher educational or occupational status, and these tensions can erupt into violence.

Ethnic minority men are constantly compared with Eurocentric models of masculinity that dictate that men should be the primary breadwinners for the family and that they should hold a position of power and control in the family. Frustration and conflict are endemic in many families of color because men typically find themselves unable to attain the same positions of power, authority, prestige, and economic stability that Anglo-American males enjoy as a result of white male privilege.

Historically, African-American women always have worked both within and outside the home. African-American men have, as a consequence, been pathologized as emasculated and irresponsible because of the significant role that these women have played as wage earners. African-American women also have been negatively stereotyped as castrating, overbearing, matriarchal, and worse simply because they have chosen to work to ensure their family's survival when salaries and jobs for men were inadequate.

Cultural traditions for Asian-American and Hispanic women have historically emphasized males playing a more dominant role in family dynamics—at least publicly—whereas women were expected to adopt a more submissive role. Recent analyses of Asian and Hispanic women indicate that in many cases, women in these families play key roles in decision making, especially regarding the care of the home and children (Canino & Canino, 1980; Kim, 1985; Root, 1996; Vasquez, 1994). Across ethnic minority families, women who work appear to be more involved in family decision making (de la Cancela, 1991). Male dominance in households is generally associated with more violence, and egalitarian relationships show the lowest rates of abuse across all racial groups (Strauss, Gelles, & Steinmetz, 1980).

There is evidence, however, for a strong cultural pull for many ethnic minority women to accord their mates deference and to allow their men to be in charge of the household, specifically because these men may have limited opportunities for autonomy and leadership in their work responsibilities and in the larger society. As an example, in traditional Asian culture, women are defined almost exclusively with respect to their spouse and household, and they are expected to be deferential and passive with men and authority figures (Lai, 1986).

It has been hypothesized that in the majority culture, changing gender roles have threatened traditional male domination of women and that men's fears of power loss may precipitate additional violence toward women (O'Neil & Harway, Chapter 2, this volume). As the previous discussion illustrates, the focus for tension in families of color may be related more to efforts to help men fulfill their role as traditional breadwinners and to try to integrate mainstream gender-role expectations with cultural mores and values. Hence, tensions related to imbalances in gender roles long have been an area of volatility for families of color, and their struggles with these issues are more complex because they involve allegiance to both societal and cultural gender-role expectations.

Cultural Stereotypes

Another factor that mediates the battering of women in families of color is cultural stereotypes. Traditional stereotypes depict Asian and Latina women as being dependent, passive, subservient, and expected to please men. These women may internalize these beliefs and, as a result, may then blame themselves when they are abused by believing that they were somehow inadequate and deficient in their response to their partners.

Interestingly, for African American women, stereotypes about them attest to their strength. However, the stresses of being unfavorably compared to Eurocentric beauty standards, being unfairly labeled as promiscuous because of their long-term history of rape, and enduring the fear of not having a mate due to the scarcity and lowered life expectancy of African American men can be internalized so that these women often blame themselves for their own abuse and failure to sustain relationships (Asbury, 1993; Braithwaite, 1981). As an example, a battered African American female explained to one of the authors that when she shared with two African American friends the fact that her spouse had beaten her on several occasions, one friend stated that it was hard to believe that a man could overpower such a strong and assertive woman, whereas another friend simply asked her, "What did you do to provoke him?"

Another cultural tradition that is particularly striking in women of color is that they have been socialized to demonstrate suffering and perseverance. In many Asian and Southeastern Asian cultures, women are expected to be stoic; to suffer in silence so as to demonstrate character, dignity, and the ability to accept one's fate; and to preserve harmony and order in the family (Ho, 1990). For Latinas, the "Marianisma" role is one in which females are deemed to be morally superior to males and to accept whatever befalls them with patience, long suffering, and lack of complaint (Falicov, 1982).

Denial, Minimization, and Tolerance of Violence and Abuse

Ethnic minority women, like other battered women, often minimize and deny escalating violence before they are willing to label this behavior as abuse (Torres, 1991). They are also subject to the cultural myths that all battered women face. These myths, as described by Bograd (1982), include the ideas that battering is rare, that it happens to women who are psychologically disturbed, that women are responsible for their battering, and that battering is somewhat a matter of course for women. As discussed by Bograd (1982), the strong allegiance clinicians, family, friends, the battered, and the batterer pay to these myths makes it more difficult for society to break the cycle of domestic violence.

Individual Factors

Individual factors refer to the individual differences found within ethnic minority groups and families. These individual differences can be reflected in personality, education, income, employment status, level of acculturation, family dynamics, and legal status with respect to citizenship and the criminal justice system. As a result of individual differences, it has been difficult to identify group patterns in domestic violence for specific ethnic minority groups. Analyses of domestic violence in ethnic minority groups is made more complex by the fact that there is so much diversity within groups. African Americans differ with respect to geographical region or origin, Native Americans have distinctive subcultures based on tribal affiliations, and Asian American and Hispanic families come from a variety of countries and continents with diverse languages, histories, cultures, and religions. All ethnic minority families and individuals can vary with respect to their acculturation to the U.S. culture; the status of migration (forced or voluntary); their legal status in this country with respect to citizenship and to the criminal justice system; the generation or years of the family's residence in the United States; and their isolation versus their ability to use social and community resources (Ho, 1990).

Lower levels of education, income, resources, and life expectancy, combined with limited employment options, systemic discrimination and racism, and dangerous neighborhoods, collectively expose many ethnic minority families to both societal and domestic violence. These families live in neighborhoods and communities in which people live desperate lives due to limited resources, and these same problems are played out within their families. Hampton and Yung (1996) have argued that both domestic and societal violence in communities of color result largely from maladaptive responses to social and economic pressures. Hence, these families face stressors on a day-to-day basis that can place them at risk for both domestic and societal violence without the necessary resources to respond adaptively to the pressures that they encounter.

THE INTERACTION OF SOCIETAL, CULTURAL, AND INDIVIDUAL FACTORS

In addition to the direct effect that societal, cultural, and individual factors have on promoting violence in the lives of women of color, these factors also interact with one another to create multiple patterns that increase the potential for violence. When these factors interact, they intensify the vulnerability of women of color and leave these women less able to protect themselves. This section describes how societal, cultural, and individual factors combine to foster and elevate violence in the lives of families of color.

Ritchie (1996) offered an elegant model of how societal, cultural, and individual factors interact and create "gender entrapment" for African American women. Ritchie uses the term *gender entrapment* to describe a complex process in which African American women who are battered become isolated, stigmatized, and emotionally and physically injured, and are unable to marshall the resources to recover and care for themselves and their families through legal means. These women go through periods of denial and shock and are often ignored, stereotyped, and not believed when they reach out to friends and families. As a result, Ritchie argues that these women are virtually forced into illegal and maladaptive coping devices such as prostitution, drug abuse, theft, property damage, and assaults and violence against others. Ritchie's analysis paints a clear portrait of how individual, cultural, and societal forces can interact to galvanize feelings of hopelessness, betrayal, and frustration on the part of battered women to a point where they lead themselves and their loved ones into new arenas of violence and harm.

An interaction of forces can be seen in theories that note how women of color continue to inhabit the lowest levels of power and prestige in a society that is dominated by racism, sexism, and classism (Lerner, 1986; Sandoval, 1990). As a result, women of color can become scapegoats for the anger of those groups who are also oppressed by white men; that is, men of color and white women (Root, 1996). This can be seen in the violence perpetrated by men of color toward women of color and in the slow response of majority women to fight violence and sexism for all women.

de la Cancela (1991) has reported that for many African American and Latina women, sexism has allowed them greater access to jobs than their male partners, although the jobs that these females typically attain are often menial and exploitative. Men of color who do not serve as breadwinners are pathologized, deemed invisible, and are criticized if they absent themselves from the family to allow their families to receive governmental services. Gelles and Strauss (1988) found that men who are unemployed or working part-time were at least twice as likely to engage in battering than were those who were employed full-time.

Several researchers have suggested that when an ethnic minority male is unable to meet the requirements for masculinity established by the dominant society, this man may engage in innovative strategies, such as colorful and stylish self-expression, that can be seen in benign areas such as attire, speech, appearance, attitudes, and behaviors that are designed to convey hypersexuality. These behaviors become menacing, however, when they use bravado, risk taking, and violence as a means to demonstrate power and control (Cazenave, 1981; Taylor, 1981).

Theorists have argued that men of color often join gangs to gain a sense of connection and affirmation that may be missing in their families, to engage in illegal activities that enable them to earn higher incomes than they could achieve legitimately, and to prove their masculinity when avenues open to majority males, such as high salaries, prestigious jobs, or academic excellence, are unobtainable (Majors & Billson, 1992).

RESILIENCY

Resiliency factors reflect resources that protect ethnic minority individuals and families from the risk factors for domestic and societal violence. These factors result from the interaction of both individual differences (such as a belief in survival or a strong faith) and cultural values and practices (e.g., valuing community, harmony, the family, and extended kinship). As an example, research has shown that because of Eurocentric values that stress individuality and autonomy, when extended family members reside with Anglo-American families, tension on the nuclear family seems to promote family violence, whereas for African Americans, living with relatives and developing friendship networks by residing in the same neighborhood over time is correlated with lower levels of domestic violence (Cazenave & Strauss, 1979). In addition, the flexible gender roles that have traditionally characterized African American and Native American families can attenuate pressures to adhere to the more rigid gender roles that are held as standard in Eurocentric families. Although patriarchal religions have contributed to the maintenance of domestic violence, women of color also have indicated that their own spiritual beliefs, practices, and faith also have provided them with the resources to endure difficulties and have, at times, empowered them to leave situations in which they were battered. Many ethnic minority women as well as nonminority women have begun to search their religious and cultural traditions for examples of strong and wise women who were viewed as powerful and in control of their lives, and they have used these women as role models to emulate, rather than religious icons that reinforce patterns of passivity, subservience, and suffering as standard for women.

Unfortunately, little attention has been directed to date to what the factors are that make ethnic minorities who face chronic stressors on a day-to-day basis either more vulnerable or more resilient. General factors that have been cited as protective factors focus on intraindividual factors, parenting, and family supports, and healthy peer, work, school, or other community relationships (Bloom, 1996). It is evident that more work needs to be conducted in the area of resiliency to identify and cultivate those unique situations or variables that prevent or ameliorate violence for ethnic minorities.

COMPARISON BETWEEN DOMESTIC VIOLENCE AND OTHER FORMS OF SOCIETAL VIOLENCE

The paucity of data on ethnic minorities and violence has led to a lack of integration in our understanding of how societal and domestic violence relate to each other. Clearly, many of the same factors that promote domestic violence at the societal, cultural, and individual levels also engender societal violence and place women of color at high risk for both types of violence. Society, however, tends to minimize the costs and consequences associated with domestic violence and focuses instead on societal violence. It is vital that researchers, practitioners, law enforcement officials, and the public in general better understand the interactions between societal and domestic violence to prevent both from occurring. In this section, we compare domestic and other forms of societal violence from the perspective of cultural and other social context factors. Although there are many distinct differences, there are also significant areas of similarity that have not been discussed at great length in the violence literature (Jenkins, 1996).

The range of criminally violent acts referred to as street crime, community violence, youth violence, and gang violence, and conducted by persons against a nonintimate (e.g., robbery and theft, simple and aggravated assault and battery, rape, stalking, arson, and homicide) are also perpetrated against intimate partners. Historically, even serious acts of domestic violence were not considered criminal offenses even though, at present, state statutes frequently consider "domestic violence" any act defined under the criminal code when it is committed against an intimate partner. The following is a discussion comparing domestic and other forms of societal violence. This brief analysis is organized along two dimensions: (1) the social characteristics and (2) the sequelae of violence.

The Social Characteristics of Violence

Social characteristics, including the nature of the relationship, gender differences, race, and socioeconomic status, are relevant when comparing domestic and other forms of societal violence. One of the defining differences between domestic violence and other forms of societal violence is the nature of the relationship between the victim and the perpetrator. Domestic violence is generally characterized as violence within an intimate relationship; that is, violence by one marital, cohabitating, or dating partner toward the other. Thus, sexual proprietary interest (Wilson & Daly, 1993) is a major factor that distinguishes the victim and offender relationship in domestic, but not in other forms of societal violence. It is important to note, however, that in many situations of societal violence, the acquaintants involved know each other and actually engage in repeated episodes of violence that escalate much in the same way that domestic violence is often displayed in intimate relationships (Jenkins, 1996).

Victimization patterns based on gender differ for intimate versus other forms of violence. Intimate violence (i.e., spouse, ex-spouse, boy/girlfriend, ex-boy/ girlfriend) accounts for 29% of violent crime toward women, but for only 4% of violent crime toward men (Bachman & Saltzman, 1995). Furthermore, in homicides among intimates, more of the victims are female (60%) than male (Dawson & Langan, 1994).

In contrast, victimization by stranger violence presents a greater risk pattern for men (49% of all violence toward men) than for women (23% of all violence toward women; Bachman & Saltzman, 1995). However, women and men are at more similar risk of violence from acquaintances (40% of all violence toward women vs. 44% toward men; Bachman & Saltzman, 1995). Thus, victims of domestic violence are more likely to be female (Bachman, 1994; Fagan & Browne, 1994), whereas generally victims of other types of violence are more likely to be male (Perkins & Klaus, 1994).

Finally, males are more likely than females to be arrested as perpetrators of all types of violent crime (Dawson & Langan, 1994; Perkins & Klaus, 1994), including domestic violence (Bourg & Stock, 1994). Comparing domestic violence against other forms of societal violence suggests that differences exist beyond gender in the social context of violence. Victimization rates among African American, Hispanic, and non-Hispanic women are similar for intimate violence (Bachman, 1994; Bachman & Saltzman, 1995; Kantor, Jasinski, & Aldarondo, 1994; Lockhart, 1985, 1991), especially when socioeconomic class is taken into account. However, research suggests that racial differences exist for perpetrators of violence toward both strangers and acquaintances (Bachman, 1994; Perkins & Klaus, 1996).

Other social factors have been found to be relevant to the comparison between domestic and other forms of societal violence. Low-income women are more likely than higher-income women to experience intimate violence, whereas rates of violence against women by strangers are evenly distributed across income groups (Bachman & Saltzman, 1995). Separated women are 25 times more likely than married women and 3 times more likely than divorced women to be victimized by an intimate (Bachman & Saltzman, 1995). Furthermore, separated women are almost twice as likely as married women to be victimized by a stranger, but less likely than divorced women (Bachman & Saltzman, 1995).

Compared with nonfamily homicides, spouse homicides less often involve either alcohol use by the defendant at the time of the killing (54.4% vs. 68.0% for spouse vs. nonfamily homicides, respectively) or defendant unemployment (25% vs. 36.6%, respectively), but more often involve a history of mental illness (12.3% vs. 2.7%, respectively; Dawson & Langan, 1994).

In summary, these findings suggest that a number of social characteristics distinguish domestic from other forms of societal violence, including gender of the victim (but not of the perpetrator), ethnic identity of the perpetrator (but not of the victim), and other perpetrator characteristics such as alcohol use, unemployment, mental illness, and victim income level. It is not clear whether these social factors are associated with the rates of occurrence of violence (or victimization) or only the rates of its detection. This information suggests that the social construction of the two forms of violence appears to differ somewhat.

Nevertheless, both domestic and other forms of societal violence share some common social characteristics, including the gender of perpetrators (i.e., increased likelihood of males) and the gender (i.e., female) and marital status (i.e., separated) of female victims. It is also important to note that men are also more likely to be in control of the weapons that are used in both societal and domestic violence and that males are also to a large degree in control of this country's criminal justice and enforcement systems (Jenkins, 1996).

The Sequelae of Violence

Various sequelae of violence against women, including victims' use of police, arrest, injury, and economic costs, are examined next. Victims of domestic and other forms of violence against women are equally likely to report the victimization to police when there is an injury (Bachman & Saltzman, 1995). However, when there is no injury, domestic violence victims are slightly more likely to report to the police (46%) than are female victims of violence by a stranger (42%), another relative (39%), or an acquaintance or friend (33%).

Rates of arrest appear to be proportionally higher for blacks than for whites. Using National Crime Victim Statistics data for the years 1987 through 1992, Bachman and Coker (1995) found that black-on-black (compared with white-on-white) violence was a significant predictor of the likelihood of arrest in domestic violence cases. Similarly, Bourg and Stock (1994) found that arrested black males and females were more likely to be charged with aggravated battery (32% and 84.6%, respectively) versus a less serious crime, than were arrested white males and females (19.5% and 26.3%, respectively). Ethnic minorities also make up a greater proportion of inmates sentenced for a violence offense (Innes & Greenfeld, 1990).

Rates of injury for female victims of domestic violence were greater for violence by an intimate (52%) than by a stranger (20%), an acquaintance or friend (26%), or another relative (38%; Bachman & Saltzman, 1995). No data exist for similar comparisons among males. The economic consequence of domestic violence is estimated to be 15% of the total crime costs (Miller, Cohen, & Wiersema, 1996), more than the proportion of total crime attributed to domestic violence (Bachman, 1994; Perkins & Klaus, 1996).

Jenkins (1996) very eloquently noted that both societal and domestic violence share the following characteristics: silence, the tendency to see perpetrators unidimensionally, and a greater comfort level with seeing crime as perpetrated by unknown strangers rather than people we know or with whom we are related. Both domestic and societal violence could not prosper without the silence, denial, and minimization long practiced by individuals closely involved with this violence, as well as public agencies and criminal justice systems. This silence is perpetuated and rationalized in domestic violence when the perpetrator is glorified for his strengths, such as his breadwinner role or his position of respect, rather than developing a more complex and comprehensive portrait that also includes his battering. In contrast, society and families want to make gang members appear unidimensional as hardened criminals, without integrating the knowledge that these gang members are family members who often provide necessary psychological and financial resources to their families.

Finally, we in society are more comfortable addressing stranger crime. Unfortunately, when crime happens to family members or acquaintances, the victim is still in many cases held responsible, albeit in subtle and often unexpressed ways. "Real" crime is crime that somehow is distal and apart from the complex of normal human relationships. Although the majority of crime is committed by people we know, this knowledge is so threatening that more resources are accorded to the rarer phenomenon of stranger crime. Perhaps society's reluctance to address domestic and societal crime more seriously when the victim and victimizer know each other reflects the knowledge that this crime is more preventable than we are willing to acknowledge, and that our silence is a manifestation of feelings of guilt and responsibility.

In summary, comparisons between the sequelae of domestic and other forms of societal violence among female victims suggest areas of difference as well as similarity. Contrary to the popular assumption that domestic violence is not "real crime," such victimization results in greater injury than other forms of violence against women and proportionally greater economic cost to society. In spite of the lack of ethnic differences found in domestic violence victimization, ethnic differences exist for data pertaining to arrest. Comparison of these findings underscores the notion that the problem of racial discrimination pervades the criminal justice system with regard to domestic as well as other forms of societal violence. Finally, both societal and domestic violence can be regarded in ways that perpetuate this violence by the inappropriate uses of silence, by viewing perpetrators unidimensionally, and by focusing more on stranger crime than crime where the victim and the victimizer know each other.

SUMMARY AND CONCLUSIONS

This discussion of domestic and societal violence has highlighted the factors that are unique to these domains as well as areas of similarity. A review of domestic violence reveals that individual, cultural, and societal elements are implicated. Due to long traditions of racism, limited information is available about the patterns of domestic violence in families of color. Furthermore, the United States society has long adhered to an implicit practice that violence toward women of color is permissible and the consequences of harming these women are minimal. Because the lives of women of color are not as highly valued as those of other groups, men of color correctly recognize that the consequences of harming these women are less than if they were to threaten the well-being of those more valued by society. The United States' tradition of devaluing the lives of women of color is in opposition to the traditions of many ethnic minority cultures, which valued women and treated them with high esteem and respect before these cultures were exposed to Western, patriarchal, and Christian values.

Practices of cultural violence and control that have been perpetrated against people of color become internalized and acted out within these communities. Men tend to act out feelings of self-hatred and limited control in violence toward women, children, and each other, whereas women express their feeling through depression, suicide, substance abuse, and, sometimes, violence. Immigrant individuals must contend with the added stresses of language barriers, isolation, fear of deportation, and individual and societal practices of backlash.

Ethnic minorities have turned inward and learned to rely on each other and their religions for survival. Unfortunately, these adaptive strategies also can prove to be maladaptive when they prevent these individuals from asking for help to end the violence that they are experiencing. The unfair treatment that ethnic minorities receive when they ask for help and the stereotyping and sensationalization of violence in their communities also minimize the probability that ethnic minority members will seek or receive the help that they need.

Structural factors intersect with cultural factors when we consider the effect of gender-role expectations in ethnic minority communities. Men and women are expected to fulfill the gender roles of the majority culture as well as their own ethnic group. The tension maintained by gender-role expectations and the social and economic barriers that ethnic minorities face perpetuate domestic violence in general, and battering in particular.

This overview of societal violence also has highlighted the fact that many of the same factors that place people of color at risk for domestic violence make them more vulnerable to societal violence as well. These factors include racism, discrimination, limited resources, poor educational opportunities, unresponsive community services, poverty, unemployment, underemployment, and fear of further victimization (Jenkins, 1996).

In reviewing the social characteristics of violence, in both societal and domestic violence, the victimizers are predominantly male. In domestic violence, the victims are typically female, but in societal violence, the victims are generally male. Race, marital status, and socioeconomic factors mediate patterns of violence for both societal and domestic violence, but the social contexts in these two types of violence are distinct. Despite stereotypes to the contrary, the costs of domestic violence are greater than those of societal violence with respect to injury to women and economic ramifications. Although there is no evidence of ethnic differences in domestic violence victimization, more ethnic minorities than majority members are arrested and prosecuted.

This discussion has clarified the idea that domestic and societal violence are significant problems in this society and that the factors that mediate their expression in communities of color relate to structural and social barriers. Violence in communities of color will not be ameliorated until the factors supporting this violence are also changed: racism, discrimination, poverty, unemployment, and equal access to educational, health, and other community resources.

In addition, more studies need to be conducted to accurately understand the prevalence, incidence, and risk factors for individuals, families, and communities for all ethnic minority groups. Rather than separating discussions of societal and domestic violence, further investigation should be conducted that illustrates where these areas overlap and where they are distinct.

Finally, we must find strategies to eradicate the practices of silence, viewing perpetrators unidimensionally, and focusing on stranger crime rather than crime involving family members or acquaintances. We must develop models that are more comprehensive and accurate in understanding crime and crime prevention. These models must not blame victims, protect victimizers, or make it comfortable for any of us to abdicate responsibility for preventing crime in either our professional or personal lives.

PART VI

Theoretical Propositions, Revised Multivariate Model of Men's Risk Factors, New Hypotheses, and Preventive Recommendations

Introduction

I n this final part, we summarize each author's critique of our preliminary model presented in Chapter 2. Using the chapter authors'
critiques, 13 theoretical propositions are presented that conceptualize the complexity of men's risk for violence against women. A revised conceptual model is
presented that describes the multiplicity of risk factors and variables related to
men's violence against women. Forty hypotheses about men's risk for violence
are enumerated, and specific variables that could be tested through research are
presented. Risk and protective factors are also discussed in the context of men's
vulnerability and resilience to victimizing women. The chapter and book close
with recommendations for preventing men's violence against women through
greater theory development, research, interventions, and advocacy.

Revised Multivariate Model Explaining Men's Risk Factors for Violence Against Women

Theoretical Propositions, New Hypotheses, and Proactive Recommendations

JAMES M. O'NEIL
MICHELE HARWAY

A lmost daily, those of us who watch the evening news are assaulted by images of the violence that permeates our society. The repetition of the graphic images on our television screens heightens our sense of vulnerability to societal violence and makes us ignore the reality that many more individuals are, in fact, victims of violence in the home rather than outside the home (Gelles & Straus, 1989). Until recently, programs to combat violence against women in general, and domestic violence in particular, were underfunded and few in number. Passage of the Violence Against Women Act has made increased funds available for domestic violence prevention programs.

Title III of the Act has made "a national commitment to condemn crimes motivated by gender in just the same way that we have made a national commitment
to condemn crimes motivated by race or religion." (U.S. Senate Judiciary
Committee, p. 41). This increased sensitivity to violence against women and the
provision of additional funding to limit the ravages imposed by such violence
will help mitigate the problem.

There is still much more work to be done to understand men's violence
against women. The goal of this book has been to address the question, "What
causes men's violence against women?" From our perspective, we need to
understand the multiplicity of risk factors that contribute to men's violence
against women so that we can appropriately target intervention programs for
men and couples. The model presented in Figure 2.1 and Chapter 2 and critiqued in the previous chapters was our attempt to capture the wide range of
factors that explain men's violence against women. Reviewing the intervening chapters has convinced us that existing models, including our own, have
not fully captured the complexity of the factors explaining men's violence
against women. The model presented in Chapter 2 was only a beginning. The
new chapters suggest that our earlier model and hypotheses need to be
revised.

In this final chapter, based on each author's contribution to the book,
we first report on new hypotheses generated about men's violence. Second,
synthesizing the new knowledge generated, we specify 13 theoretical propositions that explain men's violence against women. Third, using these
propositions, we present a new, revised conceptual model that explains the
multiplicity of risk factors and variables that contribute to men's violence
against women. Using this model, we list 40 hypotheses about men's risk for
violence against women. Further, we enumerate specific variables related to
each risk factor that could be tested in research. The revised model, theoretical propositions, and hypotheses are designed to advance research and further
theory development. Fourth, we discuss risk and protective factors as they
predict vulnerability and resilience in men prone to violence against women.
We close the chapter and the book with recommendations to prevent men's
violence against women.

CHAPTER AUTHORS' CONTRIBUTIONS

Each of the chapter authors has provided important input to our thinking about the
factors related to men's violence against women and to the modification of our
original model presented in Chapter 2. All four of the content areas described in
Chapter 2 were expanded considerably by our coauthors. Based on these new
ideas and the critiques of the earlier model, we now propose numerous theoretical

propositions that expand the model and hypotheses originally described in Chapter 2. Thirteen theoretical propositions about men's risk for violence are presented next, along with 40 hypotheses that could be tested in research.

THEORETICAL PROPOSITIONS EXPLAINING MEN'S RISK FACTORS FOR MEN'S VIOLENCE AGAINST WOMEN

From our perspective, the most useful way to revise the original model presented in Chapter 2 is to theorize about the multiple risk factors for men's violence against women. Table 12.1 lists 13 theoretical propositions about men's risks for violence against women. Propositions 1 through 5 represent overall propositions about men's risks for violence against women. These five overall propositions are

TABLE 12.1. Theoretical Propositions Explaining Men's Risk for Violence Against Women

Overall Propositions of Men's Risk Factors

1. Multiple risk factors explaining men's violence against women interact, vary, and overlap in complex ways.

2. Differentiating the predisposing risk factors from the triggering risk factors explains the multiple sources of men's violence against women more fully.

3. Men's risk for violence against women is contextual, situational, and idiosyncratic.

4. Men's risk factors can be identified, which potentially will decrease the probability of violence against women.

5. Future study on the risk factors of men's violence against women needs to be multidisciplinary, interdisciplinary, and collegial.

Specific Propositions of Men's Risk Factors

6. Societal violence, discrimination, and cultural oppression directly affect men's risk for violence against women.

7. Racial, cultural, ethnic, class, age, economic, and sociocultural factors are contextually related to men's risk for violence against women.

8. Power and control issues are critical in explaining men's risk for violence against women.

9. Biological, hormonal, anatomical, neuroanatomical, and cultural and evolutionary factors predispose men to risk factors that can trigger violence against women.

10. Men's and women's socialization, specifically gender-role socialization and conflict, predispose men to risk factors that can trigger men's violence against women.

11. Men's conscious and unconscious psychological processes, particularly cognitive and emotional processing, predispose men to risk factors that can trigger men's violence against women.

12. Psychosocial factors and situations predispose men to risk factors that can trigger men's violence against women.

13. Couples' interactional, relational, systemic, and developmental contexts predispose men to risk factors that can trigger men's violence against women.

discussed first and provide a foundation for our revised model explaining men's risk for violence against women. Propositions 6 through 13 describe specific risk factors of the new model. Propositions 6 through 8 expand the macrosocietal hypotheses presented in Chapter 2, indicating how the overall society contributes to men's risk of violence against women. Proposition 9 focuses on the biological risk factors and adds two new dimensions not discussed earlier. Proposition 10 discusses how socialization factors, particularly gender-role socialization issues, contribute to men's risk for violence against women. Propositions 11 and 12 establish a psychological risk factor and a psychosocial risk factor for men's violence. Both of these propositions represent new content areas not discussed in Chapter 2. Finally, Proposition 13 explains how the relational risk factors are relevant to understanding the interactional, systemic, and developmental issues of men's violence against women.

GENERAL PROPOSITIONS EXPLAINING MEN'S RISK FOR VIOLENCE AGAINST WOMEN

Proposition 1: Multiple risk factors explaining men's violence against women interact, vary, and overlap in complex ways.

One important conclusion emerges from our chapter authors' critiques of our earlier hypotheses enumerated in Chapter 2. Most existing models have failed to capture the complexity of risk factors explaining men's violence against women. Like Gelles (in Chapter 4), we know that no single theory adequately explains such a complex phenomenon as men's violence against women. A multiplicity of risk factors that are complexly interrelated represent the greatest explanatory power in answering the question, "What causes men's violence against women?"

The multiplicity of risk factors explaining violence against women is complex and multifaceted. How do the risk factors interact and overlap with one another? For example, how can one adequately separate the effect of the macrosocietal, relational, socialization, psychological, psychosocial, and biological factors? How do the risk factors of society (macrosocietal factors) interact with the rest of the risk factors? How can the effects of the psychological factor be separated from the socialization and biological factors? How do all of these risk factors affect the relational and systemic dynamics of the couple? Furthermore, within the individual man, how do men's cognitions, emotions, and behaviors interact with each other? How does men's unconsciousness affect the other risk factors? These questions represent the sources of "risk variance" for men who are potentially violent. These questions also reflect difficult theoretical issues and pose considerable methodological challenges for researchers.

We struggled with these questions as we pondered a new revised model. There is no simple way to explain the interaction of the risk factors and how they overlap and vary. As researchers, we approached these dilemmas with a methodological perspective. We have conceived of our new model as "sources of risk variance" that could be tested through multiple regression, discriminant function techniques, path analyses, and structural equation modeling. Our criterion variable, accordingly, is whether a man becomes violent toward his partner. The predictor variables are those multiple risk factors that predict men's violent behavior. As with any other theoretical model, however, identifying 100% of the risk variance in predicting violence is impossible. Typically, identifying the variables that account for 40% of the variance is an enviable result. Such a result indicates that the model developed is a powerful one in explaining the phenomenon under consideration. Much more commonly, as little as 10–20% of the variance is accounted for by the identified variables.

We hope that the risk factors, hypotheses, and variables we include in our revised model account for a larger proportion of the variance than in previous models. We also must acknowledge the fact that even when 40% of the variance is captured by any model, that leaves 60% of the variance unaccounted for. Thus, our revised model is likely to leave out unidentified risk factors and variables that could be implicated in men's violence.

Proposition 2: Differentiating the predisposing risk factors from the triggering risk factors more fully explains the multiple sources of men's violence against women.

The understanding of men's violence against women can be enhanced by differentiating between men's predisposition to violence and the actual triggering effects of violence. There is a difference between learning to be violent (being predisposed) and actually committing acts of violence. Predisposing risk factors are redefined as macrosocietal, biological, socialization, psychological, psychosocial, relational, and other background factors that promote the use of violence. These factors increase the probability of men's violence when triggering situations occur. Predisposing factors are not usually sufficient in themselves to cause the outbreak of violence. By contrast, triggering risk factors are those situational cues and events in the immediate experience of the man (and in some cases the couple) that explain men's violence. Triggering factors represent catalysts for the immediate outbreak of a violent episode.

The relationship between predisposition to violence and the actual triggering process is self-evident. Being predisposed to use violence as a relational tool increases the probability of violence being triggered. It is more complicated to explain the circumstances under which predisposition to violence results in an actual violent act. All the chapter authors were asked to address specific hypotheses that focused primarily on predisposing factors, triggering factors, or both kinds of factors. Five of the chapters primarily emphasized predisposing risk factors (Gelles, Chapter 4; Sanchez-Hucles & Dutton, Chapter 11; Silverstein,

Chapter 6; Greene, Chapter 5; and Nutt, Chapter 8). The other four chapters emphasized both predisposing and triggering factors about men's violence (Marin & Russo, Chapter 3; O'Neil & Nadeau,   Chapter 7; Anderson & Schlossberg, Chapter 9; and Rigazio-DiGilio & Lanza, Chapter 10).

In each of these chapters, how predisposition to violence actually leads to the triggering of violence was not described with much specificity. When and under what conditions does the cumulative predisposition to violence become a psychological or physical assault? O'Neil and Nadeau provided the most explicit connection between predisposing and triggering dynamics. In their analysis, they explained how men's sexist gender-role socialization predisposes men to violence and how a breakdown of psychological defenses can actually cause violence against women. We believe that analyzing the relationship between any predisposing risk factors and triggering risk factors can help theoreticians, researchers, and practitioners become more precise in their understanding of the etiology of men's violence against women and its prevention.

Proposition 3: Men's risk for violence against women is contextual, situational, and idiosyncratic.

We assume that violence against women is contextual, idiosyncratic, and highly situational. By this, we mean that men's risk for violence against women is activated by a host of societal, individual, psychological, biological, psychosocial, and relational contexts. These multiple contexts interact with the specific dynamics of the couple. Numerous chapter authors indicated that battering is highly contextual and is affected by a host of variables, both inside the batterer and in his external world. Sanchez-Hucles and Dutton's chapter discusses many historical, societal, cultural, racial, ethnic, and structural contexts to understand men's risk for violence against women. Contexual was also defined by other authors using the following terms: *environmental and social contexts* (Silverstein, Chapter 6), *wider contextual and ecological issues* (Rigazio DiGilio and Lanza, Chapter 10), *social and relational context, multiple levels of contexts, and batterer contexts* (Anderson and Schlossberg, Chapter 9), and *patriarchy, sexism, and stereotypes as contextual factors* (O'Neil & Nadeau, Chapter 7, and Nutt, Chapter 8). Across the chapters, the following contextual risk variables were discussed: culture, patriarchy, sexism, gender-role socialization and stereotypes, male domination and privilege, power, family of origin, poverty, race, class, ethnicity, sexual orientation, discrimination, alcohol and drugs, stress, lack of support, and marital conflict. This is only a partial list of contextual risk variables discussed by our chapter authors. Future models explaining men's violence against women should identify as many contextual and situational risk variables as possible. We will elaborate on these risk variables later in the chapter.

Proposition 4: Men's risk factors can be identified, which potentially will decrease the probability of violence against women.

Understanding men's risk factors is critical to explaining violence against women. Gelles, in Chapter 4, reviews some of these risk factors. In our revised model, we add hypotheses about psychological, socialization, psychosocial, relational, and biological risk factors. Coie et al. (1993) described risk factors as ". . . variables associated with a high probability of onset, greater severity, and longer duration of major mental health problems" (p. 1013). They also indicated that models explaining risk factors include complex interactions among genetic, biomedical, and psychosocial dimensions. In our revised model, we depict a complex interaction among the macrosocietal, relational, psychological, socialization, psychosocial, and biological risk factors for violent men. We also enumerate many risk variables related to men's violence against women that could be tested through research. Finally, later in the chapter, we discuss risk factors in the context of men's resilience and vulnerability to violence against women.

Proposition 5: Future study on the risk factors of men's violence against women needs to be multidisciplinary and collegial.

We support new models that explain men's risk for violence that are multidisciplinary. Given the complexity of men's risk for violence, multiple theories are needed. This implies that sociological, psychological, biological, evolutionary, and family systems and relational theories need to be integrated. In Chapter 1, we indicated that the previous theories on the causes of violence against women sometimes appeared fragmented, rigidly bound by discipline or political agendas, and developed in reaction to the predominant paradigm of each decade. Furthermore, different theoretical and research perspectives have been controversial and have generated negative conflicts between social scientists. These conflicts have sometimes sharply divided colleagues into separate theoretical–political camps. These professional dynamics have not always advanced our understanding of men's risk for violence and have sometimes left viewpoints unexplored or underdeveloped. Strict, discipline-based theories, political thinking, or both, have sometimes characterized the debates, have not always promoted the multivariate explanations of men's violence against women. We think it is time for theoreticians, researchers, and practitioners to move on with more collaborative, constructive, and interdisciplinary dialogues about the causes of men's violence.

These five propositions provide a theoretical foundation for a revised multivariate model to explain men's risk for violence against women. In the next few sections, we present this new model. Furthermore, we discuss Propositions 6 through 13 and generate additional hypotheses about violence against women using the revised multivariate model described in the following section.

A REVISED MULTIVARIATE MODEL EXPLAINING MEN'S RISK FOR VIOLENCE AGAINST WOMEN

Figure 12.1 depicts a revised model of the multiplicity of risk factors that contribute to men's violence against women.

This revised model is based on the chapter authors' critique of our earlier model and our own rethinking of the multiplicity of risk factors that act and interact to explain men's violence against women. The model is more systemic and considers more specifically how the multiple factors relate to each other. Only through research can we verify whether these relationships are valid.

Seven factors are shown in Figure 12.1 that explain men's risks for violence against women. They include factors such as

1. macrosocietal;

2. relational;

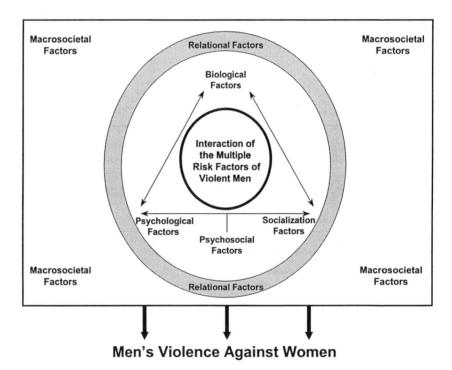

Figure 12.1. Revised multivariate model explaining men's risk factors for violence against women.

3. biological;

4. psychological;

5. socialization;

6. psychosocial; and

7. interacting risk.

First, we operationally define each of these factors and then explain how they relate to each other as depicted in Figure 12.1. In some cases, the factors have been redefined and expand on the earlier definitions found in Chapter 2.

DEFINITION OF MULTIPLE RISK FACTORS IN FIGURE 12.1

The macrosocietal risk factors are all the conditions and values in the larger society that directly or indirectly predispose men to violence against women. More specifically, these factors include all the institutional structures developed during our history and in the present that oppress and discriminate against women. These institutional structures specifically include not only sexist and patriarchal structures, but also the other forms of personal, institutional, and cultural oppression. For example, racism, classism, homophobia and heterosexism, ethnocentrism, ageism, and institutionalized forms of poverty all represent aspects of the macrosocietal factors that can promote violence against women. The macrosocietal risk factors also include how oppressive institutional structures victimize men through racism, classism, ageism, homophobia, and ethnocentrism. When these negative institutional structures are internalized by men, they also can be externalized through violence against women (see Sanchez-Hucles & Dutton, Chapter 11). The relational risk factors are defined as the ongoing interactions and interpersonal patterns between partners that predispose and/or trigger violence against women. These factors represent each partner's personal history, family-of-origin background, and personal affective and cognitive characteristics as they interact in the relational dynamic. The biological risk factors represent a man's entire evolutionary, physiological, neuroanatomical, genetic, and hormonal dimensions that may predispose and/or trigger men's violence against women. The psychological risk factors include men's cognitive and affective processes that result in attitudes, values, and behaviors that predispose and/or trigger violence against women. These factors can be conscious or unconscious and are developed in early childhood, during adolescence, and over a person's life span. The socialization risk factors are defined as the internalization of values, attitudes, and behaviors that predispose men to violence against women. Socialization occurs primarily in the context of learned roles, particularly gender roles in the family, with peers, in schools, and in the larger society.

A complex and ongoing interaction exists between the macrosocietal, socialization, and psychological risk factors. Therefore, we also include a psychosocial risk factor in Figure 12.1 to capture this interaction. Psychosocial theory defines human experience as an interaction of a person's needs and abilities with societal expectations, demands, and restraints (Newman & Newman, 1995). Likewise, men's risk for violence against women can be conceptualized as an interaction between a man's personal, social, and psychological characteristics and societal structures that cause stress, strain, and personal problems. Psychosocial factors are defined as the interaction of a man's overall socialization and psychological processes in the context of the larger society. The social part of psychosocial is all the societal and demographic influences that shape a man's personal socialization. Examples of these factors include race, class, ethnicity, gender-role stereotypes, age, socioeconomic level, occupational level, earning power, and other factors that define a man's relationship with the larger macrosocietal system. In many cases, a man's personal identity is defined by these demographic factors and societal norms. The psychological part of the psychosocial factor is a man's personal experience of these factors. In other words, the social factors have a direct and indirect effect on a man's psychological functioning and well-being. These psychosocial risk factors are particularly important if they are diminishing or destructive, or restrict the man's growth and development. For example, when these factors produce racism, sexism, classism, ethnocentrism, and poverty, the result can be very destructive on a man's self-identity. Men can experience low self-esteem, limited self-efficacy and power, hopelessness, apathy, and sometimes violence against women.

All the factors defined earlier are potential risk factors for men's violence against women. The macrosocietal, biological, psychological, relational, psychosocial, and socialization risk factors represent the diverse sources of men's violence against women. As will be shown later in the chapter, these risk factors can be operationalized as testable hypotheses and as specific variables that explain violence against women. In the next section, we discuss how these multiple risk factors overlap and complexly interact with one another, as depicted in Figure 12.1.

THE INTERACTIVE RELATIONSHIPS OF THE
RISK FACTORS PRESENTED IN FIGURE 12.1

The model presented in Figure 12.1 shows how multiple risk factors interact and are embedded within each other. We describe these risk factors from the global macrosocietal factor (on the outside of Figure 12.1) to men's specific risk factors (on the inside of Figure 12.1). The macrosocietal factor represents the most general factor that influences all the rest of the factors. As can be seen in Figure 12.1, the macrosocietal factors envelop all the rest of the factors. The macrosocietal factors represent a societal context for violence against women. This societal context includes the social, political, and economic realities that women and men face on a daily basis. The relational factor is the next overarching contextual dimension that explains men's violence against women. The relational factors are embedded within this macrosocietal context and, therefore, establish a direct connection between the larger society and people's personal relationships. The relational factors also encircle the biological, psychological, socialization, and psychosocial factors. The three bidirectional arrows in the middle of Figure 12.1 indicate that these factors interact directly with one another. Violence against women results from the effects of men's psychological learning experiences, socialization experiences, and biology within a relationship, all in the context of the larger macrosocietal dimension. All of these factors interact and contribute to the multiplicity of risks for men's violence against women (see the center of Figure 12.1). The macrosocietal, relational, biological, socialization, psychological, and psychosocial risk factors represent the sum total of the causative agents that contribute to men's violence against women.

The chapter authors' critiques of our earlier model and the new ideas in each chapter support the foregoing conceptual model. Using these critiques and our own ideas, we now operationalize Figure 12.1 through further theoretical propositions and hypotheses about the causes and risk factors of men's violence against women. In the next few sections, we return to the specific theoretical Propositions 6 through 13 shown earlier in Table 12.1. These eight propositions discuss how the macrosocietal, socialization, relational, biological, psychological, and psychosocial risk factors contribute to men's violence against women. Immediately after each of these propositions, we present specific hypotheses focused on the question, "What causes men's violence against women?"

MACROSOCIETAL PROPOSITIONS AND HYPOTHESES

The critical macrosocietal question in Chapter 2 was, "How does the larger society contribute to men's violence against women?" Nearly all the authors identify macrosocietal factors as contributors to men's violence against women. The chapter authors have expanded the macrosocietal factors beyond our initial hypothesis that patriarchal, institutional structures cause men's violence against women. The macrosocietal factors discussed by the chapter authors include the following dimensions: societal violence; patriarchal values; gender-role stereotypes; mass media; masculine mystique and value system; male dominance, privilege and entitlement; institutional forms of racism, sexism, classism, and ethnocentrism; discrimination and cultural oppression; subordination of women; economic factors; poverty; and sociobiological and evolutionary factors. All of these macrosocietal concepts have been hypothesized as direct or indirect contributors to men's risk for violence against women. Furthermore, many of these macrosocietal factors have been discussed as directly affecting men's and women's gender-role socialization and couples' systemic and interactional patterns. In the next section, we enumerate three macrosocietal propositions that extend our earlier understanding of the macrosocietal factor presented in Chapter 2.

Macrosocietal Propositions

Proposition 6: Societal violence, discrimination, and cultural oppression directly affect men's risk for violence against women.

We agree with Sanches-Hucles and Dutton and the other chapter authors that violence against women needs to be understood in the context of societal violence and oppression. Violent crime in the larger society has a direct effect on violence in people's private lives. Multiple forms of violence, cultural oppression, and discrimination contribute to violence against women. Macrosocietal factors are now expanded to include all forms of oppression such as racism, sexism, classism, ageism, ethnocentrism, and homophobia and heterosexism. How these institutionalized and personal forms of oppression relate to violence is an essential part of any comprehensive multivariate model. The relationship between violence and oppression in the larger society and violence between partners expands our multivariate model considerably.

Proposition 7: Racial, cultural, ethnic, class, age, economic, and sociocultural factors are contextually related to men's risk for violence against women.

A second important proposition is that racial, cultural, ethnic, class, age, economic, and sociocultural factors represent important contexts in explaining men's violence against women. Sanchez-Hucles and Dutton provide a comprehensive explanation of how cultural, racial, and sociocultural factors contribute to violence against women of color. These factors affect women in different ways, depending on race, class, and ethnicity. Marin and Russo, Rigazio-DiGilio and Lanza and Anderson and Schlossberg also emphasized these important contextual factors in explaining violence against women. Furthermore, they indicate that these factors have been underdeveloped and should be studied systemically. In our multicultural society, any comprehensive model that explains violence against women requires a comprehensive understanding of these sociocultural factors.

Proposition 8: Power and control issues are critical in explaining men's risk for violence against women.

From our review of the chapters, it is clear that power and control dynamics are critical to understanding violence against women. Institutionalized and oppressive structures in society support the subordination of women, resulting in men having power over and control of women. Power at the macrosocietal level includes patriarchal, sexist, racist, ethnocentric, and classist institutional structures that oppress women and men. Power inequities between men and women are observed in nearly every social, political, and economic aspect of our society. Sexist portrayals of women in the media and the economic impoverishment of women are two examples of how the power issues at the macrosocietal level become personal realities in women's lives. Power and control are also directly related to the specific interactions when men dominate and oppress women.

Nearly every chapter included power as a critical variable in explaining men's violence. For example, the following power terminology was used: *power imbalances* (Silverstein, Chapter 6), *inequitable power relationships* (Marin & Russo, Chapter 3), *power conflicts and abuses* (O'Neil & Nadeau, Chapter 7), *power as a contextual variable* (Anderson & Schlossberg, Chapter 9), *balance of power and control* (Rigazio-DiGilio & Lanza, Chapter 10), and *unequal power relationships* (Nutt, Chapter 8). Any new model explaining men's violence against women needs to include how power relates to macrosocietal, relational, psychological, socialization, psychosocial, and biological factors.

Macrosocietal Hypotheses

Table 12.2 enumerates six macrosocietal hypotheses that operationalize the three macrosocietal propositions.

The macrosocietal hypotheses have been expanded considerably to include many more aspects of our larger societal dynamics. Societal violence, culture, oppression, poverty, unemployment, and the media have been added to our original macrosocietal factor. Many women and men are not fully aware of how these larger societal dynamics directly and indirectly influence their daily lives. Many

---

TABLE 12.2. Macrosocietal Hypotheses Explaining Men's Risk for Violence Against Women

Hypothesis 1: Historical patterns in American society have normalized and glorified violence, therefore predisposing men to violence against women.

Hypothesis 2: Patriarchal, racist, classist, homophobic, heterosexist, ethnocentric, and economically oppressive institutional structures interact with historical patterns and predispose men to violence against women.

Hypothesis 3: Sexist institutional structures in society support unequal power relationships between the sexes, thereby predisposing men to violence against women.

Hypothesis 4: Sexism, racism, classism, ethnocentrism, homophobia and heterosexism, and other forms of discrimination predispose oppressed men to violence against women.

Hypothesis 5: Poverty and unemployment predispose men to violence against women.

Hypothesis 6: The media's negative portrayal of women predisposes men to violence against women.

couples are unaware of how these macrosocietal factors shape destructive life events that result in violence. Further theoretical development and analysis of the macrosocietal propositions and hypotheses are needed to understand fully how overall societal values and structures contribute to men's violence against women.

BIOLOGICAL PROPOSITIONS AND HYPOTHESES

The original biological question posed in Chapter 1 was, "Is men's violence against women biologically caused?" The biological, neuroanatomical, genetic, hormonal, and evolutionary factors were found by our chapter authors to have only limited support in explaining men's violence. In fact, as both Marin and Russo (Chapter 3) and Silverstein (Chapter 9) caution, the evidence from biology is weak and much of it is not specific to domestic violence (see Greene, Chapter 5). Moreover, these authors caution against establishing causal connections between biology and men's violence using correlational data. Silverstein rejected biological explanations of men's violence, particularly evolutionary psychology's focus on genetic and natural selection factors. Instead, she invites us to focus on how biology interacts with environmental, cultural, and contextual factors in explaining men's violence. Her analysis adds to the recent and controversial explanations of men's violence from an evolutionary perspective (Archer, 1994c, 1996; Daley & Wilson, 1994). In Chapter 5, Greene indicates that there is partial support for neuroanatomical and biological factors because brain damage contributes to men's violence against women. Research evidence has shown that abnormal brain dysfunction and brain damage is associated with men's violence against women (Rosenbaum & Hoge, 1989; Rosenbaum et al., 1994; Warnken, Rosenbaum, Fletcher, Hoge, & Adelman, 1996).

Biological Proposition

Proposition 9: Biological, hormonal, anatomical, neuroanatomical, and cultural and evolutionary risk factors predispose and trigger men's violence against women.

Biologically based theories and research on men's violence are complex issues and in their earliest stages of development. Numerous chapter authors have indicated that biologically based factors are important to consider in any heuristic exploration of men's violence. Both Gelles (Chapter 4) and Greene (Chapter 5) indicate that researching the biological bases of men's violence holds promise in the future. Consequently, the biological area should not be dismissed, but more fully explored. New areas of biological and physiological research on men's violence are emerging (see Gottman, Jacobson, Rushe, Shortt, Babcock, LaTaillade, & Waltz, 1995) and could open up this area for more comprehensive theory and study.

Biological factors are particularly important when they are studied in the context of the interaction of men's emotional, behavioral, and cognitive functioning. Furthermore, these biological dimensions need to be studied as they operate in the situational and relational aspects of the spousal relationship. Although evidence about how biological factors affect men's violence is currently quite limited, any full model of men's violence needs to include a biologically focused analysis.

Biological Hypotheses

Table 12.3 lists three biological hypotheses focused on men's violence against women.

TABLE 12.3. Biological Hypotheses Explaining Men's Risk for Violence Against Women

Hypothesis 7: Hormonal levels and other neuroanatomical factors predispose and/or trigger men's violence against women.

Hypothesis 8: Men's head injuries and brain dysfunctions predispose and/or trigger violence against women.

Hypothesis 9: Cultural evolution and its interaction with biological factors predispose and/or trigger men's violence against women.

The biological hypotheses also have been expanded to include head injuries and cultural evolution. Even though the biological hypotheses received the least support in our revised model, they no doubt will play a critical role in future research on men's violence. Advances in assessing biological and brain processes now allow researchers more direct access to the bio-psycho-social dynamics of men's violence against women. In the future, we predict that these advances will allow more biological hypotheses to be tested, particularly in the context of the psychological and relational dynamics of men and women.

SOCIALIZATION AND GENDER-ROLE SOCIALIZATION PROPOSITION AND HYPOTHESES

In Chapter 2, the socialization question was, "Do men's gender-role socialization and conflict cause men's violence against women?" Nearly every author discussed how socialization, especially gender-role socialization, was important in explaining men's violence against women. Both O'Neil and Nadeau (Chapter 7) and Nutt (Chapter 8) provide concepts that considerably expand the gender-role socialization hypotheses. In both chapters, men's and women's gender-role socialization is directly associated with the macrosocietal aspects of patriarchy and sexism. Nutt's chapter provides valuable information on how gender-role socialization and sexism predispose women to men's violence. O'Neil and Nadeau explain how men's patriarchal sexism and gender-role socialization act as primary causes of violence against women at both the conscious and unconscious levels.

Socialization and Gender-Role Socialization Proposition

> **Proposition 10:** Men's and women's socialization, specifically gender-role socialization and conflict, predispose men to risk factors that predispose and/or trigger men's violence against women.

How socialization, particularly gender-role socialization, predisposes and triggers violence against women is a critical proposition in any multivariate model. In our revised model, we expand the gender-role socialization factors to include all aspects of socialization including socialization to violence. Furthermore, we include not only men's gender-role socialization, but also aspects of women's gender-role conditioning that may predispose them to violence by men (see Nutt, Chapter 8).

Both men and women in adulthood experience unresolved gender-role conflicts from their earlier relationships with the opposite and the same sex. Nutt puts forward numerous hypotheses about how women are predisposed to men's violence through their gender-role socialization and patterns of gender-role conflict. This socialization creates unequal power bases with men that prohibit setting appropriate boundaries against men's violence. She identifies numerous patterns of gender-role conflict that may predispose women to men's violence including

1. being valued for personal appearance;
2. living through others and sacrificing personal needs;
3. having lower academic and career expectations;
4. exhibiting socialized passivity, learned helplessness, and disempowerment; and
5. experiencing losses of self-esteem.

O'Neil and Nadeau have proposed 10 hypotheses on how men's gender-role socialization can predispose men to violence against women and actually trigger it. Their model provides much more specificity on how men's sexist gender-role socialization predisposes them to violence. Additionally, they provide new concepts (distorted gender-role schemas, fear of femininity and emasculation, gender-role conflict, and self-protective defense mechanisms) that explore how gender-role socialization contributes to men's violence against women. In the context of the macrosocietal factor, they integrate gender-role socialization and psychological factors with the relational dynamics of couples.

Socialization and Gender-Role Socialization Hypotheses

Table 12.4 lists eight socialization hypotheses about men's violence against women. These hypotheses now include overall socialization in addition to our

TABLE 12.4. Socialization and Gender-Role Socialization Hypotheses Explaining Men's Risk for Violence Against Women

Hypothesis 10: Contextual variables in men's gender-role socialization interact with and affect men's predisposition to violence against women. Some of these variables include race, class, ethnicity, age, nationality, sexual orientation, family of origin, and geographic location.

Hypothesis 11: Socialization to dominating and aggressive play in the family of origin predisposes men to violence against women.

Hypothesis 12: Stereotypic and sexist gender-role attitudes and behaviors toward women, learned during gender-role socialization, predispose men to violence against women.

Hypothesis 13: A man's threatened gender-role identity can predispose and/or trigger violence against women.

Hypothesis 14: Distorted gender-role schemas, fear of femininity and emasculation, and other emotions, learned during gender-role socialization, predispose men to violence against women.

Hypothesis 15: Patterns of gender-role conflict (i.e., control, power, homophobia and heterosexism, and restrictive emotionality), learned during gender-role socialization, predispose men to violence against women.

Hypothesis 16: Self-protective defense mechanisms and other defenses, learned during gender-role socialization, can predispose men to violence against women.

Hypothesis 17: Sexist and stereotypic gender-role socialization of women, producing gender-role conflict, can predispose women to become victims of men's violence.

earlier area of gender-role socialization. Contextual variables in socialization are now included as important factors to explain how race, class, ethnicity, and other categories may affect socialization to violence. Family of origin and socialization to play were also added as critical variables to be considered. The revised gender-role hypotheses have much more specificity and more precisely articulate how men's psychological, psychosocial, and gender-role dynamics predispose men to violence or trigger it. The increased number of psychometric measures for assessing masculine ideology and gender-role conflict should allow for more expansive tests of these gender-role hypotheses in the future (O'Neil, Good, & Holmes, 1995; Thompson & Pleck, 1995). Finally, we have added a hypothesis on how women's gender-role socialization may predispose them to become victims of men's violence.

PSYCHOLOGICAL AND PSYCHOSOCIAL PROPOSITIONS AND HYPOTHESES

In our early model presented in Chapter 2, we had no distinct psychological factor or psychosocial factor contributing to men's violence. Men's psychological issues were implied in both the socialization and relational content areas. In our revised model, we include a separate psychological factor and also a psychosocial factor explaining men's violence against women. The critical psychological question is, "How do men's psychological processes, including thinking, feeling, and behaving, result in violence against women?" The critical psychosocial question is, "How do the effects of the larger society interact with men's psychological and social experiences to result in violence against women?"

Psychological Proposition

Proposition 11: Men's conscious and unconscious psychological processes, particularly cognitive and emotional processing, predispose men to risk factors that can trigger men's violence against women.

Nearly all of our chapter authors discuss psychological processes as causative factors when explaining men's violence against women. The psychological process of learning to be violent was expanded considerably by the chapter authors. Most authors discussed how men's cognitive and affective processes result in violent behavior toward women. Gelles (Chapter 4) and Anderson and Schlossberg (Chapter 9) cite research indicating that men's violence toward women can result from boys being abused in their childhood or by observing battering in their family. Experiencing or learning about violence as a family norm appears to be a factor that differentiates some batterers from nonbatterers. From this perspective, learning to be violent has early familial connections for some, but not for all, batterers. Gelles also cites evidence that psychopathology and personality disorders typify some batterers. These data suggest that psychological processes and disturbances play a role in explaining some kinds of violence against women. Nonetheless, these data fail to explain batterers who have no psychopathology or who come from nonviolent family backgrounds. Gelles also cites research on how men's psychological processes of feeling, thinking, and behaving are related to men's violence. For example, the following psychological risk factors have been associated with battering: low self-esteem, depression, unassertativeness, insufficient problem-solving skills, and problems with intimacy.

Numerous chapter authors cite men's cognitive and affective processes as being related to battering. Marin and Russo (Chapter 3) indicate that understanding men's cognitive processes is critical to understanding the emotional experiences that lead to violence. O'Neil and Nadeau (Chapter 7) theorize that men learn distorted gender-role schemas that produce fears about femininity and fears about emasculation. These fears are part of men's gender-role conflict and can activate strong, negative emotions toward women (anger, fear, guilt, shame, loss, and self-protective defenses). Rigazio-DiGilio and Lanza (Chapter 10) describe four cognitive developmental orientations and four cognitive developmental structures that may explain men's violence. In each of the orientations and structures, cognitive and emotional processing are directly related to men's violence against women. Marin and Russo also discuss men's lack of empathy and sensitivity to others as critical psychological dimensions of men's violence.

The psychological dimensions of men's gender-role socialization and conflict were reviewed by O'Neil and Nadeau. They discussed how men's unresolved emotions from gender-role conflict and threats to men's gender-role identity may cause violence toward women. The psychological threat of emasculation and deep negative feelings result in self-protective defense strategies and defense mechanisms with partners. When the defenses no longer work, violence was hypothesized to occur more often. These concepts add unconscious and defensive processes to our psychological understanding of men's violence.

From our perspective, the psychological aspects of battering relate to men's

1. deficits in cognitive processing;
2. deficits in emotional processing;
3. deficits in cognitive and affective processing of gender-role schemas related to masculinity and femininity; and
4. deficits in effective interpersonal communication and problem-solving during spousal conflicts.

These four deficits are complexly interrelated and have not been fully addressed by theoreticians and researchers. These deficit areas result in psychological and psychosocial risk factors for men who are violent against women.

Psychosocial Proposition

Proposition 12: Psychosocial factors and situations predispose men to risk factors that can trigger men's violence against women.

As defined earlier, psychosocial factors imply the effects of men's overall socialization and psychological processes in the context of the larger society. Furthermore, the psychosocial factor includes all the societal and social influences that shape a man's identity in relation to women. Our definition of psychosocial factors included a wide variety of contextual variables in a man's life. These contextual variables include the effects of certain demographic categories (race, class, ethnicity, age, and socioeconomic level) and the effects of the larger society in terms of sexism and patriarchy, racism, classism, ethnocentrism, ageism, and other kinds of personal and institutional oppression. The effects of these psychosocial factors are experienced psychologically by men during socialization in the larger society, in their family, with peers, and specifically in relationship to women. Many of the chapter authors imply directly or indirectly that psychosocial factors affect men's development and potential for violence against women.

Many chapter authors indicate that the psychosocial aspects of patriarchy contribute to men's violence. These authors indicate that men learn patriarchal scripts and values, misogynistic attitudes toward women, expectancies for male entitlement, privilege, and dominance. Silverstein (Chapter 6) hypothesizes that male dominance is the primary factor in men's violence against women. Sanchez-Hucles and Dutton (Chapter 11) specifically discuss the effects of the psychosocial learning from the following societal and cultural factors: prejudice, discrimination, racism, classism, poverty, and unemployment. Gelles (Chapter 4) enumerates and reviews six social factors as risk markers of higher rates of men's violence against women. These social factors include age, unemployment, income, stress and marital conflict, social isolation, and alcohol and drug use. Both Anderson and Schlossberg (Chapter 9) and Rigazio-DiGilio and Lanza (Chapter 10) provide a social and cultural context that has psychosocial implications for men's violence against women. Finally, O'Neil and Nadeau (Chapter 7) and Nutt (Chapter 8) also discuss how gender-role socialization, as a psychosocial process, contributes to men's violence against women.

Psychological and Psychosocial Hypotheses

Table 12.5 enumerates 11 psychological and psychosocial hypotheses that explain men's violence against women. Most of these hypotheses emphasize how men's psychological processes contribute to violence against women. Little is known about batterers' cognitive and emotional processing before the violence, during the violence, and after the violence has occurred. How distorted thinking or intense emotions operate in a man's internal processing are currently not understood. Conscious and unconscious mechanisms of batterers are complicated and largely unknown. Further, how psychosocial factors (discrimination, stress, unemployment, poverty, and isolation) affect emotional and cognitive functioning has been studied infrequently.

RELATIONAL PROPOSITION AND HYPOTHESES

The previous relational question in Chapter 2 was, "Do men's and women's verbal and interpersonal interactions cause men's violence against women?" Numerous chapter authors imply that interactional and relational issues contribute to men's violence. Anderson and Schlossberg's systems perspective and Rigazio-DiGilio and Lanza's cognitive developmental framework expand this content area considerably. Both chapters bring greater attention to the interactional, systemic, and developmental dynamics of the couple at behavioral, cognitive, and emotional levels. Furthermore, this interactional and systemic emphasis focuses on how the couple thinks, feels, and behaves during battering situations. Interactional and systemic paradigms of partner abuse have been controversial, and these chapters could help structure constructive dialogues on this important topic.

TABLE 12.5. Psychological and Psychosocial Hypotheses Explaining Men's Risk for Violence Against Women

---

Hypothesis 18: Observing, experiencing, or learning about violence in the family of origin predisposes men to violence against women.

Hypothesis 19: Deficits and problems in men's cognitive processing predispose and/or trigger men's violence against women.

Hypothesis 20: Deficits and problems in men's emotional processing predispose and/or trigger men's violence against women.

Hypothesis 21: Unconscious psychological processes and defenses predispose and/or trigger men's violence against women.

Hypothesis 22: Unexpressed emotions (fear, anger, shame, guilt, loss, jealousy, and hate) can predispose and/or trigger men's violence against women.

Hypothesis 23: Psychological breakdown of men's self-protective defensive strategies and other defenses predisposes and/or triggers men's violence against women.

Hypothesis 24: Men's power and control problems are salient, psychologically powerful dynamics that predispose and/or trigger men's violence against women.

Hypothesis 25: Men's use of psychological violence predisposes and/or triggers men's violence against women.

Hypothesis 26: Men's psychopathology and personality disorders predispose and/or trigger men's violence against women.

Hypothesis 27: Certain psychological risk factors predispose and/or trigger men's violence against women. Some of these psychological risk factors include low self-esteem, depression, psychopathology, power and control problems, lack of empathy, stress, unassertiveness, problem-solving deficits, intimacy problems, gender-role conflict, homophobia and heterosexism, and witnessing or experiencing violence in the family of origin.

Hypothesis 28: Certain psychosocial risk factors predispose and/or trigger men to violence against women. Some of these psychosocial risk factors include age, unemployment, low income, stress and marital conflict, poverty, low occupational prestige, social isolation, alcohol and drug use or abuse, sexist gender-role socialization, racism, classism, ethnocentrism, and other forms of oppression.

Relational Proposition

> **Proposition 13:** Couples' interactional, relational, systemic, and developmental contexts predispose men to risk factors that can trigger men's violence against women.

We assume that any multivariate model should assess the systemic, developmental, and relational contexts of violence and the specific patterns of interaction that cause battering (see Anderson & Schlossberg, Chapter 9; Rigazio-DiGilio & Lanza, Chapter 10; and O'Neil & Nadeau, Chapter 7). In our preliminary model, as well as in our revised model, we emphasize how couples' interactions may affect relational violence.

We are not suggesting that characteristics of those relationships cause violence. However, we do think it is important to examine what happens in relationships to understand how couples' interactions contribute to the outbreak of violence. This kind of interactional and systemic examination can focus on both the predisposing and triggering aspects of men's violence. Such a conceptualization in no way shifts the burden of blame onto the relationship or on the woman who is a part of that relationship. We believe that the perpetrator of violence is always responsible for the act itself. However, a systemic, interactional, and developmental approach does allow us to examine the relational conditions under which violence might be facilitated or inhibited.

Relational factors have been one of the least studied but most controversial areas for researchers and theorists. Until recently, this was a difficult area to consider because relational analyses were viewed as blaming the victim or excusing men's violence against women. Stevens (1994) pointed out that psychology has been reluctant to get off the "tightrope" that investigates interactional patterns in couples. He encourages violence experts to get off the tightrope to understand better why and how violence occurs. From his perspective, this will ultimately help women protect themselves better. He warns, however, that getting off the tightrope is not without danger: it can be easily misunderstood. Studying interactional dynamics of battering can be interpreted erroneously as blaming the victim or finding excuses for men's violence against women. Even with these dangers, Stevens's domestic violence tightrope is being visited by some scholars (Cahn & Lloyd, 1996). In this volume, the chapter authors have opened up this area for further exploration and discussion (see Anderson & Schlossberg, Chapter 9; O'Neil & Nadeau, Chapter 7; Rigazio-DiGilio & Lanza, Chapter 10).

Relational Hypotheses

Based on this proposition, we enumerate 12 relational and interactional hypotheses about men's violence against women. Table 12.6 presents these hypotheses that focus on men's violence from relational and interactional perspectives. This content area was expanded from 5 original hypotheses to 12 hypotheses describing the relational and interactional aspects of men's violence. These hypotheses focus attention on both partners' behaviors and how the couple's interaction relates to men's violence against women. Social, relational, and systemic contexts are the focus of these hypotheses explaining men's violence. Hypothesized areas of importance include patterns of interactions, unresolved family-of-origin issues, unresolved past problems, different patterns of communication, different cognitive orientations and structures, power and control issues, partners' use of psychological violence, and the stressful life events of couples.

Studying violent relationships has been complicated by the fact that our existing methodologies require us to examine a relationship at a point in time, rather

TABLE 12.6. Relational Hypotheses Explaining Men's Risk for Violence Against Women

Hypothesis 29: Partners' relational and systemic contexts may predispose and/or trigger men's violence against women.

Hypothesis 30: Partners' patterns of interactions and conflicts may predispose and/or trigger men's violence against women.

Hypothesis 31: Partners' unresolved family-of-origin conflicts predispose and/or trigger men's violence against women.

Hypothesis 32: Partners' reexperience of past negative emotions and situations predisposes and/or triggers men's violence against women.

Hypothesis 33: Partners' diverse patterns of interpersonal communication predispose and/or trigger men's acts of violence against women.

Hypothesis 34: Partners' cognitive and developmental orientations and structures may predispose and/or trigger men's violence against women.

Hypothesis 35: Partners' phase of relational development may predispose and/or trigger men's violence against women.

Hypothesis 36: Partners' fear of losing power and control predisposes and/or triggers men's violence against women.

Hypothesis 37: Partners' power and control conflicts predispose and/or trigger violence against women.

Hypothesis 38: Partners' abuses of power predispose and/or trigger men's violence against women.

Hypothesis 39: Partners' psychological violence predisposes and/or triggers men's violence against women.

Hypothesis 40: Partners' stressful events may predispose and/or trigger men's violence against women.

---

than over time. Breunlin, Schwartz, and Mac Kune-Karrer (1992) noted that "[f]amilies transact their business in real time by emitting a stream of behavior . . . some of these behaviors appear to repeat themselves over time and to be related to one another . . . preselection of sequences on the basis of a model often limits the therapist's field of vision and creates blind spots" (pp. 91–92). Breunlin et al. discussed the limitations of selecting just a sequence of the family's interactions during a therapeutic assessment. The same limitation exists when assessing sequences of interaction with violent couples. In fact, there are four classes of sequences that are useful for relational therapists, as well as for relational researchers to consider. Breunlin et al. labeled these sequences as

1. S1, "relatively brief sequences of face-to-face interaction" (p. 93);

2. S2, "aspects of the family's routine and periods that range from one day to a week" (p. 93);

3. S3, "the ebb and flow of some condition or problem in the family and periods ranging from several weeks to a year" (pp. 93–94); and

4. S4, "transgenerational sequences, wherein events occur from one generation to the next." (p. 94).

Couples experiencing relationship violence need to be assessed in terms of whether they are experiencing S1, S2, S3, or S4 sequences. The sequences may represent interactions in which violence is triggered by a specific behavior demonstrated by the partner. Much of the discussion about whether the victim is responsible for a given man's violence presupposes that some behavior on the women's part is the trigger for the man's violent behavior. Jacobsen, Gottman, Waltz, Rushe, and Babcock (1994) have demonstrated quite convincingly that there is no specific behavior that the victim exhibits that is responsible for a man's abusive behavior. In fact, men who are abusive seem to behave in such a manner regardless of whether the recipient is placating or provoking. However, examining S2, S3, and S4 sequences may explain what aspects of the relationship might contribute to a man's abusive behavior. Looking at what each partner brings to the relationship in terms of transgenerational history (S4), examining the history of interaction of the partners with each other (S3), and looking at how they routinely interact (S2) may help us understand better the extent to which relational factors are involved in men's violence against women. As we indicated earlier, however, our examination of relational factors in no way absolves a violent individual from the responsibility for the violence.

MEN'S RISK AND PROTECTIVE FACTORS AND THEIR RELATIONSHIP TO VULNERABILITY AND RESILIENCE TO VIOLENCE

In the model just described, we concentrated on identifying the risk factors that might contribute to men's violence against women. The 40 hypotheses imply that predicting men's violence can be improved by understanding the biological, socialization, psychological, psychosocial, relational, and macrosocietal factors. The predictability of men's violence varies widely depending on the situation, the man, the couple's dynamics, and the factors implied in our multivariate model. Multivariate predictions help us understand the functioning of groups of people, but not necessarily how single individuals think and behave. All the risk factors imply is that the individual man's vulnerability for violence can be assessed. This vulnerability can be predicted by the number of risk factors and their interactions. Vulnerability is also affected by exposure to counterbalancing protective factors in the man's life. These protective factors include a man's personal assets, supports in the environment, and his capacity to be resilient.

Figure 12.2 provides a visual representation of how men's risk factors relate to protective factors and men's resilience and vulnerability to violence against women.

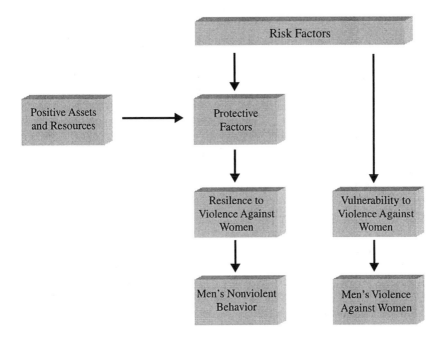

Figure 12.2. The impact of protective factors on men's risk for violence.

Figure 12.2 depicts two separate outcomes of men's risk for violence. Although the figure represents a rather simple idea, it is one that is nonetheless an important part of any discussion of men's risk for violence. On the left side of the diagram, the risk factors are shown to be mediated by men's positive assets and resources that serve as protective factors. These protective factors result in men's resilience to violence against women and in nonviolent behavior. On the right side of Figure 12.2, men's risk factors are shown without positive assets and resources and in the absence of protective factors. Without the protective factors, men's vulnerability to violence increases and can result in violence against women. The concepts in Figure 12.2 are explained more fully in the following paragraphs.

The positive counterparts to men's risk factors are men's assets and personal resources (Masten, 1994). Assets include personal characteristics such as high intelligence or exceptional talent, high socioeconomic status, physical attractiveness, self-efficacy, and loving parents. Not every man with these assets and resources is invulnerable to risk. How do individual men use their assets to counter the risk of violence? Simply stated, men counter risk for violence when they convert their positive assets and resources into protective factors. Cohler (1987) described the process of using one's assets and transforming them into protective factors as "the capacity to maintain feelings of personal integration and sense of competence when confronted by particular adversity" (p. 389). This process determines whether a man will become vulnerable to violence or resilient to it.

Gilgun (1996) referred to protective factors as "assets that individuals actively use to cope with, adapt to, or overcome vulnerability or risks" (p. 397). She indicated that individuals can use their assets in ways that protect them against the risk factors. Furthermore, individuals may be exposed to multiple protective factors that interact with each other. Gilgun noted that "[l]ike risk factors, protective factors reside within individuals, families, and other social groups and communities" (p. 397). She explained, for example, that a child who develops a protective factor such as secure attachments, is likely to be responsive and engaging with nonfamily members and to develop strong trusting relationships with extrafamilial individuals. Those relationships, in turn, are likely to further enhance an optimistic outlook and a coping style that leads to even more positive outcomes. Many authors have discussed the protective factors of childhood (Cowen, Wyman, Work, & Parker, 1990; Garmezy & Masten, 1994; Kaufman & Zigler, 1987; Masten, 1989, 1994; Masten, Best, & Garmezy, 1991; Rutter, 1987; Werner & Smith, 1982, 1992). These childhood protective factors may also have implications for men's vulnerability to violence. The major protective factors discussed in the child-development literature include self-efficacy, parental affection, trust, and supportive relationships with adults inside and outside the home.

Exposure to risk factors while possessing protective factors results in resilience. Resilience has been discussed in the literature in the context of protective factors. Masten, Best, & Garmezy (1991) defined resilience as coping with or overcoming adversity. Resilient individuals are those who experience adversity and potential negative outcomes, but, contrary to expectations, remain remarkably intact and even develop new strengths and abilities. Resilience at one point during life does not necessarily mean that it will translate to other situations (Luthar, Doernberger, & Zigler, 1993). Furthermore, vulnerability can be mediated by resilience when a man has social, emotional, and economic resources available to him.

Several factors have been suggested that produce resilience. Garmezy (1983) discussed resilience in the context of early life experiences. Three factors account for the relative invulnerability of resilient children to stress. These include certain personality dispositions in early life, including being autonomous, active and socially responsive; having supportive parents and a close family, and experiencing external support from peers and teachers. Siebert and Siegel (1996) described survivors of major crises as individuals who overcome crises through their own effort, experience positive value in their experience, and identify previously unknown strengths and abilities. Thus, another explanation for the development of resilience is related to unusual life challenges. Higgins (1994) attributed resilience to exceptional individuals who have high IQs, exceptional talents, developed inner resources, high levels of ego development, close relational ties, political and social activism, and higher financial status than their family of origin. Moreover, Higgins indicated that resilient individuals have 10 traits including cognitive flexibility, information-seeking, reflective planning abilities, positive appraisal of experiences, relational competence, extended support systems, internal locus of control, helpfulness in childhood, high self-esteem, good impulse control, special talents and resources, and the ability to marshall these traits.

Thus predicting the likelihood that an individual man may become violent toward women involves assessing the number of risk factors to which he has been exposed, their sequences or interaction with his unique psychological vulnerability to such risk factors, and the exposure he has to protective factors singly or in combination. The absence or possession of the protective factors is directly related to men's resilience and vulnerability to violence against women. Therefore, preventing men's violence directly relates to promoting men's protective factors and resilience during the early school years and throughout men's lives.

The hypotheses listed in this chapter do not include any predictions on how protective factors lead to resilience in men prone to violence. Making these predictions constitutes the next step in the expansion of the model, thus providing a challenge to theorists to create testable hypotheses in this vital area. Any multivariate model that proposes to answer the question, "What causes men's violence against women?," needs to focus on the concepts presented in Figure 12.2.

RECOMMENDATIONS TO PREVENT MEN'S VIOLENCE AGAINST WOMEN

We end this book with some specific recommendations for the prevention of men's violence against women. How do we acquire a better understanding of men's risk factors? How can men develop greater degrees of resilience that decrease their vulnerability to violence? What do violent men need to know about their behavior during their rehabilitation? What do future theorists, researchers, clinicians, and all helping professionals need to do in combating men's violence against women?

Many of the chapter authors make recommendations on how to prevent men's violence and protect women who are potential victims. Marin and Russo (Chapter 3) specifically recommend generating hypotheses that explain how to inhibit men's violence. Sanchez-Hucles and Dutton (Chapter 11) emphasize understanding the resilience factors that protect ethnic minority individuals and families from the risk of both domestic and societal violence. Nutt (Chapter 8)

recommends empowering women by educating them to the consequences of gender-role socialization and conflict. Silverstein (Chapter 6) emphasizes transforming the socialization of girls by developing a new gender ideology that legitimizes
female cooperation and coalitions. She also addresses the patriarchal conditions
that contribute to male dominance and asks how we can change those conditions.
Rigazio-DiGilio and Lanza (Chapter 10) recommend using cognitive developmental theory to help couples understand how psychological and physical violence occur. Anderson and Schlossberg's (Chapter 9) system analysis supports
assessing the complex interactions and contexts that put women at risk. O'Neil
and Nadeau (Chapter 7) suggest helping men understand their gender-role socialization, gender-role conflict, and other personality defenses that predispose them
to violence against women. Furthermore, they propose 10 gender-role related
hypotheses and a conceptual model that could be translated into quantitative and
qualitative research. Anderson and Schlossberg (Chapter 9) and Rigazio-DiGilio
and Lanza (Chapter 10) also pose specific research questions that address the
complex issues of relational violence and how it may be prevented.

All of these recommendations have significant prevention, educational, and
research implications. Next, we expand on these recommendations and discuss
critical areas for researchers, clinicians, educators, and public policy experts to
consider in combating men's violence against women.

THEORY AND MODEL DEVELOPMENT

The prevention of violence against women can be advanced by further development of theoretical models that explain the causative risk factors of men's violence. The revised model in Figure 12.1 is our attempt to depict graphically the
multiplicity of risk factors that interact with one another and cause men's violence against women. From our perspective, the model is heuristic, but far from
complete. Further discussion, debate, and dialogue by family violence
researchers and clinicians are likely to produce revisions in the model as empirical data and new knowledge are generated. The five general propositions, eight
specific propositions, and the factors presented in Figure 12.1 will need further
expansion and more discussion.

We recognize that some of the concepts and hypotheses that we have proposed
in this book may be controversial. We do not necessarily agree with every
hypothesis stated about the multiplicity of risk factors contributing to men's violence against women. We do feel that it is important to enumerate all the possible
hypotheses that may explain men's violence against women so that, in the future,
theorists and researchers can discuss, operationalize, and test them.

There are numerous areas where further theorizing is needed. First, theory
needs to explain more fully how the risk factors interact with one another. This
interaction needs to be assessed across a wide variety of contexts including race,

class, age, ethnicity, sexual orientation, and other diversity variables. Second, more theory is needed to explain how the predisposing risk factors relate to actual triggering dynamics. Greater understanding of how predisposing and triggering risk factors interact could result in explaining complex cause–effect relationships. Likewise, a further delineation of how contextual and situational variables predispose and activate men's violence is essential. The risk factors of men's violence against women also can be conceptualized in explaining other forms of men's violence including child abuse, incest, murder, suicide, and elder abuse. All of the preceding theoretical recommendations could assist in the fuller conceptual development of men's risk factors.

In the macrosocietal content area, there is a great need to understand how the larger society contributes to men's violence against women. Our chapter authors have just barely "scratched the surface" on how societal institutions, discrimination, and oppression contribute to men's violence. How racial, cultural, ethnic, class, age, economic, and sociocultural factors are contextually related to men's violence is highly underdeveloped and needs much more theoretical elaboration. A part of this needed elaboration entails understanding how societal power and control of women is transferred to individual couples' power-control dynamics, resulting in violent interactions.

The interactive nature of the biological, psychological, socialization, psychosocial, and relational risk factors pose considerable theoretical challenge. To study interacting risk factors, theorists will need to isolate more than single factors in their analyses. Theory is needed that provides simultaneous discussions of all factors and particularly how they interact. This kind of theory may be years away from being derived and may depend on the development of more robust meta-theories of men's violence against women.

RESEARCH AND TESTING HYPOTHESES ON MEN'S RISK FACTORS FOR VIOLENCE AGAINST WOMEN

Both quantitative and qualitative research is another area that can help us understand the risk factors of men's violence against women. The 40 hypotheses listed in Tables 12.2 through 12.6 provide an overall set of hypotheses to be tested across the 6 content areas. There are a host of risk variables implied in our 40 hypotheses in Tables 12.2 through 12.6. Reviewing the hypotheses, we counted over 60 independent variables that either predispose or activate men's violence against women. All of these independent variables have a common dependent variable: men's violence against women. Table 12.7 lists these risk variables across the six content areas. We conceptualize this list as "sources of risk variance" for men's violence against women. These variables could be used in quantitative and qualitative research designs, thereby translating the multivariate model presented in Figure 12.1 to actual research. In some cases, the variables

TABLE 12.7. Independent Variables Explaining Men's Risk for Violence Against Women Across Six Factors

Macrosocietal Variables
- Historical and societal patterns that glorify violence against women
- Patriarchal, racist, classist, homophobic, ethnocentric, heterosexist, and economically oppressive institutional structures
- Institutional structures that promote unequal power between men and women
- Poverty
- Unemployment
- Negative portrayal of women in the media

Biological Variables
- Hormonal levels
- Neuroanatomical processes
- Head injuries
- Brain behavior
- Cultural and evolutionary processes of men and women

Socialization and Gender-Role Socialization Variables
- Men's gender-role socialization processes
- Women's gender-role socialization processes
- Contextual variables that interact with men's and women's gender-role socialization processes
- Boys' and men's socialization to dominating and aggressive play
- Family-of-origin socialization experiences
- Sexist attitudes and behaviors
- Threats to men's gender-role identity
- Distorted gender-role schemas
- Fears of femininity
- Fears of emasculation
- Patterns of gender-role conflict
- Defenses and self-protective defenses

Psychological Variables
- Observing and experiencing violence in the family of origin
- Deficits of methods of cognitive processing
- Deficits of methods of emotional processing
- Unconscious processes
- Unexpressed emotions
- Breakdown of defenses and self-protective defensive strategies
- Power and control problems
- Psychological violence
- Psychopathology
- Low self-esteem
- Depression
- Lack of empathy
- Stress
- Unassertiveness
- Deficits or restrictions in problem-solving skills
- Intimacy problems
- Gender-role conflict
- Homophobia and heterosexism

TABLE 12.7. *(Continued)*

Psychosocial Variables
- Age
- Unemployment
- Low income
- Low occupational prestige
- Stress and marital conflict
- Sexist gender-role socialization
- Social isolation
- Alcohol and drug use or abuse
- Poverty
- Racism, classism, ethnocentrism, and other forms of oppression

Relational Variables
- Relational and systemic contexts
- Patterns of interactions
- Unresolved family-of-origin conflicts
- Past negative emotions and situations
- Patterns of interpersonal communication
- Cognitive and developmental orientations and structures
- Phase of relational development
- Fear of losses of power and control
- Power and control conflicts
- Abuses of power
- Psychological violence
- Stressful events

listed need to be more specifically operationalized before actually selecting research designs and assessment measures. Furthermore, like the factors themselves, there is some overlap in the variables across the six content areas in Table 12.7. This implies that some of the variables have multiple sources in the model and also interact complexly with one another.

Not all of these variables will be testable in the same way. For example, many macrosocietal hypotheses and variables may lend themselves to research approaches traditionally associated with sociology, anthropology, political science, economics, and history. Research approaches using surveys, participant and observation interviewing, and epidemiological and historical approaches can be employed to answer the question, "How does the larger society contribute to men's violence against women?"

The biological hypotheses need more elaboration and specification. Physiological theories and research approaches need to be combined with psychological and socialization factors to understand the complex interactions among physiological responses and cognitions, affect, and behavior. Some of this research is beginning to be implemented (Gottman et al., 1995; Jacobson et al., 1994). We agree with Walker's (1995) reactions to Gottman et al.'s (1995) research on the physiological similarities and differences in types of batterers' anger. She indicated that physiological differences among batterers ". . . can no longer be ignored by those involved in domestic violence research and treatment, even though the results are tentative, may be politically incorrect, and seem counterintuitive in certain places" (p. 269).

The socialization, psychological, psychosocial, and relational hypotheses could be tested through both qualitative and quantitative research. Given the wide array of qualitative approaches and standardized empirical tests, researchers can design empirical studies to test these hypotheses. Testing these hypotheses and risk variables would be most useful when they are in a situational context and when they differentiate between predisposing and triggering factors causing men's violence.

PREVENTION AND TRAINING PROGRAMS

Another area where the multivariate model may be useful is with prevention programs for men and women. These programs need to emphasize how to enhance men's positive assets and resources, develop men's protective factors, and increase men's resilience to violence against women. We recommend programs in schools in the early grades to help children understand how interpersonal violence occurs. Our model could be simplified and broken down for presentation in the schools, where children could learn that relationships are complex, multifaceted, and can lead to stress and conflict. Knowing at an early age how to set limits when psychological and physical violence affect interpersonal interactions would do much to help men and women become proficient at healthy relationships.

One pivotal area of focus is boys' and girls' gender-role socialization processes. Boys and girls can learn how gender-role stereotypes and socialization processes are central to interpersonal dynamics, resulting in both psychological and physical violence. Nutt, in Chapter 8, reviewed many of these issues for girls and women over the lifespan. O'Neil and Nadeau, in Chapter 7, presented an in-depth analysis of how boys' and men's gender-role socialization experiences can predispose them to violence and also trigger it. Interventions focused on these areas of socialization could do much to inhibit the volatile dynamics that can occur for middle-school children, teenagers, and adults. At the same time, middle-school- and high-school-aged children need interventions that will counter the prevailing norms regarding violence as portrayed in the media, through popular music, and at the cinema. The current culture exposes children to a great deal more violence than that experienced by previous generations. Moreover, repeated exposure to violent movies, songs, talk shows, and news reports normalizes violence and desensitizes children to its existence. Boys, in particular, need to learn to ignore current cultural messages that "a REAL man never lets others see that he is hurt, but instead fights to protect himself and to exact revenge."

Children need tools to protect themselves against prevailing cultural messages and to learn alternative conflict resolution strategies to help defuse potentially violent situations.

Similar interventions also could be developed for batterers themselves and their families. Violent men can learn about how sexist gender-role socialization relates to power, control, and other gender-related issues that inhibit effective and nonviolent problem solving. Limited data exist on whether batterers understand why they commit acts of violence against women. Some men know that they use violence to exert power and control over women. Others learn that violence occurs to defend against their own unacceptable feelings (Harway & Evans, 1996). Still other men may have limited awareness of how cognitive, affective, and biological processes result in psychological and physical assault. These men may have only fragments of understanding about their violence and therefore are vulnerable to commit repeated assaults.

Interventions with batterers can explain how a multiciplicity of factors may predispose men to violence and also actually trigger it. Of course, this kind of intervention could be effective only after the man stops the battering and demonstrates that he can control his violent behavior. Then, the hypotheses and factors could be explained to batterers as one way for them to understand the causes of their violence. These kind of interventions would not explain away or condone men's violence in any way. To the contrary, we are suggesting that men identify and take responsibility for the predisposing and triggering factors of their violence against women. If O'Neil and Nadeau are right in Chapter 7, these kinds of interventions may be met with psychological defenses that prohibit men from exploring the real sources of their violence. Consequently, men may need education in how psychological defenses and other unconscious processes operate when exploring personally threatening topics. These kinds of programs would move past traditional interventions with batterers that focus on anger management, emotional awareness, stress management, and improved communication, negotiation, and problem-solving skills.

One caution should be offered about interventions that are strictly cognitive in nature when working with batterers. We have speculated that a multiplicity of factors account for an individual man's propensity to become violent. When a man's violence is not caused by faulty thinking, programs that operate primarily at a cognitive level cannot alone help a man stay free of violence. Depth psychotherapy experiences may be necessary to help men unlearn counterproductive psychological and relational behaviors and to undo the damage of traditional gender-role socialization. In many cases, only in psychotherapy can a man begin to understand fully the complex interplay between macrosocietal factors and personal development, and learn to separate himself from their influence. Furthermore, medication or behavior modification may be needed to counteract biological contributions to men's violent behavior.

Prevention strategies could also include interventions that help men clarify their motives for using violence. Tedeschi and Felson (1994) theorized that there are three primary motives for using violence including controlling the behavior of others, restoring justice, and asserting and protecting one's identity. All three of these motives are relevant to understanding men's violence against women. Programs focused on helping men understand their motives for violence against women need to be created. For example, O'Neil and Nadeau, in Chapter 7, theorized that men's violence emanates from threats to gender-role identity that cause emasculation, fears of femininity, and gender-role conflict. If this hypothesis proves to be true, then programs for men could focus on core male-identity issues and specifically how men perceive threats to their masculine gender-role identity. Furthermore, when men's gender-role identities are based on restrictive and sexist gender-role stereotypes, men may need to examine distorted gender-role schemas related to power, control, emotionality, and sexuality. At a core level, distorted gender-role schemas may need to be examined, changed, and replaced with more healthy conceptions of masculinity for men to become resilient in conflict situations with women. This implies that prevention specialists need to be experts at helping men resolve their gender-role conflict and resocializing themselves. Foremost, it will mean the creation of paradigms of positive masculinity to replace sexist and restrictive notions of manhood. Positive paradigms of masculinity could focus on topics such as healthy emotionality, noncompetitive relationships, empathy for others, friendships, and new conceptions of power and control. Learning from these topics holds promise for helping men develop resilience and nonviolent problem solving during conflicts with women. Men can understand how they have been socialized to violence during their gender-role socialization. Through this learning, they can find nonviolent ways to solve their conflicts with women.

Helping professionals in many different disciplines also need training in understanding the complexity of men's violence against women. Teachers, lawyers, judges, clergy, and medical and mental health personnel all need to recognize that although violence against women is complex, it can be understood and prevented. This implies that social scientists, particularly mental health professionals, need to become more involved in creating and delivering educational and preventive programs for other professionals and the larger society.

ADVOCACY, ALLIANCES, AND PUBLIC POLICY INITIATIVES

The primary purpose of this book has been to advocate for greater attention to the causes of men's violence against women. We believe that this advocacy can best occur with better theories, research, and prevention and training programs that focus on explaining the complexity of partner violence. Ideally, advocacy should come from men themselves, because violence against women is a serious male problem. More men need to be advocates for explaining the causes of male violence and to be involved in comprehensive prevention efforts. Furthermore, advocacy for preventing violence against women is best realized when alliances exist between men and women. These alliances need to continue to explore how men and women can work together in understanding partner violence. Additionally, collaborative efforts across academic disciplines explaining how men's violence has multivariate sources are strongly recommended. Collegial efforts focused on better theory and more sophisticated research can stimulate public policy and legislation that protect women and resocialize men to nonviolent ways to solve interpersonal problems. This is more likely to occur with interdisciplinary dialogues where theoretical and research knowledge is used to inform the public on how men's violence is complexly woven into the social fabric of our society. As Senator Joseph Biden, Jr., states in the foreword to this book, the academic community has much to contribute to decreasing men's violence against women.

As the research and theory are developed over the coming years, methods to translate new knowledge into public policy are extremely critical. Public policy at the national, state, regional, and local levels can educate the public to understand that violence against women tears away at the soul of our families and our society. Because violence against women touches everyone and is our collective societal problem, it follows that everyone needs to find a way to be part of the solution. The conspiracy of silence with men's violence against women appears to have been broken in the 1990s. We now need to ensure that there is no conspiracy to impede progress in understanding the causes of men's violence and implementing comprehensive prevention programs.

REFLECTIONS AND CONCLUDING COMMENTS ON UNDERSTANDING A MULTIVARIATE MODEL TO EXPLAIN MEN'S VIOLENCE AGAINST WOMEN

Writing this book over the last 5 years has been a unique experience for both of us. Since 1993, we have had many phone calls, e-mails, and faxes as we dialogued about the causes of men's violence against women. The revised model in this chapter represents where we end and where we hope that you the reader will continue the dialogue, research, and theory development. Violence against women over the last 5 years has become more of a national issue, but the battering continues in all of our communities. One of the greatest mysteries of our time is why men violently hurt those women they are closest to. We are still a long way from answering the question, "What causes men's violence against women?" This book was our attempt to move along the dialogue on this critical question. We hope that the book opens up more extensive discussion between men and women, promotes more research, and stimulates prevention interventions with children and adults on nonviolent ways to solve human problems.

References

AAUW Educational Foundation. (1992). *How schools shortchange girls*. Washington, DC: Author.

Abramowitz, S., Weitz, L., Schwartz, J., Amira, S., Gomes, B., & Abramowitz, C. (1975). Comparative counselor references toward women with medical school aspirations. *Journal of College Student Personnel, 16*, 128–130.

Adams, D. (1988). Treatment models of men who batter. In K. Yllö & M. Bograd (Eds.), *Feminist perspectives on wife abuse* (pp. 176–200). Newbury Park, CA: Sage.

Adams, D. (1992). Biology does not make men more aggressive than women. In K. Bjorkqvist & P. Niemala (Eds), *Of mice and women: Aspects of female aggression* (pp. 17–26). San Diego, CA: Academic Press.

Albee, G. W. (1981). The prevention of sexism. *Professional Psychology, 12*, 20–28.

Alexander, K., & Cook, M. (1982). Curricula and coursework: A surprise ending to a familiar story. *American Sociological Review, 47*, 626–640.

Alington, D. E., & Troll, L. E. (1984). Social change and equality: The roles of women and economics. In G. Baruch & J. Brooks-Gunn (Eds), *Women in mid-life* (pp. 181–202). New York: Plenum.

Allen, P. G. (1986). Violence and American Indian women. In M. C. Burns (Ed), *The speaking profits us: Violence in the cries of women of color*. Seattle, WA: Center for the Prevention of Sexual and Domestic Violence.

American Psychological Association. (1994). *Violence and the family*. Washington, DC: Author.

American Psychological Association. (1996). *Violence and the family report of the American Psychological Association Task Force on Violence and the Family*. Washington, DC: Author.

Anderson, S. A., Rigazio-DiGilio, S. A., & Kunkler, K. P. (1995). Training and supervision in marriage and family therapy: Current issues and future directions. *Family Relations: Journal of Applied Family and Child Studies, 44*, 489–500.

Anderson, S. A., & Sabatelli, R. M. (1995). *Family interaction: A multigenerational, developmental perspective.* Needham Heights, MA: Allyn & Bacon.

Arch, E. C., & Cummins, D. E. (1989). Structured and unstructured exposure to computers: Sex differences in attitude and use among college students. *Sex Roles, 20,* 245–254.

Archer, C. (1984). Children's attitudes toward sex role division in adult occupational roles. *Sex Roles, 10,* 1–10.

Archer, J. (1991). The influence of testosterone on human aggression. *British Journal of Psychology, 82,* 1–28.

Archer, J. (1994a). Violence between men. In J. Archer (Ed.), *Male violence* (pp. 121–140). London: Routledge.

Archer, J. (1994b). Power and male violence. In J. Archer (Ed.), *Male violence* (pp. 310–331). London: Routledge.

Archer, J. (Ed.). (1994c). *Male violence.* London: Routledge.

Archer, J. (1996). Sex differences in social behavior: Are the social role and evolutionary explanations compatible? *American Psychologist, 51,* 909–917.

Arnold, F., & Kuo, E. C. (1984). The value of daughters and sons: A comparative study of the gender preferences of parents. *Journal of Comparative Family Studies, 15,* 299–318.

Asbury, J. (1987). African American women in violent relationships: An explanation of cultural differences. In R. J. Hampton (Ed.), *Violence in the Black family: Correlates and consequences* (pp. 89–105). Lexington, MA: Lexington Books.

Asbury, J. (1993). Violence in families of color in the United States. In R. L. Hampton, T. P. Gullota, G. R. Adams, E. H. Potter, & R. P. Weissberg (Eds.), *Family violence: Prevention and treatment* (pp. 159–178). Newbury Park, CA: Sage.

Avis, J. M. (1988). Deepening awareness: A private guide to feminism critique. *Journal of Psychotherapy and the Family, 3*(4), 15–46.

Avis, J. M. (1992). Where are all the family therapists? Abuse and violence within families and family therapy's response. *Journal of Marital & Family Therapy, 18*(3), 225–232.

Avis, J. M. (1994). Advocates versus researchers—A false dichotomy? A feminist, social constructionist response to Jacobson. *Family Process, 33,* 87–91.

Azrin, N. H., Hutchinson, R. R., & McLaughlin, R. (1965). The opportunity for aggression as an operant reinforcer during aversive stimulation. *Journal of the Experimental Analysis of Behavior, 8,* 171–180.

Babcock, J. C., Waltz, J., Jacobson, N. S., & Gottman, J. M. (1993). Power and violence: The relation between communication patterns, power discrepancies and domestic violence. *Journal of Consulting and Clinical Psychology, 61*(1), 40–50.

Bachman, R. (1994). *Violence against women: A national crime victimization survey report.* Washington, DC: U.S. Department of Justice, Bureau of Justice Statistics.

Bachman, R., & Coker, A. L. (1995). Police involvement in domestic violence: The interactive effects of victim injury, offender's history of violence, and race. *Violence and Victims, 10*(2), 91–106.

Bachman, R., & Saltzman, L. E. (1995). *Violence against women: Estimates from the Redesigned Survey (NCJ #154348).* [Bureau of Justice Statistics special report.] Washington, DC: U.S. Department of Justice.

Bagarozzi, D. A., & Anderson, S. A. (1989). *Personal, marital, and family myths: Theoretical formulations and clinical strategies*. New York: Norton.

Baker, R. R., & Bellis, M. A. (1993). Human sperm competition: Ejaculate manipulation by females and a function for the female orgasm. *Animal Behavior, 40*, 887–909.

Bard, M., & Sangrey, D. (1986). *The crime victims' book* (2nd ed.). New York: Brunner/ Mazel.

Barnett, O. W., & Hamberger, L. K. (1992). An assessment of maritally violent men on the California Psychological Inventory. *Violence and Victims, 7*, 15–28.

Barnett, O. W., Miller-Perrin, C. L., & Perrin, R. D. (1997). *Family violence across the lifespan*. Thousand Oaks, CA: Sage.

Bartle, S. E., & Rosen, K. H. (1994). Individuation and relationship violence. *American Journal of Family Therapy, 22*, 222–236.

Beere, C. A., King, D. W., Beere, D. B., & King, L. A. (1984). The sex-role egalitarianism scale: A measure of attitudes toward equality between the sexes. *Sex Roles, 8(7/8)*, 563–576.

Belenky, M. F., Clinchy, R. M., Goldberger, N. R., & Tarule, J. M. (1986). *Women's ways of knowing*. New York: Basic Books.

Bem, S. (1993). *The lenses of gender*. New Haven, CT: Yale University Press.

Bem, S. L. (1981). Gender role schema theory: A cognitive account of sex typing. *Psychological Review, 88*, 354–364.

Bem, S. L. (1983). Gender schema theory and its implications for child development: Raising gender-aschematic children in a gender-schematic society. *Signs: Journal of Women in Culture and Society, 8*, 598–616.

Bennett, N. (1986, February 14). They're falling in love again, say marriage counselors [Personal interview with L. Peterson]. *Stamford Advocate*, p. A1.

Bergman, B. K., & Brismar, B. G. (1992). Can family violence be prevented? A psychological study of male batterers and battered wives. *Public Health, 106*, 45–52.

Berkowitz, L. (1993). *Aggression: Its causes, consequences, and control*. New York: McGraw-Hill.

Berlin, I. N. (1987). Effects of changing Native American cultures on child development. *Journal of Community Psychology, 15*, 299–306.

Berliner, L. (1990). Domestic violence: A humanist or feminist issue? *Journal of Interpersonal Violence, 5(1)*, 128–129.

Betz, N. E. (1993). Women's career development. In F. L. Denmark & M. A. Paludi (Eds.), *Psychology of women: A handbook of issues and theories* (pp. 627–684). Westport, CT: Greenwood.

Betz, N. E., & Fitzgerald, L. F. (1987). *The career psychology of women*. Orlando, FL: Academic Press.

Biden, J. R., Jr. (1993). Violence against women: The congressional response. *American Psychologist, 48* (10), 1059–1061.

Birns, B., Cascardi, M., & Meyers, S. (1994). Sex-role socialization: Developmental influences on wife abuse. *American Journal of Orthopsychiatry, 64*, 50–59.

Bjorkqvist, K., Nygren, T., Bjorklund, A., Bjorkquist, S. (1994). Testosterone intake and aggressiveness: Real effect or anticipation? *Aggressive Behavior, 20*, 17–26.

Bloom, M. (1996). Primary prevention and resilience; changing paradigms and changing lives. In R. L. Hampton, P. Jenkins, & T. P. Gullotta (Eds.), *Preventing violence in America* (pp. 87–114). Thousand Oaks, CA: Sage.

Bograd, M. (1982). Battered women, cultural myths and clinical interventions: A feminist analysis. In F. Curtis, M. Downes, M. G. Hutchinson, D. McIntosh, J. Richard, E. Rothblum, & G. Washor-Liebhar (Eds.), *Current feminist issues in psychotherapy* (pp. 69–78). New York: Haworth.

Bograd, M. (1984). Family systems approaches to wife battering: A feminist critique. *American Journal of Orthopsychiatry, 54*, 558–568.

Bograd. M. (1987). Case commentary on neutrality versus social control: A systemic approach to violent couples. *Family Therapy Networker, 11*(3), 56–57.

Bograd, M. (1988a). Feminist perspectives of wife abuse: An introduction. In K. Yllö & M. Bograd (Eds.), *Feminist perspectives on wife abuse*. Newbury Park, CA: Sage.

Bograd, M. (1988b). Power, gender and the family: Feminist perspectives on family systems theory. In M. A. Dutton & L. E. A. Walker (Eds.), *Feminist psychotherapies: Integration of therapeutic and feminist systems* (pp. 118–133). Norwood, NJ: Ablex.

Bograd, M. (1992). Values in conflict: Challenges to family therapists' thinking. *Journal of Marital and Family Therapy, 18*(3), 245–256.

Booth, A., & Osgood, D. W. (1993). The influence of testosterone on deviance in adulthood: Assessing and explaining the relationship. *Criminology, 31*, 93–117.

Booth, A., Shelley, G., Mazur, A., Tharp, G., & Kittok, R. (1989). Testosterone and winning and losing in human competition. *Hormones and Behavior, 23*, 556–571.

Bordelon, K. W. (1985). Sexism in reading materials. *Reading Teacher, 38*, 792–797.

Bourg, S., & Stock, H. V. (1994). A review of domestic violence arrest statistics in a police department using a pro-arrest policy: Are pro-arrest policies enough? *Journal of Family Violence, 9*(2), 177–189.

Boyd-Franklin, N. (1989). *Black families in therapy: A multisystems approach*. New York: Guilford.

Braithwaite, R. L. (1981). Interpersonal relations between Black males and Black females. In L. E. Gary (Ed.), *Black men* (pp. 83–97). Beverly Hills, CA: Sage.

Breines, G., & Gordon, L. (1983). The new scholarship on family violence. *Signs: Journal of Women in Culture and Society, 8*, 490–531.

Breunlin, D. C., Schwartz, R. C., & Mac Kune-Karrer, B. (1992). *Metaframeworks: Transcending the models of family therapy*. San Francisco: Jossey-Bass.

Brice-Baker, J. R. (1994). Domestic violence in African–American and African–Caribbean families [Special issue: Multicultural views on domestic violence]. *Journal of Social Distress and the Homeless, 3*, 23–38.

Brisson, N. J. (1981). Battering husbands: A survey of abusive men. *Victimology: An International Journal, 6*, 338–344.

Brooks, G., & Silverstein, L. B. (1995). Understanding the dark side of masculinity: An interactive systems model. In R. F. Levant & W. S. Pollack (Eds.), *A new psychology of men* (pp. 280–333). New York: Basic Books.

Brown, D. G. (1958). Sex-role development in a changing culture. *Psychological Bulletin, 4*, 232–242.

Brown, G. L., Ebert, M. H., Goyer, P. F., Jimerson, D. C., Klein, W. K., Bunney, W. E., & Goodwin, F. K. (1982). Aggression, suicide, and serotonin: Relationship to CSF amine metabolites. *American Journal of Psychiatry, 139*, 741–746.

Brown, J. K., & Kerns, V. (1985). *In her prime: A new view of middle-aged women*. South Hadley, MA: Bergin & Garvey.

Browne, A. (1992). Violence against women: Relevance for medical practitioners. *Journal of the American Medical Association, 267*, 3184–3189.

Brownmiller, S. (1975). *Against our will: Men, women and rape.* New York: Simon & Schuster.

Brownmiller, S. (1984). *Femininity.* New York: Fawcett Columbine.

Bruch, H. (1985). Four decades of eating disorders. In D. M. Garner & P. E. Garfinkel (Eds.), *Handbook of psychotherapy for anorexia nervosa and bulimia* (pp. 7–18). New York: Guilford.

Bulhan, H. A. (1985). *Franz Fanon and the psychology of oppression.* New York: Plenum.

Burman, B., John, R., & Margolin, G. (1992). Observed patterns of conflict in violent, nonviolent, and nondistressed couples. *Behavioral Assessment, 14*, 15–37.

Burns, D. (1980). *Feeling good: The new mood therapy.* New York: Signet Books.

Burns, M. C. (Ed.). (1986). *The speaking profits us: Violence in the cries of women of color.* Seattle, WA: Center for the Prevention of Sexual and Domestic Violence.

Busch, R., Robertson, N., & Lapsley, H. (1993). Domestic violence and the justice system: A study of breaches of protection orders. *Community Mental Health in New Zealand, 7*, 26–44.

Bush, D. M., & Simmons, R. G. (1987). Gender and coping with the entry into early adolescence. In R. C. Barnett, L. Biener, & G. K. Baruch (Eds.), *Gender and stress* (pp. 185–217). New York: Free Press.

Buss, D. M. (1988). The evolution of human intrasexual competition: Tactics of mate attraction. *Journal of Personality and Social Psychology, 54*, 616–628.

Buss, D. M. (1989). Sex differences in human mate preferences: Evolutionary hypotheses tested in 37 cultures. *Behavioral and Brain Sciences, 12*, 1–49.

Buss, D. M. (1995). Psychological sex differences: Origins through sexual selection. *American Psychologist, 41*, 164–168.

Caesar, P. L. (1988). Exposure to violence in families-of-origin among wife abusers and maritally non-violent men. *Violence and Victims, 3*, 49–63.

Cahn, D. D., & Lloyd, S. A. (1996). *Family violence from a communication perspective.* Thousand Oaks, CA: Sage.

Canino, I., & Canino, G. (1980). Impact of stress on the Puerto Rican family: Treatment considerations. *American Journal of Orthopsychiatry, 50*, 535–541.

Cantor, D. W., Bernay, T., & Stoess, J. (1992). *Women in power: The secrets of leadership.* Boston: Houghton Mifflin.

Cantos, A., Neidig, P., & O'Leary, K. D. (1993). Men and women's attributions of blame for domestic violence. *Journal of Family Violence, 8*, 289–302.

Cappell, C., & Heiner, R. B. (1990). The intergenerational transmission of family aggression. *Journal of Family Violence, 5*, 132–152.

Carden, A. D. (1994). Wife abuse and the wife abuser: Review and recommendations. *The Counseling Psychologist, 22*(4), 539–582.

Carlson, N. R. (1994). *Physiology of behavior* (5th ed.). Boston: Allyn and Bacon.

Carter, B., & McGoldrick, M. (1989). Overview: The changing family life cycle—a framework for family therapy. In B. Carter & M. McGoldrick (Eds.), *The changing family life cycle: A framework for family therapy* (2nd ed.). Needham Heights, MA: Allyn & Bacon.

Cascardi, M., & O'Leary, K. D. (1992). Depressive symptomatology, self-esteem, and self-blame in battered women. *Journal of Family Violence, 7*, 249–259.

Cate, R. M., Henton, J. M., Christopher, F. S., & Lloyd, S. (1982). Premarital abuse: A social psychological perspective. *Journal of Family Issues, 3*, 79–90.

Cazenave, N. (1981). Black men in America: The quest for manhood. In H. P. McAdoo (Ed.), *Black families* (pp. 176–185). Beverly Hills, CA: Sage.

Cazenave, N. A., & Strauss, M. (1979). Race, class, network embeddedness, and family violence: A search for potent support system. *Journal of Comparative Family Studies, 10*, 280–300.

Cervantes, N. N., & Cervantes, J. M. (1993). A multicultural perspective in the treatment of domestic violence. In M. Hansen & M. Harway (Eds.), *Battering and family therapy: A feminist perspective* (pp. 156–174). Newbury Park, CA: Sage.

Chaffin, R. J., & Winston, M. (1991). Conceptions of parenthood. *Journal of Applied and Social Psychology, 21*, 1726–1757.

Chartier, B. M., Graff, L. A., & Arnold, W. J. (1986). *Male socialization and hostility toward women.* Paper presented at the 47th annual meeting of the Canadian Psychological Association, Toronto, Ontario.

Cheatham, H., Ivey, A., Ivey, M., Pedersen, P., Rigazio-DiGilio, S., Simek-Morgan, L., & Sue, D. (1997). Multicultural counseling and therapy. I: Metatheory—taking theory into practice. In A. Ivey, M. Ivey, & L. Simek-Morgan (Eds.), *Counseling and psychotherapy: A multicultural perspective* (4th ed., pp. 133–169). Needham Heights, MA: Allyn and Bacon.

Chen, S. A., & True, R. H. (1995). Asian/Pacific Island Americans. In L. D. Eron, J. H. Gentry, & P. Schlegel (Eds.), *Reason to hope: A psychosocial perspective on violence and youth* (pp. 145–164). Washington, DC: American Psychological Association.

Chester, B., Robin, R., Koss, M., & Goodman, D. (1994). Grandmother dishonored: Violence against women by male partners in American Indian communities [Special issue: Violence against women of color]. *Violence and Victims, 9*, 249–258.

Chodorow, N. (1978). *The reproduction of mothering: Psychoanalysis and the sociology of gender.* Berkeley: University of California Press.

Chrisler, J. C., Johnson, I. K., Champagne, N. M., & Preston, K. E. (1994). Menstrual joy: The construct and its consequences. *Psychology of Women Quarterly, 18*, 375–387.

Clark, R., Lennon, R., & Morris, L. (1993). Of Caldecotts and kings: Gendered images in recent American children's books by Black and non-Black illustrators. *Gender & Society, 7*, 227–245.

Cohler, B. (1987). Adversity, resilience, and the study of lives. In E. J. Antony & B. Cohler (Eds.), *The invulnerable child* (pp. 363–424). New York: Guilford.

Coie, J. D., Watt, N. F., West, S. G., Hawkins, J. D., Ramey, S. L., Shure, M. B., & Long, B. (1993). The science of prevention: A conceptual framework and some directions for a national research program. *American Psychologist, 48*(10), 1013–1022.

Coleman, D., & Straus, M. A. (1983). Alcohol abuse and family violence. In E. Gottheil, K. Druley, T. Skoloda, & H. M. Waxman (Eds.), *Alcohol, drug abuse, and aggression* (pp. 104–124). Springfield, IL: C.C. Thomas.

Coleman, D., & Straus, M. A. (1986). Marital power, conflict, and violence. *Violence and Victims, 1*, 139–153.

Coleman, V. E. (1996). Lesbian battering: The relationship between personality and the perpetration of violence. In L. K. Hamberger & C. Renzetti (Eds.), *Domestic partner abuse* (pp. 77–101). New York: Springer.

Combrinck-Graham, L. (1985). A developmental model for family systems. *Family Process, 24*(2), 139–150.

Connors, J., & Harway, M. (1995). A male–female abuse continuum. *Family Violence & Sexual Assault Bulletin, 11*(1–2), 29–33.

Cordova, J. V., Jacobson, N. S., Gottman, J. M., Rushe, R., & Cox, G. (1993). Negative reciprocity and communications in couples with a violent husband. *Journal of Abnormal Psychology, 102*(4), 559–564.

Covey, H. C. (1988). Historical terminology used to represent older people. *Gerontologist, 28*, 291–297.

Cowan, G. (1984). The double standard in age discrepant relationships. *Sex Roles, 11*, 17–24.

Cowan, G., Warren, L. W., & Young, J. L. (1985). Medical perceptions of menopausal symptoms. *Psychology of Women Quarterly, 9*, 3–14.

Cowen, E. L., Wyman, P. A., Work, W. C., & Parker, G. R. (1990). The Rochester child resilience project: Overview and summary of first-year findings. *Development and Psychopathology, 2*, 193–212.

Craven, D. (1996). *Female victims of violent crime.* Washington, DC: U.S. Department of Justice, Office of Justice Programs.

Cross, R. K., & Markus, H. R. (1993). Gender in thought, belief, and action: A cognitive approach. In A. Beall & R. J. Sternberg (Eds.), *The psychology of gender* (pp. 55–98). New York: Guilford.

Crossman, R. K., Stith, S. M., & Bender, M. M. (1990). Sex role equalitarianism and marital violence. *Sex Roles, 22*, 293–304.

Crowell, N. A., & Burgess, A. W. (1996). *Understanding violence against women.* Washington, DC: National Academy Press.

Cummings, E. M., & Davies, P. (1994). *Children and marital conflict: The impact of family dispute and resolution.* New York: Guilford.

Dabbs, J., Frady, R., Carr, T. S., & Besch, N. F. (1987). Saliva testosterone and criminal violence in young adult prison inmates. *Psychosomatic Medicine, 49*, 174–182.

Dabbs, J. M., Jurkovic, G. J., & Frady, R. L. (1991). Salivary testosterone and cortisol among late adolescent male offenders. *Journal of Abnormal Child Psychology, 19*, 469–478.

Dabbs, J. M., & Morris, R. (1990). Testosterone, social class, and antisocial behavior in a sample of 4,462 men. *Psychological Science, 1*, 209–211.

Dabbs, J. M., Ruback, R. B., Frady, R. L., Hooper, C. H., & Sgoutas, D. S. (1988). Saliva testosterone and criminal violence among women. *Personality and Individual Differences, 9*, 269–275.

Daitzman, R., & Zuckerman, M. (1980). Disinhibitory sensation seeking, personality, and gonadal hormones. *Personality and Individual Differences, 9*, 269–275.

Daley, M., & Wilson, M. (1994). Evolutionary psychology of male violence. In J. Archer (Ed.), *Male violence* (pp. 253–288). London: Routledge.

Darwin, C. (1871). *The descent of man and selection in regard to sex* (Vol. 1). London: John Murray.

David, D. S., & Brannon, R. (1976). *The forty-nine percent majority: The male sex role.* Reading, MA: Addison-Wesley.

Dawkins, R. (1982). *The extended phenotype. The gene as the unit of selection.* San Francisco: Freeman.

Dawson, J. M., & Langan, P. A. (1994). *Murder in families* [Bureau of Justice Statistics special report]. Washington DC: U.S. Department of Justice.

Dean, K., & Malamuth, N. (1997). Characteristics of men who aggress sexually and of men who imagine aggressing: Risk and moderating variables. *Journal of Personality and Social Psychology, 72*, 449–455.

Deffenbacher, J. L. (1992). Trait anger: Theory, findings and implications. In C. D. Spielberger & J. N. Butcher (Eds.), *Advances in personality assessment* (Vol. 9, pp. 177–201). Hillsdale, NJ: Erlbaum.

DeJong, J., Virkkunen, M., & Linnoila, M. (1992). Factors associated with recidivism in a criminal population. *Journal of Nervous and Mental Disease, 180*, 543–550.

de la Cancela, V. (1991). Working affirmatively with Puerto Rican men: Professional and personal reflections. *Journal of Feminist Family Therapy, 2*, 195–212.

Delk, J. L., Madden, R. B., Livingston, M., & Ryan, T. T. (1986). Adult perceptions of the infant as a function of gender labeling and observer gender. *Sex Roles, 15*, 527–534.

Dell, P. (1989). Violence and the systemic view: The problem of power. *Family Process, 28*, 1–14.

de Waal, F. B. M., & Lanting, F. (1997). *Bonobo. The forgotten ape*. Berkeley: University of California Press.

Diamond, J. (1992). *The third chimpanzee*. New York: Harper Perennial.

Dobash, R. E., & Dobash, R. P. (1977). Wives: The "appropriate" victims of marital violence. *Victimology, 2*, 426–442.

Dobash, R. E., & Dobash, R. P. (1979). *Violence against wives: A case against the patriarchy*. New York: Free Press.

Dobash, R. E., & Dobash, R. (1992). *Women, violence, and social change*. New York: Routledge.

Doumas, D., Margolin, G., & John, R. (1994). The intergenerational transmission of aggression across three generations. *Journal of Family Violence, 9*, 157–175.

Dowling, C. (1982). *The Cinderella complex*. New York: Pocketbooks.

Doyle, J. A. (1995). *The male experience*. Madison, WI: Brown & Benchmark.

Ducat, S. J. (1994). *Correlates of gender gap in politics: Fear of men's femininity, male gender role conflict, and homophobia*. San Francisco, CA: New College of California.

Dunn, K. (1994). Why do women remake their bodies to fit the fashion? In K. M. Hicks (Ed.), *Misdiagnosis: Woman as a disease* (pp. 95–97). Allentown, PA: People's Medical Society.

Dutton, D. (1994). The origin and structure of the abusive personality. *Journal of Personality Disorders, 8*, 181–191.

Dutton, D. (1995). Trauma symptoms and PTSD-like profiles in perpetrators in intimate abuse. *Journal of Traumatic Stress, 8*, 299–316.

Dutton, D. G. (1985). An ecological nested theory of male violence toward intimates. *International Journal of Women's Studies, 8*(14), 404–413.

Dutton, D. G. (1988). *The domestic assault of women: Psychological and criminal justice perspectives*. Boston, MA: Allyn & Bacon.

Dutton, D. G. (1994). Patriarchy and wife assault: The ecological fallacy. *Violence and Victims, 9*(2), 167–182.

Dutton, D. G. (1995). *The batterer: A psychological profile*. New York: Basic Books.

Dutton, D. G., Saunders, K., Starzomski, A., & Bartholomew, K. (1994). Intimacy-anger and insecure attachments as precursors of abuse in intimate relationships. *Journal of Applied Social Psychology, 24*, 1367–1386.

Dutton, D. G., & Starzomski, A. J. (1993). Borderline personality in perpetrators of psychological and physical violence. *Violence and Victims, 8*, 327–337.

Dutton, M. A. (1992). Assessment and treatment of PTSD among battered women. In D. Foy (Ed.), *Treating PTSD: Cognitive and behavioral strategies* (pp. 69–98). New York: Guilford.

Dworkin, A. (1974). *Woman hating.* New York: E. P. Dutton.

Dwyer, D. C., Smokowski, P. R., Bricout, J. C., & Wodarski, J. S. (1995). Domestic violence research: Theoretical and practical implications for social work. *Clinical Social Work Journal, 23*, 185–198.

Easteal, P., & Easteal, S. (1992). Attitudes and practices of doctors toward spouse assault victims: An Australian study. *Violence and Victims, 7*, 217–228.

Edleson, J. L., Eisikovits, Z. C., Guttmann, E., & Sela-Amit, M. (1991). Cognitive and interpersonal factors in women abuse. *Journal of Family Violence, 6*(2), 167–182.

Edleson, J. L., & Tolman, R. M. (1992). *Intervention for men who batter: An ecological approach.* Newbury Park, CA: Sage.

Edwards, A. (1991). Male violence in feminist theory: An analysis of the changing conceptions of sex/gender violence and male dominance. In J. Hamner & M. Maynard (Eds.), *Women, violence, and social control* (pp. 13–29). Atlantic Highlands, NJ: Humanities Press.

Edwards, J., Fuller, T., Vorakitphokatorn, S., & Sermsi, S. (1992). Female employment and marital instability: Evidence from Thailand. *Journal of Marriage and the Family, 54*, 59–68.

Eisler, R. M. (1995). The relationship between masculine gender role stress and men's health risk: The validation of a construct. In R. Levant & W. Pollack (Eds.), *A new psychology of men.* New York: Basic Books.

Elbow, M. (1977). Theoretical considerations of violent marriages. *Social Casework, 58*, 515–526.

Elbow, M. (1982). Children of violent marriages: The forgotten victims. *Social Casework: The Journal of Contemporary Social Work, 63*, 465–471.

Elias, M. (1981). Serum cortisol, testosterone, and testosterone binding globulin responses to competitive fighting in human males. *Aggressive Behavior, 7*, 215–224.

Elliot, F. A. (1976). The neurology of explosive rage: The dyscontrol syndrome. *Practitioner*, pp. 217–224.

Ellis, L. (1991). Monoamine oxidase and criminality: Identifying an apparent biological marker for antisocial behavior. *Journal of Research in Crime and Delinquency, 28*, 227–251.

Ellsworth, P. C. (1994). William James and emotion: Is a century of fame worth a century of misunderstanding? *Psychological Review, 101*, 222–229.

Erikson, E. H. (1964). The inner and outer self: Reflections on womanhood. *Daedelus, 93*, 582–606.

Erikson, E. H. (1968). *Identity, youth, and crisis.* New York: Norton.

Fagan, J. A., & Browne, A. (1994). Violence between spouses and intimates: Physical aggression between women and men in intimate relationships. In A. J. Reiss, Jr., & J. A. Roth (Eds.), *Understanding and preventing violence* (Vol. 3, pp. 115–292). Washington, DC: National Academy Press.

Falicov, C. (1982). Mexican families. In M. McGoldrick, J. Pearce, & J. Giordano (Eds.), *Ethnicity and family therapy.* New York: Guilford.

Faludi, S. (1991). *Backlash: The undeclared war against American women.* Garden City, NY: Doubleday.

Fanon, F. (1963). *The wretched of the earth.* New York: Grove.

Feinman, S. (1981). Why is cross-sex-role behavior more approved for girls than for boys? A status characteristic approach. *Sex Roles, 7,* 289–300.

Feiring, C., & Lewis, M. (1987). The child's social network: Sex differences from three to six years. *Sex Roles, 17,* 621–636.

Feld, S. L., & Straus, M. A. (1989). Escalation and desistance of wife assault in marriage. *Criminology, 1,* 142–161.

Feldman, C. M., & Ridley, C. A. (1995). The etiology and treatment of domestic violence between adult partners. *Clinical Psychology: Science and Practice, 2,* 317–348.

Felson, R. B., & Tedeschi, J. T. (1993). A social interactionist approach to violence: Cross-cultural applications. *Violence and Victims, 8,* 295–310.

Ferraro, K. (1988). An existential approach to battering. In G. T. Hotaling, D. Finkelhor, J. Kirkpatrick, & M. Straus (Eds.), *Family abuse and its consequences: New directions in research.* Newbury Park, CA: Sage.

Finkelhor, D. (1983). Common features of family abuse. In D. Finkelhor, R. J. Gelles, G. T. Hotaling, & M. A. Straus (Eds.), *The dark side of the family: Current family violence research* (pp. 17–30). Beverly Hills, CA: Sage.

Finkelhor, D., & Hotaling, G. (1984). Sexual abuse in the national incidence study of child abuse and neglect: An appraisal. *Child Abuse & Neglect: The International Journal, 8,* 23–33.

Finn, J. (1986). The relationship between sex role attitudes and attitudes supporting marital violence. *Sex Roles, 14,* 235–244.

Fitzgerald, L. F., & Crites, J. O. (1980). Toward a career psychology of women: What do we know? What do we need to know? *Journal of Counseling Psychology, 27,* 44–62.

Fitzgerald, L. F., & Nutt, R. L. (1986). The Division 17 principles concerning the counseling/psychotherapy of women: Rationale and implementation. *The Counseling Psychologist, 14,* 180–216.

Flynn, C. P. (1990). Relationship violence by women: Issues and implications. *Family Relations, 39,* 194–198.

Fodor, I. G., & Thai, J. (1984). Weight disorders: Overweight and anorexia. In E. A. Blechman (Ed.), *Behavior modification with women.* New York: Guilford.

Foley, R. (1995–1996). The adaptive legacy of human evolution: A search for the environment of evolutionary adaptedness. *Evolutionary Anthropology, 4,* 194–203.

Ford, J., Rompf, E., Faragher, T., & Weisenfluh, S. (1995). Case outcomes in domestic violence court: Influences of judges. *Psychological Reports, 77,* 587–594.

Foucault, M. (1988a). Power and strategies. In C. Gordon (Ed.), *Power/knowledge: Selected interviews and other writings 1972–1977 by Michel Foucault* (pp. 143–145). New York: Pantheon.

Foucault, M. (1988b). Truth and power. In C. Gordon (Ed.), *Power/knowledge: Selected interviews and other writings 1972–1977 by Michel Foucault* (pp. 109–133). New York: Pantheon.

Fox, M. F. (1989). Women and higher education: Gender differences in the status of students and scholars. In J. Freeman (Ed.), *Women: A feminist perspective* (4th ed., pp. 217–235). Mountain View, CA: Mayfield.

Frederick, C. M., & Grow, V. M. (1996). A mediational model of autonomy, self-esteem, and eating disordered attitudes and behaviors. *Psychology of Women Quarterly, 20,* 217–228.

Fredrickson, B. L., & Roberts, T. (1997). Objectification theory: Toward understanding women's lived experiences and mental health risks. *Psychology of Women Quarterly, 21,* 173–207.

Freedman, R. (1986). *Beauty bound.* Lexington, MA: D. C. Heath.

Freiberg, P. (1991). Self-esteem gender gap widens in adolescence. *APA Monitor, 22*(4), 29.

Freire, M. (1991). *Violence in the lives of refugee women.* Paper presented at Violence in the lives of immigrant and refugee women: Cross-cultural views conference, Hispanic Council of Metropolitan Toronto.

Friedan, B. (1993). *The fountain of age.* New York: Simon & Schuster.

Friedman, A. R. (1992). Rape and domestic violence: The experience of refugee women [Special issue: Refugee women and their mental health: Shattered societies, shattered lives: I]. *Women and Therapy, 13,* 65–78.

Frieze, I. H., & Browne, A. (1989). Violence in marriage. In L. Ohlin & M. H. Tonrey (Eds.), *New approaches to social problems: Applications of attribution theory* (pp. 79–108). Chicago: University of Chicago Press.

Furuichi, T., & Ihobe, H. (1994). Variation in male relationships in bonobos and chimpanzees. *Behavior, 130,* 212–228.

Gagneux, P., Woodruff, D. S., & Boesch, C. (1997). Furtive mating in female chimpanzees. *Nature, 387,* 358–359.

Gangestad, S. W. (1993). Sexual selection and physical attractiveness: Implications for mating dynamics. *Human Nature, 4,* 205–236.

Gaquin, D. A. (1977–1978). Spouse abuse: Data from the national crime survey. *Victimology: An International Journal, 2,* 632–642.

Gardiner, S., & McGrath, F. (1995). Wife assault: A systemic approach that minimizes risk and maximizes responsibility. *Journal of Systemic Therapies, 14*(1), 20–32.

Garmezy, N. (1983). Stressors of childhood. In N. Garmezy & M. Rutter (Eds.), *Stress, coping, and development in children.* New York: McGraw-Hill.

Garmezy, N., & Masten, A. S. (1994). Chronic adversities. In M. Rutter, E. Taylor, & L. Hersov (Eds.), *Child and adolescent psychiatry.* Oxford, England: Blackwell.

Gazmararian, J. A., Adams, M. M., Saltzman, L. E., Johnson, C. H., Bruce, F. C., Marks, J. S., & Zahniser, S. C. (1995). The relationship between pregnancy intendedness and physical violence in mothers of newborns. *Obstetrics & Gynecology, 85,* 1031–1038.

Geffner, R., Mantooth, C., Franks, D., & Rao, L. (1989). A psychoeducational conjoint therapy approach to reducing family violence. In P. Caesar & L. Hamberger (Eds.), *Treating men who batter.* New York: Springer.

Geffner, R., & Rosenbaum, A. (1992). Brain impairment and family violence. In D. I. Templer, L. C. Hartlage, & W. G. Cannon (Eds.), *Preventable brain damage* (pp. 58–71). New York: Springer.

Geis, F. L. (1993). Self-fulfilling prophecies: A social psychological view of gender. In A. Beall & R. J. Sternberg (Eds.), *The psychology of gender* (pp. 9–54). New York: Guilford.

Gelles, R. J. (1974). *The violent home.* Beverly Hills, CA: Sage.

Gelles, R. J. (1979). *Family violence.* Beverly Hills, CA: Sage.

Gelles, R. J. (1985). *Intimate violence in families.* Beverly Hills, CA: Sage.

Gelles, R. J. (1993a). Alcohol and other drugs are associated with violence—they are not its cause. In R. Gelles & D. Loseke (Eds.), *Current controversies on family violence* (pp. 31–46). Newbury Park, CA: Sage.

Gelles, R. J. (1993b). Through a sociological lens. In R. Gelles & D. Loseke (Eds.), *Current controversies on family violence* (pp. 31–46). Newbury Park, CA: Sage.

Gelles, R. J., & Cornell, C. P. (1990). *Intimate violence in families.* Newbury Park, CA: Sage.

Gelles, R. J., Lackner, R., & Wolfner, G. D. (1993). *Risk-markers of men who batter.* Report prepared for the State of Connecticut, Superior Court, Family Division.

Gelles, R. J., & Loseke, D. R. (1993). *Current controversies on family violence.* Newbury Park, CA: Sage.

Gelles, R. J., & Maynard, P. E. (1995). A structural family systems approach to intervention in cases of family violence. In S. M. Stith & M. A. Straus (Eds.), *Understanding partner violence: Prevalence, causes, consequences and solutions.* Minneapolis, MN: National Council on Family Relations.

Gelles, R. J., & Straus, M. R. (1979). Determinants of violence in the family: Toward a theoretical integration. In W. R. Burr, R. Hill, F. I. Nye, & I. L. Reiss (Eds.), *Contemporary theories about the family* (Vol. 1, pp. 549–581). New York: Free Press.

Gelles, R. J., & Straus, M. R. (1989). *Intimate violence: The causes and consequences of abuse in the American family.* New York: Simon & Schuster.

George, L. K., Winfield, I., & Blazer, D. G. (1992). Sociocultural factors in sexual assault: Comparison of two representative samples of women. *Journal of Social Issues, 48,* 105–125.

Gerber, G. L. (1991). Gender stereotypes and power: Perceptions of the roles in violent marriages. *Sex-Roles, 24*(7–8), 439–458.

Giles-Sims, J. (1983). *Wife beating: A systems theory approach.* New York: Guilford.

Gilgun, J. F. (1996). Human development and adversity in ecological perspective, part 1: A conceptual framework. *Families in Society: The Journal of Contemporary Human Services, 77*(7), 395–402.

Gilligan, C. (1982). *In a different voice: Psychological theory and women's development.* Cambridge, MA: Harvard University Press.

Gilligan, J. (1996). *Violence: Our deadly epidemic and its causes.* New York: Putnam.

Gilmore, D. D. (1990). *Manhood in the making.* New Haven: Yale University Press.

Gitlin, M. J., & Pasnau, R. O. (1989). Psychiatric syndromes linked to reproductive function in women: A review of current knowledge. *American Journal of Psychiatry, 146*, 1413–1422.

Goldberg, H. (1982). The dynamic of rage between the sexes in a bonded relationship. In L. R. Barnhill (Ed.), *Clinical approaches to family violence* (pp. 60–67). Rockville, MD: Aspen Systems Corporation.

Goldberg, H. (1993). Masculine process/masculine pathology: A new psychodynamic approach. *Journal of Mental Health Counseling, 15*, 298–307.

Golden, C. J., Jackson, M. L., Peterson-Rohne, A., & Gontkovsky, S. T. (1996). Neuropsychological correlates of violence and aggression: A review of the clinical literature. *Aggression and Violent Behavior, 1*, 3–25.

Goldner, V. (1985a). Warning: Family therapy may be hazardous to your health. *Family Therapy Networker, 9*(6), 19–23.

Goldner, V. (1985b). Feminism and family therapy. *Family Process, 24*, 31–47.

Goldner, V. (1992). Making room for both/and. *Family Therapy Networker, 16*(2), 54–61.

Goldstein, D., & Rosenbaum, A. (1985). An evaluation of self-esteem of maritally violent men. *Family Relations, 34*, 426–428.

Gondolf, E. W. (1988). Who are those guys? Toward a behavioral typology of batterers. *Violence and Victims, 3*, 187–204.

Gondolf, E. W. (1993). Treating the batterer. In M. Hansen & M. Harway (Eds.), *Battering and family therapy: A feminist perspective*. Newbury Park, CA: Sage.

Gondolf, E. W., & Fisher, E. R. (1988). *Battered women as survivors: An alternative treating learned helplessness*. Lexington, MA: Lexington Books.

Good, G., Dell, D. M., & Mintz, L. B. (1989). Male roles and gender role conflict: Relationship to helpseeking in men. *Journal of Counseling Psychology, 3*, 295–300.

Good, G. E., Heppner, M. J., Hillenbrand-Gunn, T., & Wang, L. (1995). Sexual and psychological violence: An explanatory study of predictors in college men. *Journal of Men's Studies, 4*, 59–71.

Goodman, L. A., Koss, M. P., & Russo, N. F. (1993). Violence against women: Physical and mental health effects: Part 1. Research findings. *Applied and Preventive Psychology, 2*, 79–89.

Goodwin, R. (1994). Putting relationship aggression in its place: Contextualizing some recent research. In J. Archer (Ed.), *Male violence* (pp. 143–152). London: Routledge.

Gottman, J. M., Jacobson, N. S., Rushe, R. H., Shortt, J. W., Babcock, J., La Taillade, J. J., & Waltz, J. (1995). The relationship between heart rate reactivity, emotionally aggressive behavior, and general violence in batters. *Journal of Family Psychology, 9*(3), 227–248.

Gould, S. J. (1997). Darwinian fundamentalists. *The New York Review of Books, XLIV*(10), 34–37.

Gowaty, P. A. (1997). Introduction: Darwinian feminists and feminist evolutionist. In P. A. Gowaty (Ed.), *Feminism and evolutionary biology* (pp. 1–18). New York: Chapman & Hall.

Grambs, J. D. (1989). *Women over forty: Visions and realities* (rev. ed.). New York: Springer.

Gray, R. (1997). "In the belly of the monster": Feminism, developmental systems, and evolutionary explanations. In P. A. Gowaty (Ed.), *Feminism and evolutionary biology* (pp. 385–414). New York: Chapman & Hall.

Greene, A. F., Coles, C. J., & Johnson, E. H. (1994). Psychopathology and anger in inter-personal violence offenders. *Journal of Clinical Psychology, 50,* 906–912.

Greene, A. F., Lynch, T. F., Decker, B., & Coles, C. J. (1997). A transtheoretical psy-chobiological characterization of interpersonal violence offenders. *Aggression and Violent Behavior, 2,* 273–284.

Greer, G. (1992). *The challenge: Women, ageing and the menopause.* New York: Knopf.

Gutierres, S. E., Russo, N. F., & Urbanski, L. (1994). Sociocultural and psychological fac-tors in American Indian drug use: Implications for treatment. *International Journal of the Addictions, 29*(14), 1761–1786.

Gutsche, S., & Murray, M. (1991). The feminist meets the cybernetician: An integrated approach to spousal violence. *Journal of Strategic and Systemic Therapies, 10*(3&4), 76–91.

Halas, C., & Matteson, R. (1978). *Paradoxes: Key to women's distress. I've done so well—why do I feel so bad?* New York: Ballantine.

Haley, J. (1973). *Uncommon therapy.* New York: Norton.

Hall, R. M., & Sandler, B. R. (1982). *The classroom climate: A chilly one for women?* [Project on the Status and Education of Women]. Washington, DC: Association of American Colleges.

Hamberger, L. K., & Hastings, J. E. (1986). Personality correlates of men who abuse their partners: A cross-validation study. *Journal of Family Violence, 1,* 323–341.

Hamberger, L. K., & Hastings, J. E. (1988). Characteristics of male spouse abusers con-sistent with personality disorders. *Hospital and Community Psychology, 39,* 763–770.

Hamberger, L. K., & Hastings, J. E. (1991). Personality correlates of men who batter and non-violent men. Some continuities and discontinuities. *Journal of Family Violence, 6,* 131–147.

Hamberger, L. K., & Renzetti, C. (1996). *Domestic partner abuse.* New York: Springer.

Hamberger, L. K., Saunders, D. G., & Hovey, M. (1992). The prevalence of domestic vio-lence in community practice and rate of physician inquiry. *Family Medicine, 24,* 283–287.

Hamilton, M. C. (1991). *Preferences for sons or daughters and the sex role characteris-tics of the potential parents.* Paper presented at the meeting of the Association for Women in Psychology, Hartford, CT.

Hampton, R. L., & Gelles, R. J. (1994). Violence toward Black women in a nationally repr sentative sample of Black families. *Journal of Comparative Family Studies, 25,* 105–119.

Hampton, R. L., Gelles, R. J., & Harrop, J. W. (1989). Is violence in black families increas-ing: A comparison of 1975 and 1985 National Survey Rates. *Journal of Marriage and the Family, 51,* 969–980.

Hampton, R. L., & Yung, B. R. (1996). Violence in communities of color: Where we were, where we are, and where we need to be. In R. L. Hampton, P. Jenkins, & T. P. Gullotta (Eds.), *Preventing violence in America* (pp. 53–86). Thousand Oaks, CA: Sage.

Hansen, M. (1993). Feminism and family therapy: A review of feminist critiques of approaches to family violence. In M. Hansen & M. Harway (Eds.), *Battering and fam-ily therapy: A feminist perspective.* Newbury Park: Sage.

Hansen, M., & Goldenberg, I. (1993). Conjoint therapy with violent couples: Some valid considerations. In M. Hansen & M. Harway (Eds.), *Battering and family therapy: A feminist perspective.* Newbury Park, CA: Sage.

Hansen, M., & Harway, M. (1993). *Battering and family therapy.* Newbury Park, CA: Sage.

Hare–Mustin, R. T. (1978). A feminist approach to family therapy. *Family Process, 17,* 181–194.

Hare-Mustin, R. T. (1983). An appraisal of the relationship between women and psychotherapy: 80 years after the case of Dora. *American Psychologist, 38,* 593–601.

Hart, S. D., Dutton, D. G., & Newlove, T. (1993). The prevalence of personality disorder among wife assaulters. *Journal of Personality Disorders, 7,* 328–340.

Harway, M., & Evans, K. (1996). Working in groups with men who batter. In M. Andronico (Ed.), *Men in groups: Insights, interventions, psychoeducational work* (pp. 357–376). Washington, DC: American Psychological Association.

Harway, M., & Hansen, M. (1993). An overview of domestic violence. In M. Hansen & M. Harway (Eds.), *Battering and family therapy: A feminist perspective.* Newbury Park, CA: Sage.

Harway, M., & Hansen, M. (1994). *Spouse abuse: Assessing and treating battered women, batterers, and their children.* Sarasota, FL: Professional Resource Press.

Harway, M., Hansen, M., Rossman, B. B. R., Geffner, R., & Deitch, I. (1996). Families affected by domestic violence. In M. Harway (Ed.), *Treating the changing family: Handling normative and unusual events* (pp. 163–190). New York: Wiley.

Harway, M., & O'Neil, J. M. (1998). Men's violence toward women: Overview and description of a multivariate model. In M. Harway & J. O'Neil (Eds.), *New perspectives on men's violence against women.* Thousand Oaks, CA: Sage.

Hashimoto, C. (1997). Context and development of sexual behavior of wild bonobos (*pan paniscus*) at Wamba, Zaire. *International Journal of Primatology, 18,* 1–23.

Hayes, H., & Emshoff, J. (1993). Substance abuse and family violence. In R. Hampton, T. Gullotta, G. Adams, E. Potter, & R. Weissberg (Eds.), *Family violence: Prevention and treatment.* Newbury Park, CA: Sage.

Healey, S. (1986). Growing to be an old woman: Aging and ageism. In J. Alexander, D. Berrow, L. Domitrovich, M. Donnelly, & C. McLean (Eds.), *Women and aging* (pp. 58–62). Corvallis, OR: Calyx.

Heesacker, M., Rigazio-DiGilio, S. A., Prichard, S., & Ivey, A. E. (1998). *The cognitive-developmental orientation scale: Test construction and investigation.* Manuscript in preparation.

Hemmer, J. D., & Kleiber, D. A. (1981). Tomboys and sissies: Androgynous children? *Sex Roles, 7,* 1205–1211.

Henton, J., Cate, R., Koval, J., Lloyd, S., & Christopher, F. S. (1983). Romance and violence in dating relationships. *Journal of Family Issues, 4,* 467–482.

Herek, G. M. (1986). On heterosexual masculinity. *American Behavioral Scientist, 29,* 563–577.

Herman, J. L. (1992). *Trauma and recovery.* New York: Basic Books.

Hess, B., & Waring, J. (1983). Family relationships of older women: A women's issue. In E. W. Markson (Ed.), *Older women: Issues and prospects* (pp. 227–251). Lexington, MA: Lexington Books.

Hewlett, B. S. (1992). Husband–wife reciprocity and the father–infant relationship among Aka pygmies. In B. S. Hewlett (Ed.), *Father–child relations: Cultural and biosocial contexts* (pp. 153–176). New York: Aldine de Gruyter.

Heyn, D. (1989). Body hate. *Ms.*, July/August, pp. 35–36.

Higgins, G. O. (1994). *Resilient adults: Overcoming a cruel past.* San Francisco: Jossey-Bass.

Hill, H., Soriano, S., Chen, A., & La Framboise, T. (1995). Sociocultural factors in the etiology and prevention of violence among ethnic minority youth. In L. D. Eron, J. H. Gentry, & P. Schlegel (Eds.), *Reason to hope: A psychosocial perspective on youth and violence* (pp. 59–100). Washington, DC: American Psychological Association.

Hill, R. (1972). *The strengths of Black families.* New York: Emerson-Hall.

Ho, C. K. (1990). An analysis of domestic violence in Asian American communities: A multicultural approach to counseling. In L. S. Brown & M. P. P. Root (Eds.), *Diversity and complexity in feminist therapy* (pp. 129–150). Binghamton, NY: Harrington Park Press.

Hochschild, A. (1989). *The second shift: Working parents and the revolution at home.* New York: Viking.

Hoff, L. A. (1990). *Battered women as survivors.* London: Routledge.

Hoffman, K., Demo, D., & Edwards, J. (1994). Physical wife abuse in a non-western society: An integrated theoretical approach. *Journal of Marriage and the Family, 56,* 131–146.

Hoffnung, M. (1984). Motherhood: Contemporary conflict for women. In J. Freeman (Ed.), *Women: A feminist perspective* (3rd ed., pp. 124–138). Palo Alto, CA: Mayfield.

Hokanson, J. E., Burgess, M., & Cohen, M. F. (1963). Effects of displaced aggression on systolic blood pressure. *Journal of Abnormal and Social Psychology, 67,* 214–218.

Holtzworth-Munroe, A., & Hutchinson, G. (1993). Attributing negative intent to wife behavior: The attributions of maritally violent versus non-violent men. *Journal of Abnormal Psychology, 102,* 206–211.

Holtzworth-Munroe, A., Markman, H., O'Leary, K. D., Neidig, P., Leber, D., Heyman, R., Hulbert, D., & Smutzler, N. (1995). The need for marital violence prevention efforts: A behavioral-cognitive secondary prevention program for engaged and newly married couples. *Applied and Preventive Psychology, 4,* 77–88.

Holtzworth-Munroe, A., & Stuart, (1994). Typologies of male batterers: Three subtypes and the differences among them. *Psychological Bulletin, 116,* 476–497.

Horney, K. (1973). *Feminine psychology.* New York: Norton.

Hornung, C., McCullough, C., & Sugimoto, T. (1981). Status relationships in marriage: Risk factors in spouse abuse. *Journal of Marriage and the Family, 43,* 675–692.

Hotaling, G. T., Straus, M. A., & Lincoln, A. J. (1990). Intrafamily violence and crime and violence outside the family. In M. A. Straus & R. J. Gelles (Eds.), *Physical violence in American families: Risk factors and adaptations to violence in 8,145 families.* New Brunswick, NJ: Transaction Publishers.

Hotaling, G. T., & Sugarman, D. B. (1986). An analysis of risk markers in husband to wife violence: The current state of knowledge. *Violence and Victims, 1,* 101–124.

Hotaling, G. T., & Sugarman, D. B. (1990). A risk marker analysis of assaulted wives. *Journal of Family Violence, 5*(1), 1–13.

Howell, M. J., & Pugliesi, K. L. (1988). Husbands who harm: Predicting violence by men. *Journal of Family Violence, 3,* 15–27.

Hrdy, S. B. (1990). Sex bias in nature and in history. A late 1980's reexamination of the "biological origins" argument. *Yearbook of Physical Anthropology, 33,* 25–37.

Hrdy, S. B. (1995). The primate origins of female sexuality, and their implications for the role of nonreceptive sex in the reproductive strategies of women. *Journal of Human Evolution, 10*, 131–144.

Hrdy, S. B. (1997). Raising Darwin's consciousness: Female sexuality and the prehominid origins of patriarchy. *Human Nature, 8*, 1–49.

Huesmann, L. R., Eron, L., Lefkowitz, M., & Walder, L. (1984). Stability of aggression over time and generations. *Developmental Psychology, 20*, 1120–1134.

Huston, A. (1983). Sex typing. In P. H. Mussen (Ed.), *Handbook of child psychology* (vol.4). New York: Wiley.

Hyde, J. S. (1991). *Half the human experience: The psychology of women* (4th ed.). Lexington, MA: D. C. Heath.

Hyde, J. S., Rosenberg, B. G., & Behrman, J. (1977). Tomboyism. *Psychology of Women Quarterly, 2*, 73–75.

Idani, G. (1991). Social relationships between immigrant and resident bonobo (*pan paniscus*) females at Wamba. *Folia Primatologica, 57*, 83–95.

Imber-Black, E. (1986). Maybe "linear causality" needs another defense lawyer: A response to Dell. *Family Process, 25*, 523–525.

Infante, D. A., Sabourin, T. C., Rudd, J. E., & Shannon, E. A. (1990). Verbal aggression in violent and nonviolent marital disputes. *Communication Quarterly, 38*, 361–371.

Innes, C. A., & Greenfeld, L. A. (1990). *Violent state prisoners and their victims.* Bureau of Justice Statistics special report (NCJ #124–133). Washington, DC: U.S. Department of Justice.

Ivey, A. E. (1986). *Developmental therapy: Theory into practice.* San Francisco: Jossey-Bass.

Ivey, A. E. (1991). *Developmental strategies for helpers: Individual, family, and network interventions.* Pacific Grove, CA: Brooks/Cole.

Ivey, A. E., & Rigazio-DiGilio, S. A. (1991). Development over the life span. In A. Ivey (Ed.), *Developmental strategies for helpers: Individual, family, and network interventions* (pp. 119–158). Pacific Grove, CA: Brooks/Cole.

Jackson, L. A. (1992). *Physical appearance and gender: Sociobiological and sociocultural perspectives.* Albany: State University of New York Press.

Jacobs, J. (1996). Psychological and demographic correlates of men's perception of and attitudes toward sexual harassment (Doctoral Dissertation, University of Southern California). *Dissertation Abstracts International, 97/05*, 117.

Jacobson, N. S., Gottman, J. M., & Short, J. W. (1995). The distinction between Type 1 and Type 2 batterers— further considerations: Reply to Ornduff et al. (1995), Margolin et al. (1995), and Walker (1995). *Journal of Family Psychology, 9*, 272–279.

Jacobson, N. S., Gottman, J. M., Waltz, J., Rushe, R., Babcock, J., & Holtzworth-Munroe, A. (1994). Affect, verbal content, and psychophysiology in the arguments of couples with a violent husband. *Journal of Consulting and Clinical Psychology, 62*, 982–988.

James, K., & McIntyre, D. (1983). The reproduction of families: The social role of family therapy? *Journal of Marital & Family Therapy, 9*, 119–129.

Jang, D., Lee, D., & Morello-Frosch, R. (1991). Domestic violence in the immigrant and refugee community: Responding to the needs of immigrant women. *Response, 72*, 2–7.

Jenkins, P. (1996). *Threads that link community and family violence: Issues for prevention* (pp. 33–52). Thousand Oaks, CA: Sage.

Johnson, E. H., & Greene, A. F. (1992). The interview method for assessing anger: Development and validation. In E. H. Johnson, W. D. Gentry, & S. Julius (Eds.),

Personality, elevated blood pressure, and essential hypertension (pp. 25–66). Washington: Hemisphere Publishing Corporation.

Johnson, M. P. (1995). Patriarchal terrorism and common couple violence: Two forms of violence against women. *Journal of Marriage and the Family, 57*, 283–294.

Jong, E. (1994). *Fear of fifty*. New York: Harper Collins.

Jordan, J. V., Kaplan, A. G., Miller, J. B., Stiver, I. P., & Surrey, J. L. (1991). *Women's growth in connection: Writings from the Stone Center*. New York: Guilford.

Jung, C. G. (1953). Animus and anima. In *Collected works* (Vol. VII). New York: Pantheon.

Kahn, A. S. (1984). The power war: Male response to power loss under equality. *Psychology of Women Quarterly, 8*, 234–247.

Kalmuss, D. (1984). The intergenerational transmission of marital violence by men. *Journal of Marriage and the Family, 46*, 11–19.

Kalmuss, D., & Seltzer, J. (1986). Continuity in marital behavior in remarriage: The case of spouse abuse. *Journal of Marriage and the Family, 48*, 113–120.

Kano, T. (1992). *The last ape: Pygmy chimpanzee behavior and ecology*. Stanford, CA: Stanford University Press.

Kantor, G. K., Jasinski, J. L., & Aldarondo, E. (1994). Sociocultural status and incidence of marital violence in Hispanic families. *Violence and Victims, 9*(3), 207–222.

Kantor, G. K., & Jasinski, J. L. (1997). *Out of the darkness: Contemporary perspectives in family violence*. Thousand Oaks, CA: Sage.

Kanuha, V. (1994). Women of color in battering relationships. In L. Comas-Diaz & B. Greene (Eds.), *Women of color: Integrating ethnic and gender identities in psychotherapy*. New York: Guilford.

Kaplan, R., O'Neil, J. M., & Owen, S. (1993). Sexist, normative, and progressive masculinity and sexual assault: Empirical research. In J. M. O'Neil & G. Good (Chairs), *Research on men's sexual assault and constructive gender role interventions*. Symposium conducted at the American Psychological Association, Toronto, Canada.

Kaschak, E. (1992). *Engendered lives: A new psychology of women's experiences*. New York: Basic Books.

Kaufman, D. R. (1995). Professional women: How real are the recent gains? In J. Freeman (Ed.), *Women: A feminist perspective* (5th ed., pp. 287–305). Mountain View, CA: Mayfield.

Kaufman, G. (1992). The mysterious disappearance of battered women in family therapists' offices: Male privilege colluding with male violence. *Journal of Marital and Family Therapy, 18*, 233–243.

Kaufman, J., & Zigler, E. (1987). Do abused children become abusive parents? *American Journal of Orthopsychiatry, 57*, 186–192.

Kaufman-Kantor, G., & Straus, M. A. (1987). The drunken bum theory of wife beating. *Social Problems, 34*, 213–230.

Keller, E. L. (1996). Invisible victims: Battered women in psychiatric and medical emergency rooms. *Bulletin of the Menninger Clinic, 60*, 1–21.

Kelly, L. (1988). *Surviving sexual violence*. Minneapolis: University of Minnesota Press.

Kerouac, S., & Lescop, J. (1986). Dimensions of health in violent families. *Health Care for Women International, 7*, 413–426.

Kilbourne, J. (1994). Still killing us softly: Advertising and the obsession with thinness. In P. Fallon, M. A. Katzman, & S. C. Wooley (Eds.), *Feminist perspectives on eating disorders* (pp. 395–418). New York: Guilford.

Kilpatrick, D. G. (1990). Violence as a precursor of women's substance abuse: The rest of the drugs-violence story. In *Critical issue—substance abuse and violence: Drugs and violent crime*. Symposium conducted at the American Psychological Association Convention, Boston.

Kim, S. C. (1985). Family therapy for Asian Americans: A strategic-structural framework. *Psychotherapy, 22*, 342–348.

Kipnis, D. (1976). *The powerholders*. Chicago: University of Chicago Press.

Kishur, G. R. (1989). The male batterer: A multidimensional exploration of conjugal violence. *Dissertation Abstracts International, 49*, 2409A. (UMI No. 8814496)

Kohlberg, L. (1976). Moral stages and moralization: The cognitive-developmental approach. In T. Lickona (Ed.), *Moral development and behavior*. New York: Holt, Rinehart & Winston.

Kolbenschlag, M. (1981). *Kiss Sleeping Beauty goodbye*. Toronto: Bantam.

Koop, C. E. (1985). *The Surgeon General's workshop on violence and the public health*. Washington, DC: U.S. Government Printing Office.

Kortenhaus, C. M., & Demarest, J. (1993). Gender role stereotyping in children's literature: An update. *Sex Roles, 28*, 219–232.

Koss, M. P. (1988). *Women's mental health research agenda: Violence against women* [Women's mental health occasional paper series]. Washington, DC: National Institute of Mental Health.

Koss, M. P., Goodman, L. A., Browne, A., Fitzgerald, L. F., Keita, G. P., & Russo, N. F. (1994). *No safe haven: Male violence against women at home, at work and in the community*. Washington, DC: American Psychological Association.

Koss, M. P., Heise, L., & Russo, N. F. (1994). The global health burden of rape. *Psychology of Women Quarterly, 18*, 509–530.

Koss, M. P., & Heslet, L. (1992). Somatic consequences of violence against women. *Archives of Family Medicine, 1*, 53–59.

Koss, M. P., Koss, P. G., & Woodruff, W. J. (1991). Deleterious effects of criminal victimization on women's health and medical utilization. *Archives of Internal Medicine, 151*, 342–357.

Kozol, W. (1995). Fracturing domesticity: Media, nationalism, and the question of feminist influence. *Signs, 20*, 646–666.

Kreuz, L. E., & Rose, R. M. (1972). Assessment of aggressive behavior and plasma testosterone in young criminal population. *Psychosomatic Medicine, 34*, 321–332.

Kunkler, K. P., & Rigazio-DiGilio, S. A. (1994). Systemic cognitive-developmental therapy: Organizing structured activities to facilitate family development. *Simulation and Gaming: An International Journal of Theory, Design, and Research, 25*, 75–87.

Kurt, J. (1995). Stalking as a variant of domestic violence. *Bulletin of the American Academy of Psychiatry and the Law, 23*, 219–230.

La Freniere, P., Strayer, F. F., & Gauthier, R. (1984). The emergence of same-sex affiliative preferences among preschool peers: A developmental/ethological perspective. *Child Development, 55*, 1958–1965.

La Fromboise, T., Choney, S. B., James, A., & Running Wolf, P. (1995). American Indian women and psychology. In H. Landrine (Ed.), *Bringing cultural diversity to feminist psychology: Theory, research and practice* (pp. 197–240). Washington, DC: American Psychological Association.

Lai, T. (1986). Asian women: Resisting the violence. In M. C. Burns (Ed.), *The speaking profits us: Violence in the lives of women of color* (pp. 8–11). Seattle, WA: Center for the prevention of sexual and domestic violence.

Laner, M. R. (1983). Courtship abuse and aggression: Contextual aspects. *Sociological Spectrum, 3*, 69–83.

Langan, P., & Innes, C. A. (1986). *Preventing domestic violence against women* [Bureau of Justice Statistics special report]. Washington, DC: U.S. Department of Justice.

Langhinrichsen-Rohling, J., Neidig, P., & Thorn, G. (1995). Violent marriages: Gender differences in levels of current violence and past abuse. *Journal of Family Violence, 10*(2), 159–176.

Lanza, A. S., Cramer, D., Kunkler, K. P., & Rigazio-DiGilio, S. A. (1994). *Part one of Connecticut's Family Violence Education Program: A systematic evaluation.* Prepared under contract with the Family Division, Superior Court, Judicial Branch, State of Connecticut.

Lanza, A. S., & Kunkler, K. P. (1994 December). *Developmental therapy (DT) and systemic cognitive-developmental therapy (SCDT): Creating An integrative framework for working with men who batter.* A presentation for the Connecticut Association for Marriage and Family Therapy's 1994 winter conference, Storrs, CT.

Lanza, A. S., Rigazio-DiGilio, S. A., & Kunkler, K. P. (1993 January). *Developmental therapy: An integrative approach to group treatment with men who batter.* Presentation for the American Association for Marriage & Family Therapy 1993 national conference, Anaheim, CA.

Lanza, A. S., Rigazio-DiGilio, S. A., & Kunkler, K. P. (1994). The assessment and treatment of relationship violence: A co-constructive developmental approach. *Family Counseling and Therapy, 2*(2), 1–24.

Lanza, A. S., Rigazio-DiGilio, S. A., & Kunkler, K. P. (1995). *Cognitive-Developmental Framework for Working with Men Who Batter: Assessment and Interventions Strategies.* A two-day professional training for the Family Division and Office of Alternative Sanctions, Judicial Branch, State of Connecticut.

Lanza, A. S., Rigazio-DiGilio, S. A., & Kunkler, K. P. (in press). Developmental counseling and therapy: An integrative approach to group treatment with men who batter. *Family Relations.*

Larner, G. (1994). Para-modern family therapy: Deconstructing post-modernism. *Australian & New Zealand Journal of Family Therapy, 15*(1), 11–16.

Lawson, D. (1989). A family systems perspective on wife battering. *Journal of Mental Health Counseling, 11*, 359–374.

Lazarus, R. S. (1991a). Cognition and motivation in emotion. *American Psychologist, 46*, 352–367.

Lazarus, R. S. (1991b). Progress on a cognitive-motivational-relational theory of emotion. *American Psychologist, 46*, 819–834.

Lee, R. S. (1995). Machismo values and violence in America: An empirical study. In L. L. Adler & F. L. Denmark (Ed.), *Violence and the prevention of violence* (pp. 11–31). Westport, CT: Praeger.

Lehr, R. F., & Fitzsimmons, G. (1991). Adaptability and cohesion: Implications for understanding the violence-prone system. *Journal of Family Violence, 6*(3), 255–265.

Lerner, H. G. (1987). Is family systems theory really systemic? A feminist communication. *Journal of Psychotherapy & the Family, 3*(4), 47–63.

Lerner, I. M. (1968). *Heredity, evolution, and society.* San Francisco: Freeman.

Lesnoff–Caravaglia, G. (1984). Double stigmata: Female and old. In G. Lesnoff–Caravaglia (Ed.), *The world of the older woman* (pp. 11–20). New York: Human Sciences.

Lesse, S. (1979). The status of violence against women: Past, present, and future factors. *American Journal of Psychotherapy, 33*, 190–200.

Levant, R. F., & Pollack, W. S. (Eds.). (1995). *A new psychology of men.* New York: Basic Books.

Levinson, D. (1989a). *Family violence in cross-cultural perspective.* Newbury Park, CA: Sage.

Levinson, D. (1989b). Integrated study of intimate violence. In L. K. Hamberger & C. Renzetti (Eds.), *Domestic partner abuse* (pp. 191–212). New York: Springer.

Levinson, D. J., Darrow, C. H., Klein, E. B., Levinson, M. H., & McKee, B. (1978). *The seasons of a man's life.* New York: Ballantine.

Lewis, D. O., Moy, E., Jackson, L. D., Aaronson, R., Restifo, N., Serra, S., & Simos, A. (1985). Biopsychosocial characteristics of children who later murder: A prospective study. *American Journal of Psychiatry, 142*, 1161–1167.

Lewis, M. (1972). Parents and children: Sex role development. *The School Review, 80*, 229–240.

Lightdale, J. R., & Prentice, D. A. (1994). Rethinking sex differences in aggression: Aggressive behavior in the absence of social roles. *Personality and Social Psychology Bulletin, 20*, 34–44.

Linnoila, M., Virkkunen, M., Scheinin, M., Nuutila, A., Rimon, R., & Goodwin, F. K. (1983). Low cerebrospinal fluid 5-hydroxyindoleacetic acid concentration differentiates impulsive from nonimpulsive violent behavior. *Life Sciences, 33*, 2609–2614.

Lloyd, S. (1991). The dark side of courtship: Violence and sexual exploitation. *Family Relations, 40*, 14–20.

Lloyd, S. (1996). Physical aggression, distress, and everyday marital interaction. In D. Cahn & S. Lloyd (Eds.), *Family violence from a communication perspective* (pp. 177–198). Thousand Oaks, CA: Sage.

Lloyd, S. A. (1990). Conflict types and strategies in violent marriages. *Journal of Family Violence, 5*(4), 269–284.

Lockhart, L. (1985). Methodological issues in comparative racial analyses: The case of wife abuse. *Social Work Research and Abstracts, 21*, 35–41.

Lockhart, L., & White, B. W. (1989). Understanding marital violence in the Black community. *Journal of Interpersonal Violence, 49*, 421–436.

Lohr, J. M., Hamberger, L. K., & Bonge, D. (1988). The relationship of factorially validated measures of anger-proneness and irrational beliefs. *Motivation and Emotion, 12*, 171–183.

Lopata, H. Z. (1979). *Women as widows*. New York: Elsevier.

Lott, B. (1978). Behavioral concordance with sex role ideology related to play areas, creativity, and parental sex-typing of children. *Journal of Personality and Social Psychology, 36*, 1087–1100.

Lovdal, L. T. (1989). Sex role messages in television commercials: An update. *Sex Roles, 21*, 715–724.

Luthar, S. S., Doernberger, C. H., & Zigler, E. (1993). Resiliency is not a unidimensional construct: Insights from a prospective study of inner-city adolescents. *Development and Psychopathology, 5*, 703–717.

Lytton, H., & Romney, D. M. (1991). Parents' differential socialization of boys and girls: A meta-analysis. *Psychological Bulletin, 109*, 267–296.

MacDonald, A. P., Jr. (1976). Homophobia: Its roots and meanings. *Homosexual Counseling Journal, 3*, 23–33.

MacEwen, K. E., & Barling, J. (1998). Multiple stressors, violence in, and marital aggression: A longitudinal investigation. *Journal of Family Violence, 3*, 73–87.

Magill, J. (1989). Family therapy: An approach to the treatment of wife assault. In B. Pressman, G. Cameron, & M. Rothery (Eds.), *Intervening with assaulted women: Current theory, research, and practice*. Hillsdale, NJ: Erlbaum.

Mahalik, J. R., & Cournoyer, R. J. (1997). *Contributions of gender role conflict to men's cognitive distortions: Implications for treatment of depression*. Chestnut Hill, MA: Boston College.

Mahalik, J. R., Cournoyer, R., DeFranc, W., Cherry, M., & Napolitano, J. (1998). Men's gender role conflict and use of psychological defenses. *Journal of Counseling Psychology, 45*, 247–255.

Maiuro, R. D., Cahn, T. S., & Vitaliano, P. P. (1986). Assertiveness deficits and hostility in domestically violent men. *Violence and Victims, 4*, 277–289.

Maiuro, R. D., Cahn, T. S., Vitaliano, P. P., Wagner, B. C., & Zegree, J. B. (1988). Anger, hostility and depression in domestically violent versus generally assaultive men and nonviolent control subjects. *Journal of Consulting and Clinical Psychology, 56*, 17–23.

Majors, R., & Billson, J. M. (1992). *Cool pose: The dilemmas of Black manhood in America*. Lexington, MA: Lexington Books.

Makepeace, J. (1981). Courtship violence among college students. *Family Relations, 30*, 97–102.

Makepeace, J. M. (1983). Life events stress and courtship violence. *Family Relations, 32*, 101–109.

Malamuth, N. M., Heavey, C. L., & Linz, D. (in preparation). *Sexual arousal to aggression, empathy level and the prediction of sexual aggression: A 10-year follow-up study*.

Malamuth, N. M., Sockoskie, R. J., Koss, M. P., & Tanaka, J. S. (1991). Characteristics of aggressors against women: Testing a model using a national sample of college students, *Journal of Consulting and Clinical Psychology, 59*, 670–681.

Margolin, G. (1988). Interpersonal and intrapersonal factors associated with marital violence. In G. T. Hotaling, D. Finkelhor, M. Straus, & J. Kirkpatrick (Eds.), *Family abuse and its consequences: New directions in research* (pp. 203–217). Newbury Park, CA: Sage.

Margolin, G., & Burman, B. (1993). Wife abuse versus marital violence: Different terminologies, explanations, and solutions. *Clinical Psychology Review, 13*, 59–73.

Margolin, G., Gordis, E. B., Oliver, P. H., & Raine, A. (1995). A physiologically based
typology of batterers—promising but preliminary: Comment on Gottman et al. (1995).
Journal of Family Psychology, 9, 253–263.

Margolin, G., John, R. S., Ghosh, C. M., & Gordis, E. B. (1996). Family interaction
process: An essential tool for exploring abusive relations. In D. Cahn & S. Lloyd
(Eds.), *Family violence from a communication perspective* (pp. 37–58). Thousand
Oaks, CA: Sage.

Marsh, C. (1993). Sexual assault and domestic violence in the African American community. *Western Journal of Black Studies, 17*, 149–155.

Martin, C. L. (1990). Attitudes and expectations about children with nontraditional and
traditional gender roles. *Sex Roles, 22*, 151–165.

Martin, D. (1983). *Battered wives*. New York: Pocket Books.

Martz, D. M., Handley, K. B., & Eisler, R. M. (1995). The relationship between feminine
gender role stress, body image, and eating disorders. *Psychology of Women Quarterly,
19*, 493–508.

Maruniak, J. A., Desjardins, C., & Bronson, F. H. (1977). Dominant-subordinate relationships in castrated male mice bearing testosterone implants. *American Journal of
Physiology, 233*, 495–499.

Masten, A. S. (1989). Resilience in development: Implications of the study of successful
adaption for developmental psychopathology. In D. Cicchetti (Ed.), *The emergence of
a discipline: Rochester Symposium on Developmental Psychopathology* (Vol. 1,
pp. 263–294). Hillsdale, NJ: Erlbaum.

Masten, A. S. (1994). Resilience in individual development: Successful adaptation despite
risk and adversity. In M. C. Wang & E. W. Gordon (Eds.), *Educational resilience in
inner-city America: Challenges and prospects* (pp. 3–23). Hillsdale, NJ: Erlbaum.

Masten, A. S., Best, K. M., & Garmezy, N. (1991). Resilience and development:
Contributions from the study of children who overcome adversity. *Development and
Psychology, 2*(4), 425–444.

Matlin, M. W. (1996). *The psychology of women* (3rd ed.). Fort Worth, TX: Harcourt
Brace.

Mazur, A., & Lamb, T. (1980). Testosterone, status, and mood in human males. *Hormones
and Behavior, 14*, 236–246.

McCall, G. J., & Shields, N. M. (1986). Social and structural factors in family violence. In
M. Lystad (Ed.), *Violence in the home: Interdisciplinary perspectives* (pp. 98–123).
New York: Bruner Mazel.

McCloskey, L. A., Figueredo, A. J., & Koss, M. P. (1995). The effects of systemic family
violence on children's mental health. *Child Development, 66*, 1239–1261.

McCloskey, L. A., Southwick, K., Fernandez, E., Eugenia, M., & Locke, C. (1995). The
psychological effects of political and domestic violence on Central American and
Mexican immigrant mothers and children. *Journal of Community Psychology, 23*,
95–116.

McHugh, M. C., Frieze, I. H., & Browne, A. (1993). Research on battered women and
their assailants. In F. L. Denmark & M. A. Paludi (Eds.), *Psychology of women: A
handbook of issues and theories* (pp. 513–552). Westport, CT: Greenwood.

McKinley, N. M., & Hyde, J. S. (1996). The Objectified Body Consciousness Scale. *Psychology of Women Quarterly, 20,* 181–215.

Medea, A., & Thompson, K. (1974). *Against rape.* New York: Farrar, Straus and Giroux.

Mednick, S. A., Gabrielli, W. F., & Hutchings, B. (1984). Genetic influences in criminal convictions: Evidence from an adoption cohort. *Science, 224,* 891–894.

Miedzian, M. (1991). *Boys will be boys: Breaking the link between masculinity and violence.* New York: Doubleday.

Miller, J. B. (1986). *Toward a new psychology of women* (2nd ed.). Boston: Beacon.

Miller, J. B. (1991). Women and power. In J. V. Jordan, A G. Kaplan, J. B. Miller, I. P Stiver, & J. L. Surrey (Eds.), *Women's growth in connection: Writings from the Stone Center* (pp. 197–205). New York: Guilford.

Miller, S. L. (1996). *Expanding the boundaries: Toward a more inclusive out of the darkness: Contemporary perspectives in family violence.* Thousand Oaks, CA: Sage.

Miller, T. R., Cohen, M. A., & Wiersema, B. (1996). *Victim costs and consequences.* Washington, DC: National Institute of Justice.

Mintz, L. B., & Betz, N. E. (1988). Prevalence and correlates of eating disordered behaviors among undergraduate women. *Journal of Counseling Psychology, 15,* 463–471.

Mitchell, V., & Helson, R. (1990). Women's prime in life: Is it the 50's? *Psychology of Women Quarterly, 14,* 451–470.

Mollica, R., Wyshak, G., & La Valle, J. (1987). The psychological impact of war trauma and torture on southeast Asian refugees. *American Journal of Psychiatry, 144,* 1567–1571.

Moltz, D. (1992). Abuse and violence: The dark side of the family. An introduction. *Journal of Marital and Family Therapy, 18*(3), 223.

Mones, A. G., & Panitz, P. E. (1994). Marital violence: An integrated systems approach. *Journal of Social Distress and the Homeless, 3,* 39–51.

Money, J., & Ehrhardt, A. A. (1972). *Man and woman, boy and girl: Differentiation and dimorphism of gender identity from conception to maturity.* Baltimore, MD: Johns Hopkins University Press.

Morin, S. F., & Garfinkle, E. M. (1978). Male homophobia. *Journal of Social Issues, 34,* 29–47.

Morley, R. (1994). Wife beating and modernization: The case of Papua, New Guinea. *Journal of Comparative Family Studies, 25,* 25–52.

Mosher, D. L., & Tomkins, S. S. (1988). Scripting the macho man: Hypermasculinity socialization and enculturation. *Journal of Sex Research, 25,* 60–84.

Moyer, K. (1987). *Violence and aggression: A physiological perspective.* New York: Paragon House.

Mullins, C. R., & Linz, D. (1995). Desensitization and resensitization to violence against women: Effects of exposure to sexually violent films on judgments of domestic violence victims. *Journal of Personality and Social Psychology, 69,* 449–459.

Murphy, C. M., Meyers, S. L., & O'Leary, K. D. (1993). Brief report: Family of origin violence and MCMI-II psychopathology among partner assaultive men. *Violence & Victims, 8*(2), 165–176.

Murphy, C. M., & O'Leary, K. D. (1989). Psychological aggression predicts physical aggression in early marriage. *Journal of Consulting and Clinical Psychology, 57,* 579–582.

National Aging Resource Center on Elder Abuse. (1990). *Elder abuse—questions and answers: An information guide for professionals and concerned citizens.* Washington, DC: Author.

Nelson, D. E., Higginson, G. K., & Grant-Worley, J. A. (1995). Physical abuse among high school students. Prevalence and correlation with other health behaviors. *Archives of Pediatric Adolescent Medicine, 149,* 1254–1258.

Newman, B. M., & Newman, P. R. (1995). *Developments through life: A psychosocial approach.* Pacific Grove, CA: Brooks/Cole.

New York City Department for the Aging (1990). *Elder abuse a profile of victims served by the New York City Department for the Aging.* New York: Author.

Nisbett, R. (1993). Violence and U.S. regional culture. *American Psychologist, 48,* 441–449.

Norton, A. J., & Moorman, J. E. (1987). Current trends in marriage and divorce among American women. *Journal of Marriage and the Family, 49,* 3–14.

Norton, I., & Manson, S. (1995). A silent minority: Battered American Indian women. *Journal of Family Violence, 10,* 307–318.

Nutt, R. L. (1991). Ethical principles for gender-fair family therapy. *The Family Psychologist, 7*(3), 32–33.

Nutt, R. L., & Gottlieb, M. C. (1993). Gender diversity in clinical psychology: Research, practice, and training. *The Clinical Psychologist, 46,* 64–73.

O'Brien, J. (1971). Violence in divorce prone families. *Journal of Marriage and the Family, 33,* 692–698.

O'Brien, M., & Huston, A. C. (1985a). Development of sex-typed play in toddlers. *Developmental Psychology, 21,* 866–871.

O'Brien, M., & Huston, A. C. (1985b). Activity level and sex stereotyped toy choice in toddler boys and girls. *Journal of Genetic Psychology, 146,* 527–534.

Ofei-Aboagye, R. (1994). Altering the strands of fabric: A preliminary look at domestic violence in Ghana [Special issue: Feminism and the law]. *Signs, 19,* 924–938.

Okun, L. (1986). *Woman abuse: Facts replacing myths.* Albany: State University of New York Press.

O'Leary, K. D. (1993). Through a psychological lens. In R. Gelles, & D. Loseke (Eds). *Current controversies on family violence* (pp. 7–30). Newbury Park, CA: Sage.

O'Leary, K. D., Malone, J., & Tyree, A. (1994). Physical aggression in early marriage: Prerelationship and relationship effects. *Journal of Consulting and Clinical Psychology, 62*(3), 594–602.

O'Leary, K. D., & Murphy, C. (1992). Clinical issues in the assessment of spouse abuse. In R. T. Ammerman & M. Hersen (Eds.), *Assessment of family violence: A clinical and legal handbook.* New York: Wiley.

O'Neil, J. M. (1981a). Patterns of gender role conflict and strain: Sexism and fear of femininity in men's lives. *Personnel and Guidance Journal, 60,* 203–210.

O'Neil, J. M. (1981b). Male sex-role conflict, sexism, and masculinity: Implications for men, women, and the counseling psychologist. *The Counseling Psychologist, 9,* 61–80.

O'Neil, J. M. (1982). Gender role conflict and strain in men's lives: Implications for psychiatrists, psychologists, and other human service providers. In K. Solomon & N. B. Levy (Eds.), *Men in transition: Changing male roles, theory, and therapy* (pp. 5–44). New York: Plenum.

O'Neil, J. M. (1990). Assessing men's gender role conflict. In D. Moore & F. Leafgren (Eds.), *Men in conflict: Problem solving strategies and interventions* (pp. 23–38). Alexandria, VA: American Association for Counseling and Development.

O'Neil, J. M. (1992). *A gender role workshop focused on sexism, gender role conflict, and the gender role journey.* Storrs, CT: University of Connecticut.

O'Neil, J. M. (1995). Fifteen years of theory and research on men's gender role conflict. New paradigms for empirical research. In R. F. Levant & W. S. Pollack (Eds.), *A new psychology of men* (pp. 164–206). New York: Basic Books.

O'Neil, J. M. (1998). *Gender role conflict research program (1978–present)* [on line]. School of Family Studies, University of Connecticut, Storrs, CT. Available: www.familystudies.uconn.edu/oneil.htm.

O'Neil, J. M., & Egan, J. (1992a). Abuses of power against women: Sexism, gender role conflict, and psychological violence. In E. P. Cook (Ed.), *Women, relationships, and power: Implications for counseling* (pp. 49–78). Alexandria, VA: American Counseling Association Press.

O'Neil, J. M., & Egan, J. (1992b). Men's and women's gender role journeys: A metaphor for healing, transition, and transformation. In B. R. Wainrib (Ed.), *Gender issues across the life cycle* (pp. 107–123). New York: Springer.

O'Neil, J. M., Fishman, D. M., & Kinsella Shaw, M. (1987). Dual-career couples, career transitions and normative dilemma: A preliminary assessment model. *The Counseling Psychologist, 15,* 50–96.

O'Neil, J. M., & Good, G. E. (1997). Men's gender role conflict: Personal reflections and overview of recent research. *Society for the Psychological Study of Men and Masculinity Bulletin, 2,* 10–15.

O'Neil, J. M., Good, G. E., & Holmes, S. (1995). Fifteen years of theory and research on men's gender role conflict: New paradigms for empirical research. In R. Levant & W. Pollack (Eds.), *The new psychology of men* (pp. 164–206). New York: Basic Books.

O'Neil, J. M., & Harway, M. (1994). Understanding male violence against female partners. In R. Levant (chair). *Women, men, change, and the family.* Invited paper and dialogue, American Psychological Association Miniconvention, Psychology looks at families: Implications for the future, Los Angeles, CA.

O'Neil, J. M., & Harway, M. (1997). A multivariate model explaining men's violence toward women: Predisposing and triggering hypotheses. *Violence Against Women, 3*(2), 182–203.

O'Neil, J. M., Harway, M., Brooks, G., & Hansen, M. (1995). *Expanding psychology's knowledge of violence against women: Psychologists dialogue.* Symposium presented at the 26th annual APA Mid-winter convention, New Orleans, LA.

O'Neil, J. M., Helms, B., Gable, R., David, L., & Wrightsman, L. (1986). Gender-role conflict scale: College men's fear of femininity. *Sex Roles, 14,* 335–350.

Otterbein, K. F. (1979). A cross-cultural study of rape. *Aggressive Behavior, 5,* 425–435.

Oyama, S. (1989). Ontogeny and the central dogma: Do we need the concept of genetic programming in order to have an evolutionary perspective? In M. R. Gunnar &

E. Thelen (Eds.), *Systems and development. The Minnesota symposium on child psychology* (Vol. 22, pp. 1–34). Hillsdale, NJ: Erlbaum.

Pagelow, M. D. (1981). *Woman-battering: Victims and their experiences.* Newbury Park, CA: Sage.

Pagelow, M. D. (1984). *Family violence.* New York: Praeger.

Pagelow, M. D. (1992). Adult victims of domestic violence: Battered women. *Journal of Interpersonal Violence, 7,* 87–120.

Parish, A. R. (1996). Female relationships in Bonobos (*pan paniscus*): Evidence for binding, cooperation and female dominance in a male philopatric species. *Human Nature, 7,* 61–96.

Pence, E., & Paymar, M. (1986/1990). *Power and control tactics of men who batter: An educational curriculum.* Duluth: Minnesota Program Development, Inc.

Peplau, L. A., & Gordon, S. L. (1985). Women and men in love: Gender differences in close heterosexual relationships. In V. E. O'Leary, R. K. Unger, & B. S. Wallston (Eds.), *Women, gender, and social psychology* (pp. 257–292). Hillsdale, NJ: Erlbaum.

Perilla, J., Bakerman, R., & Norris, F. (1994). Culture and domestic violence: The ecology of abused Latinas. *Violence and Victims, 9,* 325–339.

Perkins, C., & Klaus, P. (1996). *Criminal victimization 1994: National crime victimization survey (NCJ #158022).* Washington, DC: U.S. Department of Justice.

Philpot, C. L., Brooks, G. R., Lusterman, D.-D., & Nutt, R. L. (1997). *Bridging separate gender worlds: Why men and women clash and how therapists can bring them together.* Washington, DC: American Psychological Association.

Piaget, J. (1954). *The construction of reality in the child.* New York: Basic Books.

Piaget, J. (1963). *The origins of intelligence in children.* New York: Norton.

Pierce, M. C., & Harris, R. J. (1993). The effect of provocation, race, and injury description on men's and women's perceptions of a wife-battering incident. *Journal of Applied Social Psychology, 23,* 767–790.

Pillemer, K. A., & Finkelhor, D. (1988). The prevalence of elder abuse: A random sample survey. *The Gerontologist, 28,* 51–57.

Pinderhughes, E. (1989). *Understanding race, ethnicity, and power.* New York: Free Press.

Pipher, M. (1994). *Reviving Ophelia: Saving the selves of adolescent girls.* New York: Ballantine.

Pittman, F. (1985). Gender myths: When does gender become pathology? *Family Therapy Networker, 9,* 25–33.

Pleck, J. (1981). *The myth of masculinity.* Cambridge: MIT Press.

Pleck, J. H. (1995). The gender role strain paradigm: An update. In R. F. Levant & W. Pollack (Eds.), *A new psychology of men* (pp. 11–32). New York: Basic Books.

Pleck, J. H., Sonenstein, F. L., & Ku, L. C. (1991). *Attitudes toward masculinity: Their impact on adolescent male–female relationships.* Paper presented at the 99th annual convention of the American Psychological Association, San Francisco, CA.

Pliner, P., Chaiken, S., & Flett, G. L. (1990). Gender differences in concern with body weight and physical appearance over the life span. *Personality and Social Psychology Bulletin, 16,* 263–273.

Plotnick, R., Mir, D., & Delgado, J. M. R. (1971). Aggression, noxiousness and brain stimulation in unrestrained rhesus monkeys. In B. E. Eleftheriou & J. P. Scott (Eds.), *The physiology of aggression and defeat*. New York: Plenum.

Plumb, P., & Cowan, G. (1984). A developmental study of de-stereotyping and androgynous activity preferences of tomboys, nontomboys, and males. *Sex Roles, 10*, 703–712.

Pollack, W. (1995). No man is an island: Toward a new psychoanalytic psychology of men. In R. Levant & W. Pollack (Eds.), *A new psychology of men* (pp. 33–67). New York: Basic Books.

Pomerleau, A., Bolduc, D., Malcuit, G., & Cossette, L. (1990). Pink or blue: Environmental gender stereotypes in the first two years of life. *Sex Roles, 22*, 359–367.

Pressman, B. (1989). Wife-abused couples: The need for comprehensive theoretical perspectives and integrated treatment models. *Journal of Feminist Family Therapy, 1*, 23–43.

Pressman, B. (1994). Violence against women: Ramifications of gender, class and race inequality. In M. P. Mirkin (Ed.), *Women in context: Toward a feminist reconstruction of psychotherapy* (pp. 352–389). New York: Guildford.

Ptacek, J. (1988). Why do men batter their wives? In K. Yllö & M. Bograd (Eds.), *Feminist perspectives on wife abuse* (pp. 133–157). Newbury Park, CA: Sage.

Purcell, P., & Stewart, L. (1990). Dick and Jane in 1989. *Sex Roles, 22*, 177–185.

Raine, A. (1993). *The psychopathology of crime: Criminal behavior as a clinical disorder*. San Diego, CA: Academic Press.

Ramirez, M., III (1991). *Psychotherapy and counseling with minorities*. New York: Pergamon.

Rando, R. A., Brittan, C. S., & Pannu, R. K. (1994). Gender role conflict and college men's sexually aggressive attitudes and behavior. In J. M. O'Neil & G. E. Good (Chairs), *Research on men's sexual and psychological assault of women*. Los Angeles, CA: American Psychological Association.

Report of the American Psychological Association Commission on Violence and Youth (1993). *Violence and youth: Psychology's response*. Washington, DC: American Psychological Association.

Report of the Task Force on Violence and the Family. (1996). *Violence and the family*. Washington, DC: American Psychological Association.

Reisenzein, R. (1983). The Schachter theory of emotion: Two deacaes later. *Psychological Bulletin, 94*, 239–264.

Rigazio-DiGilio, S. A. (1993). Family counseling and therapy: Theoretical foundations and issues of practice. In A. Ivey & L. Simek-Downing (Eds.), *Counseling and psychotherapy: A multicultural perspective* (3rd ed.). Needham Heights, MA: Allyn & Bacon.

Rigazio-DiGilio, S. A. (1994a). A co-constructive integration of treatment for individuals, families, and networks. *Journal of Mental Health Counseling, 16*(1), 43–73.

Rigazio-DiGilio, S. A. (1994b). A co-constructive-developmental approach to ecosystemic treatment. *Journal of Mental Health Counseling, 16*, 43–74.

Rigazio-DiGilio, S. A. (in press a). Systemic cognitive-developmental therapy: A counselling model and an integrative classification schema for working with partners and families. *International Journal for the Advancement of Counselling*.

Rigazio-DiGilio, S. A. (in press b). From microscopes to holographs: Clients and therapist development within a social constructivist paradigm. In T. Sexton & B. Griffin (Eds.), *Constructivist thinking in counseling and supervision.* New York: Teacher's College Press.

Rigazio-DiGilio, S. A., & Anderson, S. A. (1991). *A cognitive-developmental model of marriage and family therapy supervision.* AAMFT Supervision Leading Edge Series, Washington, DC.

Rigazio-DiGilio, S. A., & Anderson, S. A. (1994). A cognitive-developmental model for marital and family therapy supervision. *The Clinical Supervisor, 11,* 93–118.

Rigazio-DiGilio, S. A., Anderson, S. A., & Kunkler, K. P. (1995). Gender aware supervision in marriage and family therapy: How far have we actually come? For special section in *Counselor Education and Supervision, 34,* 344–355.

Rigazio-DiGilio, S. A., Daniels, T. G., & Ivey, A. E. (in press). Systemic cognitive-developmental supervision: A developmental-integrative approach to psychotherapy supervision. In C. E. Watkins, Jr. (Ed.), *Handbook of psychotherapy supervision.* New York: Wiley.

Rigazio-DiGilio, S. A., Goncalves, O., & Ivey, A. E. (1995). Developmental counseling and therapy: A framework for individual and family treatment. In D. Capuzzi & D. Gross (Eds.), *Counseling and psychotherapy: Theories and interventions.* Columbus, OH: MacMillan/Merrill.

Rigazio-DiGilio, S. A., Goncalves, O. F., & Ivey, A. E. (1996). From cultural to existential diversity: The impossibility of an integrative psychotherapy within a traditional framework. *Applied and Preventative Psychology: Current Scientific Perspectives, 5,* 235–248.

Rigazio-DiGilio, S. A., & Ivey, A. E. (1990). Developmental therapy and depressive disorders: Measuring cognitive levels through patient natural language. *Professional Psychology: Research and Practice, 21,* 470–475.

Rigazio-DiGilio, S. A., & Ivey, A. E. (1991). Developmental counseling and therapy: A framework for individual and family treatment. *Counseling & Human Development, 24*(1), 1–19.

Rigazio-DiGilio, S. A., & Ivey, A. E. (1993). Systemic cognitive-developmental therapy: An integrative framework. *Family Journal: Counseling for Couples and Families, 1*(3), 208–219.

Rigazio-DiGilio, S. A., & Ivey, A. E. (1995). Individual and family issues in intercultural counselling and therapy: A culturally-centered perspective. *Canadian Journal of Counselling, 29,* 244–261.

Rigazio-DiGilio, S. A., & Ivey, A. E. (1997). The helping interview: A cognitive-developmental approach. In O. Hargie (Ed.), *The handbook of communication skills* (pp. 409–429). New York: Routledge.

Rigazio-DiGilio, S. A., Ivey, A. E., & Locke, D. C. (in press). Continuing the post-modern dialogue: Enhancing and contextualizing multiple voices. *Journal of Mental Health Counseling.*

Rigazio-DiGilio, S. A., Lanza, A. S., & Kunkler, K. P. (1994). The assessment and treatment of relationship violence: A co-constructive developmental approach. *Family Counseling and Therapy, 2*(2), 1–24.

Rimonte, N. (1989). Domestic violence against Pacific Asians. In Asian Women United of California (Eds.), *Making waves* (pp. 327–337). Boston: Beacon.

Ritchie, B. (1996). *Compelled to crime: The gender entrapment of Black battered women.* New York: Routledge.

Roberts, A. R. (1987). Psychological characteristics of batterers: A study of 234 men charged with domestic violence offenses. *Journal of Family Violence, 2*, 81–93.

Robinson, C. C., & Morris, J. T. (1986). The gender-stereotyped nature of Christmas toys received by 36-, 48-, and 60-month-old children: A comparison between nonrequested and requested toys. *Sex Roles, 15*, 21–32.

Rodin, J., Silberstein, L. R., & Striegel–Moore, R. H. (1984). Women and weight: A normative discontent. In T. B. Sonderegger (Ed.), *Psychology and gender: Nebraska Symposium on Motivation* (pp. 267–307). Lincoln: University of Nebraska Press.

Roopnarine, J. L. (1986). Mothers' and fathers' behaviors toward the toy play of their infant sons and daughters. *Sex Roles, 14*, 59–68.

Root, M. P. P. (1996). Women of color and traumatic stress in "domestic captivity": Gender and race as disempowering statuses. In A. J. Marsella, M. J. Friedman, E. T. Gerrity, & R. M. Scurfield (Eds.), *Ethnocultural aspects of posttraumatic stress disorder: Issues, research and clinical applications* (pp. 363–388). Washington, DC: American Psychological Association.

Rose, R., Bernstein, I., & Gordon, T. (1975). Consequences of social conflict on plasma testosterone levels in rhesus monkeys. *Psychosomatic Medicine, 37*, 50–61.

Rosenbaum, A., Geffner, R., & Benjamin, S. (in press). A biopsychosocial model for understanding relationship aggression. *Journal of Aggression, Maltreatment & Trauma.*

Rosenbaum, A., Hoge, S. K., Adelman, S. A., Warnken, W. J., Fletcher, K. E., & Kane, R. (1994). Head injury in partner-abusive men. *Journal of Consulting and Clinical Psychology, 62*, 1187–1193.

Rosenbaum, A., & O'Leary, K. D. (1981). Marital violence: Characteristics of abusive couples. *Journal of College Student Development, 1*, 63–71.

Rosenbaum, A. S., & Hoge, S. K. (1989). Head injury and marital aggression. *American Journal of Psychiatry, 146*, 1048–1051.

Ross, M., & Olson, J. M. (1981). An expectancy-attribution model of the effects of placebos. *Psychological Review, 88*, 408–437.

Rostosky, S. S., & Travis, C. B. (1996). Menopause research and the dominance of the biomedical model 1984–1994. *Psychology of Women Quarterly, 20*, 285–312.

Rounds, D. (1994). *Predictors of homosexual intolerance on a college campus: Identity, intimacy, attitudes toward homosexuals and gender role conflict.* Unpublished Master's thesis, Department of Psychology, University of Connecticut.

Rubin, J. Z., Provenzano, F. J., & Luria, Z. (1974). The eye of the beholder: Parents' views on sex of newborns. *American Journal of Orthopsychiatry, 44*, 512–519.

Russell, D. (1975). Rape: *The victim's perspective.* New York: Stein and Day.

Russo, N. F. (1979). Overview: Sex roles, fertility, and the motherhood mandate. *Psychology of Women Quarterly, 4*, 7–15.

Russo, N. F., Denious, J., Keita, G. P., & Koss, M. P. (1997). Intimate violence and black women's health. *Women's Health: Research on Gender, Behavior, and Public Policy, 3*(3–4), 315–348.

Russo, N. F., & Green, B. L. (1993). Women and mental health. In F. L. Denmark & M. A. Paludi (Eds.), *Psychology of women: A handbook of issues and theories* (pp. 379–436). Westport, CT: Greenwood Press.

Russo, N. F., Koss, M. P., & Goodman, L. (1995). Male violence against women: A global health and development issue. In L. L. Adler & F. L. Denmark (Eds.), *Violence and the prevention of violence* (pp. 121–127). Westport, CT: Praeger.

Rutter, M. (1987). Psychosocial resilience and protective mechanism. *American Journal of Orthopsychiatry, 57,* 316–331.

Sabourin, T. C., Infante, D. C., & Rudd, J. E. (1993). Verbal aggression in marriages: A comparison of violent, distressed but nonviolent, and nondistressed couples. *Human Communication Research, 20,* 247–267.

Sadker, M., & Sadker, D. (1994). *Failing at fairness: How America's schools cheat girls.* New York: Scribners.

Sadker, M. P., & Sadker, D. M. (1982). *Sex equity handbook for schools.* New York: Longman.

Saltzberg, E. A., & Chrisler, J. C. (1995). Beauty is the beast: Psychological effects of the pursuit of the perfect female body. In J. Freeman (Ed.), *Women: A feminist perspective* (5th ed., pp. 306–315). Mountain View, CA: Mayfield.

Sanday, P. R. (1981). The socio-cultural context of rape: A cross-cultural study. *Journal of Social Issues, 37,* 5–27.

Sandoval, C. (1990). Feminism and racism: A report on the 1981 National Women's Studies Conference. In G. Anzaldúa (Ed.), *Making face, making soul (Hacienda caras): Creative and critical perspectives by women of color* (pp. 55–71). San Francisco: Aunt Lute Foundation.

Sapolsky, R. (1997). Testosterone rules. *Discover, 18,* 45–50.

Saunders, D. (1980). The police response to battered women: Predictors of officers' use of arrest, counseling, and minimal action. *Dissertation Abstracts International, 40,* 6446A.

Saunders, D. G. (1992). Woman battering. In R. T. Ammerman & M. Hersen (Eds.), *Assessment of family violence: A clinical and legal handbook.* New York: Wiley.

Scanzoni, J. (1979). Social processes and power in families. In W. R. Burr, R. Hill, F. I. Nye, & I. Reiss (Eds.), *Contemporary theories about the family.* New York: Free Press.

Schachter, S., & Singer, J. E. (1962). Cognitive, social, and physiological determinants of emotional states. *Psychological Review, 69,* 379–399.

Schlegel, A., & Barry, H. (1986). The cultural consequences of female contributions to subsistence. *American Anthropologist, 88,* 142–150.

Serra, P. (1993). Physical violence in the couple relationship: A contribution toward the analysis of context. *Family Process, 32,* 21–33.

Sheehy, G. (1992). *The silent passage.* New York: Random House.

Sheffield, C. J. (1995). Sexual terrorism. In J. Freeman (Ed.), *Women: A feminist perspective* (5th ed., pp. 1–21). Mountain View, CA: Mayfield.

Shidlo, A. (1994). Internalized homophobia: Conceptual and empirical issues in measurement. In B. Greene & G. M. Herek (Eds.), *Lesbian and gay psychology: Theory, research, and clinical applications* (pp. 176–205). Newbury Park, CA: Sage.

Siebert, A., & Siegel, B. S. (1996). *The survivor personality: Why some people are stronger, smarter, and more successful at handling life's difficulties . . . and how you can be too.* New York: Berkley Publication Group.

Signorielli, N., & Lears, M. (1992). Children, television, and conceptions about chores: Attitudes and behaviors. *Sex Roles, 27,* 157–170.

Simons, R. L., Wu, C. I., & Conger, R. D. (1995). A test of various perspectives on the intergenerational transmission of domestic violence. *Criminology, 33,* 141–170.

Sinnott, J. D. (1984). Older men, older women: Are their perceived roles similar? *Sex Roles, 10,* 847–856.

Smith, M. (1991a). Patriarchal ideology and wife beating: A test of a feminist hypothesis. *Violence and Victims, 5,* 257–273.

Smith, M. (1991b). Male peer support of wife abuse: An exploratory study. *Journal of Interpersonal Violence, 6,* 512–519.

Smuts, B. (1992). Psychological adaptations, development and individual differences. *Behavioral and Brain Sciences, 15,* 396.

Smuts, B. (1995). The evolutionary origins of patriarchy. *Human Nature, 6,* 1–32.

Smuts, B. B., & Gubernick, D. J. (1992). Male–infant relationships in nonhuman primates: Paternal investment or mating effort? In B. S. Hewlett (Ed.), *Father–child relations: Cultural and biosocial contexts* (pp. 1–31). New York: Aldine de Gruyter.

Song, Y. I. (1986). *Battered Korean women in urban America: The relationship of cultural conflict to wife abuse.* Unpublished doctoral dissertation, Department of Psychology, Ohio State University, Colombus, Ohio.

Sonkin, D. J., Martin, D., & Walker, L. (1985). *The male batterer.* New York: Springer.

Sontag, S. (1972). The double standard of aging. *Saturday Review,* pp. 29–38.

Sorensen, S. B., & Telles, C. A. (1991). Self reports of spousal violence in a Mexican American and non-Hispanic White population. *Violence and Victims, 6,* 3–15.

Sork, V. L. (1997). Quantitative genetics, feminism, and evolutionary theories of gender differences. In P. A. Gowaty (Ed.), *Feminism and evolutionary biology* (pp. 86–115). New York: Chapman & Hall.

Spence, J. T., & Helmreich, R. (1978). *Masculinity & femininity: Their psychological dimensions, correlates and antecedents.* Austin: University of Texas Press.

Spielberger, C. D., Johnson, E. H., Russell, S. F., Crane, R., Jacobs, G. A., & Worden, T. J. (1985). The experience and expression of anger: construction and validation of an anger expression scale. In M. A. Chesney & R. H. Rosenman (Eds.), *Anger and hostility in cardiovascular and behavioral disorders* (pp. 5–30). New York: Hemisphere/McGraw-Hill.

Sprenkle, D. H. (1994). Wife abuse through the lens of "systems theory." *The Counseling Psychologist, 22,* 598–602.

Staples, R. (1976). Race and family violence: The internal colonialism perspective. In L. Gary & L. Brown (Eds.), *Crime and its impact on the Black community* (pp. 85–96). Washington, DC: Howard University.

Staples, R. (1990). Changes in black family structure: The conflict between family ideology and structural conditions. In C. Carlson (Ed.), *Perspectives on the family: History, class, and feminism* (pp. 281–293). Belmont, CA: Wadsworth.

Stark, E., Flitcraft, A., & Frazier, W. (1979). Medicine and patriarchal violence: The social construction of a "private" event. *International Journal of Health Services, 9,* 461–493.

Stark, E., & Flitcraft, A. (1988). Violence among intimates: An epidemiological review. In V. B. Van Haselt, R. L. Morrison, A. S. Bellack, & M. Herson (Eds.), *Handbook of family violence* (pp. 213–293). New York: Plenum.

Stark, E., & Flitcraft, A. (1996). *Women at risk.* Thousand Oaks, CA: Sage.

Stark, E., Flitcraft, A., Zuckerman, D., Grey, A., Robinson, J., & Frazier, W. (1981). *Wife abuse in a medical setting: An introduction for health personnel* (Monograph No.7). Washington, DC: Office of Domestic Violence, DHHS.

Steinmetz, S. K. (1977). Wife-beating, husband-beating: A comparison of the use of physical violence between spouses to resolve marital fights. In M. Roy (Ed.), *Battered women: A psychosocial study of domestic violence* (pp. 63–67). New York: Van Nostrand Reinhold.

Steinmetz, S. K. (1987). Family violence: Past, present, and future. In M. B. Sussman, & S. K. Steinmetz (Eds.), *Handbook of marriage and the family* (pp. 725–765). New York: Plenum.

Stern, M., & Karraker, M. K. (1989). Sex stereotyping of infants: A review of gender labeling studies. *Sex Roles, 20,* 501–522.

Stets, J. E. (1990). Verbal and physical aggression in marriage. *Journal of Marriage and the Family, 52,* 501–514.

Stevens, M. A. (1994). Stopping domestic violence: More answers and more questions needed. *The Counseling Psychologist, 22*(4), 587–592.

Stordeur, R. A., & Stille, R. (1989). *Ending male violence against their partners: One road to peace.* Newbury Park, CA: Sage.

Storms, M. D., & Nisbett, R. E. (1970). Insomnia and the attribution process. *Journal of Personality and Social Psychology, 16,* 319–328.

Straus, M. A. (1973) A general systems theory approach to a theory of violence between family members. *Social Science Information, 12,* 105–250.

Straus, M. A. (1979). Measuring intrafamily conflict and violence: The conflict tactics (CT) scales. *Journal of Marriage and the Family, 41,* 75–88.

Straus, M. A. (1980). Wife-beating: How common and why. In M. A. Straus & G. T. Hotaling (Eds.), *The social causes of husband–wife violence* (pp. 23–36). Minneapolis: University of Minnesota.

Straus, M. A. (1990). Measuring intrafamily conflict and violence: The conflict tactic (CT) scale. In M. A. Straus & R. J. Gelles (Eds.), *Physical violence in American families* (pp. 29–47). New Brunswick, NJ: Transition Publishing.

Straus, M. A., & Gelles, R. J. (1986). Societal change and change in family violence from 1975 to 1985 as revealed in two national surveys. *Journal of Marriage and the Family, 48,* 465–479.

Straus, M. A., & Gelles, R. J. (1988). How violent are American families? Estimates from the National Family Violence Resurvey and other studies. In G. T. Hotaling, D. Finkelhor, J. T. Kirkpatrick, & M. A. Straus (Eds.), *Family abuse and its consequences* (pp. 14–36). Newbury Park, CA: Sage.

Straus, M. A., & Gelles, R. J. (1990). *Physical violence in American families: Risk factors and adaptation to violence in 8,145 families.* New Brunswick, NJ: Transaction.

Straus, M. A., Gelles, R. J., & Steinmetz, S. (1980). *Behind closed doors: Violence in the American family.* Garden City, NY: Anchor.

Straus, M. A., & Hamby, S. L. (1997). Measuring physical and psychological maltreatment of children with the conflict tactic scales. In G. K. Kantor & J. L. Jasinski (Eds.), *Out of the darkness: Contemporary perspectives on family violence.* Thousand Oaks, CA: Sage.

Straus, M. A., & Kaufman-Kantor, G. (1992, July). *Change in spouse assault rates from 1975 to 1992: A comparison of three national surveys in the United States.* Paper presented at the 13th World Congress of Sociology, Bielefeld, Germany.

Strauss, M., & Smith, C. (1990). Violence in Hispanic families in the United States: Incidence rates and structural interpretations. In M. A. Strauss & R. J. Gelles (Eds.), *Physical violence in American Families: Risk factors and adaptations in 8,145 families* (pp. 341–368). New Brunswick, NJ: Transaction.

Sturm, J. T., Carr, M. E., Luxenberg, M. G., Swoyer, J. K., & Cicero, J. J. (1990). The prevalence of Neisseria Gonorrhoea and Chlamydia trichomatous in victims of sexual assault. *Annals of Emergency Medicine, 19*, 142–144.

Sudarkasa, N. (1981). Interpreting the African Heritage in Afro American family organization. In H. P. McAdoo (Ed.), *Black families* (2nd ed., pp. 37–53). Beverly Hills, CA: Sage.

Sue, S., & Okazaki, S. (1990). Asian American educational achievements: A phenomenon in search of an explanation. *American Psychologist, 45*, 913–920.

Sullivan, C., Basta, J. Tan, C., & Davidson II, W. S. (1992). After the crisis: A needs assessment of women leaving a domestic violence shelter. *Violence and Victims, 7*(3), 267–275.

Svare, B., & Kinsley, C. H. (1987). Hormones and sex-related behavior. In K. Kelley (Ed.), *Females, males, and sexuality: Theories and research* (pp. 13–58). Albany: State University of New York Press.

Symons, D. (1979). *The evolution of human sexuality.* New York: Oxford University Press.

Taylor, R. L. (1981). Psychological modes of adaptation. In L. E. Gary (Ed.), *Black men* (pp. 141–158). Beverly Hills: Sage.

Tedeschi, J. T., & Felson, R. B. (1994). *Violence, aggression, & coercive actions.* Washington, DC: American Psychological Association.

Teens express themselves (1988). *The State* [Columbia, SC], p. 2A.

Tellegen, A., Bouchard, T. J., Wilcox, K. J., Segal, N. L., Lykken, D. T., & Rich, S. (1988). Personality similarity in twins reared apart and together. *Journal of Personality and Social Psychology, 53*, 1031–1039.

Thompson, B. (1994). Food, bodies, and growing up female: Childhood lessons about culture, race, and class. In P. Fallon, M. A. Katzman, & S. C. Wooley (Eds.), *Feminist perspectives on eating disorders* (pp. 355–378). New York: Guilford.

Thompson, E. H., & Pleck, J. H. (1995). Masculine idealogies: A review of research instruments on men and masculinity. In R. Levant & W. Pollack (Eds.), *The new psychology of men.* New York: Basic Books.

Thorne-Finch, R. (1992). *Ending the silence: The origins and treatment of male violence against women.* Toronto: University of Toronto Press.

Thornhill, R., & Thornhill, N. W. (1992). The evolutionary psychology of men's coercive sexuality. *Behavioral and Brain Sciences, 15*, 363–375.

Tolman, R. (1989). The development of a measure of psychological maltreatment of women by their male partners. *Violence and Victims, 4*(3), 159–177.

Tolman, R. M., & Bennett, L. W. (1990). A review of quantitative research on men who batter. *Journal of Interpersonal Violence, 5*, 87–118.

Torres, S. (1987). Hispanic-American battered women: Why consider cultural difference? *Response to the Victimization of Women and Children, 10*, 20–21.

Torres, S. (1991). A comparison of wife abuse between two cultures: Perception, attitudes, nature and extent. *Issues in Mental Health Nursing for the 90's: New concepts. New Theories, 12*, 113–131.

Turner, A. K. (1994). Genetic and hormonal influences on male violence. In J. Archer (Ed.), *Male violence* (pp. 233–252). London: Routledge.

Unger, R., & Crawford, M. (1992). *Women and gender: A feminist psychology*. New York: McGraw-Hill.

Urberg, K. A. (1982). The development of the concepts of masculinity and feminity in young children. *Sex Roles, 6*, 659–668.

U.S. Department of Justice. (1980). *Intimate victims: A study of violence among friends and relatives*. Washington, DC: Government Printing Office.

U.S. Department of Justice. (1984). *Attorney General's task force on family violence: Final report*. Washington, DC: U.S. Department of Justice.

U.S. Department of Justice. (1994). *Domestic violence: Violence between intimates*. Washington: U.S. Department of Justice, Bureau of Justice Statistics.

U.S. Department of Justice. (1996). *Uniform crime reports for the United States, 1995*. Washington, DC: U.S. Department of Justice, Federal Bureau of Investigation.

U.S. Department of Labor. (1994). *1993 handbook on women workers: Trends and issues*. Washington, DC: U.S. Government Printing Office.

U.S. Senate Judiciary Committee (1990). *Report No. 101-545 accompanying S.2754 (The Violence Against Women Act of 1990)*. Washington, DC.

U.S. Senate Judiciary Committee (1991). *Report No. 102-197 accompanying S.15 (The Violence Against Women Act)*. Washington, DC.

van der Kolk, B. A. (1988). Trauma in men: Effects on family life. In M. B. Straus (Ed.), *Abuse and victimization across the lifespan* (pp. 170–185). Baltimore, MD: Johns Hopkins University Press.

Vasquez, M. (1994). Latinas. In L. Comas-Diaz, & B. Greene (Eds.), *Women of color: Integrating ethnic and gender identities in psychotherapy* (pp. 114–138). New York: Guilford.

Virkkunen, M., DeJong, J., Bartko, J., Goodwin, F. K., & Linnoila, M. (1989). Relationship of psychobiological variables to recidivism in violent offenders and impulsive fire setters. *Archives of General Psychiatry, 44*, 241–247.

Virkkunen, M., Rawlings, R., Tokola, R., Poland, R. E., Guidotti, A., Nemeroff, C., Bissette, G., Kalogeras, K., Karonen, S., & Linnoila, M. (1994). CSF biochemistries, glucose metabolism, and diurnal activity rhythms in alcoholic, violent offenders, fire setters, and healthy volunteers. *Archives of General Psychiatry, 51*, 20–27.

Volavka, J. (1995). *Neurobiology of violence*. Washington, DC: American Psychiatric Press.

Volavka, J., Martell, D., & Convit, A. (1992). Psychobiology of the violent offender. *Journal of Forensic Science, 37*, 237–251.

Walker, B. A., Reis, S. M., & Leonard, J. S. (1992). A developmental investigation of the lives of gifted women. *Gifted Child Quarterly, 36*, 201–206.

Walker, L. E. (1979). *The battered woman*. New York: Harper & Row.

Walker, L. E. (1981). Battered women: Sex roles and clinical issues. *Professional Psychology, 12*, 81–91.

Walker, L. E. (1984). *Battered woman syndrome*. New York, NY: Springer.

Walker, L. E. (1989). *Terrifying love: Why battered women kill and how society responds.* New York: Harper & Row.

Walker, L. E. (1991). Posttraumatic stress disorder in women: Diagnosis and treatment of battered women syndrome. *Psychotherapy, 28,* 21–29.

Walker, L. E. (1992). Battered women syndrome and self-defense. *Notre Dame Journal of Law, Ethics, and Public Policy, 6,* 321–334.

Walker, L. E. A. (1995). Current perspectives on men who batter—implications for intervention and treatment to stop violence against women: Comment on Gottman et al. (1995). *Journal of Family Psychology, 9,* 264–271.

Walker, L. E. A., & Browne, A. (1985). Gender and victimization by intimates. *Journal of Personality, 53,* 179–195.

Wallace, R., & Nosko, A. (1993). Working with shame in the group treatment of male batterers. *International Group Psychotherapy, 43,* 45–61.

Walsh, W. B., & Osipow, S. H. (1994). *Career counseling for women.* Hillsdale, NJ: Erlbaum.

Walters, G. D. (1992). A meta-analysis of the gene–crime relationship. *Criminology, 30,* 595–613.

Warnken, W. J., Rosenbuam, A., Fletcher, K. E., Hoge, S. K., & Adelman, S. A. (1996). Head-injured male: A population at risk for relationship aggression. In L. K. Hamberger & C. Renzetti (Eds.), *Domestic partner abuse* (pp. 103–124). New York: Springer.

Weis, J. G. (1989). Family violence research methodology and design. In L. Ohlin & Tonry, M. (Eds.), *Family violence* (pp. 117–162). Chicago: University of Chicago Press.

Weitzman, J., & Dreen, K. (1982). Wife beating: A view of the marital dyad. *Social Casework, 463*(5), 259–265.

Werner, E. E., & Smith, R. S. (1982). *Vulnerable but invincible: A longitudinal study of resilient children and youth.* New York: McGraw-Hill.

Werner, E. E., & Smith, R. S. (1992). *Overcoming the odds: High-risk children from birth to adulthood.* Ithaca, NY: Cornell University Press.

Whitaker, C. (1976). The hindrance of theory in clinical work. In P. J. Guerin, Jr. (Ed.), *Family therapy: Theory and practice.* New York: Gardner Press.

Whitbourne, S. K., & Hulicka, I. M. (1990). Ageism in undergraduate psychology texts. *American Psychologist, 45,* 1127–1136.

Whitchurch, G., & Pace, J. (1993). Communication skills training and interpersonal violence. *Journal of Applied Communication Research, 21,* 96–102.

White, E. C. (1990). Love doesn't always make it right: Black women and domestic violence. In E. C. White (Ed.), *The Black woman's health book: Speaking for ourselves* (pp. 92–97). Seattle, WA: Seal Press.

White, F. J. (1996). *Pan Paniscus* 1973 to 1996: Twenty-three years of field research. *Evolutionary Anthropology, 6,* 11–17.

Whitman, S., Coleman, T. E., Patmon, C., Desai, B. T., Cohen, R., & King, L. N. (1984). Epilepsy in prison: Elevated prevalence and no relationship to violence. *Neurology, 34,* 775–782.

Widom, C. S. (1988). Sampling biases and implications for child abuse research. *American Journal of Orthopsychiatry, 58,* 260–270.

Wilson, M., & Daly, M. (1993). Spousal homicide risk and estrangement. *Violence and Victims, 8*(1), 3–16.

Wilson, M., Daly, M., & Scheib, J. E. (1997). Femicide: An evolutionary psychological perspective. In P. A. Gowaty (Ed.), *Feminism and evolutionary biology* (pp. 431–465). New York: Chapman & Hall.

Woffordt, S., Mihalic, D. E., & Menard, S. (1994). Continuities in marital violence. *Journal of Family Violence, 9*, 195–225.

Wolf, N. (1991). *The beauty myth.* New York: William Morrow.

Wolf-Smith, J. H., & LaRossa, R. (1992). After he hits her. *Family Relations, 41*, 324–329.

Wong, R. R. (1995). *Family and Conciliation Courts Review, 33*, 110–128.

Wrangham, R. (1987). The significance of African apes for reconstructing human social evolution. In W. P. Kinzey (Ed.), *The evolution of human behavior: Primate models* (pp. 51–71). Albany: State University of New York.

Wrangham, R. (1993). The evolution of sexuality in chimpanzees and bonobos. *Human Nature, 4*, 47–79.

Wrangham, R., & Peterson, D. (1996). *Demonic males. Apes and the origins of human violence.* Boston: Houghton Mifflin.

Wyatt, G. (1994). Sociocultural and epidemiological issues in the assessment of domestic violence. *Journal of Social Distress and the Homeless, 3*, 7–21.

Yllö, K. (1983). Using a feminist approach in quantitative research. In D. Finkelhor, R. Gelles, M. Straus, & G. Hotaling (Eds.), *The dark side of families: Current family violence research* (pp. 277–288). Beverly Hills, CA: Sage.

Yllö, K. (1984). The status of women, marital equality and violence against wives: A contextual analysis. *Journal of Family Issues, 5*, 307–320.

Yllö, K. (1988). Political and methodological debates in wife abuse research. In K. Yllö & M. Bograd (Eds.), *Feminist perspectives on wife abuse* (pp. 28–50). Newbury Park, CA: Sage.

Yllö, K. (1993). Through a feminist lens: Gender, power, and violence. In R. Gelles & D. Loseke (Eds.), *Current controversies on family violence* (pp. 47–62). Newbury Park, CA: Sage.

Yllö, K., & Bograd, M. (Eds.). (1988). *Feminist perspectives on wife abuse.* Newbury Park, CA: Sage.

Young, C. (1986). Afro-American family: Contemporary issues and complications for social policy. In D. Pilgrim (Ed.), *On being Black: An in-group analysis.* Bristol, IN: Wyndham Hall.

Younger, B. (1994). Violence against women in the workplace. *Employee Assistance Quarterly, 9*, 113–133.

Yung, B. R., & Hammond, W. R. (1994). Native Americans. In L. D. Eron, J. H. Gentry, & P. L. Schlegel (Eds.), *Reason to hope: A psychosocial perspective on youth and violence* (pp. 133–144). Washington, DC: American Psychological Association.

Yung, J. (1991). The social awakening of Chinese American women as reported in Chung Sai Yat Po, 1900–1911. In C. Du Bois & V. L. Ruiz (Eds.), *Unequal sister: A multicultural reader in U.S. women's history* (pp. 195–207). New York: Routledge.

Zihlman, A. L. (1997). Women's bodies, women's lives: An evolutionary perspective. In M. E. Morbeck, A. Galloway, & A. L. Zihlman (Eds.), *The evolving female. A life history perspective* (pp. 185–197). Princeton, NJ: Princeton University Press.

Index

About the Contributors

Stephen A. Anderson, Ph.D., is a Professor in the University of Connecticut's School of Family Studies, where he teaches and supervises students in the school's accredited doctoral and master's degree programs in marriage and family therapy. With Dr. Dennis Bagarozzi, he is the coauthor of *Personal, Marital, and Family Myths: Theoretical Formulations and Clinical Strategies* and coeditor of *Personal Myths: Psychotherapy Implications.* He is also the coauthor (with Ronald Sabatelli) of *Family Interaction: A Multigenerational, Developmental Perspective.* He has served on the editorial boards of *Family Relations,* the *Journal of Systemic Therapies,* and the *Teachers' College Press Series on Counseling and Human Development.* He is a Clinical Member and Approved Supervisor in the American Association for Marriage and Family Therapy. At present he serves as consultant to the Domestic Violence Program at Stafford Human Services in Stafford Springs, Connecticut, where he is also engaged in research designed to identify typologies of violent couples.

Joseph R. Biden, Jr., has served in the United States Senate since January, 1973. Now the senior Democrat on the Foreign Relations Committee and a member of the Judiciary Committee, he has earned international recognition as a policy innovator, effective legislator, and party spokesman on issues ranging from international relations and arms control to crime prevention and drug control.

Since 1991, he has been an Adjunct Professor at the Widener University School of Law, where he teaches a seminar in constitutional law. He is widely recognized as one of the Senate's leading foreign policy experts, and he has published numerous editorials and articles, nationally and internationally, on international relations.

Senator Biden lives in Wilmington, Delaware, and commutes to Washington when the Senate is in session. He is married to the former Jill Jacobs, and has three children: Beau, Hunter, and Ashley.

Mary Ann Dutton, Ph.D., is a clinical psychologist and forensic consultant who specializes in the area of intimate violence. She has published in both psychology and legal professional journals. Her research is focused primarily on issues related to domestic violence. She has written *Empowering and Healing the Battered Woman: A Model of Assessment and Intervention,* and is currently working on another book titled (tentatively) *Understanding the Diversity of Battered Women's Response to Violence.* She also has written about the application of scientific knowledge concerning domestic violence in the courtroom in the form of expert testimony in cases involving domestic violence, in particular, *Understanding Women's Responses to Domestic Violence: A Redefinition of Battered Woman Syndrome.* She authored two reports for the U.S. Department of Justice concerning the validity, use, and effect of expert testimony concerning battering and its effects in criminal trials.

She has served over the past 12 years as a consultant and expert witness to attorneys in legal cases involving domestic violence and/or sexual assault. Currently, she holds a position as Professorial Lecturer of Law at the National Law Center, The George Washington University, and also serves as the Director of Research at The Center, Post-traumatic and Dissociative Disorders Program.

Richard J. Gelles, Ph.D., is the Joanne and Raymond Welsh Chair of Child Welfare and Family Violence in the School of Social Work of the University of Pennsylvania.

His book, *The Violent Home*, was the first systematic empirical investigation of family violence and continues to be highly influential. He is author or coauthor of 23 books and more than 100 articles and chapters on family violence. His latest books are *The Book of David: How Preserving Families Can Cost Children's Lives* (1996) and *Intimate Violence in Families,* third edition (1997). He was a member of the National Academy of Science's panel on "Assessing Family Violence Interventions." He was also the Vice President for Publications for the National Council on Family Relations.

Anthony F. Greene, Ph.D., received the Doctor of Philosophy in Clinical and Health Psychology from the University of South Florida in 1988. His first academic appointment was as Assistant Professor in the Medical Psychology track of the Clinical and Health Psychology department at the University of Florida. He is currently in the Regional Faculty for the Clinical Psychology doctoral program of the Fielding Insti-tute, and has adjunct appointments at the University of Florida, in addition to full-time clinical work in the Student Mental Health Service at the University of Florida. He has published numerous journal articles and chapters in the areas of health, interpersonal violence, psychopathology, and the assessment of anger.

Michele Harway, Ph.D., is Director of Research and Core Faculty at the Phillips Graduate Institute (formerly California Family Study Center), in Encino, California. Her work has focused on domestic violence research, research on women's development, on training mental health professionals to recognize and intervene with perpetrators, and on survivors of domestic violence as well as their children. She is the editor and author of six previous books including *Battering and Family Therapy: A Feminist Perspective* (with M. Hansen), *Spouse Abuse: Assessing and Treating Battered Women, Batterers and Their Children* (also with M. Hansen), and *Treating the Changing Family: Handling Normative and Unusual Events.* She is a member of the Consulting Faculty of the Fielding Institute, and she maintains a private psychotherapy practice. She is a fellow of the American Psychological Association in Divisions 35, 43, and 51 (Divisions on the Psychology of Women, Family Psychology, and Society for the Psychological Study of Men and Masculinity, respectively). She was named Family Psychologist of the year in 1998 by the American Psychological Association's Division of Family Psychology. She is president-elect of Division 43 of APA (Family Psychology).

A. Stephen Lanza, M.A., L.M.F.T., is a Connecticut licensed marital and family therapist and a divorce mediator in private practice, and serves as a Special Master in the Connecticut Family Courts. Additionally, he is the editor of the professional publications of the Connecticut Association for Marriage and Family Therapy and serves on its Board of Directors. Formerly a Lecturer in the School of Family Studies at the University of Connecticut's Storrs campus, he is now an adjunct faculty member at the University's regional campus in

Stamford. He was the former Director of the Family Violence Project at the University of Connecticut, School of Family Studies, and is currently the Coordinator of Research and Training for the same project. He is the Coordinator of the Domestic Violence Program serving the greater Fairfield, Connecticut, area. He has developed and been the clinical director of domestic violence treatment programs serving the Stafford and Mansfield, Connecticut, areas. His publications in the area of relationship violence include monographs, training tapes, and statefunded research projects and evaluation reports. He has presented at the national and regional levels and has taught both graduate and undergraduate students in the area of family violence and men's violence against women at three major Northeast universities. Since 1989, he has facilitated group treatment programs for men who batter and over that time, has worked with hundreds of men, women, and couples experiencing violence and abuse.

Amy J. Marin, Ph.D., is a Professor of Psychology at Phoenix College, where she teaches courses in social psychology and the psychology of gender. Her research interests focus on the relationship of gender and ethnic identities to achievement and health-related behaviors and outcomes.

Rodney A. Nadeau, M.A., is a Ph.D. Candidate in the Marriage and Family Therapy Program at the University of Connecticut. From 1992 to 1997, he was Coordinator of the Family Violence Program at the Frederick Humphrey Center for Marital and Family Therapy. He also has 10 years of clinical experience working with couples and families and has made several presentations on the topic of family violence at both the state and national levels. Currently, he is Director of the Youth Challenge Program at a Youth Service Bureau in Hebron,

Connecticut. In this program, he has been working with children and families identified as having problems with anger and aggression.

Roberta L. Nutt, Ph.D., is Professor of Psychology and Director of the Counseling Psychology doctoral program, which emphasizes family psychology and women's and gender issues, at Texas Woman's University. She is past president of the Family Psychology Division of the American Psychological Association, Chair of the section on Feminist Professional Training and Practice of the Psychology of Women Division, former Chair of the Counseling Psychology Division Committee on Women, and former Chair of the Texas State Board of Examiners of Psychologists. She is coauthor of the book *Bridging Separate Gender Worlds: Why Men and Women Clash and How Therapists Can Bring Them Together* and the *Division 17 Principles Concerning the Counseling/ Psychotherapy of Women: Rationale and Implementation.* She has written and presented widely in the area of gender-sensitive psychotherapy.

James M. O'Neil, Ph.D., is Professor of Family Studies and Educational Psychology at the University of Connecticut, Storrs. In 1975, he received his Ph.D. from the University of Maryland's Counseling and Personnel Services Department. A licensed psychologist in private practice, he also provides counseling, psychotherapy, and consultation services in South Windsor, Connecticut, and in the greater Hartford area. He is a fellow of the American Psychological Association in Divisions 17, 35, 43, 51, and 52. In 1988, he coedited a special

issue of *The Counseling Psychologist* on "Victimization and its Aftermath." He is one of the founding members of the Society for the Psychological Study of Men and Masculinity (SPSMM), Division 51 of the American Psychological Association. SPSMM named him Researcher of the Year in 1997 for his 20-year research program on men's gender-role conflict. His research programs relate to men and masculinity, gender-role conflict, psychology of men and women, and violence and victimization. He is the author of the *Gender Role Conflict Scale*, a widely used measure of men's conflict with their gender roles. He has published over 40 journal articles, 13 book chapters, and his first book, *Organizational Consultation: A Casebook*, was published in 1992. In 1991, he was awarded a Fulbright Teaching Scholarship by the Council for International Exchange of Scholars, to lecture in the former Soviet Union. He lectured at the Moscow State Pedagogical University from February through April 1992, on the topics of psychological counseling, psychology of gender roles, and victimization. He also conducted research on Russian men's gender-role conflict and psychological violence. In 1995, he was recognized as a Teaching Fellow by the University of Connecticut for outstanding excellence and dedication to the teaching profession.

Sandra A. Rigazio-DiGilio, Ph.D., is an Associate Professor in the COAMFTE-accredited masters and doctoral marriage and family therapy programs at the University of Connecticut. Additionally, she holds a joint appointment in the Department of Psychiatry. She is a licensed psychologist and a licensed marriage and family therapist.

She is currently serving a 3-year term on the AAMFT Board of Directors. Additionally, she serves on the Editorial Board for the *Journal of Counseling and Development*, is the Associate Editor of the Teacher's College Press Book Series on *Counseling and Development*, and is the Associate Editor of the Practice Section for the *Journal of Mental Health Counseling*.

She has published over 35 chapters and articles focused on an integrative, co-constructive, developmental model of therapy and an accompanying supervisory model. Both have been positively reviewed as nonpathological models and metaframeworks that (1) are gender and culture sensitive; (2) can be easily learned, applied, and researched; and (3) can be used by therapists and supervisors as a guide to tailor their work to the unique needs of those seeking service. There are several research projects currently under way to determine each model's effectiveness with different treatment and supervisory populations.

Nancy Felipe Russo, Ph.D., is Regents Professor of Psychology at Arizona State University, where she conducts research on the relationship of gender and mental health, including the causes, consequences, and correlates of violence against women. A former member of the American Psychological Association Task Force on Male Violence Against Women, she currently serves as Editor of the *Psychology of Women Quarterly.* Her honors include the APA's Distinguished Contributions to Psychology in the Public Interest Award.

Janis Sanchez-Hucles, Ph.D., is Professor of Psychology at Old Dominion University in Norfolk, Virginia, and a clinical psychologist in private practice in Virginia Beach, Virginia. She is also a faculty member for the Virginia Consortium for Clinical Psychology and a Community Faculty Member for Eastern Virginia Medical School. Her research has focused on clinical training, women of color and families, diversity, attachment, feminism, and issues pertaining to urbanicity and violence, and she has become a

national speaker and trainer in the areas of diversity, clinical training, ethnic minority issues, and the psychology of women. She is a fellow of the American Psychological Association (APA), and she has served on an APA Presidential Task Force on Violence and the Family, on the APA Council of Representatives representing the Division of the Psychology of Women, and she currently cochairs the APA's Committee on Urban Initiatives. She is of African American and Cuban descent.

Margaret C. Schlossberg is a doctoral student in the School of Family Studies at the University of Connecticut. She received a master's degree in Marriage and Family Therapy at the University of Connecticut in 1992. She has played an integral part in the University of Connecticut's (UConn's) School of Family Studies Research Project on Domestic Violence in conjunction with UConn's Departments of Family Studies, School of Education, School of Social Work, and the Institute of Public Service. She has also served as the primary research assis-

tant to a multidisciplined research project on Youth Violence in Connecticut. Furthermore, she has worked as a clinician at diverse sites in Connecticut and recently received the Connecticut Association of Marriage and Family Therapy's 1997 Student of the Year Award. Her other research interests have included collaboration in medical family therapy and training, and supervision in marriage and family therapy. She has presented her research at both state and national conferences.

Louise B. Silverstein, Ph.D., is Assistant Professor at the Ferkauf Graduate School of Psychology at Yeshiva University. She is the cofounder of the Yeshiva Father-hood Project, which is a qualitative research study of fathering from a multicultural perspective. She is also the Codirector of the Yeshiva-Ackerman Family–School Collaboration Project, which provides specialized training to doctoral students in building family–school partnerships.

She is a past president of the American Psychological Association's Division of Family Psychology and Chair of the Feminist Family Therapy Task Force within the Division of the Psychology of Women. She is a family therapist in private practice in New York City.